A Mother's Job

A Mother's Job

THE HISTORY OF DAY CARE, 1890–1960

Elizabeth Rose

New York Oxford

Oxford University Press

1999

Oxford University Press

Oxford New York
Athens Auckland Bangkok Bogotá Buenos Aires Calcutta
Cape Town Chennai Dar es Salaam Delhi Florence Hong Kong Istanbul
Karachi Kuala Lumpur Madrid Melbourne Mexico City Mumbai
Nairobi Paris São Paulo Singapore Taipei Tokyo Toronto Warsaw

and associated companies in
Berlin Ibadan

First issued as an Oxford University Press paperback, 2003
Published by Oxford University Press, Inc.
198 Madison Avenue, New York, New York 10016

Library of Congress Cataloging-in-Publication Data
Rose, Elizabeth R.
A mother's job : the history of day care, 1890–1960 / Elizabeth Rose.
p. cm.
ISBN 0-19-511112-5 0-19-516810-0 (pbk.)
1. Day care centers—United States—History. 2. Day care centers—Pennsylvania—Philadelphia—History. 3. Nursery schools—United States—History. 4. Nursery schools—Pennsylvania—Philadelphia—History. I. Title.
HQ778.63.R65 1999
362.7'12'0974811—dc21 97-52021

1 3 5 7 9 8 6 4 2

Printed in the United States of America
on acid-free paper

To the memory of my grandmother,
Frieda Covner Rose
zichrona l'bracha
and
To my children,
Eli and Eva

Acknowledgments

Many people have nurtured both me and this project as it grew into a book. Marjorie Murphy at Swarthmore College first inspired me to go on to do graduate work in history, both by her own example and by the respect with which she treated my early efforts. At Rutgers, I was blessed with supportive advisors: special thanks are due to Suzanne Lebsock and Alice Kessler-Harris for their encouragement as I tried to combine motherhood and intellectual work. Many thanks to the Society of American Historians, whose recognition greatly increased my confidence in the project and made it possible to really start thinking of it becoming a book. The Vanderbilt history department has offered a supportive environment in which to transform the manuscript from dissertation to book. Financial support from Rutgers University, the Indiana University Center on Philanthropy's Governance of Nonprofit Organizations Fellowship Program, and the Vanderbilt University Research Council gave me the gift of time to research, write, and rewrite.

The support I received from friends and colleagues has been equally important. Sally Steffen not only gave me a home base in Philadelphia, but also gave of her friendship, listening to my stories at the end of each day of research and helping me over some stumbling blocks. Sharla Fett has been a pillar of support for me since our first day of graduate school and continued to send thoughtful comments and vital encouragement over the phone lines after we moved apart. Dissertation support groups at Rutgers and at the University of Wisconsin provided crucial help, and I would like to thank Joe Broderick, Annette Igra, Lynn Mahoney, and Erika Rappaport at Rutgers and Andrea Freedman, Deirdre Maloney, Lian Partlow, Ayesha Shariff, Landon Storrs, Nancy Taylor, and Susan Traverso at Wisconsin. Bill Ladd was a patient and helpful computer consultant (as well as housemate) when I was trying to analyze my data. Eileen Boris, Dawn Greeley, Joanne Goodwin, Linda Gordon, and Julia Wrigley also gave generously of their time to read and comment on part or all of the manuscript at different stages.

Many archivists in Philadelphia and elsewhere were very helpful to me. I owe a special debt to Lily Schwartz of the Philadelphia Jewish Archives Center at the Balch Institute Library, who first guided me to the Neighborhood Centre papers. Special thanks are also due to Margaret Jerrido, Brenda Galloway-Wright, and George Brightbill at Temple

University's Urban Archives, and to the staff of the National Archives for helping to find materials and for providing pleasant working environments.

Being immersed in the history of day care has made me acutely aware of the debt I owe to the people who have provided care for my children. In chronological order, I thank the staff of the Strawberry Hill Day Care Center in Nashville, the Magic Penny Day Care Center in Madison, the Vanderbilt University Child Care Center (especially Claudia Moore, Tonya Hall, Betty Douglas, Dena Kaye Abdulla, Ginette Cambronero, Lisa Zacarelli, Jennifer Stark, and Glenda Williams), and Rosalie Rowan and Sheila Saad at the Brightwood Playschool in Nashville. All of these people have provided loving care, helping my children, my family, and me to flourish.

Most of all, I must thank my various families. Ann and David Rose, as always, provided a steady stream of encouragement and love. Their own love of history is contagious, and has sparked my own. The Dougherty family did me the favor of not asking too often how the project was going and has also been a wonderful source of support. Jack Dougherty has helped with this project in innumerable ways, from helping me formulate arguments to helping me arrange photographs. Since we became parents four years ago, we have lived out in our personal lives many of the central issues in this book. Jack's commitment to truly sharing the work of parenting has made all kinds of things possible. But most important, his love has sustained me for the past ten years.

Little did I realize, when I first embarked on this project, how deeply I would come to care about day care. Eli Dougherty Rose, who was born in the middle of this project, and Eva Rose Dougherty, who was born at its end, have made me a more passionate historian and helped me understand my subject. But more important, they have brought great joy to my life. I dedicate this book to them, as well as to the memory of my grandmother, with the hope that they will always be both cared for and caring.

Nashville, Tennessee E.R.
September, 1997

Contents

Note on Case Records

Names of day nursery clients and their relatives in all the case records used in this book have been changed in order to preserve client confidentiality. Where case records were systematically numbered, I have referred to the original case number in the footnotes; in the case of the Wharton Centre case records, I have created a five-digit number based on the number of the folder and the order of the records within the folder. (Thus Wharton case 20309 is located in folder 203, and is the ninth record in that folder.) Case records from the Neighborhood Centre Day Nursery used in this study were chosen by a 10% sample. In order to preserve the sense of the language, I have not corrected grammatical errors or abbreviations from the case records.

A Mother's Job

There is a broader motherhood than the motherhood that mothers one's own; there is the spirit of the Lord that is the mother that mothers all children, and it is because the world lacks that, that the conditions of the children of this country has not been better.

—Hannah Schoff, president of the
National Congress of Mothers, 1905

She was a miracle to me, but when she was eight months old I had to leave her daytimes with the woman downstairs to whom she was no miracle at all.

—Tillie Olsen,
Tell Me a Riddle, 1956

Introduction

In 1994, a young college student named Jennifer Ireland found herself at the center of a national debate about day care. Ireland was a teenage mother who had graduated from high school with honors and won a scholarship to the University of Michigan. She took her two-year old daughter, Maranda, with her to Ann Arbor, and enrolled her in the university's day care center. But when Maranda's father, faced with child support claims, appealed for custody, Ireland found that her decision to send the child to day care while she attended classes tipped the scales against her. The judge awarded custody to the father, who had promised that his mother would stay home to take care of Maranda, while he worked and attended a local community college. Judge Raymond Cashen wrote in his decision that although Maranda had a deep bond with her mother, and her day care arrangements were good, staying with her meant that she would be "in essence raised and supervised a great part of the time by strangers." With her father, on the other hand, she would be reared by her grandmother, a full-time homemaker who would "devote her entire time to raising the child when the father was not available."[1]

Although Cashen's ruling showed the continuing power of the idea that day care is inherently bad for children, and that mothers who rely on day care are neglectful, the public outcry about the case challenged these judgements. Within days, the *Washington Post*, the *New York Times*, and the *Los Angeles Times* all issued editorials condemning the judge's decision, while the legal clinic representing Ireland received three hundred calls in two days offering emotional and financial support. The American Civil Liberties Union, the National Organization for Women, the United Auto Workers, and other national organizations jointly filed a friend of the court brief siding with Ireland.[2] Commentators rejected the message that Cashen appeared to be sending to women across the socioeconomic spectrum—that a mother's job was really in the home. "Women across the country are frightened by this ruling," Kim Gandy of the National Organization for Women told reporters. "I have a two-year-old myself, and the idea that somebody could come and say that I'm a bad mother because she's in day care part-time is a very scary thought."[3] The *New York Times* focused on the importance of day care to poorer women, calling the ruling "an affront and threat to the millions of women for whom day care is the difference between ignorance and an education, poverty and a decent income, dependency and self-reliance."[4] Julie Field, director of the legal clinic that took on Ireland's case, asked, "What does [Cashen's ruling] say to professional mothers like me? What does that say to the scores of women on public assistance who are being told to go out and get a job and better themselves?"[5] Columnist Anna Quindlen called it an "outrage" and found the judge's explanation that Jennifer Ireland could not possibly do justice to her studies and her daughter at the same time "deeply offensive" not only to Ireland but to all "those of us with rigorous jobs and small children."[6] An article in a Madison, Wisconsin, newspaper showed how much this issue seemed to cut across class lines; it reassured readers that such a case could not happen in Madison, since "so many judges have children who are in day care."[7] Ultimately, both the appeals court and the state supreme court found that Cashen's ruling had been inappropriate: with instructions that day care could not be grounds for denial of custody, the case was remanded to the circuit court and assigned to another judge. The Michigan Supreme Court wrote that "placement of a child in a good day-care setting can have many benefits and is in no sense a sign of parental neglect."[8]

The "Baby Maranda" case drew national attention because it exposed Americans' contradictory feelings about day care and motherhood. In the words of a *Washington Post* reporter, the case "stoked the guilt and anxiety and outrage of a country that struggles constantly with the question of what to do with the kids."[9] Many Americans share Cashen's assumption that care by relatives is inherently superior to care by "strangers," despite evidence to the contrary, and many working parents—especially mothers—feel that they should, in fact, be staying home with their children rather than going out to work.[10] Although the definition of a good mother as a full-time caregiver at home remains powerful, however, it coexists with a contradictory idea: that a mother's job is to provide materially for her children. Although Cashen seemed to feel that Ireland's decision to go to college would make it impossible for her to be a good mother, others saw her determination to pursue an education as part of her maternal responsibility. For instance, one woman wrote in a letter to the *Detroit Free Press*, "This young woman appears to be doing everything she can to ensure a bright future for her child," and the editorial agreed: "Ms. Ireland is more likely to be an effective mother if she pursues her education and equips herself to earn a better living and to build a better life."[11]

In this current period of welfare "reform," the message that a mother's first duty is support, not nurture, has become particularly strong for poor single mothers. These women are compelled to put their children in day care and go out to work in order to avoid becoming a burden on the taxpayers. While women like Jennifer Ireland could lose custody of their children for spending too much time away from them, columnist Katha Pollitt noted, "We don't hear too much about whether stressed-out moms, and daycare, and coming home to an empty, cookieless apartment, and constantly shifting babysitting arrangements are bad for poor kids. On the contrary . . . [a mother's] long hours on the job and frazzled mothering are supposed to be sources of pride for the whole family."[12] Many commentators noted that Jennifer Ireland was being punished for finishing school and staying off welfare—at a time when politicians and policymakers were debating how to get more single mothers to do the same thing.

Finally, although many people feel that day care is inferior to family care by mothers or other relatives, others promote day care as an educational experience that is beneficial to children, not just to their parents. The idea that day care is good for children was widespread enough that Maranda's father, Steven Smith, felt that he had to justify *not* sending the child to day care. "People say she'll learn so much in day care and learn to cooperate. But there are kids in our neighborhood she can play with, and it's not like I can't teach her to paste and cut and color and read and all that other stuff."[13] Recent discoveries about the cognitive development of very young children have added to the perception that quality day care can promote children's development—conflicting with the persistent belief that children are always better off at home.[14]

Why do we have such contradictory attitudes toward day care and mothers' work? A thoughtful look back at the history of day care can help us understand where we are today, and where we might want to go in the future. Although most people think of day care as a purely contemporary issue, in fact it has a long history in this country—a history that has profoundly shaped current attitudes and practices. *A Mother's Job* explores that history in one city, Philadelphia, over a span of seventy years, tracing the gradual transformation of day care from a charity for poor single mothers to a socially legitimate need of "normal" families, and even a potential responsibility of the state. Day care is simultaneously attacked and defended today because, even though its meaning has changed over time, it has never been completely transformed.

When elite women in Philadelphia created day nurseries for the children of wage-earning mothers in the late nineteenth century, they sought to take children off the streets and to enable mothers to keep their families together. But by defining day care as a charity for women who were driven into the labor force by economic desperation, these philanthropic reformers attached a stigma to day care that it still carries today. Day nursery leaders' deep ambivalence about encouraging mothers to become breadwinners led them to define their institutions narrowly and to avoid championing day care or pushing for its expansion. Rather than celebrating the wages they enabled mothers to earn, day nursery managers emphasized the "home" they provided for children and their success in assimilating immigrants and African-Americans. By contrast, the working-class and poor mothers who used the nurseries often had a broader view of their need for day care, seeing their wage work as an extension, not an abdication, of their responsibilities as mothers. These mothers, alienated from the charitable day nurseries, made other arrangements for their children if they could.

In the 1910s and 1920s, day nurseries, criticized by professional social workers who frowned on mothers' employment, fell into disregard. But at the same time, a new institution with a new definition of day care emerged. Nursery schools, which focused on affluent children's education rather than on poor mothers' employment, avoided the stigma of charity that tainted the day nurseries. Arguing that group care could be educational and beneficial for children, the nursery schools challenged the assumption that a mother's care was always best, and ultimately helped transform attitudes toward day care in general.

Further challenges to the model of charitable day care grew out of the crises of economic depression and war. By disturbing the stability of the male breadwinner/female caretaker paradigm, the Great Depression of the 1930s called into question the balance between women's paid and unpaid labor. While wives took on the burden of family support, private day nurseries expanded their scope, throwing aside earlier understandings of their mission. At the same time, the federal government sponsored public nursery schools throughout the country, bringing to a much wider audience the idea that group care for children could be desirable. World War II inspired further questions about the traditional division of labor within the family, as men left for war and the federal government urged women to lend their labor to the war effort. Conflict between child welfare advocates and representatives of defense industries about who had a stronger claim to mothers' labor created a confused and disorganized policy. While this debate went on around them, women in Philadelphia took advantage of the greater legitimacy of maternal employment, expressing their conviction that their wage work would benefit their families and that day care would be good for their children. Married women, professional couples, and women who did not absolutely "have" to work increasingly used Philadelphia day nurseries for their children during the war years.

At the same time, the federal government created publicly funded day care centers in the Philadelphia schools during the war, further legitimizing day care. These centers defined day care as a public service for which parents paid, not a charity bestowed on the worthy poor by the benevolence of the wealthy. When the future of the centers was jeopardized after the war ended, mothers in Philadelphia led public demonstrations and lobbying campaigns that ultimately forced the city government to continue funding these centers through the 1950s. In these demonstrations and negotiations, mothers displayed a new sense of entitlement, arguing that they had a *right* to publicly provided day care. Meanwhile, mothers applying to both private and public day care agencies expressed a new sense that their wage work was a legitimate way to improve their families' quality of life, and that day care would benefit their children. Despite calls for women to return to full-time motherhood after the war, the transformation in ideas about women's wage work and day care thus gained momentum in the postwar years. By the 1950s a new interpretation of day care emerged, which challenged but did not displace the older vision of day care as a charity for poor single mothers. This legacy of competing visions of day care and motherhood has helped to create the day care dilemmas of the 1990s.

Since ideas about good and bad mothering, children's needs, and mothers' responsibilities are always at stake in discussions of day care, examining the interactions between mothers and day care institutions enables us to pay close attention to the ways in which the experience and practice of motherhood have varied across lines of class and race, as well as over time. While middle-class white mothers were expected to devote all their energies to child care, rely on doctors and other experts, and concern themselves with their children's emotional and psychological growth, working-class definitions of good mothering often differed. The women who brought their children to the day nurseries in this study also prided themselves on being good mothers, but they often earned this distinction by the sacrifices they made to provide economically for their children rather than by their continuous presence and involvement in all aspects of their children's lives.

Other aspects of what it means to be a "good mother" have changed significantly from one generation to another. In fact, the very idea that haunts many working mothers today—that children need a full-time mother—was the particular creation of the urban middle class in the early nineteenth century. While these mothers focused their lives around nurturing their children's bodies and souls, most American mothers, whether they lived in urban working-class neighborhoods, slave quarters on southern plantations, or midwestern farms, continued to devote most of their energy to working to keep children clothed and fed, and relied on other women and older children to provide whatever child care was necessary.[15] So the redefinition of "a mother's job" that began during the course of this book, and with which we as a society are still struggling, is only another chapter in a long history.

Until very recently, day care was largely ignored by scholars. Most of the day care history that existed treated history as a backdrop for discussions of contemporary policy debates, thus doing little to help us fully understand the nuances and complexities of past developments.[16] Recent works by historians and sociologists that have paid more attention to day care have tended to focus on the national stage and on philanthropists, educators, and policymakers rather than on mothers, thus leaving us without an understanding of how day care functioned in particular contexts and of what role it played in the daily lives of ordinary people.[17]

By combining a local story with national debates, *A Mother's Job* seeks to give a fuller account of the changing meaning and practice of day care over a long time span. Looking at the history of day care in one city gives us a detailed and concrete picture of how day care programs worked and how families used them, allowing us to understand how day care fit into the context of daily life in a particular place. With its long tradition of philanthropy, Philadelphia was one of the major centers of the day nursery movement, and local archives have preserved a rich and varied written record. The story of day care in Philadelphia seems to be representative of the experience of other large cities, although we must await further research to know for sure what was "typical." Focusing on a city that was an important site of European immigration in the early twentieth century and of African-American migration throughout the century also enables us to see how race and ethnicity structured both working-class family life and the provision of day care. Using Philadelphia as a case study, this book reaches outward to explore national debates about day care, women's wage work, and child welfare.

In writing this history of day care, my approach has been shaped by the conviction that we cannot understand the complexities of social welfare programs and policy without incorporating the experiences, viewpoints, and "voices" of people who used these programs. In order to illuminate the experience of day care clients, this book draws on more than a thousand case records in addition to the standard sources (annual reports, board meeting minutes, publications, and correspondence) generated by twelve Philadelphia day nurseries, government agencies, and other social welfare agencies concerned with day care. It argues that the perceptions and decisions of ordinary working-class and poor families played a significant role in shaping the policies and practice of day care programs. I thus join other historians who have explored the interactions between welfare institutions and their clients, revising simplistic analyses of welfare agencies as tools with which elites exercise "social control" over the poor. Like these other historians, I have tried to trace the relationship between the moral codes of working-class clients and those of official institutions—recognizing that these "moral vernaculars" are sometimes, but not invariably, in conflict.[18]

Case records, created by social workers at the charitable day nurseries, can be a gold mine for historians. They not only give valuable social facts about the people who sought day care, but also enable us to explore the reasons that people gave for seeking day care, how they explained their children's needs as well as their own, how they presented their feelings about paid work and motherhood, their responsibilities to their children and other family members, and their relationships with social workers and others who sought to help them. As social workers probed into mothers' conflicts with family members, neighbors, and welfare agencies, they recorded different conceptions of women's work, motherhood, fatherhood, and children's needs. Using these case records thus allows us to hear social workers, parents, and children talking about day care and its meaning. Integrating this sort of material with discussions of day care policy and popular attitudes toward wage-earning mothers allows us to gain a much richer understanding of the changing meaning and uses of day care.

Case records of welfare agencies must, of course, be used with caution. As is true of most historical sources that record the lives of the poor, these records offer a very partial rendering of the "voices" of day nursery families. In discussing her use of similar records, historian Regina Kunzel quotes a sociologist who wrote in 1928, "The characters in case records do not speak for themselves. They obtain a hearing only in the translation provided by the language of the social worker." Like the unmarried mothers in Kunzel's case records, the experience of day care families that comes through the case records "was mediated several times over—shaped by the kinds of questions asked, by who was asking, by the [client's] relationship with the social worker, and by what that worker considered important enough to record."[19] But the many biases in these records do not render them worthless, for they can provide glimpses into the words and worlds of clients as well as those of social workers. We cannot think of the day nursery case records as an opportunity to eavesdrop directly on working-class women's conversations about paid work and motherhood. But by reading these records carefully and critically, we can trace the different expectations, identities, and strategies that these women revealed as they presented themselves in the office of a day nursery social worker. The different "scripts" that they used, the reasons they gave for needing care for their children, and the ways in which they claimed a right to assistance tell us much about their lives and identities.

In writing this book, I have also been concerned with the ways in which definitions of motherhood shape welfare institutions and social policy. My analysis has been influenced by a rapidly growing body of literature on the history of women's role in building the "welfare state." In the late nineteenth and early twentieth century, white middle-class women carved out a place for themselves in the public domain by arguing that women had a special responsibility for child welfare. College-educated women who were barred from male professions were able to create new roles for themselves as child welfare advocates, social workers, kindergarten teachers, factory investigators, public health nurses, nutritionists, and home economists. Although most were not mothers themselves, these women drew on the language of motherhood to justify their presence in the public sphere, arguing that it was their duty to extend their maternal compassion and nurturance into the broader society. Insisting that motherhood was a vital service to the state that required recognition and support, they mobilized women across the country to gain public attention for the needs of mothers and children. They even gained a foothold in the federal government when the Children's Bureau, which would become a strong advocate for child welfare, was created in 1914.[20] Historians have recently coined the term *maternalism* to describe these female reformers and their political philosophy.[21] Although scholars use the term somewhat differently, all agree rhetoric of motherhood, and the activities of women who used that rhetoric, h power in making claims on the state and helped transform the relationship b state and citizen in the years from 1880 to 1920.

Although maternalist reformers led the way to a welfare state at a time when other sorts of demands for social provision and government regulation fell on deaf ears, the very political efficacy of maternalism came at a price.[22] Reformers achieved great gains by appealing to conventional definitions of motherhood and family life; they could not question those definitions without losing their legitimacy. Maternalism gave elite women a rationale for creating day care institutions, thus recognizing and meeting a concrete need long before it was put on the public agenda. But with their commitment to full-time motherhood supported by a male breadwinner, maternalists also found it impossible to see mothers as workers, and thus could not truly support day care. Intent on valorizing the unpaid work of motherhood, most remained hostile to day care throughout the period of this study, discouraging mothers from taking on paid work on top of the burdens they carried at home. When grinding poverty or wartime emergencies made women's paid labor desirable, day care was defended as a temporary necessity, but rarely as a positive good. By portraying women's mothering work as inherently in conflict with their wage work, maternalist reformers denied poor and working-class women's own definitions of motherhood, as well as their need for assistance. In an attempt to valorize the work of mothering and meet the needs of children, these reformers ended up reducing the options available to women who needed or wanted to support, as well as to care for, their children.

Day care has a complex history, one that it is important for us to understand if we are to come to terms with some of the pressing social issues of our day. Day care has had many different purposes and meanings, for it is intertwined with questions about children's needs, the value of paid and unpaid work, and the responsibilities of mothers, fathers, and government. The history of day care does not suggest that it is a panacea for social ills: while some advocates of day care have sought to foster women's economic independence, others have aimed to benefit employers or the state, reduce the welfare rolls, dictate family forms to the poor, increase the power of experts, and force women to work outside the home. Although day care has not always been a means of benefiting women and children, however, I write from the conviction that it can be, and that it is an essential part of efforts to value the work of raising children and give people choices of ways to combine that work with other aspects of their lives. As day care becomes more and more central to the lives of American families, it becomes even more important for us to understand its history in order to make wise decisions about caring for our children. Perhaps a deeper awareness of day care's early history in this country can help us today explore ways of valuing *and* sharing the work of raising children.

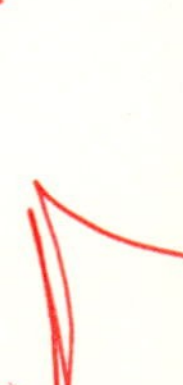

I

ESTABLISHING DAY CARE, 1890–1930

1

"Foster Mothers"

Creating Day Nurseries

Day care emerged out of pity in nineteenth-century Philadelphia—pity for children who played on city streets while their mothers went out to work to support them. The female philanthropists who established the first day nurseries wanted to bring these poor children in from the streets and create surrogate homes to shelter, nourish, and train them. In the process, they hoped to transform not only the children but their families as well, bringing immigrants and African-Americans into the "respectable" working class. By taking on "a mother's job," however, these elite women did not mean to encourage other women to become breadwinners. They saw mothers' wage work as an unfortunate necessity, a heroic response to the tragedy of poverty, not as a means to improve the lives of women or their families. The nurseries they established throughout the city thus offered day care as a charity for women who went to work out of economic desperation, not as a means of redefining motherhood.

A visitor to any of Philadelphia's working-class neighborhoods in 1890 might encounter children in the streets peddling fruit, selling newspapers, carrying large bundles of clothes for their mothers to work on at home, rocking small babies, and playing games like kick-the-can in between delivery wagons, horsecars, pushcarts, and ice trucks. These children were subject to physical dangers, such as being hit by streetcars, and they were exposed to the seamier side of city life as they mingled with prostitutes, chased policemen, and played around the doors of neighborhood saloons.[1] For many children, the city streets served as both playground and workplace; it was also the source of much of their wordly education.

The visitor who watched children peddling goods on street corners, caring for their younger siblings, doing the marketing, or even going to work themselves might learn that these working-class neighborhoods were made up of people whose ideas about childhood, work, and family responsibility were quite different from those conventionally celebrated by more affluent, native-born white Americans. The Russian Jewish boy selling rags, the Italian girl carrying garments on which she and her mother would work at home, and the African-American child reluctantly watching over her baby brother were all doing their bit for the family economy, which for most urban working-class families at the turn of the century required contributions from everyone. African-

Americans, restricted to low-paying jobs and expensive housing, often needed the wages of every available worker to survive; those too young to work were assigned to care for the very young. In immigrant and native-born white families, men and older children worked as much as they could, handing over their pay envelopes to the woman of the household, whose job was to "manage," stretching the family's cash to pay the landlord and the insurance collector, ensure that the children were adequately fed and clothed, and make the required contributions to lodges, churches, and kin or neighbors in need. In addition to their primary tasks of housekeeping and child-rearing (which might include hauling water up three flights of stairs, bargaining with grocers, and boiling diapers), mothers might also try to bring more cash into the household themselves, by taking in boarders, doing piece work for garment manufacturers, peddling, or taking in laundry. When times got bad, they would go out to work themselves.

So, many working-class and immigrant children did not inhabit a special world of their own protected from the harsh realities of adult life, and their mothers had worries that extended beyond nurturing children's development and supervising their play. Children did not spend all their free time in a home clearly separated from the outside world; rather, life in the small apartment homes spilled out into streets, alleys, and courtyards. Furthermore, both African-American and white working-class families were accustomed to sharing their living space with relatives or others. From a fairly early age, children were expected to "help out," whether through paid or unpaid labor.

When middle- and upper-class Philadelphians visited these neighborhoods around the turn of the century, and saw children in the streets, they saw not children behaving properly by helping out their families, but children neglected and abandoned to the dangers of the streets. In their eyes, children's presence in the streets was evidence of the inadequacy of working-class family life and the social chaos wrought by industrialization, urbanization, and immigration. While the conviction that poor people had inadequate homes and families was not new, the idea acquired a new urgency at the turn of the century as the city developed into a modern metropolis and manufacturing center. In order to keep children off the streets and create a kind of a public child's world for urban working-class children, reformers established day nurseries, as well as public playgrounds, settlement houses, and kindergartens; they organized clubs for boys and girls, enforced school-attendance laws, lobbied to restrict child labor, and created juvenile courts.

Through these efforts, reformers drew public attention to serious dangers threatening children in the city. But their focus on children also carried symbolic meaning. While adults were often held responsible for the poverty in which they lived, children seemed to be innocent victims. Moreover, saving the children meant saving the future; to reformers preoccupied with efficiency, social engineering, and the environmental causes of poverty, focusing on children seemed to be a way to eradicate deep-rooted social problems. Most of all, the sight of poor children in the streets suggested to many reformers a world turned upside down. Children belonged in the home, in a child's world physically and morally distinct from that of adults. Historian Christine Stansell's observations about an earlier generation of urban reformers hold true for the Progressive reformers as well: they valued a "particular geography of social life" that clearly separated the home from the world outside. The home was sacred, enclosed, protected, and privatized; "presided over by women, inhabited by children, frequented by men," it alone could preserve "those social virtues endangered by the public world of trade, in and politics" that the streets represented.[2] Thus the sight of children playing streets was not only disturbing because of the potential for physical danger, but because it suggested urban chaos, lost childhood, family breakdown, and the destruction of the home. In the eyes of reformers, children on the streets were *by definition* neglected and unloved. Reformers thus sought to reshape the social geography of poor neighborhoods, creating separate spaces for children, as well as encouraging working-class mothers to create attractive domestic space within their small living quarters so that children would stay out of the public world of the streets.

Most of the children playing on the city streets had mothers, relatives, or neighbors watching them from a window or courtyard. But those children whose mothers were at work seemed to be particularly vulnerable, and particularly in need of rescue. Married women's wage work expanded rapidly at the turn of the century, almost doubling from 1890 to 1920 in the country as a whole. As Philadelphia became an important center of industry, the ranks of working women grew rapidly. From 1850 to 1880, while the city's population doubled, the number of adult women employed in industrial jobs more than tripled. Only a few cities in the country attracted a larger proportion of wage-earning women.[3] In the six industrial sections of Philadelphia that investigator Gwendolyn Hughes studied in 1918–19, one in five married women was gainfully employed.[4] Mothers whose families needed their wages labored in the textile and hosiery mills in the north of the city and in the garment, cigar, and paper box factories in the south; they sold goods in large department stores and smaller shops, worked in laundries and restaurants, scrubbed offices in the central downtown, and cooked, cleaned, and cared for other people's children in private homes throughout the city.

Rates of women's employment, and the types of work in which women engaged, varied with ethnicity, race, and neighborhood. Rates of wage-earning by married women ranged from 28% among Irish families to as little as 7% among Poles.[5] While Kensington's native-born American and northern European women worked in textile mills or other factories, the Slovakian mothers of the northeastern section were more likely to work in domestic service or laundries, and the Polish, Italian, Hungarian, Russian, and Jewish mothers of the southeastern part of the city were often "mistresses of small shops, grocery or delicatessen, as a rule with an occasional news stand or notions store."[6] Italian and Polish wives were more likely to take in homework or boarders than to go out to work in a factory.[7] Similarly, among immigrant Jews, work in a family business—even if it was the marginal, low-status business of peddling fruit or operating a notions stand—was considered preferable to working in a factory.[8] All these women worked for a variety of reasons: to supplement their husbands' inadequate earnings; to support their children when husbands died, deserted, or lost their jobs; to pay off debts or medical expenses; or simply because a job became available. Above all, mothers went out to work to help provide for their families, for wage work was one way of meeting their responsibility to their children.

But reformers feared that by going out to work, mothers were actually abdicating their maternal responsibility, which was to provide full-time nurturing and housekeeping. Indeed, the idea of a mother going out to work in order to provide for her children violated conventional understandings of motherhood itself and suggested the breakdown of the social system in which men provided while women cared for the family. The mother who was also a factory worker was seen as an aberration; social worker

Helen Glenn Tyson wrote in 1925, "The mother in industry has always seemed a kind of 'social accident,'" creating "a bewildering problem in our industrial society today."[9] Just like children in the streets, the image of mothers in factories suggested that something had gone wrong in the modern city. At a conference called by the Women's Bureau in 1922, Secretary of Labor James Davis made this point eloquently:

> The spectacle of American mothers torn from their children while they strive in the toil and turmoil of industry to earn a livelihood for themselves and their little ones is an indictment of our modern civilization, a shame that cries to Heaven for vengeance, a menace to the whole structure of our national life. . . . An economic structure which is anywhere based upon the labor in industry of the mothers of the Nation is false and sooner or later it will come crashing down about our heads.[10]

There was something especially disturbing about the idea of mothers working in factories and industrial plants; it was "the mother in industry," not in domestic service, shopkeeping, or clerical work, that was the focal point of reformers' attention in these years. For the factory represented the height of modernity, technology, and science harnessed to the demands of the marketplace, while motherhood was the touchstone of social values that would guard against the excesses of the marketplace. Service work, which drew on more traditional conceptions of femininity, was not as threatening. This distinction also had a racial component, for it was the presence of white mothers in factories, not of African-American mothers in domestic work, that seemed to threaten the social fabric.

Progressive-era reformers agreed that motherhood and wage work should not be combined, for the "double burden" of breadwinning and maintaining a home was too heavy a load. John Martin, writing in *The Survey* in 1916, argued that mothers and industry simply did not mix: "Always will the pains and exhaustions and anxiety of pregnancy and child-bearing and baby-tending vitally handicap mothers in industry and push them down to the bottom of the industrial pit. . . . Never can they be prosperous, happy, contented and healthy in industry."[11] Labor reformer Florence Kelley put the argument more succinctly, writing, "The working mother is handicapped by her own nature."[12] It became commonplace to warn that "to be the breadwinner and the home-maker of the family is more than the average woman can bear."[13] Studies of infant mortality conducted by the federal Children's Bureau that correlated high infant death rates with mothers' wage work reinforced the idea that combining motherhood and wage work was harmful to the health of both mothers and children.

Children on the streets and mothers in the factories were thus equally out of place. Many reformers felt that mothers who went out to work not only risked their health but also deprived their children of a "normal" childhood and family life. For just as a family without a breadwinner was an "unhallowed thing," a home without a full-time mother was cold and empty, not really a home at all.[14] To the women who founded day nurseries in Philadelphia, the children of working mothers seemed homeless and motherless; through the day nursery they tried to provide a surrogate home and surrogate mothering to these children. The Franklin Day Nursery, for example, stated blankly that the children who attended the nursery "have no mothers. They are dead or working ten and twelve hours a day in shops and mills."[15] According to this formulation, a wage-earning mother may as well be dead, for her children were effectively orphaned by her long absence from home.

Above all, the nurseries aimed to shield children from the physical gers of the streets. A poem included in the Jane D. Kent Day Nursery's s port in 1886 suggests the anxiety about the presence of children on city vated many of the women who founded day nurseries. Using t Zechariah's vision of heaven, "And the streets of the city shall be full of bo playing in the streets thereof," the poet contrasts the prophet's vision of children playing on the streets of heaven with her vision of the dangerous streets of the earthly city:

> I notice now on every street,
> The little ones I daily meet;
> And oft I wonder if above
> Their feet shall tread the paths of love
>
> . . . .
>
> Alas! on earth in every street
> Lie evil snares for little feet.
> 'Tis from these very snares of sin
> The "nursery" seeks to draw them in;
> And guard them till they pass away
> To streets where "boys and girls" may play.[16]

Only in heaven could children safely play in the streets; while on earth, they would need to be protected, "drawn in" from the dangers of the streets to the safety of the nursery. The image of the protective home and the dangerous outside world was also invoked by the president of the Baldwin Day Nursery, when she wrote in 1917 that the nursery existed because death, desertion, and illness were "operating to drive the child's natural protector in the home out into the industrial world."[17]

Wage-earning mothers also worried about their children, fearing for their safety and concerned that they would grow "wild" without a mother's daily attention. When Helen Glenn Tyson interviewed one hundred mothers using Philadelphia day nurseries in 1919, she was struck by the mothers' concern with their children's physical safety. These women particularly valued the day nursery, they told Tyson, because "the children were 'safe' in the nursery; they were 'off the streets'; the mother 'knew where they were.'" The mothers also worried that, while they were working, they could not give their children the supervision and affection that they needed.[18] While the majority of breadwinning mothers were able to make arrangements with female kin or neighbors to care for their children, some were unhappy with this care; to others, it was simply not available. Thus, when elite women looked at the "homeless" children of working mothers and decided to establish day nurseries, they were meeting a real need, despite the class- and culture-specific nature of their concern. The institutions that they created may not have been exactly what the working mothers would have wanted, had they been asked. But the mothers would make use of them nevertheless.

"Accidental Philanthropy": The Beginnings of Day Nurseries

"The day nursery," Helen Glenn Tyson commented in her 1925 survey of day nurseries in Pennsylvania, "is the most accidental form of philanthropy imaginable. It comes into existence in the most casual fashion. . . . As church workers, nurses, and settlement workers have gone in and out of the homes of the poor they have seen these neglected little ones, and it has been a simple and natural thing to group them under the care of a kindly woman, who is paid a small sum to mother and feed them through the day."[19] From 1880 to 1920, day nurseries multiplied in Philadelphia's varied neighborhoods, founded by a range of people who found themselves going "in and out of the homes of the poor." Despite the diversity of their origins, however, all these nurseries shared a common purpose: to get the children of working mothers off the streets and into a supervised, structured environment.

Tyson's description of the founding of day nurseries perfectly fits the history of one of the first day nurseries in the United States. In 1863, Hannah Biddle, member of one of Philadelphia's most prominent families, was supervising the Sunday school at an Episcopalian church located in the heart of fashionable Rittenhouse Square.[20] According to an account recorded some forty years later, in visiting the families of the Sunday school children, Biddle found children locked into rooms alone; sometimes she could see them through the windows as she knocked on the door. She recalled, "I was moved with pity for the forlorn children who were left all day, either shut up in their homes, or allowed to wander about the streets between school hours, without suitable food and completely demoralized. I thought of the Creche I had seen in Paris and was sure that was the best way to brighten the lives of these children."

It is not clear to what degree the conditions Biddle observed were related to the social chaos caused by the Civil War, but we can certainly speculate that the wave of women's voluntarism that the war produced, combined with her family's tradition of civic leadership and noblesse oblige, encouraged her to create a solution. As she indicated, Biddle's solution was inspired by the French *crèches*, nurseries organized and funded by city governments and charitable women, which had begun in Paris in the 1840s.[21] She may not have been aware of day nurseries founded in Troy, New York, and in New York City in the 1850s, although it is tempting to think that her relatives may have been among the Quaker women who founded the country's first day nursery as part of their workroom for poor widows at the House of Industry in Philadelphia in 1795.[22] The ways in which Biddle's nursery was organized suggests that its founders also modeled their new institution on orphanages, the premier child-caring institutions of the nineteenth century. With these varied sources of inspiration, Hannah Biddle decided to take action: she "invited twelve ladies to form a board," rented a house, and hired a caretaker, and thus created the institution that for years was simply called the Day Nursery.[23]

Two other nurseries were founded in Philadelphia before 1880, but it was during the 1880s and 1890s that the number of day nurseries in the city really began to grow. In 1902, the Day Nursery reported: "There are now seventeen Nurseries in Philadelphia alone, and all are prosperous. This increase shows conclusively that the idea of nursery care and protection for children, during the enforced absence of their mothers, has taken deep hold of the popular mind and meets a manifest want."[24] The decision to change the nursery's name to the First Day Nursery in 1916 showed the board's consciousness of being part of a larger movement. When Josephine Dodge, president of the newly formed National Federation of Day Nurseries, came to Philadelphia in 1898, there were enough nurseries to warrant forming a local association, the Philadelphia Association of Day Nurseries (PADN). The expansion of day nurseries in the city reached its peak in the

1910s; by 1920, fifty nurseries had been established.[25] The growth of day nurseries in Philadelphia was part of a national trend: in 1892, when the first Conference of Day Nurseries was held in New York City, at least ninety nurseries had been established throughout the country, and by 1912 there were five hundred.[26]

Philadelphia day nurseries were founded in various ways. Some grew out of the work of Sunday schools, settlement houses, or kindergartens. For instance, the Young Women's Union Day Nursery was established as part of a Jewish settlement house that started as a kindergarten in a poor immigrant neighborhood.[27] Women were often supported in their venture by neighborhood clergy: for instance, Hannah Biddle established the First Day Nursery "under the auspices" of Bishop Stevens, while the women who founded St. Nicholas and Frankford day nurseries were aided by their respective ministers.[28] Although nurseries like the Young Women's Union and the Baldwin Day Nursery operated in connection with settlement houses, most were freestanding and independent of other agencies. Other nurseries were founded by groups of friends from elite private schools: thus the Jane D. Kent Nursery was established by a group of women who had known each other at the Friends Central School, and the Baldwin Day Nursery was founded by students at the Baldwin School, a girls' prep school located in the affluent suburb of Bryn Mawr.[29]

More nurseries were founded directly by the PADN, which launched a campaign to establish new nurseries shortly after its founding. In 1903, board members "called attention to the fact that . . . only 300 children were daily receiving care in day nurseries" and "made a plea for the establishment of new nurseries in the congested districts."[30] In 1905, the association circulated a letter to the principals and attendance officers of every school in the city about the need for nurseries, emphasizing that school-age children were being kept home to care for younger siblings. The letter was sent by the president of the Board of Education on official letterhead, thus bearing "the stamp and seal of authority" and was so effective that proposals were made for establishing eight new nurseries. "The problem now facing us," the PADN reported in 1905, "is—how to get these nurseries started without money enough in our treasury to 'back' the new ventures."[31] Over the next five years, spurred on by the "untiring labor" of PADN president Mrs. W. W. Frazier and by the help of a special fund devoted to that purpose, five new nurseries were founded.[32] Demand still outpaced supply, however, and the organization continued to receive appeals from child welfare organizations citing the need for nurseries in other parts of the city.[33]

Nurseries sprouted up in different neighborhoods to serve different sections of Philadelphia's working class. Kensington, where the Baldwin Day Nursery and the Kensington Day Nursery were established, was the center of Philadelphia's immense textile industry: hosiery, wool, carpet, silk, and other textile mills dominated the landscape.[34] Rows of brick or frame two-story dwellings surrounding the mills housed the families of English, Scotch, Welsh, and Irish immigrants and their descendants. The textile mills employed many women: Gwendolyn Hughes found that this area had the highest percentage (25%) in the city of married women employed in 1918.[35] In a survey conducted for the U.S. Children's Bureau in 1928, Clara Beyer described the Kensington area as an "old, highly industrialized section" in which mothers "have worked in the mills from generation to generation" when family needs dictated, although most did not work when their children were small unless they absolutely had to.[36] Two-thirds of the mothers applying to the Baldwin Day Nursery in the 1910s and 1920s worked in factories, the highest rate of industrial employment of any of the nurseries for which information is available.

By contrast, the African-American families who were streaming into Philadelphia from Virginia, North and South Carolina, and Georgia—and those whose families had been in the city for generations—were shut out of most factories, working instead at unskilled jobs in the interstices of the city's industrial economy. The resulting low wages and irregular employment for men meant that these families were more likely to send mothers as well as fathers out to work on a regular basis. In the Seventh Ward, which W. E. B. DuBois described as the center of African-American life in Philadelphia, mothers went out to work in large numbers in order to supplement the small wages of men who worked as day laborers, stevedores, porters, and custodians. Other studies of the city's African-American population found that married women's employment was common: in 1911, 54% of African-American families in Philadelphia had wives working, and in 1928, African-American mothers were more than twice as likely to be employed as white mothers.[37]

When African-American women in Philadelphia did go out to work, it was most often as a domestic servant. Seventy-one percent of the African-American mothers using the St. Nicholas Day Nursery in the 1910s worked as domestics, with the rest working in laundries or cigar factories; in the Seventh Ward, DuBois reported that 88.5% of Negro women worked as domestics, while others did laundry work, made dresses, or cleaned by the day.[38] Domestic work was often a woman's only option, although many might have agreed with the woman who told a Consumer's League investigator in 1918 that "she would rather starve than work as a domestic." When African-American women were employed in other industries, they were segregated into the dirtiest and most unpleasant part of the work: stripping tobacco leaves, scrubbing pans in bakeries, bundling soiled laundry, sewing cheap garments, pressing clothes, or scrubbing railroad terminals, cars, and waiting rooms.[39]

Many domestic servants were required to live at their employers' houses and had to board their children with other women or keep them with relatives. But those who did return to their own homes each night could bring their children to the day nurseries at the Benezet Settlement House, the Lincoln, the St. Nicholas, or the Women's Union day nurseries. The Women's Union Day Nursery was unusual not only in Philadelphia, but nationally, for it was organized, funded, and managed by African-American women. The nursery was a project of the Women's Union Missionary Society, an organization of African-American women from different religious denominations throughout the city founded in 1873 to help women "who are dependent on their own exertions for support." After conducting an employment office and two small industrial schools, the group, under the leadership of schoolteacher Julia Jones, opened the day nursery in 1893. Among the fund-raising efforts for the nursery was an 1897 poetry reading by Paul Dunbar.[40] In 1909, W. E. B. DuBois heralded the nursery as one of the most successful in the country, meeting a "crying need" among Negroes.[41] The composition of its board in 1926 suggests its grassroots origin: the board members, including two social workers, two public school teachers, a dressmaker, and the wives of a caterer, a butler, an auto mechanic, a Post Office clerk, and a salesman, lived in the neighborhood of the nursery.[42] This list of occupations suggests that the nursery board members were among the middle and upper classes of Philadelphia's African-American community, who lived among the poorer black families in the city's central African-American neighborhood.

Also streaming into South Philadelphia during these years—and sometimes displacing African-American residents—were Jewish immigrants from Russia, Poland, and Eastern Europe; Italian immigrants recruited from Sicily and southern Italy by the Pennsylvania Railroad; and immigrants from Slovakia, Poland, Hungary, and other parts of Europe. In the Jewish section of South Philadelphia where the Young Women's Union Day Nursery was established, immigrant women worked in small sweatshops or factories, peddled goods in the street, operated small stores, or took in homework. In this crowded neighborhood, which had quickly become the center of immigrant Jewish life in Philadelphia, Jews from Eastern Europe tried to re-create something of the world they had known in Europe, with their storefront synagogues and lively open-air market. The Young Women's Union, made up of women from some of the most elite German-Jewish families in the city, hoped to help assimilate these immigrants by providing services to their children.

East European Jewish immigrants sometimes resented the efforts of their more affluent brethren and quickly established their own network of charitable institutions. In 1911, the Downtown Hebrew Day Nursery was founded by East European immigrant women who "saw the need for day care . . . and did something about it"; a newspaper article celebrating the nursery's fiftieth anniversary explained the nursery's origins as "an essentially helpful-neighbor operation."[43] When some of these immigrants achieved a small measure of upward mobility and moved to the Strawberry Mansion neighborhood, "wives of business men and store-keepers in that vicinity" founded the Hebrew Day Nursery of Strawberry Mansion in 1923.[44] A poem read in honor of the nursery's twenty-fifth anniversary recalled how these neighborhood women, meeting with their baby buggies in Fairmount Park, talked about the children whose working mothers could not bring them to the park:

> Have you ever been so very ambitious
> As to wheel your child and carry knishes
> To the bandstand in the Fall and Spring
> In Fairmount Park to have your fling?
>
> . . . .
>
> They knew how much their children derived
> While less fortunate ones were being deprived.
> Since working mothers were unable to come,
> Their children played on the streets for fun.
> Their children played on the streets for their fun.
> And from this concern borne under a tree
> Evolved the plan for our nursery.[45]

To the west of the Jewish district of South Philadelphia, Italian women brought their children to the day nursery at St. Anthony's Church, the House of Industry Day Nursery, or the San Cristoforo Nursery; by 1920 they could go to the nursery at St. Mary Magdalen de Pazzi Church, a center of the Italian neighborhood.[46] Irish, Hungarian, Polish, and Slovakian women brought their children to charitable and church-sponsored day nurseries in various areas of the city while they went to work cleaning houses, rolling cigars, working in laundries, or running newsstands. And native-born white saleswomen and clerical workers, as well as factory workers, in the central downtown brought their children to the First Day Nursery and the Jane D. Kent Nursery.

The nurseries that formed the PADN were overwhelmingly Protestant; although they saw themselves as nonsectarian and many of their clients were Catholic or Jewish, the nurseries were founded, funded, and usually staffed by Protestants, and some included "religious instruction" as part of their mission.[47] For instance, the Baldwin Day Nursery, which was closely connected to a Presbyterian settlement house and had a substantial number of Catholic children among its charges, reported in 1927 finding "great opportunity for character strengthening in a little family altar around which all gather each day."[48] Mothers' meetings associated with the nursery were described as "women's temperance socials," Gospel meetings which always included an opportunity to take the total abstinence pledge, as well as "short, practical Bible lessons, and much hymn singing."[49]

The Protestantism of these nurseries worried some Catholics, who began to establish their own day nurseries in response.[50] The pastor of the Cathedral parish, disturbed by the number of children "roaming around the streets," decided that the parish needed a nursery. He approached a "pious lady of the parish," Miss Grace Town, who had been a schoolteacher and "had quite a lot of time on her hands." They rented a small house and hired a nurse and two assistants, but when reports reached the pastor that the children were not being well cared for, he asked for help from the Sisters of Charity, who conducted an orphanage nearby. In 1903, two Sisters were sent to the nursery, which Miss Town had been keeping in operation with her own funds.[51]

Although the Cathedral Day Nursery had been the city's only Catholic nursery when it was founded in 1897, that was soon to change. At churches throughout the city, parish priests asked religious orders of women to conduct day nurseries. For instance, soon after St. Malachy's Convent was opened in 1915, the rector of the parish asked the Sisters of Mercy to operate a nursery "in order to enable working Mothers to provide a safe place for the small children."[52] St. Joseph's Day Nursery was founded "at the earnest solicitation" of priests from three parishes and was conducted by the Missionary Sisters of St. Francis.[53] The suffering of children orphaned by the 1918 flu epidemic provided the impetus for the founding of day nurseries at St. Monica's and St. Casimir's (the latter was specifically for Lithuanian children and was partially funded by "the various Lithuanian societies").[54] By 1923, twelve new Catholic nurseries had been established, and two more were founded before 1930.

In addition to providing care for children, the Catholic nurseries sought to promote piety among their charges. By attending the Cathedral Day Nursery, the *Catholic Charities Yearbook* claimed, "many children were . . . rescued from the influence of non-Catholic nurseries, which abounded in the central part of the city." Religious instruction was an important part of what went on inside the nursery, as the *Yearbook* commented:

> There is another side to the Catholic day nursery—the spiritual side. Many of these little children learn for the first time how to make the Sign of the Cross and how to say their prayers. There are also cases where the children of careless and indifferent Catholics would have otherwise been lost to the faith if it were not for the fostering care they receive in the nursery.[55]

To help achieve these ends, the Cathedral Day Nursery included among its furnishings a statue of the Sacred Heart and the Stations of the Cross.[56]

Mothers were also "rescued" through the work of the nursery. Sister Lizzie Patterson explained that the day nursery had been the means of many conversions: "Through the children the hearts of the mothers are reached and brought to their sense of duty towards God." Mothers' meetings, Sister Lizzie wrote, were "the cause of untold good as Father Kelley takes this opportunity of pointing out to them [the mothers] their duty towards God and their children."[57] Teaching religious lessons through home visiting was particularly important because most of the families using the Cathedral nursery did not attend church. Similarly, the *Yearbook* noted that by visiting children's homes, "the Sisters of St. John's Nursery . . . are able to do a great deal of good not only to the little ones who are in their care, but to their parents as well, and through their influence have in many cases brought guardians who were careless and indifferent about their religious duties back to the sacraments."[58] The Sisters also visited the homes of other poor Catholics in the parish; Sister Frances Finley remembered that "S[iste]r Lizzie was a byword in the Parish. . . . When anyone was in need the first thing people would tell them was to go to Sr Lizzie she helps everybody."[59]

Philadelphia's Catholic day nurseries, concerned with providing specifically Catholic care for children, kept their distance from the Protestant and Jewish nurseries grouped together in the PADN. The PADN invited the Cathedral Day Nursery to join the association in 1900, but it never did.[60] The Catholic nurseries were content to provide shelter, care, and religious instruction for the children of their parishes, and they seem to have remained relatively isolated from the debates among day nursery founders, social workers, and reformers that affected those nurseries more closely tied to the organized day nursery movement.

In addition to the day nurseries that have left written records, there may have been many informal child-care arrangements sponsored by churches and individuals. A study of Philadelphia's day nurseries conducted in 1916 found twenty-two nurseries belonging to the PADN and thirteen independent nurseries; another study in 1919 came up with similar numbers. The independent nurseries, which were run by Catholic churches, Protestant missions such as the Salvation Army and the Bedford Street Mission, and individuals, left few traces in the historical record.[61] Only one or two nurseries that were run as business operations have been documented, and then only because someone associated with one of the charitable day nurseries was investigating the poor conditions in these for-profit nurseries. After describing unsanitary and generally unsatisfactory conditions at one nursery, the 1916 Child Federation report commented, "The woman responsible for this piece of 'charity' keeps a downtown office, from which she distributes a magazine which is sold 'for the benefit of the children of this city.'"[62] This may have been the same nursery that Helen Tyson noted in another report was run by "one woman—for begging purposes."[63] In another case, conditions at the Sunshine Nursery were bad enough in 1916 to warrant a complaint to the Chamber of Commerce. Several mothers using the nursery reported to the Society for Organizing Charity that the "children were neglected, and that [owner] Mrs. Clark profits by this 'pseudo-philanthropic enterprise.'"[64] A preliminary investigation by the Department of Health and Charities showed it to be "a more or less fake institution."[65] Although further reports confirmed this conclusion, the nursery continued to operate until a juvenile court judge ordered it to be closed in 1924, calling it a "disgrace to the city."[66] This nursery's history is recorded only because of the publicity surrounding the complaint—it is quite possible that other for-profit nurseries existed in the city during this period, joining the ranks of boarding-

houses, orphanages, and informal arrangements with kin and neighbors that wage-earning mothers relied on to provide care for their children.

An "accidental philanthropy," day nurseries multiplied in Philadelphia from 1880 to 1920. The nurseries that would become part of the urban landscape in many of the city's working-class neighborhoods were nurtured by a variety of people: elite women, Protestant and Catholic clergy, settlement workers, Sunday school teachers, church groups, immigrant aid societies, and neighborhood women. As time went on, however, the diverse origins of these nurseries faded and they became more standardized. While the Catholic nurseries retained their distinct mission and character, the nurseries that joined the PADN gradually grew to resemble each other, establishing definitions of purpose and standards of practice that would in turn influence the independent nurseries as well.

The Ladies of the Board

Philadelphia's day nurseries came to resemble each other in part because of the commonalities among the people who ran them. First of all, day nursery managers were women. Day nurseries stood out among Progressive-era institutions in being a women's charity: while other welfare organizations were founded and governed by men and women working together, day nursery boards were peopled almost exclusively by women.[67] The maternalist impulse that motivated day nursery founders—to get children off the streets and provide them with surrogate homes and mothers—must have seemed the appropriate province of women. Even when men were the initiators of a nursery, as with some of the church-linked nurseries, they recruited women to put their idea into practice.

Second, with only a few exceptions, day nursery managers were among the most elite women in the city. Many of the leading upper-class families in Philadelphia featured in sociologist E. Digby Baltzell's study *Philadelphia Gentlemen* were represented on at least one of the day nursery boards.[68] Seventy percent of the officers of the PADN were listed in the exclusive *Social Register* or the *Blue Book* for Philadelphia. In the eighteen nurseries that belonged to the PADN from the 1880s through the 1910s (excluding the three member nurseries whose Jewish or African-American board members would have been automatically excluded), 53% of the board members were listed in one of these guides; every nursery board had at least one member of high enough social standing to be listed, and in eight of the nurseries, more than three-quarters of the board members were listed. Many of these women belonged to exclusive organizations such as the Colonial Dames of America and the Acorn Club, while their husbands, graduates of the University of Pennsylvania, Haverford, Swarthmore, Princeton, or Yale, belonged to the city's best-known country clubs and organizations.[69] Even at the handful of PADN nurseries that did not have such elite boards, the board members still came from well-to-do families. For instance, the husbands of the board members of St. Nicholas Day Nursery included lawyers, investment bankers, and vice presidents of Strawbridge & Clothier department store, the Philadelphia Electric Company, and the Philadelphia Traction Company.[70]

Day nursery boards were filled with people who had longstanding ties to each other.

Like other German-Jewish philanthropies in the city, the board of the Young Women's Union—made up of women whose families owned major department stores and cigar, meat-packing, and paper factories in the city—was linked by a "spider web" of business and family relationships. Founded by Fanny Binswanger, daughter of a leading Jewish businessman-philanthropist, and Rosena Fels, sister of the soap manufacturer who would soon become one of Philadelphia's best-known philanthropists, the Young Women's Union was also supported by Binswanger's aunt, and its first corresponding secretary was soon to marry her brother.[71] Such family ties ensured that control of day nurseries, as well as of other charities, would remain within a closed circle of like-minded people. Similarly, Alice Griswold of the Franklin Day Nursery wrote in 1917, "We have all been friends for so long—one can scarcely tell at a meeting who is chairman of what. . . . Occasionally a change takes place, or a new member joins our board, but she soons adds her friendly spirit to the others and on goes our work as heartily as ever."[72]

Charitable work, an expression of the concept of noblesse oblige, was an expected part of these women's lives, an important indicator of their upper-class status. Philanthropy played a status-building role among the city's Protestant elite; this was true to an ever greater degree in Philadelphia's Jewish community, where philanthropic service was more important than bloodlines in establishing high social standing.[73] One nursery manager, looking back in 1940, recalled that in her youth, a woman "supported and worked for only one charity by which she was known"; that is, her charitable work became an important part of her reputation as an upper-class woman.[74] In 1913, the society page of the *Philadelphia Record* featured an article about the First Day Nursery. The nursery was "Supported by Society Women Who Take Great Personal Interest in the Work"; "every afternoon some of the best-known society matrons and debutantes can be seen in the recreation rooms of the nursery, telling stories to the older children, or in the dormitories, coddling the babies." The article concluded by saying, "There is no institution more popular among society women and none more enthusiastically maintained by their personal efforts," and listed the names of prominent society women who "spend an afternoon each week in comforting and amusing the little children of the slums."[75] Such volunteerism was an central part of upper-class women's lives: it gave them a socially acceptable—even mandatory—sphere of public activity, allowing them to take on all the responsibilities of managing a major institution without challenging the idea that women did not belong in the public realm of business and politics. Charitable activity was an important outlet for women's energies; for instance, Fanny Binswanger organized the Young Women's Union after her father forbade her to go to college. By devoting themselves to charitable causes like day nurseries, such women asserted their leadership as members of the city's upper class while staying within the boundaries of proper womanly behavior.[76]

As time went on, the status of the day nursery as a field of charity for "society matrons and debutantes" sometimes drew sharp criticism. In a 1926 editorial entitled, "Wake Up, Managers," the newsletter of the National Federation of Day Nurseries complained that "there are many hundreds of managers in this country who know and care little about the work. Many of these women are railroaded onto the board because they can afford to give money and prove to be deadwood as far as improving the nursery is concerned."[77] In introducing Ethel Beer's 1938 book, *The Day Nursery*, educator Patty Hill wrote approvingly, "The sentimental and oft disturbing efforts of debutantes and their ambitious mammas seeking an emotional outlet for their own starved lives are also bitterly assailed."[78] Indeed, Beer, herself a day nursery board member in New York City, criticized wealthy women who turned their own children over to nurses and servants, but gladly accepted the invitation to be part of a day nursery board.

As Beer pointed out, serving on a day nursery board had a social function that went beyond an individual woman's concern with the plight of poor children. She explained, "As a rule, a Day Nursery Board is a close corporation bound together by ties of family and acquaintances. The selection of its members, therefore, has a social basis. Very rarely does the Board reject a proposed member. Sometimes the membership is inherited, that is, a mother may be succeeded by her daughter, an aunt by a niece."[79] This observation is borne out in the records of Philadelphia's day nurseries. A 1960 newspaper article about the history of the Lincoln Day Nursery showed a picture of Mrs. Benjamin West Frazier, Jr., next to Mrs. G. Harrison Frazier, Jr., and noted, "Their husbands, who are first cousins, are grandsons of the woman who founded the nursery 71 years ago. Since the day nursery was organized in 1889, there has always been a Frazier or two on the board."[80] Similarly, an article about the fiftieth anniversary of the First Day Nursery commented, "The children and grandchildren of the founders of the nursery are still looking after its welfare, and the same old family names are among its managers and active workers."[81] Service on this day nursery board was part of the life of women in the inner circles of Philadelphia's fashionable society, where attention to "the same old family names" was crucial. Memberships were passed from mother to daughter as part of the duties of upper-class womanhood. For instance, at the First Day Nursery, "Mrs. Maxwell Wyeth was unanimously elected to the board to fill the place left vacant by the death of Mrs. Wyeth Sr."[82] In fact, extending membership to female relatives of women already serving on the board was so common that occasionally a mistake was made: At a 1918 meeting, the First Day Nursery board learned that "Mrs. Harrison Frazier had been notified of her election to the board," although it was her daughter, Miss Harriet Frazier, who had actually been approved for membership.[83]

The elite standing of many day nursery board members, and their access to the wealth of their families, was vital, since board members were responsible for raising the funds necessary to operate the nurseries, as well as for overseeing their daily operations. In the early years, many managers were actively involved in running the nurseries, although the founders of the Jane D. Kent Nursery, who (according to a newspaper article many years later) at first "worked in shifts to care for the children," were unusual.[84] Like nineteenth-century housewives, most managers saw their job as supervising the workings of the nursery household, rather than actually doing the work itself. The managers' duties could involve anything from inspecting the premises and advising the matron to visiting nursery families, sewing clothes for the children, bringing special gifts, or reading them stories. Managers might come to the nursery daily, although weekly visits were the norm: a report of the Young Women's Union in 1896 mentioned, "Some members of the Nursery Committee are constantly on hand, either to investigate cases before admittance or to assist in some other manner those who come under the society's charge."[85] The sewing the board members did for the children was a gesture of charity, like the sewing circles prevalent among many classes of women throughout the nineteenth century. For instance, in 1915, the managers of the Baldwin Day Nursery agreed to "hold an all day meeting at the house of Mrs. Wilson . . . to cut out and sew aprons in the morning, stay for lunch and hold the business meeting in the afternoon."[86] Perhaps by giving up their leisure to make clothes for these children, board members also laid claim to a kind of surrogate motherhood.

While day nursery managers performed a number of roles, however, their primary job was to raise money. Most of the day nurseries charged a small fee—usually between five and ten cents a day—but these fees were largely symbolic, intended to preserve the idea that the day nursery was not "pauperizing" poor families by giving them something for nothing. (Of course to families struggling to make ends meet, even a very small fee was more than symbolic, often becoming another burden. And the parents' fees did constitute a small but important part of many nurseries' budgets, despite their status as purely charitable institutions.)[87] Most of the money necessary to operate the nurseries, however, had to come from other sources. Sometimes a board member would give some of her own income to keep a nursery afloat. For instance, the Ways and Means Committee of the Baldwin Day Nursery announced in 1922 that fund-raising was not an immediate need, as "Mrs. Pew had very generously offered to finance the nursery during July and August."[88]

For both major and minor donations, managers relied primarily on their personal and family connections, soliciting annual subscriptions and emergency funds to meet immediate needs, as well as major legacies and bequests.[89] Most day nurseries relied on fund-raising "entertainments" held by the managers to generate most of their income. For instance, the fund-raising efforts of the Baldwin Day Nursery included a benefit performance of the Savoy Opera Company in 1911, a bridge party at the Bellevue-Stratford Hotel in 1913, a "Bal Masque" at the Merion Cricket Club in 1915, and a tableaux and dance at the Ritz-Carlton Hotel in 1917.[90] Day nursery supporters who remembered the nurseries in their wills often sustained them financially for years. A history of the First Day Nursery explained that although the institution had been pressed for money early in its existence, "slowly and surely it progressed, . . . and today it is receiving substantial help from the legacies of those who were its friends in its early struggles for existence. It has never closed its doors."[91] Indeed, much of the nursery's income from the mid-1880s through the 1910s came from numerous bequests of more than one thousand dollars. A newspaper article in 1913 explained, "So generously were the appeals for help responded to by the friends of the institution that during its history of half a century there has never been the need of making an appeal to the public."[92] The Young Women's Union also benefited from legacies and effective private fund-raising networks: in 1896, the annual report explained, "the executors of the estate of the late Simon Muhr recently offered $5000 for a building or endowment fund with the sole condition that an equal amount be raised within a specified time. Through the efforts of a small committee of gentlemen, not only the amount required was raised, but considerably more."[93]

Such spectacular gifts could not be counted on, however, and day nursery managers had to keep raising money to meet routine expenses. Regular donations came through annual subscriptions and appeals made by individual managers to their family and friends. At a meeting of the Baldwin Day Nursery in May 1921, for instance, "a list of former contributors during May was read so that each member could write to those who had contributed through her."[94] At a 1903 meeting, board members discussed "the low state of the funds" and planned visits to the mills of the district as well as to ministers of nearby churches "to ask them to help us with a donation day."[95] Support from local mill owners was sought again in 1917, when "Mrs. Coffin suggested writing personal notes to managers of mills in Kensington asking for contributions."[96]

While day nursery boards frequently faced shortfalls, the managers' networks usually produced help. For instance, during the summer of 1902, "some anxiety was occasioned by the low ebb of the funds" of the Baldwin Day Nursery. Mr. E. R. Strawbridge, a department store owner whose wife was a frequent contributor to the nursery, donated money to print up a fund-raising appeal that was mailed to one thousand potential supporters.[97] But the nursery still needed money for a new building; in 1904, Esther Kelly reported,"Toward the needed amount for the building, about $10,000, there has been rec'd up to this present time $35." With no funding in sight, Kelly put her faith in God: "These needs, together with the current expenses of the coming year, we leave in the hands of Him who has provided during the past years, and of those good friends whom He has sent to help to carry on this work."[98] And indeed, two years later, she could report a complicated real estate transfer that resulted in a new building for the nursery—made possible by a gift to the settlement house with which the nursery was affiliated, as well as by the financial support of Kelly's new husband, and a timely loan from the nursery's attorney.[99] Nurseries with less elite boards had to make more public appeals: perhaps the most creative grassroots fund-raising appeal was that of the Frankford Day Nursery, which raised $12,123 in twelve days to pay for a building with the sale of bricks. "With a slogan 'Everybody Buy a Brick in the Nursery' in store windows, on the sides of local trucks, and even as a song in the Marshall [public] school, the goal was reached."[100]

Unlike the PADN-affiliated nurseries, which were governed by boards of lady managers and funded through their personal connections to wealth, Catholic day nurseries were funded by donations from parishioners and from the church hierarchy. Day-to-day decisions were made by the nuns who ran the nurseries, but they were dependent on their superiors within the religious order, and even more on the pastor, bishop, and parishioners for support. Most fund-raising for the Catholic nurseries was done through the parish church that sponsored the nursery. St. Malachy's Day Nursery, for example, was "supported by the members of St. Malachy's parish, as the small offerings received from the parents of the children would not be sufficient to finance the nursery."[101]

While church officials donated building space, the "ladies of the parish" often played an important role in raising money to meet daily expenses. For instance, when the Daughters of Charity, who were summoned to take over the Cathedral Day Nursery, first arrived, they were disheartened to find six undernourished-looking children and nothing in the place to eat. At first they relied on small donations from individuals (the local grocer sent some food, and "a lady of the Parish" sent what was left over from her dinner every day) and on the proceeds from a salvage bureau they had started to help support the nursery. When they needed a larger building, however, "some kind ladies of the parish" helped procure the funds necessary for renovation. Other Catholic charitable groups, such as the Conference of St. Vincent DePaul and the Knights of Columbus, helped periodically, but it was the efforts of women parishioners that sustained the nursery. Sister Frances Finley remembered, "Several ladies of the parish kept giving Card parties and Bazaars for the Nursery."[102] In 1923 the *Catholic Charities Yearbook* reported that the nursery's main income came from these women's weekly euchre card parties, as well as the annual donation day, when "an appeal to the people of the parish and to friends from other parts of the city is made." Finally, a sewing circle, "composed of young ladies from the Cathedral parish," gathered every week to make clo nursery children.[103] Similarly, St. Monica's Day Nursery received support auxiliary, which held fund-raising card parties "to defray the current expenses. some of the Protestant nurseries, the Cathedral Day Nursery also benefited from bequests; Sister Lizzie Patterson recorded that "occasionally the Day Nursery has been remembered in the wills of good Catholics."[105]

The Mission of Day Nurseries

The women who founded the day nurseries soon had to face a troubling question: what if offering care to the children of working mothers actually encouraged more women to go out to work? Their belief in the importance of mothering, which had led them to establish the nurseries in the first place, meant that they did not want to encourage women to work for wages. So day nursery managers emphasized that the nurseries were to serve only poor mothers working out of absolute economic necessity; in their publicity they often emphasized the heroic figure of the struggling widow or deserted wife, who could not be blamed for working. Because most day nursery managers were ambivalent about maternal wage-earning, even in the face of dire economic conditions, they tended to emphasize their service to children rather than the paid work for mothers that they made possible. Fearing the negative consequences of taking on "a mother's job," day nursery managers simultaneously stressed the homelike nature of their nurseries and sought to reshape the homes from which day nursery children came.

Day nurseries were intended for working mothers, but not for all working mothers. In order to be sure that women who were looking for a way to free themselves of daily responsibility for their children did not use the nurseries, day nursery managers limited their charity to women in specific circumstances. The mission statement of the San Cristoforo Day Nursery, a nursery founded by the PADN to serve an Italian neighborhood, was typical of other charitable day nurseries (and in fact was repeated word for word in the annual reports of many PADN member nurseries):

> The object of the Day Nursery is to receive and care for, during the day, the young children of poor working-women, whose employment calls them from their homes, and who would otherwise be obliged to leave their children entirely without protection and subject to the perils of fire and accident.[106]

Many nurseries were careful to state that they would not accept children of mothers who worked for any reason but dire financial necessity. The president of the Franklin Day Nursery explained in 1912 that "if the support of the family no longer falls on the mother, those children must withdraw . . . ; the Nursery must never deteriorate into a mere receiving station for children, to free mothers from their duties."[107] Similarly, in describing St. Malachy's Day Nursery, the *Catholic Charities Yearbook* warned, "Mothers who are not obliged to work to support their children or those who desire . . . merely to free themselves from the responsibilities of a home are not permitted to place their children."[108] We can speculate that nurseries founded by African-American women (such as the Women's Union Day Nursery) were less troubled by fears of women going out to work, but unfortunately the few records that have survived do not provide much evidence of the founders' attitudes or the nursery's policies. Supporters of day nurseries frequently felt the need to prove that the existence of the nurseries was not a factor encouraging women to leave their children to take up wage work. In a 1925 study, social worker Helen Tyson reminded her readers that "the fear that the existence of the day nurseries may induce mothers to place their children in order to enter industry . . . has no foundation in fact."[109] Yet fears abounded that women who did not "have" to work would take advantage of the nurseries. For instance, a speaker addressing the PADN in 1923 warned of the "danger of freeing the mother from maternal responsibilities and not working for the interests of the home."[110]

In annual reports and other publicity intended to elicit donations, day nursery supporters addressed this fear by highlighting the heroic figure of the struggling widow or deserted wife, who could not be condemned for working. For instance, in 1900 the Baldwin Day Nursery described its clients as widows and deserted women who were "needy, helpless, mutely-appealing." Another Baldwin report presented day nursery families as victims of fate, "staggering under some of life's heaviest handicaps."[111] A poem written to celebrate the twenty-fifth anniversary of the Strawberry Mansion Day Nursery recalled that "the method used in admission" in the nursery's early years gave preference to cases of desperation and tragedy:

> D.D.D. was the key to the code
> Desperate, deserted and destitute.
> The louder the wails, the shorter the road,
> That led to this child care institute[112]

Catholic nurseries also highlighted the desperation and sacrifices of nursery mothers. In 1923, the *Catholic Charities Yearbook* described the typical woman the nurseries served as a "good mother" who was a "victim of various kinds of misfortune," but considered "no toil too great and no hours too long if by any means her babes can be returned to her when the day is done."[113]

The struggling single mother was also the central figure in Marion Kohn's descriptions of Jewish immigrant nursery families, even when that image did not fit reality. In her 1913 report to her board at the Young Women's Union, Kohn claimed that more than half of the children cared for at the nursery "came from homes where the father had deserted," although according to Kohn's own figures, no more than a quarter of the families applying for nursery care fit that description. Kohn went on to tell the story of Edith, an eighteen-year-old mother whose husband had deserted: "It is not easy to work ten hours a day, to leave the baby at the Nursery early in the morning, to come for it in the evening, then return to one's squalid tenement, to build the fire and prepare the frugal meal—in warm weather and in cold, in storm and in sunlight, day after day. . . . Most of our mothers are not as young as Edith, but they are like her—all struggling and self-sacrificing—women to whom the highest tribute should be paid."[114] Again in 1914, Kohn emphasized the plight of the nursery mother and sang her praises:

> Who is the parent of the Nursery child? and from whence does she come? She is, in 75 percent of our homes, the deserted mother. In many instances she has come from Russia with her children to meet her husband in America, and when deserted, there are no relatives to whom she may turn. Starvation or the world of industry face her, and choosing the latter, she comes to us. . . . Too high a tribute cannot be given to the Nursery mother whose

> every day living means sacrifice and loving devotion to her children, and sometimes, almost super-human effort to keep her family together.[115]

Kohn wrote these words at a time when desertion was becoming a major issue of concern to social welfare workers, especially within the Jewish world, and the specter of the Old World woman rejected by her Americanized husband evoked fears that immigration was dissolving sacred social bonds. The deserted mother in her description is a victim who must find a way to support her children, not a mother who willingly leaves her children in the care of others.

Mothers, whether deserted women or widows, were the central figures in day nursery reports, but struggling fathers also appeared and were also praised for their determination to keep their families together. Single fathers represented a tiny fraction of the families applying for day nursery care (averaging 1.8% at five nurseries), but were appealing figures to day nursery managers. Thus the Baldwin Nursery's annual report in 1900 referred not only to "the widow and deserted mother," but also to the "much-perplexed and overwrought widower" as needing the nursery's help. The report did not include in this brief sketch of the nursery's clientele the much more frequent—and troubling—cases of women who worked because their husbands earned insufficient wages.[116] A father's duty was support, not daily care, and while the father who wanted to keep his family together after his wife's death or desertion was seen as admirable, such an attempt was not expected of most fathers. Instead, they were encouraged to hire a housekeeper or place the children in foster care or an orphanage. Helen Glenn Tyson questioned whether "it is ever advisable for a father alone to try to keep his family together," citing the cases of six father-only families using Philadelphia day nurseries. All these fathers "had great trouble about the laundry and mending, and the cooking was an impossibly difficult problem." She concluded that the "motherless" children in these families "were not receiving the protection and care due all little children."[117] While mothers could, with the help of the nursery, fill a father's shoes, fathers could not take the place of mothers. Remarriage was often the preferred solution, and the Baldwin Nursery reported proudly in 1914 that a widower with six children who had been using the nursery married a widow who was using the nursery for her child. While the nursery itself could not replace the children's mother, by facilitating this marriage, "the Nursery had provided a good mother in that case."

Bad fathers also appeared in day nursery reports. They were the silent presence behind the many stories of the struggles of deserted mothers, mothers who left their husbands because of abuse, or mothers whose husbands refused to support them. Sometimes they were a visible presence as well. In the same report that told of the widower finding a new mother for his children at the nursery, the Baldwin managers told the story of a couple that had separated and was again living together, using the nursery.

> The father forbade the boys to help their mother in what he called "woman's work," however ill and tired she might be; and he himself never lifted a finger. After being in the Nursery, the mother's retort was that the Matron would not let the boys remain if they did not do their share of work at home. That silenced the father, because he was ready enough for the woman to do a man's work in supporting the family."[118]

As victims of lazy, irresponsible, or violent men, mothers could gain the sympathy of day nursery managers, who found it easier to condemn individual men than to probe the structural roots of poverty.

While day nursery managers praised the sacrifices made by wage-earning mothers and, by providing care for their children, encouraged them to support their families, they believed that both children and mothers suffered from the "social accident" that forced a mother to leave her home to seek work. Their reports expressed their hope that day nursery families could be restored "to normal conditions," with a breadwinning father enabling the mother to be at home with her children. These women were strong believers in the family wage, hoping that the families they served would attain that ideal of a male wage generous enough to support a family; although they were daily confronted with the effects of women's low wages, they never called for equal pay. Day nursery women believed in the importance of motherhood, and to them, motherhood meant full-time devotion to children. Women who could not afford that version of motherhood were to be pitied, and their children helped, but they were not to be encouraged to keep working if there was any alternative.

Day nursery reports frequently repeated the idea that families in which mothers had to work were deprived of "normal" family life. For instance, Marion Kohn of Neighborhood Centre Day Nursery declared, "I can imagine no life more abnormal than that of the Day Nursery mother and child."[119] She frequently described the goal of the nursery as "the re-establishment of a family to normal conditions," "home rehabilitation," or "building up the home," implying that the homes of her clients had somehow been destroyed when mothers went out to work.[120] Likewise, the Baldwin Day Nursery claimed in 1918, "It is the abnormal life that seeks our help, the unfortunate, the bruised, the down-hearted and discouraged men and women, with burdens too great to be borne alone, the children deprived of the wholesome conditions of normal family life."[121] Nursery workers were delighted when a mother who had been using the nursery returned to her "normal" status as full-time mother. For instance, the visitor for the First Day Nursery reported enthusiastically in 1917 on the Fowles family: "Everything is *lovely* here at present. Mr. F has been working regularly, since he came out of the House of Correction and giving Mrs. F about $9/wk. Mrs. F has been able to give up mill work and remain at home."[122] When the Franklin Day Nursery organized an "alumni party" in 1925, the managers were proud to report

> that of the thirty-five [children who returned for the party] everyone had a trade, and none were day laborers; that everyone lived in a house or apartment, and not in rooms, and that none of the young men who were married were allowing their wives to work as their own mothers had had to do.[123]

And Marion Kohn concluded the story of how a couple was reunited by the day nursery by saying, "And now we say with some thankfulness, too, that another family has been saved to society."[124]

Despite their commitment to the family wage, full-time motherhood, and rescuing children from the streets—all relatively popular ideas—day nursery managers faced several problems in winning support for their efforts. At a time when the presence of mothers in industry was criticized as evidence of the ravages of industrialization, the day nursery made it easier for mothers to manage the logistics of making a living by working outside the home. At a time when there was great enthusiasm in reform circles for closing down orphanages and placing children in private homes, day nursery founders were creating new institutions modeled on the orphanage. In order to cope with these difficulties, day nursery managers made two rhetorical moves: they focused on meeting the needs of children rather than on enabling mothers to earn wages, and they emphasized over and over again the homelike nature of the nurseries they were creating. They also justified the nurseries by describing the ways in which contact with the nursery improved the homes of families who used it.

Day nursery founders and supporters addressed their own profound ambivalence about maternal employment by focusing on meeting the needs of the children rather than on helping mothers to earn wages and support their families. Indeed, there is a deafening silence in day nursery reports and publicity about mothers' paid work, a silence that seems puzzling when we remember that the nurseries were founded to enable mothers to work. Of course, this emphasis on children was part of a much broader tendency among women reformers of this era to emphasize children's needs as a way of garnering public support for welfare measures, a strategy that historian Linda Gordon has recently labeled "putting children first": "As I imagine it, women held up children in front of them, plump little legs and adorable wide eyes inducing a suspicious gatekeeper to open a door to the public treasury."[125] Children were innocent, appealing, and worthy objects of charity, while parents were more complicated. Focusing on children may also have been a way of presenting the *institution* itself as worthy of aid; managers were proud of the buildings and furnishings they had provided, and pictures of groups of children inside the nursery showcased these efforts better than focusing on the mothers.

But the emphasis on children also served to downplay the fact that the day nursery served working mothers. Women were presented in these reports as mothers needing safe care for their children and as wives abandoned or disappointed by their husbands, but never as workers. This was part of a broader tendency within a maternalist discourse that defined women as mothers, real or potential, and (while making passionate pleas for the value of the nurturing work women did as mothers) ignored the fact that mothers were also workers.[126] Had day nursery founders sought to encourage mothers to support their children through wage work, or redefined motherhood to include supporting as well as nurturing children, day nursery reports might have depicted mothers' workplaces, shown photographs of a mother proudly opening her own pay envelope, or even displayed pictures of a mother with her children in the home made possible by her wages. Instead, the text and photographs of the reports focus solely on the nursery, depicting children sleeping, eating, and playing in their surrogate home. Both mothers and children were cast in passive rather than active terms, as seemed appropriate for objects of charity.

Rather than directing attention toward working mothers, day nursery managers focused on the nurseries themselves as surrogate homes providing surrogate mothering. For instance, the 1917 report of the Baldwin Day Nursery described a family with two boys who came to the nursery, and commented: "To correct, to guide and to develop these boys into upright citizens, to bring them to a strong and healthy manhood, is the aim of their mother and the aim also of their foster mother, the Baldwin Day Nursery."[127] Another report claimed that, for children who "lacked a mother's care," the Baldwin Nursery "supplied the parent that was missing."[128] By defining themselves as "foster mothers," nursery founders expressed their conviction that the children they served were indeed orphans, suffering from their mothers' need to go out to work.

Over and over again, nursery reports spoke of efforts to make the nurseries "a home" for the children who spent time there. To women anxious about creating cold institutions, the word *home* suggested comfort, beauty, safety, morality, nurture, and health. Because nurseries were presented as an alternative to orphanages, it seemed particularly important to stress their homelike environment. In her annual report in 1904, the matron of the Baldwin Nursery explained, "The older children go from the nursery to the public schools, as from a happy home."[129] The managers of the nursery invited subscribers to visit at any time, "but particularly during some birthday celebration or other festivity, when they can see the children at their games and realize that the Nursery is to them a happy, cheerful home."[130] Similarly, when the managers of the Lincoln Day Nursery praised their matron, it was for her qualities as a surrogate mother: "Mrs. Holt's understanding interest in the moral and physical welfare of each child, and her attitude of affection for each, make the children respond as to a mother, and eradicate as much as is possible institutional defects."[131]

In order to make it clear that day nurseries were not drawing children out of nurturing homes to place them in heartless institutions, day nursery reports often contrasted the bleak homes of their clients with the warm atmosphere of the nursery, a reversal of the usual dichotomy between "home" and the outside world. Nurseries were presented as being safe havens from the outside world, havens that poor children's homes could not provide. Thus the First Day Nursery explained in 1890: "Day after day the children wend their way from the courts and narrow streets in all kinds of weather often from cheerless homes, to receive shelter, warmth and nourishing food at the Nursery, whose doors are ever open to those who need its fostering care."[132] The children's homes are equated with the "cheerlessness" of the outside world, but the nursery is a real home, providing not only shelter but nourishing care. Similarly, in a dramatic portrait of a nursery mother's day, Marion Kohn of Neighborhood Centre juxtaposed the homelike qualities of the nursery with the hostile nature of the outside world and the bleakness of the mother's own home:

> The driving sleet beats against the window; and Mrs. Fein starts from her sleep, knowing it is day. No light from the wintry sky filters in through her tenement window. . . . After a scant breakfast, she wraps the baby in a shawl, bids the other little ones follow, and hurries into the street. . . . Together they walk through the cold driving storm and when, at length, the nursery is reached, there is warmth and kindness and cheer. . . . At last she leaves her children with a feeling of safety that for them, at least, a helpful provision is made. She goes to the factory where all day, the busy whir of machinery, the anxiety of the "piece worker" and the orders of the foreman add not the most tuneful harmony to her motherhood.[133]

The contrast between the nursery and the outside world was also drawn in a Baldwin Day Nursery report in 1902:

> Perhaps the best view of the work of the nursery is when, amid the screams of the great factory whistles blowing on every side their summons to work, mother and child are seen for a brief moment together at the door of the nursery, before the former hurries on to reach the factory gate in time; or when, at the end of the day, while the streets are full of workers hurrying homeward, the mothers again raise the nursery latch to greet their children.[134]

These descriptions firmly establish that the world of children and mothers sh distinct from the world of the factory; the nursery takes the place of the home viding a refuge from the "screams of the great factory whistles" and the "busy whir of machinery." While the nursery provides a surrogate home, the mother takes on the father's role in moving back and forth between the worlds of home and work.[135] In the passage from the Baldwin report, the mother stands at the threshold between the two worlds at the nursery door before she passes through the factory gate, and at the end of the day, she crosses the threshold again by raising the nursery latch.

Day nursery managers sought not only to provide a "home" for the children of working mothers, but to reshape the homes from which the children came by influencing both the children and their mothers. They hoped to use the nursery as a model home to teach mothers efficient, sanitary, and modern techniques of housekeeping and child-rearing, and to instill in the children a love of cleanliness, order, nutritious food, good manners, and patriotism. One Franklin Day Nursery report spoke of its efforts to transform the children:

> What a fine lot of healthy, happy looking children you say. . . . Can these be the children of those weary looking mothers? Is it possible these bright, clean faces have come out of such homes. . . ? But it is all too true. Those three live with their mother in a bathroom, a board covers the tub and is used as a bed. That child is one of five or seven—all occupy one room with a consumptive father no longer able to work. Those children have a drunken mother. . . . This is the material we are turning into healthy, useful boys and girls.[136]

Similarly, an early report of the First Day Nursery spoke not only of inculcating in the children "habits of truthfulness, honesty and cleanliness," but hoped that the training the children received would extend "its silent influence to the inmates of their homes" as well.[137]

Within the nurseries, rigid structuring of time and space, and close attention to order, hygiene, and obedience were meant to socialize children to habits of self-discipline and self-control, enabling them to take their places in an industrial culture in which punctuality and order were prized. The House of Industry Day Nursery described the "surplus energy of the seething mass of black-eyed, restless Italian tots" being diverted into "useful and helpful channels that it is hoped will be carried into the homes" and explained that "these boisterous, undisciplined children" were in particular need of the discipline of the nursery.[138] Many saw these lessons in cleanliness, order, and homemaking as one of the central purposes of the day nurseries. A survey of the city's day nurseries in 1916 commented, "The nursery is potentially the greatest power for good in the life of an impoverished family since, through its control of the children, it has a greater influence than either the settlement or the school." This report listed among the legitimate functions of the day nursery "to instill in the child habits of order, cleanliness, courtesy and obedience and to instruct the mother . . . in proper feeding, bathing and general care of her children."[139]

Day nursery workers placed great faith in the idea that children would carry the lessons of the nursery back into their homes. They hoped that after experiencing life in the nursery, children would insist that their mothers conform to nursery standards of hygiene and nutrition at home. The Franklin Day Nursery reported,

> Here in the Nursery [the children] get their first glimpse of home life as it ought to be for them—warmth, nourishment, and lessons not only in the a, b, c's of books but the a, b c's

> of conduct, truth, obedience and clean habits. How quickly they yield to the influence, you can see, and it is encouraging to notice how earnestly their parents try to live up to the rules of the Nursery and help the work begun there.[140]

At Catholic nurseries, too, great emphasis was placed on learning habits of order and cleanliness, and on unlearning "impressions he has already formed, or is apt to form, from the streets":

> The Sisters train the children . . . in the ways of cleanliness and in good manners. . . . The children learn to keep clean and to go to sleep at the right moment. They are glad and proud to eat nicely, to hold the spoon well and spill nothing, to make no crumbs, to say, "Thank you," after being helped, and to pass things to one another. . . . This sort of work is the salvation, spiritual, physical and mental, of the children from their cradles and up to the beginning of their school years.[141]

The "success stories" that day nursery managers included in their annual reports suggest their hopes of taking the children of working mothers off the streets and turning them into members of the "respectable" working class. In a 1913 report, the Baldwin Nursery reported that in one family, the children whose widowed mother had sent them to the nursery while she went out to work "are now helpful and affectionate, a pleasure and a support to their mother, who is able to give up the mill and devote her time to making their homes comfortable. This is the result of [the nursery's] ten years of care of their health, of their minds, of their characters." The children in another family, "instead of being the product of a disorderly home, growing up under a drinking father and mother, without church or training," had turned out well: "the two girls are both members of a neighboring church, neat, attractive, self-respecting, and respected by all who know them."[142]

Mothers of the Nation

By creating nurseries for Italian, Polish, Jewish, and African-American children, these elite, mostly Anglo-Saxon, women hoped to instill in children and their parents values and patterns of living that would make them into familiar and nonthreatening members of the "respectable" working class. This goal was accentuated in nurseries serving new immigrants and African-Americans, for these families seemed particularly distant from the racialized ideal of family life that the day nursery tried to promote. Day nursery founders thus took part in what Gwendolyn Mink has called "women's politics of racial uplift": a campaign led by elite or white middle-class women to absorb "new races" into the American polity by reshaping immigrant and African-American motherhood. The apparent universality of motherhood, Mink notes, "implied the possibility of a universal maternal virtue"; through assimilation of middle-class American styles of mothering, any race could be redeemed.[143]

But day nursery founders, like many other Progressives, were more interested in absorbing immigrants into the American mainstream than in absorbing African-Americans. African-Americans, with their high rates of maternal employment, probably had a greater objective need for day nurseries than any other group in the city. Indeed, the importance of day nurseries to Philadelphia's African-American community was such that when John Emlen of the Armstrong Association (a predecessor League) set out to list "institutions and agencies for relief and for social b blacks in Philadelphia, day nurseries topped the list.[144] Despite the fact African-American women were more likely to be breadwinners than thei counterparts, however, most nurseries were established to serve immigrants the Philadelphia day nursery scene in 1919, Helen Glenn Tyson found thirty-six nurseries in the city, of which only five admitted African-American children.[145] A wave of migration from the South in the late 1910s doubled Philadelphia's African-American population (already the largest of any northern city), putting increased pressure on local social institutions. Yet the influx of migrants into the city did not spur the creation of many more nurseries. In 1928, the *Bulletin* quoted the president of the PADN as saying that "the influx of colored people from the South was causing a problem for the association. She said the need was for many more colored nurseries."[146]

Why did the women who founded day nurseries pass over the needs of African-Americans and focus instead on European immigrants? The vision of motherhood and family life that animated the women who founded day nurseries was race- as well as class-specific; as historian Eileen Boris writes, "Within the word 'mother,' as used by many reformers and makers of public policy, lurked the referent 'white.'"[147] Historian Gwendolyn Mink argues that efforts to transform the motherhood of European immigrants "marked them as assimilable," preparing them "to claim whiteness."[148] Immigrant women, despite their wage-earning and their foreign ways, were seen primarily as mothers who could be redeemed through Americanization. But if wage work vitiated motherhood, then African-American women, seen primarily as workers, could not truly and fully be mothers. Moreover, most white Progressive reformers felt that African-Americans were beyond the reach of assimilation: slavery had destroyed their family structure, their individual psyches, and their capacity to instill moral values and self-control in their children. One Boston settlement worker explained that, unlike immigrants, African-Americans "cannot be raised by a process of assimilation," as their race is "so foreign." Even NAACP founder Jane Addams spoke of the "lack of restraint" in African-American families, and Frances Kellor, founder of the National League for the Protection of Colored Women, wrote, "There is no race outside of barbarism where there is so low a grade of domestic life, and where the child receives so little training, as among the negroes," for "in slavery, the negro knew no domestic life."[149] The fact that so many African-American mothers worked at a time when mainstream visions of motherhood were tied to domesticity only reinforced the idea that they were not, and could not become, "true" mothers.

Black clubwomen sought to change the terms of this discourse by emphasizing African-American mothers' devotion to their children, despite their need to leave them by day to earn wages. Women organized in the National Association of Colored Women (NACW), and in local clubs "defied the denial of the status of mothers" to African-American women, claiming for themselves the virtues of nobility, self-sacrifice, and nurturing love typically associated with white motherhood.[150] While insisting on their commonalities with white mothers, however, African-American clubwomen like Mary Church Terrell also drew attention to the difference in black women's experience of motherhood. Addressing the National Congress of Mothers in 1899, Terrell asked her white listeners to contrast "the feelings of hope and joy which thrill the heart of the white mother with those which stir the soul of her colored sister. . . . As a mother of the oppressed race clasps to her bosom the babe which she loves as fondly as you do yours, her heart cannot thrill with joyful anticipations of the future."[151] Part of the sorrow that "stirred the soul" of Terrell's African-American mother may have been realizing the need to leave her child without adequate supervision so she could earn wages to support it. Recognizing that most African-American mothers were breadwinners, Terrell urged women in the NACW to put the creation of day nurseries and kindergartens at the top of their list of priorities. Addressing the organization's second convention in 1899, Terrell referred to the day nursery as "a charity of which there is an imperative need among us." Visiting a day nursery, she had been "shocked at some of the miserable little specimens of humanity, brought in by mothers, who had been obliged to board them out with either careless or heartless people." Establishing day nurseries, Terrell explained, was an ideal project for African-American clubwomen, for nurseries

> would not only save the life, and preserve the health of many a poor little one, but it would speak eloquently of our interest in our sisters, whose lot is harder that our own, but to whom we should give unmistakable proof of our regard, our sympathy, and our willingness to render any assistance in our power. . . . To each and every branch of the Association, then, I recommend the establishment of a day nursery, as a means through which it can render one of the greatest services possible to humanity and the race.[152]

African-American women's clubs and church societies, made up of women who were often wage-earning mothers themselves, did take Terrell's plea to heart. African-American women created day nurseries throughout the country and were probably responsible for providing most of the day nurseries available to black children.[153] But with limited resources, they could not possibly meet the demand. In Philadelphia, the Women's Union Day Nursery is the only African-American-run nursery whose records have survived. Its report in 1926 proclaimed, "The Women's Union Day Nursery . . . has the proud distinction of being the only nursery in Pennsylvania for colored children that is managed by a Board of Directors of the same race."[154] The nursery's board, as we saw earlier, emerged from the interdenominational Women's Union Missionary Society and consisted of women typical of the African-American middle class: teachers, social workers, hairdressers, and wives of postal workers, caterers, and butlers.

Other Philadelphia nurseries serving African-American children were founded and managed by elite white women. The St. Nicholas, the Lincoln, and the Jenkintown nurseries were all created by members of the PADN specifically to serve African-American children, and they seem to have operated similarly to the PADN nurseries that served white children. PADN board members were preoccupied with control of these black nurseries, assuming that African-Americans could not manage on their own. In announcing the creation of the Lincoln Day Nursery at a PADN meeting, one of its founders said, "The Lincoln Day Nursery is under the control of white managers, and bids fair to be a power for good in its neighborhood."[155] Most striking was a request from a Camden, New Jersey, nursery for information on "how to start a colored day nursery in connection with a white [nursery] . . . with colored matron and managers, but under the supervision of managers of white nursery."[156] Miss Julia Jones, president of the Women's Union nursery, was "requested to write a paper on the subject." The paper that she read at the next general meeting, however, was entitled, "How to Nursery," and in describing the paper, no mention was made of ensurin Rather, she gave "a short account of the inception and organization Missionary Union Day Nursery," which "illustrated what can be done by astic women."[157] Even nurseries controlled by white boards could be s need to provide role models to poor African-American families: in 1916, t Nursery reported that "three talks were given to the Mothers' Club by women physicians of their race."[158] On the other hand, attempts to promote African-American dignity could be seriously undermined by events like the "Pickaninny Dance," a major fundraiser for the St. Nicholas Day Nursery in 1915.[159]

While a few day nurseries existed to serve African-Americans, the majority of Philadelphia's nurseries were established in order to care for the children of European immigrants and native-born whites. A list of "nationalities represented" in twenty-one PADN nurseries in 1926 included Italian, Russian, Jewish, Lithuanian, Polish, Romanian, Irish, English, Scottish, Ukranian, Hungarian, German, Spanish, and Portuguese, as well as "American" and "Colored American."[160] Catholic nurseries also served different immigrant groups, especially when parishes were created for specific nationalities.[161] Although they clearly existed to serve Catholic children, many of these nurseries also accepted non-Catholics living in the parish. According to the 1923 *Catholic Charities Yearbook*, the twelve Catholic nurseries in Philadelphia cared "for the children of all nationalities and races."[162] The *Yearbook* commented that at Our Lady of Mercy Day Nursery, "The broad views of the reverend founder are reflected in the work, as children of all creeds are eligible—the last received was a child of Hebrew parents."[163]

Day nurseries, like the kindergartens and settlement houses with which they were often associated, were intended to be centers of Americanization, as well as child welfare stations. Some, like Neighborhood Centre, were established specifically for the purpose of Americanizing immigrants, while others adopted Americanization as they went along, as part of a general program of neighborhood uplift. Marion Horwitz of the Franklin Day Nursery (which served Italian and Russian immigrants as well as native-born whites) wrote that "everyone who is interested in the making of Americans" should visit the nursery to discover how it fulfilled its mission of "instilling in little boys and girls the principles of cleanly, orderly, ambitious, patriotic American manhood and womanhood." The most inspiring sight a visitor might encounter, she proposed, would not be the clean cribs, motherly nurses, toys, or nourishing food that the nursery provided, but rather the sound of as many as one hundred children, "warm and clean and well fed, because the Nursery has made them so," singing "My Country, 'Tis of Thee," and pledging allegiance "to their Flag."[164]

Among the lessons that nursery children were meant to carry back to their parents was the idea that the hygienic, orderly, child-centered way of life that the nurseries advocated was particularly "American." Everything from table manners to daily baths to relying on a doctor's advice was defined as the American way of doing things and was taught to immigrant children and mothers along with English and lessons in civics. The Joy Day Nursery, which served an immigrant neighborhood of people from Poland, Lithuania, and the Ukraine, suggested in a 1929 report that all nurseries would do well to focus on Americanization:

> Probably every Nursery aims to make its influence reach out through the children to their homes. We can do real service for the foreign population of our neighborhood by a simple, practical demonstration of American ways of living. We begin with the . . . tots, giving them a start in habits of tidiness and table manners.[165]

Children who spent time in day nurseries in Philadelphia were surrounded by American flags (a fund-raising circular for Neighborhood Centre's day nursery featured a photograph of a group of small immigrant children waving American flags), learned patriotic songs, and learned to celebrate American civic holidays, especially Washington's and Lincoln's birthdays, Thanksgiving, and the Fourth of July. In the nurseries, children learned to associate American flags, American food, and "correct" English speech with cleanliness, order, thrift, and adherence to rules. The House of Industry, whose day nursery and settlement house served an Italian neighborhood, explained in 1917, "by observing the National Holidays and explaining . . . the significance of these Holidays, we strive to do our part in the work of Americanization."[166] Another report described how, with the help of a kindergarten teacher,

> the surplus energy of the seething mass of black-eyed, restless Italian tots, is fast being diverted into useful and helpful channels that it is hoped will be carried into the homes. . . . This training is urgently needed by these boisterous, undisciplined children, who are accustomed to get from their parents what they want by screaming until they get it.[167]

In a common rhetorical move, this report linked the children's nationality to their characters and to the inadequate parenting they received at home, but hoped that experience in the nursery would help transform both the children and their parents.

While the House of Industry report noted that settlement staff gave "talks and lectures . . . about other lands, the great men and women they have produced, so that these foreign-born women may feel that we respect their memories and ideas," other day nurseries embarked on Americanization campaigns with less sensitivity.[168] For instance, the secretary of the National Federation of Day Nurseries wrote in 1912, "A considerable percentage of foreign-born mothers are too ignorant to feed or care for their children in a wholesome way." And a former day nursery worker wrote in the social welfare journal *Charities*, "Let the most ignorant and wretched come and we will show them a better way. They are but children themselves, but with a duller perception. The more ignorant they are, the less Americanized they are, the more they need the influence of the day nursery."[169] This sort of patronizing attitude may have been behind the trouble faced by the San Cristoforo Day Nursery. Founded in 1907 by the women of the PADN, the nursery was "intended primarily for Italian children, as it is situated in the heart of Little Italy." Although its opening was announced enthusiastically at a PADN meeting, within five years the nursery was in crisis. In 1913 an annual report explained that the nursery had moved out of its original Italian neighborhood "because it was found by the Board of Managers that certain local difficulties made it impossible to do satisfactory work in that district." While the report did not specify what the "local difficulties" were, it seems quite possible that they had to do with a gap between the expectations of the elite Protestants on the nursery's board and the Italian immigrants they planned to serve. The San Cristoforo Nursery subsequently moved to "a portion of the city mainly inhabited by North of Ireland people, of a respectable class." The managers had been "greatly encouraged in finding a class of people who" (perhaps unlike the Italians in the previous location), "are responsive and grateful, and show every dispositio to accept the help given as an assistance towards eventual self-reliance."[170]

Americanization seemed particularly imperative to the founders of the Young Women's Union Day Nursery (later Neighborhood Centre). The Young Women's Union, which started as a free kindergarten and eventually became a full-fledged settlement house, was founded by German-Jewish women to Americanize and uplift East European Jewish immigrants. These affluent German-Jewish women shared the attitudes of the elite African-American women who founded the black women's club movement, knowing that they were judged by "the masses of our women," and therefore obliged to "go down among the lowly, the illiterate, and even the vicious, to whom we are bound by the ties of race and sex, and put forth every possible effort to uplift and reclaim them."[171] In the same way, elite German-Jewish women felt a need, both out of charity and self-preservation, to "reclaim" the immigrant women who would represent Jewish womanhood in America. The day nursery that grew out of these women's efforts was intended in part "to make of the children good American citizens, to imbue them with the best American ideals," as one of its founders wrote in 1910.[172] A poem written for the organization's twenty-fifth anniversary celebration suggested how these women combined a maternalist sensibility with the creation of a modern Jewish-American identity:

> For in your hearts you heard the cry
> Of little children in their need;
> The street waif's moan, the mother's sigh—
> A blind world with no hand to lead;
> And all your woman's spirit rose
> To hush its cries, to sooth its woes
> . . . .
> Sons have you reared to voice your praise
> And daughters conscious of their race,
> Through whom, in God's appointed ways,
> A modern Israel takes its place[173]

The "modern Israel" that was taking its place at the Young Women's Union, however, was not the same as the one envisioned by many of the nursery's immigrant clients. The YWU's day nursery sought to teach cleanliness, child care, cooking, thrift, patriotism, and moral family life while providing care for children. Although the nursery, and the settlement of which it was a part, was founded in part to combat Christian missionary efforts in the immigrant neighborhood, settlement workers sometimes engaged in a kind of missionary work of their own: trying to wean immigrant children away from the Orthodox Judaism of their parents, replacing it with the more "modern" and Protestant-influenced Reform Judaism practiced by most German Jews. While settlement workers understood Yiddish, and could translate when necessary, they disdained the immigrants' language as "jargon," and did not seek to pass it—or any other aspect of East European Jewish culture—on to the next generation. Similarly, the settlement studiously avoided any contact with the Zionist movement, although commitment to Zionism was a significant part of most immigrants' Jewish identity.

In response to these differences, most immigrants turned away from the settlement house and instead nurtured their own institutions, which offered a more familiar understanding of Jewish identity.[174] While many immigrants were eager to become Ameri-

nt to do so on their own terms, and while they made use of the day nurs- .ained their own vision of what it meant to be Jewish in America. East Eu- rants and German-Jewish philanthropists did agree, however, on the need y Jewish nurseries. Sometimes this had to do with the exclusion of Jewish n other day nurseries, but more often it had to do with a distrust of the motives o. .he Protestant (sometimes church-affiliated) nurseries and with a desire to have children raised in a Jewish environment. For instance, Minnie Kaplan applied to the Young Women's Union Nursery in 1917, saying "that she was desirous of having the children attend a nursery that was directed by Jewish people."[175] Immigrants also founded their own day nurseries — the Downtown Hebrew, the Hebrew, the Strawberry Mansion, and later the Northern Hebrew — which enabled them to provide care for their children in a more familiar context.

Nurseries, then, were in part an attempt to absorb the families of the poor into the American mainstream by transforming the practice of working-class motherhood. As such, they sought to bridge racial and ethnic as well as class differences. Founded and managed by some of Philadelphia's most elite women, the charitable day nurseries made it clear that they did not intend to alter the conventional division of labor between men and women. The nurseries would serve only the most deserving poor mothers and would not encourage any mother to work for wages if there was any alternative. Day nursery leaders focused their energy on the "desperate, deserted, and destitute," and stressed the value of the surrogate home they provided to children, rather than the freedom they offered to mothers. By bringing children off the streets and into an environment that valued order and cleanliness, day nursery founders hoped to provide a home for the children of working mothers and transform the homes from which they came. Their success, of course, was only partial, for it relied on the willingness of poor women to have their child-rearing practices and patterns of family life transformed.

2

Using Day Nurseries

Created as a charity and modeled on the orphanage, the day nursery never became very popular with wage-earning mothers. Although many mothers worried about finding care for their children, they often hesitated to rely on the nurseries for help. Despite day nursery managers' emphasis on making the nurseries into "homes," in practice most nurseries were highly regimented institutions, operated by an overworked staff in cramped physical quarters, and the women who used them were not allowed to forget that they were receiving charity. Women who had few other resources did rely on the nurseries, but usually only for short periods of time and for the children most obviously in need of care. Nurseries elicited a variety of responses from the women who relied on their charity: some expressed gratitude while others fought with nursery workers for control of their children. Ultimately, however, the women who used the charitable day nurseries did not set the terms that shaped the provision of care for their children.

Breadwinning Mothers

As we have seen, women from many different segments of Philadelphia's working class used day nurseries in the early twentieth century—from the English millworkers of Kensington to African-American domestic servants on Lombard Street, native-born saleswomen to immigrant sweatshop workers. Indeed, the variety of working-class families who used the nurseries suggests how vulnerable even the more comfortable and "respectable" workers in the city were to economic crisis. Despite important differences in their resources, status, future possibilities, and habits of daily life, these women shared a common experience of going out to work and needing care for their children. Without a reliable and adequate male wage to depend on, they could not devote themselves to unpaid housework and child care in the home; rather, they had to meet their normal responsibilities at home on top of the duties of being a supplemental or substitute breadwinner for their families. These women also had in common that by going out to work they were violating expectations—sometimes their own, sometimes those of others—about proper family roles.

Because they appeared to violate conventional definitions of motherhood, working mothers and those who sought to represent them to the public needed to prove that they went out to work because they had to. Sympathetic observers such as Gwendolyn Hughes and Helen Tyson stressed that mothers worked from economic necessity, not out of caprice, greed, or disregard for their children's needs. By emphasizing the sacrifices that working women made in order to help support their children, commentators reinstated these women as "good mothers" despite their daily absence from home. Katharine Anthony, an advocate of state support for all mothers, wrote in her study *Mothers Who Must Earn*, "Too often we hear these women spoken of as if some perversity of interest drove them to neglect their homes and go out to work at the expense of their homes and children. It is for the sake of the children that they work, as mothers have from time immemorial."[1] Echoing this view, the U.S. Women's Bureau based its advocacy of women's wage work on research showing that most women worked in order to help support their families and that women gave more of their wages to the family than did men. Bureau investigators argued that since women played an important role in supporting dependents, they should be "accorded the recognition" that went along with that responsibility.[2] Neither spokeswomen for working mothers nor most working mothers themselves spoke very loudly in public about the self-esteem and increased domestic power that might also be by-products of women's wage work.[3]

Gwendolyn Hughes, who surveyed 728 wage-earning mothers in Philadelphia in 1918–19 as part of her graduate work in social economy at Bryn Mawr, found that the dream of being supported by a man's "family wage" was elusive for many working families. "The struggle to live on the husband's wage, in most industrial families, is a failure," Hughes wrote, pointing to a different study of 11,073 families in Philadelphia which found that only 6% were supported by the husband alone.[4] The families that Hughes interviewed saw no options other than mothers' wage-earning, for revenue from relatives or lodgers was neither sufficiently widespread nor substantial enough to serve as a substitute for a mother's wages.[5] Thirty-five percent of the women she studied were single mothers (22% were widows and 13% had been deserted), while 29% were working because their husband's wage was insufficient, either because of an emergency or on a regular basis. Fourteen percent of husbands were ill and unable to work, and 11% of the women had nonsupporting husbands.

More than ten years after Hughes did her interviews, other studies also presented mothers' wage work as a fulfillment of family responsibility. After interviewing more than two thousand immigrant women in Philadelphia and the industrial Lehigh Valley, Women's Bureau investigator Caroline Manning concluded, "All 'needed to help a little out'— husbands ill, husbands out of work or on part time, rent to pay, and children to feed were indeed common to all." Her respondents seemed to find it "only natural" that husbands could not make enough to support their families. She recounted the words of immigrant men and women who explained, "A family can't get ahead unless the wife works"; "Necessary to help. Short money all the time"; and those of a widow who supported herself and her two children, who simply said, "Must work— no work, no eat."[6] African-American women found it even more necessary to supplement their husbands' earnings; a study of working mothers in Philadelphia found that larger proportions of African-American women with husbands worked for wages than did married white women.[7]

Women applying to day nurseries in Philadelphia had even fewer options and resources to draw on than other wage-earning mothers. Helen Tyson claimed that it was "the resourceless mother; the one without friends and relatives; and especially the mother without even the partial help of a man" who typically used the day nursery.[8] Indeed, the day nursery population seems to have been poorer than the total population of wage-earning mothers in Philadelphia. Widowed, deserted, separated, divorced, and unmarried mothers joined women whose husbands earned insufficient wages, whose husbands were unemployed, ill, incapacitated, in prison, or simply refused to support their wives and children. Sixty percent of the women applying to six day nurseries worked for wages because they were single mothers (either through widowhood, desertion, separation, divorce, or because they had never married), compared to 35% of the women in Hughes's study; and while 11% of Hughes's women worked out of preference (to save money for a house or to buy "extras" for the family), only 3% of the women applying to six day nurseries gave this explanation.[9] Tyson found that three-quarters of the day nursery families she interviewed were living below the poverty line. Even in the families that were "normally constituted," with mother and father living together, she commented, "The disquieting fact presents itself that when the husband's wage is considered in relation to the size of the family in only 8 cases could it possibly have been adequate to provide the minimum wants of the group." While men's wages were inadequate to support a family, however, women's wages were much lower. Only about a third of the women in this group of one hundred families were earning "a wage approximately adequate for self-support," and only three of the mothers "would seem to have received a wage sufficient to allow any margin for the support of their children."[10] Women's low wages, depressed partly because of the common assumption that women worked only for "pin money," meant that the economic hurdles that these women faced were huge: historian David Montgomery notes that in the 1900s, "the Department of Labor concluded that 74.3 percent of the women in factories and 66.2 percent of those in stores earned less than a 'living wage.'"[11]

Working mothers themselves were careful to stress that they worked out of economic necessity. In describing their situation to day nursery social workers or board members, women nearly always presented themselves as being forced to go out to work, explaining that their labor was the only thing that could keep their families from dire poverty. For instance, a woman applying to the Neighborhood Centre nursery explained that if she were not able to work, "they will be forced to sell their furniture and give up their home."[12] In another case, Rosa Kutner told how her husband, who had immigrated to the United States from Russia three years before "in search for a better livelihood," had left her for another woman. Outraged, her family in Russia raised enough money to send her and her four-year old daughter to Philadelphia, but her husband refused to resume living with her, or to support his daughter. Thrown on her own resources, Mrs. Kutner would have to go to work.[13] Women whose husbands lived with them were not immune from financial crisis either. Applying to the First Day Nursery in 1919, Mrs. Sturn said she needed to go out to work and place her four children at the nursery, since her husband "only gave her $7 last week and the store bill was $17." She showed her agreement with the day nursery's assumption that the husband should support his family by saying, "Thought she would try him again and stay home but he won't do what is right."[14] The desperation felt by many mothers trying to make ends meet was expressed eloquently by one, who wrote to the social worker at Neighborhood

Centre, "Miss Cohen what should I do I have to give eat a whole family. It is coming Passover and we need everything. . . . I should dye from hunger/haven't any relations. But I want to work and make a living for my children." Looking at her new baby and thinking about the poverty he faced, this woman later wrote, "My baby is pretty. I wish he would have the luck [good fortune] the way he has prettiness."[15]

While many reformers assumed that a mother's employment made it impossible for her to mother her children, most working-class mothers saw their paid work as an expression of love, sacrifice, and devotion to their children. Although they worried about their children, they did not think that they were inadequate mothers because they went out to work. To these women, wage work was an extension of family responsibility, a way to help out one's husband in his task of supporting the family, and a fulfillment of a mother's duty to her children. A lazy or indifferent mother would "put her children away" in an orphanage or foster home, but a "good" mother would, in the words of the woman quoted above, work to "make a living for my children." As historian Ellen Ross writes about working-class mothers in London during the same period, "The work and love were inseparable. . . . The good mothers . . . 'worked for' their children as the term went, rather than, as we do, ministering to their feelings or becoming their friends."[16]

This was no easy task: working long hours at tedious, back-breaking jobs for low pay, and coming home to a full day's worth of household work was difficult, and most women did not relish it. Gwendolyn Hughes estimated that laundry would take women two or three evenings a week, and food preparation, including marketing, as much as four hours a day. Keeping a household running often involved elaborate advance planning: Hughes described one employed mother who washed and dressed her children for school at night before they went to bed, since she would be gone in the morning.[17] Many of the wage-earning mothers whom Helen Tyson interviewed in 1919 complained that combining wage work with motherhood made it difficult to keep their homes up as they wished. One said she "works all the time and then cannot keep things decent," while another complained that she "cannot keep sewing done and children and house clean." Not surprisingly, these women were physically run down, and many mentioned problems such as "nervousness," "backache," and "constant headache."[18] Being supported by a man's wages seemed like an attractive alternative: one immigrant woman, a shirtwaist operator who brought her child to Neighborhood Centre, said freely "that she was tired of working, and wanted to marry as soon as an opportunity presented itself." She even tried to get her daughter placed in foster care so that she would have a better chance of remarriage, since "no man wanted to marry a woman who had a child." Her story apparently ended happily: she told the social worker that she was engaged to a man who had a seven-room house, had deposited money in the bank in her name, and was interested in giving her daughter a musical education.[19]

Most day nursery mothers, of course, could not count on such luck. African-American women, who often faced a lifetime of combining wage work with motherhood, may have been equally eager to escape the "double burden" of paid and unpaid labor, but were less likely to see marriage as an escape route. Although black mothers' wage work was accepted, even expected, most African-Americans did not see it as desirable.[20] While they celebrated women's achievements in business and education and valued women's economic independence, many African-Americans agreed with W. E. B. DuBois and Augustus Dill, who wrote in 1914, "Black mothers who ought to be home training their children are away at work."[21] For instance, Lucy Slowe, dean of women at Howard University, called for campaigns to "build up public sentiment for paying heads of families wages sufficient to reduce the number of Negro women who must be employed away from home to the detriment of their children and of the community in general."[22] African-American mothers themselves often shared this view: in his study of Philadelphia's Seventh Ward, DuBois reported, "Nearly all the housewives deplore the lodging system and the work that keeps them away from home."[23] The pain of leaving their children to inadequate care so they could spend their days taking meticulous care of their employers' children ran deep for many African-American women.

While most working-class and poor mothers in Philadelphia did not particularly want to work for wages, when they did go out to work, they saw their work as the fulfillment of their family obligations, not its abdication. Women reported the positive and negative effects of their wage work as being almost equal, recognizing both the problems that their long hours of absence caused for their children and the value of their earnings in meeting their families' needs. While 37.9% of the wage-earning mothers in Hughes's study reported "injurious effects of wage earning," especially noting the effect of their absence on their children, 37.3% reported beneficial effects, especially "providing necessities."[24] As we have seen, most of the women using day nurseries worked out of clear financial necessity. But sometimes, against the advice of middle-class reformers, they worked in order to provide an extra margin of comfort or security for their families. For instance, Mrs. Goldstein had originally sought care for her Jacob because her unemployed husband had deserted the family. When the nursery social worker visited her home a few months later, however, she found that Mr. Goldstein had returned and had found employment. "When Mrs. G was asked why she had not told us of her husband's whereabouts, she said that she was anxious to work so that they might save money enough to rent a small house."[25] Knowing that day nursery workers might frown on this explanation, Mrs. Goldstein simply did not inform the social worker of the change. (Indeed, she was right to be circumspect about this information, since as soon as the social worker learned the real situation, the child was dismissed from the nursery.)

Mrs. Goldstein's decision to continue working, seen negatively by the day nursery, may have been widely approved by her peers. In surveying Jewish day nurseries for the Bureau of Jewish Children, Neighborhood Centre worker Marion Kohn reported that immigrant neighbors felt that "the woman who wishes to go out to work because her standards are high, and the amount her husband earns is insufficient for the family's support," should be helped by a day nursery. They would have understood the women who told Caroline Manning that they worked in order to help buy a home, or who, when asked why they went out to work, simply said, "Big pile of debts at store and house to pay."[26] The sentiment of the Bureau for Jewish Children, however, "was that a better position should be secured for the man, and that the mother should stay at home with her children. Only in rare cases of physical or mental disability of the father, should the mother be encouraged to leave her home."[27] At the Baldwin Day Nursery, 6% of the women applying for day nursery care in the early 1920s gave as their reason that they needed to work to pay off debts or to save money to buy a home, and others who cited "insufficient income" sometimes referred to needs such as canceling debts, saving for a home, or saving enough money to enable the family to move. Similarly, some of Caroline Manning's respondents spoke of saving "for a better life," or at least to tide the family over emergencies such as illness and unemployment. Having come to America to improve their lives, they considered working to be one way to achieve that goal. Thus one woman explained that her family might be able to live on her husband's wages; "but bad for the children. They never be Americans, and where I go when old?" Others were willing to work themselves in order to improve their children's chances: one immigrant woman said of her son, "He must not work in the mill but be an American."[28]

The ethos of sacrificing in order to provide for children's education may have been a particularly important motivation for many African-American mothers, and a way of explaining their wage work to themselves and others. This commitment extended back several generations. For instance, one North Carolina mother stated in 1869, "I don't care how hard I has to work if I can only send Sallie and the boys to school looking respectable."[29] Indeed, African-Americans' commitment to educating their children seems to have inspired mothers to go out to work themselves rather than take their children out of school: a government survey in 1911 showed that only 13% of African-American families in Philadelphia, compared to 50% of Irish and 23% of Italian families, had children earning wages.[30] (This pattern was probably reinforced by the relative paucity of job opportunities for African-American children, compared to white. DuBois commented that because of restricted opportunity, African-American children's chief employment was helping around the house while mothers worked.)[31] Historian Elizabeth Pleck has suggested that this commitment to children's education was part of an overall strategy for family betterment that had implications for child care as well. African-American children were reared for independence, encouraged to go to school and become socially mobile, ensuring the support of their parents in old age. Italian children, on the other hand, who "were never left alone" as children, were raised to submerge their needs to those of their parents; they were expected to work at an early age and turn over their wages to their families. Pleck suggests that African-American mothers, given the heritage of work and child care patterns under slavery, were less likely than others to connect their physical presence with good parenting, believing that "an obedient youngster remained out of trouble when left alone." The good mother was the one who worked hard to provide for her children, not necessarily the one who was always there.

Thus, while many of the women who used the day nurseries shared the day nursery founders' sense that a mother's wage work was unfortunate, they recognized the contribution that her work could make to a family, and acknowledged a broader definition of the conditions that could make a mother's wage-earning necessary. In their "moral vernacular," motherhood was not only about nurturing, but also about providing. As they explained their situations to day nursery investigators, they tried to elicit sympathy and help by stressing the unfortunate conditions that forced them to go out to work; but they also felt they deserved credit for struggling to provide for their children. Indeed, like Mrs. Goldstein, they sometimes deliberately tailored their explanations of their need to work to fit day nursery workers' expectations, emphasizing their economic desperation and leaving out other reasons for working that were less likely to gain them sympathy and help from day nursery board members.

Minding the Children: Working Mothers' Child Care Arrangements

Just as mothers who went out to work retained responsibility for laundry, cooking, and housework, so it was their responsibility to find—and then worry about—daily care for their children. Fathers made only 3% of 501 applications to four day nurseries from 1900 to 1929, and these were almost all cases where the mother was ill or absent. In trying to make arrangements for their children, mothers typically turned first to their sisters, mothers, landladies, or neighbors. Gwendolyn Hughes found that 72% of the working mothers she studied were able to arrange to have an adult living in the household (often a relative) care for their children. These mothers, she noted, "consider themselves fortunate" and often made comments such as, "Oh, mother looks after my boy as well as I could."[32] Later studies confirmed that care by relatives and neighbors was the most common solution. According to a 1927 newspaper article, 65% of Philadelphia's wage-earning mothers left their children with relatives, 13.5% with neighbors, and 15% without any supervision.[33] Immigrant women were even more likely to turn to family members and neighbors: Caroline Manning's 1930 study of immigrant women in Philadelphia and the Lehigh Valley found that more than 90% of these wage-earning mothers relied on relatives, older siblings, or neighbors to care for their children.[34]

African-American mothers also relied on kin and neighbors for child care. Since their housing options were more restricted and more expensive than those of whites, African-Americans were more likely than other groups to share living quarters with boarders, relatives, or other families. Mary White Ovington, in her study of African-Americans in New York City, noted that "elderly colored women are often seen bringing up little children."[35] A surplus of African-American women over African-American men in Philadelphia, as in other northern cities, meant that these boarders tended to be female, providing a potential pool of child caretakers. Indeed, single African-American women migrating north were often expected to take over the care of their relatives' children almost as soon as they arrived. Isetta Peters, who migrated from South Carolina to Washington, D.C., during this period explained: "So, you got here and met people. The next day you watched the childrens. That's right, the next day. Oh, they'd always be other peoples' babies with your peoples for you to mind. . . . Whoever had somebody that's where all them left they babies. See, they all had to work so they all helped bring up somebody [from the South] to watch the babies." Bernice Reeder recalled that when her brother and his wife were trying to convince her father to allow Bernice to come north with them, "Ma-Sis started to cry when she was telling how she'd have to leave their two young ones alone if I didn't come. Finally Daddy broke down and said I could go."[36] But kinswomen were often eager to get to work themselves and could not be counted on forever.

Neighbors and relatives played a major role in providing child care, even in families that used Philadelphia's day nurseries. Neighbors were especially willing to help out at times of crisis. For instance, when Mr. Lippmann came to the office of the Neighborhood Centre Day Nursery in 1924, he explained that he "was having much difficulty to make an adjustment in America. He said if it were not for the neighbors he could not get along. The children slept with a neighbor many nights as it was necessary for him and his wife to go to the wharf at four o'clock in the morning" to pick up the fruit they would spend the day peddling.[37] Landladies and neighbors may also have been *landsleit* (from the same town or region of the "old country") and often helped out when they could. For instance, when Sarah Sikofsky was sent to a sanitarium for tuberculosis, she wrote to the day nursery visitor, "About Sam, my landlady is perfectly willing to take care of him, only if his board is paid. She will keep him nice & clean."[38] (In asking for help, Sarah was careful to appeal to the visitor's presumed interest in hygiene as a measure of good care for children.) But while neighbors could help out temporarily, relatives, especially aunts and grandmothers, were more likely to take on long-term child-care responsibilities. Often, only some of the children in a family would attend a day nursery, while others were cared for by relatives. Relatives cared for almost half of the siblings of children who attended the Baldwin Nursery and accounted for half of the care provided to the children at the Baldwin and at the Neighborhood Centre nurseries either before or after their attendance at the nursery.[39]

Although supervision by kin and neighbors was central to many working mothers' child care plans, some mothers found this care to be unreliable and unsatisfactory. Relatives did not always provide good care, and depending on them often generated friction and tension. For instance, when Mrs. Atchick came to the Neighborhood Centre Nursery, she complained that her husband's sister had sent her son "back to her in a very neglected condition with all of his dirty laundry, child had been unnecessarily chastised about every move."[40] Several of the mothers who talked with Helen Tyson in 1919 said they preferred the nursery to the care of relatives: "You can't depend on a relative," "At the nursery there is no partiality," and above all, "At the nursery, the children were safe."[41]

Taking over the care of a sister's or daughter's child added significantly to a woman's work and could exacerbate already existing family tensions that led to arguments about how much relatives owed each other. For instance, Mrs. Mayberry's mother and sister had been caring for her children while she was in a sanitarium for tuberculosis. Mrs. Mayberry told the visitor from the First Day Nursery about "a very unkind letter which she rec'd from her sister." In this letter, the sister told Mrs. Mayberry that "she was not really sick and had better get home soon and take care of her children and not expect as much from her relatives etc."[42] Similarly, when the Neighborhood Centre Nursery worker talked with Celia Gelman's mother, she "stated that she was ill and not even able to take care of her own children, that she had done enough for Mrs. Gelman and her family since her daughter's marriage." Celia's father was more sympathetic and had taken care of his granddaughter for two weeks, but his other children, sharing their mother's view, had returned the girl to her mother without his knowledge.[43]

More often, however, the problem was that relatives were already overburdened with their own jobs and families and were unable to take on the long-term care of children whose mothers needed to work for wages. Helping out in an emergency was one thing, but taking on long-term responsibility was more of a sacrifice. Knowing that day nursery social workers would ask about getting help from relatives, women applying to day nurseries were quick to explain that resources within the extended family were already stretched to the limit. Thus a woman whose husband was on strike explained to the Neighborhood Centre visitor that her husband could not take care of the children since he was out looking for work; his parents were too old to care for them, and her sisters "have families and cannot care for children."[44] In 1921, the Neighborhood Centre worker called on the sister of a woman who had applied for nursery care, needing to go out to work since her husband, a clothing operative, was on strike. The visitor reported, "Five children occupy one room, and she and her husband the other. . . . Mrs. G states that she would be only too glad to take care of her sister's children, except that she does not have the room for them and also that the family live on a very busy street, and the children would need supervision which Mrs. G feels she would not be able to give them with her home and store duties. She is woman's only relative."[45]

So even when mothers preferred the care of a relative, it was not always available. This was especially true for mothers who had recently come to Philadelphia, whether from Hungary or from rural North Carolina, sometimes without a well-developed network of support. These women had to rely on finding a neighborhood woman who boarded children, risk leaving the children alone, or place them in institutions. Boarding, enabling children to stay nearby, was the most popular option and offered mothers flexibility and greater control over the care their children received. These arrangements could be quite positive, as in the memories of one woman who grew up in the mill town of Lawrence, Massachusetts: "We'd go there early in the morning, where a woman, a neighbor, would take care of us. She'd send us out to school and back, have our lunch—very common. It would always be a woman that was in the building. You were brought up as if you were her child."[46] Boarding children could be part of working mothers' arrangements to pool resources with neighbors. Rachel M., a African-American woman in West Philadelphia, took care of five children while their mothers worked as domestics; one was her adopted daughter and another the son of another adopted daughter. When Rachel was ill, one of the mothers came and stayed with her "and they put their earnings together and they live in common."[47] In her study of working mothers in Chicago, Children's Bureau investigator Helen Wright observed that most women who "boarded" other women's children were either family members or neighbors, "friends of the mothers who agreed to care for the children partly as an act of neighborly kindness and partly because they were glad to receive a little extra money to eke out a scanty income."[48]

But things were not always so rosy. In the best of cases, neighbors and landladies were often casual about their supervision of other women's children. Caroline Manning feared that a landlady who was "watching a little the children" was not watching them enough.[49] One Philadelphia mother, who went out to work because her husband had been unemployed for seven months, told a day nursery visitor that she had left her daughter with her landlady, "but the child was so poorly cared for, that she feared an accident might happen to her."[50] Another woman complained that the woman with whom she boarded her child drank and provided inadequate care.[51] Some women who boarded children came to the attention of child welfare investigators because they used the title of "day nursery." One such place, investigated in 1916 by the Child Federation, was a "so-called nursery . . . opened by a woman simply for the sake of increasing her personal income." She charged the African-American mothers ten cents a day, and "when she goes to market or wants to do an errand of any kind, the babies are left alone."[52] Such expansions of the common practice of "boarding" children were probably common but did not leave many traces. In surveying day nurseries throughout the state of Pennsylvania in 1925, Helen Glenn Tyson found "that a number of institutions call themselves day nurseries that in reality are boarding homes for children, while informal neighborhood groupings of children, especially among the colored population, exist in numbers."[53]

Some mothers risked leaving their children alone, like Anna Lippman, who tied baby Mitchell to his chair so he would not fall off and left her two preschoolers playing while she went to work at her husband's produce stand. When the day nursery social worker visited the home, the baby "had been crying and calling for his mother," and the four-year old girl "told worker that she did not know where her mother was."[54] An immigrant mother who spoke with Caroline Manning explained how she closed up the house before leaving for her job in the hosiery mill: "I give them their breakfast, put the meal on the table for them, hide the matches, knives, and everything that could hurt them, lock the front door and the gate in the back yard, and go away."[55] African-American reformers pointed to similar conditions as part of the reason for high rates of child mortality among urban blacks: Mary Church Terrell reported in 1901, "The infants of wage-earning mothers are frequently locked alone in a room from the time the mother leaves in the morning until she returns at night," and Rosa Morehead Bass wrote, "We find great mortality among the children of the poor. Even before they can make their wants known, the mother is compelled to leave them daily, and a surprising number are burned to death."[56]

Many children, especially those over six years old, were expected to care for themselves. African-American working mothers trained their children early to care for themselves and for each other. Sadie Mosell observed that children in the African-American Philadelphia families she studied often prepared meals and purchased food for the family, and Mary Ritter Beard noted that African-American children were often "kept at home to care for younger members of the family while the mother is away at work."[57] A quarter of the children of immigrant working women in Caroline Manning's study were unsupervised during their mothers' absences; most of these were between seven and twelve years old. Drawing on traditions in which children were expected to contribute to the family economy from an early age, many working-class parents did not see a problem with these arrangements. For instance, in the rural South, it was common for African-American children to take responsibility at home while their mothers worked in homes of whites. All girls over age six or seven routinely helped the adult women with child care (or, as one put it, "washed, watched, and whipped" the children younger than herself); by the age of ten they would be training for "work out."[58] Some mothers did worry about their unsupervised school-age children: for instance, one African-American mother in Chicago was concerned when her youngest, a seven-year-old girl, was dismissed early from school and had no place to go until her older brother came home with the key. One very cold day, a neighboring barber saw her and took her into his shop to keep her warm. Finally the mother became so worried about the situation that she stopped working altogether.[59]

The needs of school-age children was an issue on which day nursery workers and their clients tended to differ, with many working-class parents assuming that such children could easily take care of themselves and even of their younger siblings, while day nursery women assumed that these children continued to need protection and supervision. Social workers and observers often worried about the effects of these arrangements on the older children as well as the younger ones; Caroline Manning cited the case of a thirteen-year-old Hungarian girl who appeared stunted, worried, and ca[...] the responsibility of caring for five younger siblings while her mother we[...] Marion Kohn of the Young Women's Union Day Nursery similarly objected [...] girl's plans to take over her mother's role of working and caring for hom[...] younger siblings while her mother was at a tuberculosis sanitorium. Visiting the home, Kohn noted that Anna, who found it difficult to "do all the work for the children," had made a "real effort" to keep things together. After trying out Anna's plan for a month, however, Kohn decided that it was unsatisfactory and arranged to have the children placed in foster homes. Anna, who had tried her best to keep the home together, became "melancholy on account of the illness of her mother, and the breaking up of her home."[61] Having taken on the responsibilities of her mother's role, it became her personal failure when the family was split up.

When all else failed, parents placed their children in orphanages, whether temporarily or for the long term. Using orphanages to care for children whose families were disrupted by poverty, illness, or unemployment was common practice at the turn of the century. Most orphanages were filled with children whose parents were not dead, but simply struggling with poverty: single fathers were especially urged to place their children in institutions.[62] Day nursery supporters often presented the nursery as an alternative to the orphanage, and many families did use the two types of care interchangeably. School-age children were especially likely to be placed in orphanages, while infants and younger children were kept with relatives and older children sent out to work.[63] For instance, siblings of children attending the Neighborhood Centre Nursery were sent to the Hebrew Orphans Home, the Hebrew Sheltering Home, and the Jewish Foster Home, or placed in foster care through the Juvenile Aid Society. Often a mother would place her older children in institutions until her situation improved and send the youngest one to the nursery.[64] Fifteen percent of the children whose siblings attended the Baldwin Nursery (but who were not themselves applying for nursery care) were living in institutions, and 7% of the Neighborhood Centre nursery children were placed in institutions either before or after their time at the nursery. Although many families used orphanages as a temporary solution, to the children who were placed there, it often felt like abandonment and family failure. Indeed, the threat of being placed in an orphanage often hung over the heads of poor children, especially those with single mothers—and was sometimes used as a threat to induce good behavior.

Foster care, which gradually came to replace the orphanages, and adoption were also options for mothers who could not both provide and care for their children. In a letter to the *Jewish Daily Forward*, a New York immigrant mother whose husband had deserted her complained,

> I am young and healthy, I am able and willing to work in order to support my children, but unfortunately I am tied down because my baby is only six months old. . . . It breaks my heart but I have come to the conclusion that in order to save my innocent children from hunger and cold I have to give them away. I will sell my beautiful children to people who will give them a home.[65]

The contrast between the care given to children in orphanages or foster homes and the lack of support given to children whose mothers were trying to support them must have seemed bitter to many struggling women. Chana Berner, for instance, tried to commit suicide in 1914 by taking gas. "When questioned later she stated that she had been sent from one place to another, . . . and then after coming to Philadelphia and not finding work, had become discouraged, believing that the children would be better provided for if she were dead."[66]

Clearly, many working mothers faced trouble in finding care for their children. The day nurseries founded by elite women from the 1880s through the 1910s offered one solution. Only a tiny fraction of the children needing care, however, ever used the nurseries. This was partly because enough nurseries were never established. But even if a massive campaign to fund charitable day nurseries had been successful, the nurseries would probably not have filled up. For the day nursery, carrying the stigma of charity and offering institutional care, offered an unattractive solution to most mothers' child care dilemmas.

The definition of day care as a charity, and the creation of orphanagelike conditions within the day nurseries, combined with the logistical difficulties involved in using the nurseries to ensure that most mothers would try to avoid the nurseries if they could. Katharine Anthony's study of 370 wage-earning mothers in Manhattan showed that only 4.6% of the nonworking children were cared for in day nurseries. Preschool children were more likely than their older siblings to be brought to a nursery (18% of these young children were attending a nursery), but most were cared for by relatives, neighbors, or "minders" hired by the mothers. Anthony explained, "The women regard the day nursery as a type of institution, and as such, distrust it."[67] This distrust of institutional care included both a dislike for the type of care that nurseries offered and a fear that contact with child-welfare workers at the nurseries would lead to their children being taken away permanently (as did happen periodically, through the nurseries' connections with the Society for the Prevention of Cruelty to Children, juvenile court, and foster placement agencies). Many families were reluctant to turn to "strangers" to care for their children, preferring the familiarity and convenience of neighborhood care. Relying on a charity that resembled an orphanage was a last resort for most mothers, who wanted to avoid the warehousing of their children as well as the humiliation of depending on charity. And since the nurseries represented not only "strangers," but charity workers from different class and cultural backgrounds, parents' fears that they might lose their children (either literally or figuratively) were often quite strong.

In Philadelphia, as in Manhattan, the proportion of working mothers using nurseries to care for their children was small: Gwendolyn Hughes's study of working mothers found only 12% of children under sixteen, and 15% of children under ten, cared for by nurseries.[68] A 1927 newspaper article claimed that day nurseries served only 5% of the twenty-five thousand married women in Philadelphia "employed by business and industry."[69] And only a few of the day nursery mothers whom Helen Tyson interviewed in 1919 chose nursery care freely: 10% "felt sure they could arrange other care for their children"; the rest regarded it as "the only possible way to keep the family together." Tyson reminded her readers that the positive attitudes toward nurseries represented in her study were a result of the mothers' long experience with the nurseries; the mothers she interviewed "had probably forgotten their first reaction to the idea of placing the children there."[70] An analysis of the case records of four Philadelphia nurseries suggest that women used nurseries mostly for younger children who were obviously in need of care; they seem to have been more willing to make other arrangements for the older children after school, including leaving them to their own devices. Children did attend nurseries in significant numbers (most nurseries took children of ten or twelve), but usually only if younger siblings were attending as we

Logistical difficulties such as getting children to the nursery in the mor viding care for them when they were ill were a significant factor in discouraging the use of day nurseries. A representative of the PADN told a reporter in 1927, "The mothers do not use the Day Nurseries because of the distance between them and their place of employment."[72] Nurseries were open long hours to accommodate working mothers' schedules, but getting children to and from the nursery could be a chore. Tyson observed that in more than half the families she studied, the children had to be taken more than five blocks, and in twenty-three families more than nine blocks, to and from the nursery each day. "Such a trip on a cold or wet morning is a real hardship for a sleepy child, and it is small wonder that the attendance at the nurseries is so irregular." One of the mothers she spoke with confirmed this, saying she "hated to drag the children to the nursery so early in the morning."[73] The task of getting children up early, fed, and dressed, and taking them to the nursery discouraged mothers with large families from using the nurseries: 79% of the mothers using four day nurseries during this period had only one or two children.[74] The care that day nurseries took to exclude children who were ill also made life difficult for nursery mothers, who lost days from work and sometimes lost jobs to stay home with sick children.

Logistical difficulties, however, were not the main reason for mothers' dislike of the day nurseries. Rather, it was the status of the nursery as a charitable institution, whose use involved constantly proving one's worthiness and need to work, that discouraged women from making greater use of the nurseries. Even families that did use the nurseries typically did not continue for long periods of time. At the Baldwin Day Nursery in the early 1920s, the average length of time a child spent at the nursery was only one and a half months. Neighborhood Centre had a larger proportion of children who "grew up in the nursery," so the average was much higher, approximately two and a half years. Even there, however, more than half the families sent children for less than one year. This high turnover rate was typical of other nurseries in the city. Helen Tyson noted in 1919, "While a few children are literally 'brought up' in the nursery, the population as a whole is a curiously fluctuating group, and varies surprisingly from week to week."[75] Again in her statewide study of nurseries in 1925, she observed, "For the one child that 'grows up in the nursery' there are fifty that stay from a week to a month."[76] Thus nurseries were used by women who were working out of financial necessity, many because they were the only support of their children. With few other options, these women chose to use the charitable nurseries, but usually relied on them only for a limited amount of time and only for the children that were most obviously in need of care.

Life Inside the Nurseries

Despite the managers' emphasis on the homelike qualities of the nurseries, most were in fact highly regimented institutions modeled on orphanages. Historian Sonya Michel describes the popular image of the day nurseries as "one of dreary, highly regimented institutions, reeking of carbolic disinfectants and overcooked vegetables, crowded with pale, listless children."[77] The rigid environment of the nurseries sprung both from design and necessity. Day nursery managers believed that an orderly, hygienic, and disciplined atmosphere would benefit children; at the same time, limited funds and staff made a degree of regimentation necessary as a practical matter. Many nurseries had inadequate physical plants and few toys, play equipment, or organized play activities. Indeed, the level of care provided in many day nurseries suggests that day nursery managers felt it did not take much to create a "home" for poor and working-class children. Wealthy women could afford to finance the nurseries at least in part because they did not seem to think that much was required. For instance, when Sister Frances Finley first arrived to help take over the work of the Cathedral Day Nursery, which parishioner Grace Town had been operating from her own funds, she was dismayed to find a small house containing "about 6 little children who looked undernourished and one tiny infant that looked like it was going to die any minute." The children ate in "a dark cellar, where the food was also prepared."[78]

Day nursery managers were proud of the orderly existence that children who attended the nurseries lived; their annual reports featured pictures of uniformed children eating, bathing, and napping in orderly rows. Like orphanages, day nurseries tried to instill in children a sense of order and discipline by running a strictly regimented routine. A description of the daily routine at the Baldwin Day Nursery was typical, suggesting the efficiency and order that nurseries hoped to provide:

> From 6:30 to 7 the mothers arrive with their little ones, whose hands and faces are then washed, the hair brushed, and aprons put on. If any of the children come without breakfast, breakfast is supplied. Then they play about till 8:45 when the school children are started for school. From 9–12 those of a suitable age are in the kindergarten. During these hours the matron washes and dresses the infants and puts them to sleep, after which she superintends the housework and makes out the daily record of attendance. At 12 the kindergarten closes, and the school children soon arriving, dinner is served. After dinner the school children return to school and all the other children are put to bed for a two hours' rest. At about 3 o'clock all are awake once more, hands and faces are washed, and then comes two hours of play. 5:00 is supper time. The mothers arrive from 5:30 to 6:30, or even later, according to the time at which they leave their work.[79]

High child-adult ratios and cramped quarters, however, often made it difficult to accomplish the nurseries' daily routine. The Cathedral Day Nursery, for instance, which reported its daily attendance as one hundred children throughout the 1920s, never had more than four Sisters as staff, and the typical PADN nursery had about three adults to minister to fifty children of varying ages. In 1905, the Baldwin Nursery's report complained that the lack of space was "an insurmountable difficulty," making it impossible to bathe the children frequently and making it necessary "to place two and sometimes three children in a crib during the rest hour."[80] Nurseries in Philadelphia were almost all housed in converted row houses that were not designed to accommodate large numbers of children. Lillian Strauss of the Child Federation concluded after surveying thirty-five nurseries in the city that eight were "unfit to house children," and twenty-three had "grave fire dangers."[81] Looking back at the early years of the Strawberry Mansion Nursery, Anna Frigond remembered a "make-shift" physical setup typical of many nurseries: a single-family house with some walls knocked out, minimal furniture, "utilitarian and severe," with long tables, hard backless benches, some cribs, and a few cast-off dolls as the only equipment.[82]

It was not just lack of resources, however, but decisions about how to spend those resources that affected children's experiences in the nurseries. As Anna Frigond noted, space for feeding, washing, and toileting took precedence over toys and play equipment; sanitation was more important than stimulation. Concerned about the possibility of spreading disease by bringing together large numbers of children, nurseries seemed to adhere to what historian Kenneth Cmiel has called the "dirt theory of disease," placing a premium on spotless environments that could be easily mopped and scrubbed.[83] In fact, these nurseries may have carried out on a larger scale the preoccupation with physical care, sanitation, and routine that was the focus of child-rearing advice during this period for all classes.[84] A description of the Downtown Hebrew and Jewish day nurseries in 1920 noted the absence of "directed play or instruction" and the inadequacy of the supplies of "toys, games and apparatus. . . . Rooms present a barren appearance, no pictures or decorations."[85] When members of the PADN visited the Forty-ninth Street Station Day Nursery, they found few toys and little play equipment in the playroom, and none at all in the backyard. On their list of recommendations, however, instituting careful record-keeping was deemed more important than securing toys and equipment. Similarly, although the Child Federation's 1916 study of Philadelphia day nurseries noted the sterility of day nursery furnishings, its major concern was with sanitary practices, especially daily wet-mopping and proper cleansing of rubber nipples and soiled diapers.[86]

The task of child care in the charitable day nurseries, according to one critical early childhood expert, consisted chiefly of "herding children, feeding one end and wiping the other."[87] At the Strawberry Mansion Day Nursery, Frigond remembered:

> It was really a matter of putting the child through his paces, feeding him, keeping him clean, putting or forcing him to sleep, and airing him. . . . After all, with no special toys or equipment . . . not only did the children lack growth opportunity as we understand it today but they did get on people's nerves. One method of lessening their nuisance value was to turn them out of doors. . . . We walked the children to the point of exhaustion or kept them in a circle playing "here comes Punchinello" and "go in and out the windows." Their stamina was greater than that of the workers and occasionally we had to sit it out while inspiring the children to go round and round.[88]

The children attending Frigond's nursery were actually quite fortunate, for they could play these outdoor games in nearby Fairmount Park. Lillian Strauss noted that in most nurseries, children were sent out to play in a brick-paved yard surrounded by buildings and fences. She described a typical playtime scene: "The nursemaid sits at one end with two or three two-year olds who are fretful and crying, while some twelve or fifteen children under four years old wander disconsolately about the enclosure." In most nurseries, no organized play was conducted; nursemaids watched the children at play in the yard or on a roof garden and the matron would "conduct a game, sing a song or put the children through a few gymnastic exercises when she can spare a few moments for it."[89] Some mothers were critical of the lack of play and exercise at the day nurseries: one mother told Helen Tyson that it was "bad for children to sit around aimlessly all day," and two others "wished the younger children could have more fresh air."[90] Eating was also a highly regimented experience: food was served at long tables, and in many nurseries the children, seated on benches, were expected to remain absolutely silent during the meal, raising their hands if they wanted anything. The idea of silent mealtimes, like other aspects of the day nurseries' routine, was probably borrowed from orphanages, where silence during mealtimes was a common rule.[91] Lillian Strauss criticized the practice in her 1916 report, writing, "The unnatural restraint is cruel and decidedly not conducive to good digestion"; elsewhere she noted that the practice "has been discarded even in prisons."[92]

Given all of this regimentation, it is not surprising that some children preferred the freedom of the streets. In 1924, Marion Kohn of Neighborhood Centre was trying to persuade Rebecca Belsky to keep her children at the nursery rather than placing them in foster care or in an institution. A friend of Mrs. Belsky, Sam "Booboo" Hart, whom Kohn described as "one of the highest priced bootleggers of the District," was interfering with Kohn's plans; he had apparently raised thousands of dollars for the Federation of Jewish Charities and was using this influence to persuade the Bureau for Jewish Children to place the Belsky children despite Kohn's advice. Kohn may have been surprised when Sam Hart explained during a meeting to discuss the situation "that he had attended the DN about thirty years ago and that he did not enjoy DN care and whenever he could he climbed over the fence and ran away." She recovered well, however, and "assured him that Nursery care had improved since then."[93]

Day nurseries were presided over by overworked and underpaid matrons who, with little training or status, faced the task of caring for large numbers of children as well as overseeing the physical work of running the nursery. While board members had periodic contact with the mothers, it was the matron who greeted mothers when they brought their children to the nursery each morning or picked them up in the evening, and who was responsible for the children for all the hours in between. Usually a single or widowed woman who lived on the premises, the matron was expected to be "the mother, nurse, and maid" of the nursery.[94]

Filling these different roles at the same time placed heavy demands on matrons' physical and emotional energies. In 1900, the Baldwin Day Nursery board commended their matron by saying, "She had been tireless by day and by night, finding nothing which she could do for the children's good either unworthy work for her to do or overmuch."[95] While matrons at most of the PADN nurseries had help from cooks, nursemaids, and/or cleaning women, they usually took some part in the cooking and cleaning as well as the work of caring for the children. The matron at the Forty-ninth Street Station Day Nursery, for instance, explained to a committee of investigators that she was substituting for the cook for the day; even when the cook was there, she "always makes the desserts and does the baking, cleans her own room."[96] When the Baldwin Nursery hired a new matron in 1908, among the items she requested was material to sew new sheets for the babies' cribs.[97] This matron had to be prepared each morning for bathing, dressing, feeding, diapering or toileting, and amusing an unknown number of children: in 1913 attendance fluctuated from a low of ten children to a high of eighty-five.[98] A report of the Jane D. Kent Nursery in 1886 explained that while the assistant matron ("a mother, indeed") was in charge of the infant room, the matron had charge of all the other children, from toddlers to nine-year-olds. She was expected not only to attend to these children's physical needs, but to squeeze in a little education as well. "After receiving [the children], giving them breakfast, washing heads, hands and faces when necessary of the morning arrivals, she has in this sunny room, blackboard, alphabet, wall tablet, and other helps toward teaching here a little and there a little."[99]

Matrons came to their jobs at day nurseries from a variety of backgrounds. In surveying thirty-five Philadelphia nurseries in 1916, Lillian Strauss of the Child Federation found a few matrons who were trained nurses, and one who was a partially trained dietitian. Most of them, however, had no special training: "they are interested women, kindly and sympathetic, who do everything in their power to improve nursery conditions, but the general attitude is that they are making a futile effort against impossible odds."[100] Anna Frigond of the Strawberry Mansion Day Nursery could serve as an example of the ideal matron. She was at once trained as a practical nurse, knowledgeable about trends in social work, *and* motherly—she remembered holding a child frightened by the sudden departure of his mother "on our lap for the entire day if he would let us, and many were the times way back when our tears were mingled with that of the child."[101]

But while some nurseries were fortunate enough to find a matron devoted to her job, the low wages and status of the position made this unlikely. For instance, one woman who worked at an independent nursery "did not seem at all interested in her work. Her only object in being there was to earn the wages, as her husband had been out of work for a year." This matron was the nursery's only employee; she did all the cooking, cleaning, and caretaking, and Lillian Strauss observed, "She kept all the children shut up in one room where she could watch them easily."[102] Reminiscing in 1949, Frigond described what she went through to hire staff for the Strawberry Mansion Nursery in its early years.

> Come sit with me behind my desk and review the reasons why would-be workers wanted to take on nursery jobs. Our first applicant does not even appear in person. . . . Her mother, recommended by a Board member, applies for her and presents these qualifications. "My daughter is a good girl, but she is not much for learning. So I won't make a bookkeeper out of her! . . . But I wouldn't like to put her in a shop. I'm sure she could help with the children." . . . Our next applicant is an old maid who has worked in a factory for many years. Says she, "I'm tired of the noise in the shop, and the boss gets on my nerves. I would like some easier work." . . . By and large, nurseries were forced to hire the old maids and the incompetents and misfits. Salaries were too low to attract more intelligent persons . . . for example, we had to hire the applicant who did not like the factory.[103]

Observers such as Lillian Strauss and Helen Glenn Tyson frequently called for the professionalization of the job of day nursery matron. Strauss noted in 1916 that the average salary paid to matrons in PADN-affiliated nurseries was just over thirty dollars a month, and commented, "It is not to be supposed that trained women can be procured for such a wage."[104] At a meeting of the PADN in 1920, Cora Baird Jeanes reminded her fellow nursery managers that in order for nurseries to enter "the foremost ranks of child welfare agencies, . . . the question of an efficient staff would have to be met. It was essential to interest young women of good education in the work," in order to secure "a higher type of personnel."[105]

The class distance between day nursery clients and day nursery matrons was often minimal, like that between working mothers and their neighbors who boarded children. In at least one case, a matron actually became a day nursery client: a couple who came to Philadelphia with their children in order to take charge of the Hebrew Day

Nursery sent their children to the Neighborhood Centre Day Nursery when that position did not work out.[106] Matrons served as the bridge between the day nursery managers and the clients of the nursery. While their own class position and life experience may have made some of them sympathetic to the challenges faced by day nursery mothers, however, they were also responsible for enforcing rules and policies established by the managers. In fact, in order to keep the nurseries running smoothly with very limited staff and resources, the matrons may have had to be stricter with both children and mothers than the managers would have been.

Despite their heavy responsibilities, the day nursery matrons were treated as servants of the board. Like good servants, Lillian Strauss found the matrons to be "almost without exception loyal to their boards of managers," so much, in fact, that she had trouble getting them to tell her anything critical about their working conditions.[107] The typical matron lived in a small room at the top of the nursery building, sometimes shared by another member of the nursery staff, or by her children who lived at the nursery with her.[108] These rooms were furnished at the pleasure of the board members: for instance, at a meeting in 1915, one of the members of the Baldwin board "made a strong plea" for making the matron's bedroom "into an attractive sitting room where she could entertain her friends in the evening. Through the generosity of some of the managers, she is to have a new window seat made [with] fresh cretonne coverings and the walls repapered."[109] At a meeting of the St. Nicholas Day Nursery board, it was reported that the matron had "asked if her dining table might be mended, and if she could have a half dozen table napkins for her personal use. She further asked for some pictures for the dining room. Mrs. Kennedy offered to donate these."[110] The managers typically presented the matron, along with the other workers, with a small Christmas gift: for instance, in 1910 the Sunnyside Day Nursery's matron and maid each received a five-dollar gold piece.[111] As with live-in domestic service, marriage often meant the end of the matron's job: when Miss Ringhoff, the matron at the Baldwin Nursery, married in 1917, the board rejected her proposal to continue her job and have her husband live at the nursery.[112]

The matrons' second-class status was also evident from the way in which they were incorporated into the PADN. When the idea was raised at an early PADN meeting of inviting the matrons to attend the organization's general meetings, it was decided to hold separate meetings for the matrons instead.[113] Rather than joining board members in their discussions about the nursery's role within the field of social work or about strategies for expanding and improving nursery care in the city, the matrons were given lectures by local experts on topics such as "food," "health," "prevention of fire," and "recreation and play."[114] Indeed, while many matrons may have had useful insights on day care policy to share with the board members, the amount of work they had to do translated into a preoccupation with practical matters, especially cleanliness and order.

Charitable Relations

Not only did day nurseries offer highly regimented care, but they did not let the children and mothers who used them forget that they were recipients of charity. Before she could bring her child to a day nursery, a mother would have to prove her worthiness, justify her reasons for going out to work, and go through an "investigation" by the matron or a member of the nursery board. On a daily basis as well, women and children who used the nurseries were reminded that they were charity cases. The entire process by which a child entered the nursery for the day was marked by rituals distinguishing the world of the nursery from the world outside. The first of these rituals was the daily medical inspection, performed by a trained nurse or a physician, or sometimes by the matron. This medical inspection was often a point of contention between mothers and nursery staff, for it was a process in which the authority of the nursery staff superseded a mother's judgment about her child's health. Distrust of mothers' abilities to sustain their children's health was pervasive. For instance, the Neighborhood Centre Nursery prepared bottles of milk for mothers to take home at night, "thereby assuring the baby of proper food."[115] At the Cathedral Day Nursery, the nuns, fearing vermin, sometimes destroyed the clothes in which the children arrived.[116]

Mothers knew that when their child "failed" a morning inspection, it was their work as mothers that had been judged inadequate; failure to pass the medical inspection also meant that a mother would lose a day of work (and possibly her job) for a condition that she did not judge to be very serious.[117] So when a morning's inspection detected lice or other evidence that a mother had not been keeping her child adequately clean, mothers often took offense. In fact, so many mothers were offended when the San Cristoforo Nursery tried to cut their children's hair short to avoid lice, that the nursery almost closed down.[118] Similarly, the First Day Nursery's visitor reported in 1919 that their cleaning woman, Mrs. Peters, who also sent her children to the nursery, was very angry when the doctor found nits and bugs in her children's hair. "I am afraid all of our efforts with Mrs. P and her children have come to an end. She has left us in high temper and withdrawn the children from our care" with a "hateful" resignation note.[119]

After the medical inspection came the daily bath and changing of clothes. Although every nursery stipulated that mothers must bring their children in clean condition, nurseries typically bathed children on arrival and dressed them in fresh clothes. Strauss observed, "In all nurseries in which infants are kept, the entire clothing of the babies is changed when they arrive in the morning, and in most of them fresh aprons are put over the ordinary clothing of other children to give the child a cleanly appearance."[120] This practice, Ellen Ross has suggested in another context, was a way in which nursery staff not only showed their lack of confidence in the mothers' ability to keep their children clean, but also laid claim to the children under their care, "muting . . . their existence as others people's daughters and sons."[121] By devoting their own physical labor to sewing nursery clothes or aprons, board members may have sought to identify themselves as these children's surrogate mothers. The nursery clothes also served to identify children as part of the institution, setting them apart from other children who might be playing on the streets. Like children attending orphanages, nursery children may have resented wearing these "special" clothes which marked them as "charity kids."[122]

Day nurseries, as we have seen, brought together some of the wealthiest women in Philadelphia with some of the city's poorest women and children. The nurseries were a social space where, to borrow the language of a reporter describing the First Day Nursery in 1913, "society women and debutantes" met the mothers and "children of the slums." As charitable institutions uniquely positioned to intervene in working-class family life, day nurseries nurtured a variety of relationships between clients and benefactors. The women who used the nurseries alternately expressed gratitude for nursery care, suggested that the nursery was different from charity, fought with nursery workers over a child's future, asked them to intercede with employers or creditors, lied about their situation in order to get help from the nurseries, relinquished control over their children's future to the guidance of nursery workers, and used the nursery as a negotiating tool in their own struggles with other family members. The day nursery became a neighborhood resource, one part of a mother's strategy for providing for her children that might include trying to get more money from an unwilling husband; getting clothes or food from relatives; swapping childcare or meals with other women; taking in homework; peddling; begging; going out to work; taking in other women's children; seeking help from unions, lodges, or mutual aid associations; remarrying or starting a relationship with a man who could offer support; sending an older child out to work; or seeking help from other charities.

Day nursery reports are filled with innumerable descriptions of what historian Ellen Ross has aptly called "rituals of benevolence," occasions at which elite women sought to make visible their generosity toward, and responsibility for, poor mothers and their children. For instance, an early report of the Jane D. Kent Nursery described mothers' trips to the seashore and "delightful visits . . . in June and July to the Zoological Garden and the Sanitarium, under the escort of the Lady managers."[123] In 1913, the children were served Christmas dinner at the nursery; each child received two articles of new clothing, a toy, a book, and a box of candy, while their mothers were given "a beautiful basket of choice fruit and a quarter pound of tea."[124] The same spirit pervaded a Hanukkah celebration at Neighborhood Centre; as a later director of the settlement house remembered,

> A prominent lady Board member would arrive in her chauffeured limousine. With her chauffeur behind her, his arms filled with boxes of candy, each tied with a neat ribbon, she would come into the gym where the boys and girls were lined up against the wall and would give each one a box handed to her by her chauffeur.[125]

Other day nursery reports document trips to the circus, Christmas stockings, picnics in the country, hayrides, Thanksgiving baskets, turkeys, parties with ice cream and cake, and periodic gifts of clothing, often sewed by the managers or by church sewing circles. A description of Our Lady of Mercy Day Nursery was typical: "The Ladies of the Alliance have been very faithful in coming to the Nursery every Wednesday evening to make frocks and other necessities for the tiny tots. On several occasions the members of the Alliance have given surprises to the children in the form of toys, candy, etc."[126]

These "rituals of benevolence" may have been intended to unite the classes, but in the tradition of charity that reinforces class distinctions. Ellen Ross, in writing about free meals provided to poor schoolchildren in London, notes that such events carried different meanings to philanthropists, mothers, and children. To the benevolent elite who provided the gifts, these occasions represented a sacramental linking of the classes, a vision of rich and poor woven together by the benevolence of the wealthy. To the mothers, these occasions were a resource to be used in their daily efforts to provide for their families; and for some of the children, Ross comments, they "were indeed a kind of sacrament, promising care and love outside their homes from those with apparently more to give than their own parents."[127] Whether they had warm feelings toward the ladies of the board or resented their pretensions, the children who attended the nurseries recognized that they were the recipients of charity: when asked to describe the Baldwin Nursery for an annual report, two twelve-year-old boys who attended the nursery explained, "The Baldwin Day Nursery is a specimen of the kindness shown by the prominent ladies and gentlemen of Philadelphia."[128] Children may well have responded to special visits from board ladies as did the children of the Hebrew Orphan Asylum of New York: eagerly, but cynically too. Hyman Bogen writes, "When visitors came, they willingly played the role of the grateful orphans in return for the goodies they knew would be forthcoming. Still, no amusement, no cake and ice cream treats, no catered banquets meant much more to them than a diversion, a transitory pleasure."[129]

In addition to providing holiday parties and special outings for nursery children and sometimes for their mothers, day nursery managers could be counted on to provide limited material assistance to poor families and intercede on their behalf with employers or creditors. For instance, the First Day Nursery's visitor reported in 1917, "Mrs. McCallahan would be glad if we would ask her employer for a raise . . . Miss Burke has sent her coal. We purchased a pair of shoes for the little girl." Board members later gave this family a box of clothing, including "a lovely muff and hat." The visitor also asked board members for clothes so that another nursery mother could send her children to Sabbath school and reported that a third mother, a dressmaker, "says she would be glad for work if any of the lady managers need her."[130] In 1913, day nursery director Marion Kohn reported that through the influence of the Day Nursery Committee Mr. Horace Fleisher had donated seventy dollars to one boy to buy out a corner on which to sell papers, and department store owner Abe Snellenberg provided after-school employment for another boy.[131] In these cases as in others, the benevolence of the board members was intensely personal: gifts were passed from a specific benefactor to a specific worthy recipient who would be expected to show appropriate gratitude, and only for a very well-defined need.

Many families who used day nurseries were uncomfortable with being defined as the object of elite benevolence and objected to the idea that the nursery was a charity. Since bringing one's children to a nursery was part of an effort to maintain self-sufficiency rather than depending on charitable support, many mothers insisted that the day nursery was a respectable solution, superior to other forms of charity. Some seemed to suggest that it was not charity at all. For instance, an Irish widow who used the Baldwin Day Nursery "had promised her husband that she would never accept charity, but that, unaided, she would bring up their children. She fully realized that the Nursery was a charity, but she hoped he would excuse it." She "resolutely" refused all other aid, including loans from the nursery, through a series of bad work, accidents, and serious illnesses.[132] Similarly, Yetta Miller sent her Daniel to the day nursery, but refused support from the United Hebrew Charities, "stating that she preferred working." Although Marion Kohn wanted to help Mrs. Miller with clothing, she "refuses to take any assistance." Even when the child's illness prompted Kohn to ask Miller to stay at home and have her income supplemented by the UHC, she refused to consider the possibility.[133] Mrs. Newman also made a distinction between the day nursery and reliance on charity. Although she did not express any qualms about sending her son Harvey to the nursery, when he turned old enough to work she insisted on sending him out, saying "that she must have help, and that she would not go to a charitable agency for financial aid."[134] Helen Tyson found that a quarter of the mothers she interviewed "regarded the nursery care quite frankly as 'charity,' but seemed to feel no hesitation about accepting it, since they, too, were doing their part to 'help along.'"[135] Others offered to pay more than they were required to in order to feel that they were not accepting charity; Marion Kohn described one couple who "assume the attitude that they do not wish to accept charity and would be glad to pay even 50 cents a day, should that be necessary for the care of the child." (While fifty cents a day may not strike us today as a princely sum, it was ten times the fee that most nurseries charged, and represented a significant sacrifice for a family whose next step if day nursery care did not work out was to sell all their furniture.)[136]

Others, aware not only of the nursery's charitable nature but of its connections to other welfare agencies, were adamant about refusing day nursery care altogether and pursued other options to support their households. When the Abelov family was reported to Neighborhood Centre as being in need, Mrs. Abelov was willing to ask that her children be taken in the nursery, because with her husband unemployed, the family had no income. But Mr. Abelov refused this arrangement, saying "that he did not wish to have his children placed in a DN, but asked that we secure employment for him, and stated he would not accept any financial assistance from this organization."[137]

If it was a mother's job to find day care and worry about it, it was also part of her job to know how to take advantage of resources like the day nursery. Day nurseries were known in their neighborhoods as places to turn in times of trouble, and information about them circulated in informal neighborhood networks as well as in official directories. Most of the mothers applying to the Baldwin Day Nursery in the early 1920s, for instance, reported that they had heard of the nursery from relatives, friends, or neighbors, or from other agencies or churches; others simply said that they "knew the neighborhood," that they knew the settlement house, or that they saw the nursery's sign and mothers picking up their children; one said she "just heard of it." The milk man, the steam heater man, the insurance man, the policeman, a landlady, an employer, and a woman in a neighborhood store all referred mothers to the nursery.

Information about how to "work the charities" by presenting oneself and one's situation in the proper light to receive help must also have circulated freely. For instance, Eva Kulofsky came to the Young Women's Union Day Nursery in 1907, saying that "she wants to put Sammy away as he is a very bad boy." Familiar with the system that offered help with children only when mothers were willing to give them up, her relatives had told her how to present her case. Mrs. Kulofsky returned later that day, however, and confessed that "her relatives had advised her to say the boy was bad so that he could be taken away from her, but he really isn't a bad boy, she would rather have him with her."[138] Another woman, who went out to work as a cloak finisher after her husband's death, later "acknowledged that she had stated that Albert was a year and half older than he really was believing that we would not take so young a child in the Nursery."[139] Other women applying for day nursery care deceived nursery workers about their husbands' whereabouts, knowing that deserted or widowed women were more likely to receive help, or about the existence of relatives; several explained that they had gotten extensive help from neighbors or landladies who later turned out to be sisters or mothers in disguise.

Many mothers expressed gratitude for the charity of the day nursery—both the daily care of their children that made it possible for them to keep their families together, and the special help that the nurseries could provide at holidays or to meet special needs. Some, like Goldie Rokofsky, found at a day nursery not only the help they needed but a sympathetic friend as well. Rokofsky, who turned to Neighborhood Centre's Marion Kohn when she was pregnant and her sick husband was unable to work, wrote in a letter to Kohn thanking her for ten dollars Kohn had sent, "I will never forget what you try so good for me." A year later, she wrote asking for advice about how to feed her family, concluding, "You are the only person in the world that could give me a good advise."[140] Another family, who had contact with the day nursery for more than ten years, expressed gratitude to the social worker, saying they "were very grateful to Neighborhood Centre for their constant interest. They said that through sincere sympathy and ready help Neighborhood Centre was giving them the courage to start anew."[141] And there were other clients who brought their children to the day nursery for many years, developed close relationships with Kohn and other settlement workers, and turned to them for advice and help on a range of issues from finding an apartment to methods of child-rearing. Of course, such expressions of gratitude, transcribed (and probably reworded) by the social worker into the family's case record, should be read carefully, for they were part of an unequal relationship in which properly expressed gratitude might ease the way for help in the future.

Although most children who attended day nurseries did not stay for long periods of time, there was an important minority that "grew up at the nursery." For a variety of reasons, this pattern seems to have been more common at Neighborhood Centre than at the other nurseries for which we have records from this time period. Some of these children seem to have adopted the nursery and the settlement house of which it was part as a second home, becoming "protégés" of day nursery social workers, and sometimes even using the nursery as a way to escape their own families. Clara Tobin, who attended the day nursery for eight years, ran away from her mother's home at the age of twelve, after spending time with Presbyterian missionaries. The nursery case record is filled with praise for Clara and her unusual sensibilities; at one point, a social worker explained that "her love of the beautiful and the symbolic explained why she had become interested in Christianity." (The criticism of immigrant Judaism implicit in this statement was not unusual among German-Jewish social workers who did not see much beauty or symbolism in immigrant religious practices.) After Clara was returned, by the joint efforts of various child welfare associations and the city detective bureau, Neighborhood Centre workers supervised her new living arrangements. "It was thought better not to have Clara live with her mother. Their personalities often clashed and while the mother admired Clara for her refinement, Clara did not admire certain crudities in her mother." Settlement workers secured a small fellowship that made it possible for Clara to attend high school and eventually made arrangements for her to live at the settlement.[142] The values that Clara had learned in the nursery probably reinforced the "refinement" that separated her from her immigrant mother, and nursery workers may have provided role models and expectations for her that were very different from what she got at home.

For young people like Clara, growing up in the nursery could mean broadened opportunities. The Day Nursery Committee raised special funds to send Samuel Katz to the National Farm School, Helen Levin to business college, and Jennie Kass, who had worked along with her mother as a nursemaid at the Day Nursery, to Temple University for training as a social worker.[143] The committee also provided hot lunches, suppers, and carfare for Dora Warkel and Alice Shamberg, day nursery graduates who were attending high school.[144] Sometimes following the path made possible by contact with the nursery and settlement house meant breaking away from the immediate demands of the family economy. Anna Penner, the teenager who had become depressed when Marion Kohn insisted on placing her younger siblings in foster care rather than allowing her to continue bearing the burden of the home, is a case in point. Although her initial identity was clearly that of the "little mother" taking on the responsibilities vacated by her sick mother, under the tutelage of the settlement house she began to envision a different future. Anna was brought to live in the settlement house and was sent back to school. She became valedictorian of her class, assisted at the settlement house, and worked at a variety of jobs that settlement workers helped her secure. A later case record notes that Anna was employed by the Hebrew Orphan Asylum, attended Hunter College, and was expected to transfer to Columbia College in the fall.[145] Like Hilda Satt Polacheck, whose relationship with Jane Addams brought her out of the garment factory and into a different world, children who developed strong ties to Marion Kohn at Neighborhood Centre could find their lives transformed.[146]

The closeness of the relationships that these children developed with the workers at Neighborhood Centre is suggested in the long letters that Samuel Katz wrote to Marion Kohn, describing the details of his everyday life at the Farm School and asking for advice about his future. In one letter he wrote, "I wish you were out here, Everything is green, violets and other wild flowers are everywhere, its just great," and in another, he asked Kohn to intercede for him when a female friend from home stopped writing to him; he closed a third letter by writing, "Best regards to everyone at the [Young Women's] Union." These relationships, of course, were not without conflict; when Samuel doubted the career plan that Kohn had laid out for him at the Farm School and suggested that the civil service might be more promising, she reprimanded him: "Wouldn't it be a better plan to trust in those for your future, who most have your interest at heart? Do you think that I would let you go to a Farm School if I believed that you were taking three years out of your life? No! It is because I am sure that my friends will see to your success. . . . Just look at the boys whom you and I know, who have not had a school chance, and think of where they are today." She closed her letter by apologizing for not answering his letter sooner: "it is just that I am busy and worrying about people who are starving around me every day."[147]

While the mothers of children who became day nursery "protégés" seem to have been glad to relinquish control over their children's future to day nursery workers who could assure them of greater opportunities, other mothers struggled with nursery workers for control over their children. They knew that the nursery, like other social welfare institutions, did not hesitate to judge them unfit mothers and to take their children away from them. Rose Schwartz, an unmarried mother who sent her daughter Beatrice to the Neighborhood Centre Nursery rather than live at home with her own mother, fought with Marion Kohn about her daughter during the whole time that she used the nursery. Beatrice had been causing trouble at the nursery, "inducing little girls to go home with her after school and telling them stories of life and its development that were most serious." Kohn, concerned about Beatrice's lack of "moral sense," and probably linking it to Rose's history of running a house of prostitution in Chicago, was eager to have the girl boarded out, but her mother "was devoted" to the child and "would not be parted from her." Kohn was "anxious to bring the case into court, believing that if Beatrice were allowed to remain with her mother, she would be lost to Society." She did not go to court at that time, but two years later another opportunity presented itself. Beatrice had fallen and broken her arm while at the nursery, and her mother decided to enter a lawsuit. "This proposition was so welcomed by Miss Kohn as an opportunity to bring the case before the court in the best interest of the child, that Mrs. Schwartz changed her plans" and withdrew her daughter from the nursery.[148]

In another case, Kohn tried to use her influence with the court to persuade a mother to stop begging and instead seek work in a factory—for not all forms of "providing" for a child were legitimate. Kohn wrote, "There was no doubt that Rebecca loved the child but her love was not that of understanding, nor did she realize that her begging plus the environment in which she was forcing Sara to live were having an adverse influence on the child's life." Although Kohn threatened to take Rebecca to court to have Sara taken away from her, Rebecca refused to seek factory work, and instead simply withdrew the child from the nursery and transferred her to another school. The case finally did come into court a few years later, and although Kohn asked the judge to take Sara away from her mother until the mother "would be willing to work and build a home," the judge refused, proclaiming "that since the mother was kind to the child it made no difference that she received her money by begging."[149] Like Rose Schwartz, Rebecca was able to maintain her claim to her child despite Kohn's belief that her maternal devotion was not enough. Other women withdrew their children from nurseries rather than subject them to medical examinations or procedures that they saw as dangerous. Thus one mother applying to the First Day Nursery "stood a little against having baby vaccinated." The visitor reported that when she called later at this woman's house, the mother "was making different arrangements, decided not to place him in nursery."[150]

Family members often used the nurseries as negotiating tools in their own family conflicts. Sometimes mothers called on the nurseries to help them exert control over their children. For instance, in 1919, the First Day Nursery's visitor reported, "The Dunley's are with us again. Mrs. D says Lydia was running the streets and dragging the children around with her. She said she would rather have her here and have her working for us, so we took them all. Lydia is 14, a large girl for the nursery, but we are going to try to teach her to work."[151] In other cases, women instructed nursery workers to restrict fathers', or other relatives', access to their children. One father wrote to the Young Women's Union in 1917 asking to know how his baby was doing. "As my wife dont want to correspond with me and I am anxious to hear how my baby is getting along. . . . I dont care that my wife dont write to me she can do as she pleases, but I feel discont[ent]ed if I don't hear from my baby, or in other words I can't make my wife to correspond with me but I think I can hear of my baby."[152] One woman who had a history of difficulty with her stepmother seemed to prefer putting her children in the custody of the day nursery rather than with her relatives and instructed the nursery to keep her stepmother from seeing them. When she was in the hospital, she left early against the advice of the doctors because "her step-mother had been reporting unfavorably about the children's condition. Mrs M could not rest until she saw them herself." She later forgave her stepmother for doing this, as she wrote to Marion Kohn:

> Dear Miss Cohn my mother and sister were cring I should forgive them what they told me about the children that they werend treated right. They are felling so bad that they passed such remorks about the children. They are sorry for it now after they found the children so sweet and dears clean. And [e]very body say how nice and fat they look. As I forgive them I hope that you will forgive them too. . . . When my family will come on Sunday please forgive them and leave them in as I see their sorry for it.[153]

In this case, Mrs. M's struggle for control was not with the nursery but with her family; in fact placing her children at the nursery gave her more power to determine when and how she would allow her relatives to involve themselves with her children.

Day nursery workers clearly tried to exert "social control" over their clients. They tried to convince or coerce adult family members into acting in specific ways: working at respectable jobs, conducting their households according to standards of "modern" motherhood and home economics, availing themselves of proper medical care, providing certain kinds of help to relatives in need, sending children to school as long as possible, carrying out proper roles within marriage, or taking legal action when marriages fell apart. These efforts at controlling adults were of a piece with day nursery workers' efforts to socialize children to habits of cleanliness, punctuality, and order within the nursery; the overall effort at social control represented by nurseries and other welfare institutions was one of the reasons that employers (such as the mill owners who were asked to contribute to the Baldwin Day Nursery), business leaders, and their wives were encouraged to support them. By helping to shape these poor families into hardworking, disciplined, and independent members of the respectable working class, nurseries would not only help reduce dependency on charity but also help create a reliable rising generation of workers and consumers.

But, as these cases demonstrate, the powers of day nursery workers were often restricted, as women who felt threatened could simply remove their children from the nursery, and judges and other welfare agencies did not always concur with a social worker's judgment. In recent years, scholars have revised simplistic analyses of social control, in which social welfare agencies, schools, and other institutions were seen as dictating the values and behavior of their clients. Rather, they have reminded us that while social control was often an important aim of reformers, social workers, and philanthropists, it was an aim that was not always realized. The putative agents of social control were not always in agreement with each other about what values and behavior they were trying to promote, much less about how to promote it. Clients exercised a certain amount of power in their dealings with these institutions, making choices and demands according to their own view of legitimate behavior, rights, and duties; and they often used these agencies for their own ends, which sometimes included trying to exercise more "social control" over their children, spouses, neighbors, and relatives.[154]

Women used the day nurseries, then, as they used other charities and social agencies —instrumentally, selectively, and on their own terms. Sending children to a charitable day nursery was one of many strategies that a hard-pressed mother might use in seeking to provide for her family, and it was not most women's first choice of care for their children. Mothers reacted to the nursery's stigma of charity and to the institutional care that it offered by turning to the nurseries only when they had no other options, using the nurseries for limited periods of time, and sending only those children who were most in need of care. Within the world of the nursery, they sought to maintain their dignity while getting the help they needed; thus a woman might express gratitude for a Thanksgiving basket one day and withdraw her child in a huff the next. In the final analysis, however, wage-earning mothers did not set the terms that defined them as noble but inadequate mothers and defined the day nursery as a piece of charity that offered a poor substitute for a real mother's care.

3

Deserving Mothers

Day Care as Welfare

Leah Nadel, a short, dark Russian-Jewish woman who neither spoke nor understood English, first came to the day nursery at the Young Women's Union in 1912, seeking care for her two children, a four-year-old boy and a three-year old girl. Her husband, described as an "inebriate," had pawned most of the furniture, and the social worker described the conditions of their two-room apartment as "miserable." The children began to attend the nursery while Leah went out to work sewing buttons in a factory. After six years spent in and out of jail and hospitals, Leah's husband died of tuberculosis. In 1920, the worker observed, "Visits made to Mrs Nadel's home always show that she is making a real effort at homekeeping." Her status as one of the "respectable poor" was further enhanced by her refusal to accept any additional charitable assistance. In 1921, the nursery received a letter from the state's Mothers' Assistance Fund, asking about Leah's character. Nursery director Marion Kohn responded that Leah Nadel was "one of the finest of our Day Nursery mothers, one of the most hard working and earnest." Three years after she became a widow and almost ten years after she took over the responsibility of supporting her children, Leah started to receive fifteen dollars a month as a mother's pension from the state.

But her basic situation did not change: she continued to work, the children continued to attend the nursery, and she continued to receive detailed advice from social workers. Although she was sometimes skeptical of this advice, she did her best. For instance, a visiting nurse reported that Leah was "interested in the various vegetables [;] although she said she is quite sure she will never learn to like them she will cook them for the children." On an earlier visit, when social worker Rosetta Stang told Mrs. Nadel, who slept in one room with the two children, that it was "unwise" to have the children sleep in the same room, she "did not understand our point of view and said that she believed that having the children sleep in the same room would strengthen their moral standards. She promised, however, to make other adjustments." And she continued to be a favorite of the day nursery social worker, who described her as "very energetic, hard working and self-respecting," devoted to her children and anxious for them to get a good education.[1]

Leah Nadel's story suggests some of the ways in which the day nurseries operated as a charity during the 1910s and 1920s. Although she did eventually become one of the struggling widows pictured in day nursery reports and fund-raising literature, Nadel's struggles to support her family began long before her husband's death. The help she received from the day nursery—and through its contacts with other social agencies—was crucial in aiding her to make a life for herself and her children. But in order to receive that help, she had to keep proving herself a "deserving" mother, keep promising that she would make "adjustments" in her housekeeping and mothering practices in order to remain in the good graces of the nursery social workers.

From their inception in the nineteenth century, day nurseries had offered care for children as a charitable gift to poor families. Because it was assumed that only the poorest and most desperate families would send mothers into the workplace, day care was linked with dire poverty and family crisis. As the world of charity changed during the 1910s and 1920s, with reformers making new claims on the state on behalf of motherhood and agreeing that mothers should not be forced to work, day nurseries increasingly fell into disregard. By arguing that the public should provide financial support to enable poor women to devote themselves to full-time mothering, reformers at once demanded more from government and promoted a narrower definition of motherhood than did day nursery supporters. The idea that motherhood encompassed providing for children as well as caring for them was consequently ignored. Also promoting a narrower definition of motherhood during this period were professional social workers, who emerged as a strong voice in the 1920s. Through careful individual counseling and organizing of community resources, social workers sought to restore poor families to "normalcy," with a breadwinning father and a full-time mother. Their commitment to this vision of family life, of course, meant that they would not encourage wage-earning mothers and would not advocate for day care.

While these efforts to promote the breadwinning father/full-time mother paradigm were only partially successful, they helped create an atmosphere in which the nurseries' efforts to enable mothers to work for wages were no longer seen as desirable: mothering, not breadwinning, became the basis for social policy toward women. The same maternalist ideology that inspired elite women to create surrogate homes for the children of working mothers also inhibited their efforts by promoting anxiety about the very idea of helping mothers to be breadwinners.[2] The adoption of mothers' pension legislation and the emergence of professional social work cast day nurseries in a negative light, causing a crisis of confidence among day nursery leaders and pushing them to limit the scope of their work.

Single Mothers: The Problem and the Solutions

During the Progressive era, public attention turned to the figure of the poor single mother, charged with both supporting and raising her children. Welfare reformers focused on single mothers not so much because their numbers were increasing as because of the threatening social breakdown they seemed to symbolize, and the way in which their presence seemed to indict the cherished American belief that working men could and would provide for their wives and children. Reformers who began with the assumption "that men paid for their families while women raised them"[3] were puzzled by the figure of the breadwinning mother, unsure how to treat her, and confused about policies that would remedy this "social accident." Some called for men to put down a security deposit for their future wives and children, while others began to insist that the public must take some responsibility for supporting these families when individual men were unwilling or unable to do so.[4]

But if the public was going to take on responsibility for poor families, what form should that assistance take? As social worker Helen Glenn Tyson wrote in 1919, the working mother "must obviously be relieved of part of her burden" if she was to raise her children to be useful citizens. "Shall she, therefore, be released from home and child care for part of the day, in order that she may go out to earn the living? Or shall economic support be assured her, so that most of her time may be given to her children?"[5] As Tyson noted, there was a debate during these years between those who wanted to establish day nurseries to serve poor mothers and those who preferred to give these mothers money to enable them to stay at home to raise their children. Mothers' pension legislation, which provided state aid to widowed mothers, quickly gained popularity because it was based on the idea of female dependence and domesticity. Women who could no longer exchange their housekeeping and mothering work for economic support from a particular man could (if they were lucky) now make the same bargain with the state, substituting one source of economic dependence for another. Day nurseries offered a different exchange, giving women help with their mothering work in order to enable them to provide economically for their children.

Women across the country who were concerned with child welfare saw mothers' pensions and day nurseries as two different—and mutually exclusive—directions for welfare policy to take. At a meeting of the PADN in 1908, a woman who had recently attended a national child welfare conference reported that "in investigating the reason for the non-existence of day nurseries in Germany, it was found that there is a pension fund of two million dollars set aside for the support of widows and destitute mothers with children."[6] In Kansas City, the United Jewish Charities decided to abandon their day nursery "because they believed that a system of pensions to the women who patronized the nursery would be better."[7]

Day nurseries were initially popular because they appealed not only to the maternal instincts of those who wished to bring neglected children in from the streets but also to a long-standing fear of promoting "dependence" on charity. By providing a surrogate mother during the day, nurseries enabled poor women to take on the role of breadwinner, supporting their families through their labor rather than relying on charity. Maintaining independence from the degrading charity of direct aid seems to have been particularly important to women like Leah Nadel, as well as to some day nursery supporters. But if Americans worried about making poor people "dependent," they also believed that wives and mothers were meant to be dependent. By the nineteenth century, Nancy Fraser and Linda Gordon have argued, dependency—previously a condition shared by most of the population—was considered proper for women, yet degrading for men. The ideal of the family wage came to represent white men's "independence," which was demonstrated by their ability to support nonemployed wives and children. Of course, men's independence was often illusory; not only did it mask their real dependence on women's unpaid labor within the home, but few men actually earned enough to single-handedly support a family. Nevertheless, it carried important ideological weight.[8]

Single mothers, with no male wage to depend on, confused these categories. As mothers caring for dependent children, and as women, they were seen to be "naturally" dependent themselves, yet they were often also workers, earning a wage like "independent" heads of families. Of course, the small wage that most women earned was itself a marker of gender difference: while a male wage was meant to support a family, a female wage was seen as "pin money," or as the bare minimum that might be necessary to support a single young woman.[9] The difficulty of supporting a family "independently" on such a wage meant that poor mothers risked merging a "good" dependency—that of the housewife and mother—with a "bad" dependency—that of the pauper dependent on charity. The breadwinning mother thus remained a puzzling figure, and reformers seemed uncertain about whether to treat her more like a breadwinner, who should be encouraged to achieve "independence," or more like a mother, who should properly be supported.

While advocates of mothers' pensions started from the assumption that mothers without husbands needed the state to step in "as a surrogate for the absent father,"[10] proponents of day nurseries assumed that what these mothers needed most of all was a surrogate *mother* to take care of their children while they took on the male breadwinning role. But proponents of both mothers' pensions and day nurseries were torn by the conflicting claims of dependent domesticity and respectable self-support. The ambivalence of politicians, social workers, and the general public toward these conflicting claims meant that neither solution was really put into practice. Ironically, women receiving pensions were urged to work for wages, while women using day nurseries were urged to return to full-time mothering.

Taking on a Father's Job: Mothers' Pensions

The fifteen dollars a month that Leah Nadel started receiving from the Mothers' Assistance Fund in 1920 was a result of political agitation by welfare reformers and middle-class women's organizations throughout the 1910s. The idea of "pensioning" widows with young children originated with some private charities around the turn of the century, was picked up by several states, and gained widespread support following the 1909 White House Conference on the Care of Dependent Children.[11] This conference, attended by President Theodore Roosevelt and leading reformers, proclaimed that the home was "the highest and finest product of civilization" and resolved that children should not be separated from their mothers on account of poverty.[12] This declaration strengthened the resolve of those private charities that were already giving pensions to mothers. For instance, the Philadelphia United Hebrew Charities reported in 1912 that it would no longer make a rule of placing children in institutions whose mothers were living but unable to support them. "If a woman is mentally, morally and physically fit to take care of her children," the organization resolved, "it is the duty of the community to supply her with financial aid necessary to keep her family intact. . . . The ideal of all human society is the preservation of the home, however humble it may be."[13]

The White House conference (despite its clear preference for privately financed mothers' aid) also galvanized a wide range of people to work for publicly financed pensions. Support for mothers' pensions came from middle-class women's organizations, especially the National Congress of Mothers and the state federations of women's clubs; juvenile court judges and county officials interested in saving money; and feminists and professional reformers who saw mothers' pensions as the opening wedge to the creation of an American welfare state. The idea of mothers' pensions spread quickly from 1911, when the first state legislation was passed; by 1920, over three-quarters of the states had adopted the measure, and four more states passed legislation before 1930.[14] Although the laws varied from state to state, they all provided a monthly stipend to women (usually widows, but in some states deserted or divorced women as well) who had children under sixteen and had no male support. In 1935, mothers' pensions were taken over by the federal government, in a section of the Social Security Act known as Aid to Dependent Children; it was later renamed Aid to Families with Dependent Children. Thus the mothers' pension legislation enacted in the Progressive era was the foundation for the entitlement program that most often comes to mind when Americans today hear the word "welfare."

The rhetoric used by some of these proponents of mothers' pension legislation promised a new relationship between women and the state, one that honored motherhood as being as significant a contribution to the state as military service. Indeed, the use of the term *pension* was a deliberate strategy to equate mothers' aid with state rewards for military service and to distance such aid from the stigma of private charity. For instance, in 1911, the president of the Tennessee Congress of Mothers declared: "We cannot afford to let a mother, one who has divided her body by creating other lives for the good of the state, one who has contributed to citizenship, be classed as a pauper, a dependent. . . . Today let us honor the *mother* wherever found—if she has given a citizen to the nation, then the nation owes something to her." Motherhood was not to be a badge of dependency but a source of citizenship.[15] William Hard, a former settlement house worker who conducted a major campaign for mothers' pensions in the pages of a women's fashion magazine, also had a grand vision of the meaning of mothers' pensions. He argued that mothers receiving pensions were employees of the state and should be treated as such: "Her true position is determined not by her poverty but by her duty. . . . To call such a person a "dependent" is to me as monstrous as to call the librarian of Congress a "dependent." He is paid for his work; she for hers."[16]

Supporters and opponents of mothers' pensions alike saw them as a step toward a system of universal social insurance in an American welfare state. Evelyn Cavin, director of the pension program in Philadelphia, suggested in 1925 that they "should be regarded just as a wedge in order to secure better state support for widows and their families," while Otto Barnard of the New York Charity Organization Society criticized mothers' aid as a step toward socialism: "It is not American; it is not virile."[17] Charity organizations, which had fought to dismantle public outdoor-relief systems in many large cities, were convinced that the mothers' pension programs represented a step backward into a governmental relief system that would inevitably be marred by corruption and political influence. Most of all, charity workers were appalled by the invocation of state aid as a right, as they believed that this mentality would lead to "pauperism" and create long-term dependence.

Most supporters of mothers' pensions, however, did not see them as an entering wedge to socialism, a way to redefine attitudes toward welfare provision, or a reconsideration of women's citizenship. The maternalist rhetoric that drew the most support lamented the folly and injustice of separating children from their mothers simply because they were too poor to care for them. For instance, one magazine article described a courtroom scene in which a judge had ordered a family broken up: "The mother begged to be allowed to keep them. The little boy threw himself into her arms, sobbing, 'Oh, mamma, I can't leave you.' But it was of no use." Another judge spoke harshly of "the collapse of all things strong and holy at such a time."[18]

Middle-class women reacted to such scenes of pathos with the knowledge of their own potential vulnerability to poverty on the loss of a male provider. They thus pushed energetically for mothers' pensions in order to enable poor women to maintain custody of their children.[19] By keeping the focus of their rhetoric on widowed mothers, proponents of mothers' pensions emphasized women's victimization and self-sacrifice rather than a claim to payment for the work of mothering.[20] They also emphasized the needs of children for their mothers' full-time care and saw mothers' pensions as a way of ensuring that poor children would have the chance to be raised to be good citizens, rather than languishing in orphanages and contributing to social unrest when they came of age. Other supporters of mothers' pensions focused on the evils of institutionalizing children, and juvenile court judges as well as county and state officials realized that it was far cheaper to pay women to keep their own children at home than to pay for children's support in orphanages or foster homes.[21]

Although mothers' pensions easily won public support by appealing to domesticity, in their implementation the idea of state-sponsored domesticity foundered on deep ambivalence about using the public purse to support poor mothers and their children.[22] The ways in which the mothers' pension programs were put into practice worked against many of their supporters' lofty goals about valuing motherhood as a state service, and even went against the more modest goals of those who wanted to make sure that mothers would be able to stay at home with their children. The pension programs were marked by inadequate funding, exclusions and restrictive rules about who was eligible to apply for pensions, and stipends so small that most recipients had to work for wages in order to get by. At the same time, the goal of dignifying the lives of poor mothers by taking relief out of the hands of private charities was soon lost, as the pensions were administered by professional social workers with close ties to private charities; by the 1920s they had been absorbed into the domain of private charity, and were accompanied by extensive "investigation" and casework.

Although mothers' pension legislation had proved quite popular, funding for the pension programs was always inadequate. States left it up to counties and municipalities to fund the programs; the result was that there was never enough money to cover all potential recipients, and most counties in the country did not even have a mothers' pension program.[23] This lack of funding and the political vulnerability of the programs meant that only the most appealing mothers would be eligible: deserted and unmarried mothers, along with some immigrant and most African-American mothers, were shunted off to find help from domestic relations courts, day nurseries, orphanages, and private charity. Only white widows of unquestionable morality seemed to have a claim on the public purse. Minorities were specifically excluded from programs in some areas; in other areas with large minority populations, programs were simply not established. When mothers from non-Anglo "racial" groups were granted pensions, they often received smaller stipends, since program designers assumed that Mexicans, African-

Americans, Italians, and Czechs needed less to live on than did native-born whites.[24] The specific exclusion of African-American mothers from many mothers' pension programs reinforced the idea that these women were primarily workers, not the sort of mothers that the public wanted to subsidize. And even for the tiny percentage of single mothers who were not only eligible, but who were lucky enough to actually receive pensions, the amount granted was so small that it was understood that they would have to seek wage work in order to make ends meet.

Exclusions and restrictions written into mothers' pension laws meant that most single mothers could not even apply for state pensions. In Pennsylvania, the Mothers' Assistance Fund (MAF) excluded women whose husbands had deserted or divorced them, women whose husbands were seriously ill or in prison, women who had never been married, and women who kept male lodgers. On top of these statewide restrictions, Philadelphia County also excluded mothers with only one child, since "the mother with one child can ordinarily provide for its support."[25] (This self-assured statement was contradicted by studies conducted by the Children's Bureau, which found that it was difficult for many women, especially African-American women, to earn enough to support themselves and one child.)[26] Women could be excluded if they had not lived in the state long enough or were not citizens, or if they were ill or lived in poor housing; they also had to prove that they were the type of moral mother who should be encouraged to raise new citizens.[27]

The result of all these restrictions, along with the lack of funds for the program, was that mothers' pensions were only available to a small fraction of the women who might have needed them. When Elizabeth Hall surveyed the families of 1,182 men between twenty and forty years of age who died in Philadelphia, she found that only 312 families qualified for MAF assistance, and of these, only one third actually received the grant after three and one-half years.[28] Similarly, out of 237 widows in Gwendolyn Hughes's study, only 9 were receiving pensions. Even mothers who did meet the eligibility requirements had difficulty actually getting a pension; in 1926, there were almost as many eligible families on the waiting list in Philadelphia as there were families receiving pensions.[29]

One of the goals of mothers' pension supporters had been to separate aid to mothers from the stigma-laden sphere of private charity. Yet in practice, the distinction between public and private aid was not at all clear. Some women actually received their state pensions through private charity organizations, while others went back and forth between public and private charity, hardly noticing the difference. Either way, the radical idea that aid to mothers was not charity, but a payment for services rendered to the state, was vitiated when it was in fact a private charitable organization that was distributing the aid. The Orphans Guardians Society, a Jewish organization in Philadelphia that pioneered the idea of supporting widows with children in their own homes, first started distributing payments from the MAF in 1918; by 1924, 17% of the organization's total budget came from the MAF.[30] Because the Orphans Guardian Society's grants were much more generous than the MAF pensions, the private agency often supplemented MAF families.[31] Up until 1929, mothers actually turned their MAF checks over to their OGS "guardian," who would then dole it out gradually; this system only changed when the director of the MAF insisted that mothers pick up the money themselves from City Hall and hold onto it.[32] Money distributed by a charitable society was a gift, no matter how regularly it came, while mothers picking up their stipends at City Hall might construe them as wages for services rendered to the city. Other private charities, especially the Society for Organizing Charity (SOC), supplemented inadequate pensions and supported those who did not meet the MAF's strict eligibility requirements.[33] Social workers at private charities often had a great deal of influence over whether a woman would receive a MAF grant; day nursery social workers regularly received form letters from the MAF requesting an account of a former client's character, and asking, "As a taxpayer, do you consider her a mother who should receive State aid?"[34]

One of the most important aspects of the private charity influence was the insistence on careful supervision of the women who received pensions. This insistence, strongly supported from the beginning by most advocates of pensions, carried the private charity tradition of oversight and constant evaluation of clients into the pension programs, undercutting their potential for dignifying motherhood as state service. Women who received pensions, like Leah Nadel, knew that they needed to please their caseworker in order to continue receiving the aid; they were not entitled to help, but had to constantly prove that they deserved it. Morality, cleanliness, budgeting, cooking, scientific child-rearing, and church attendance were all factors to be considered, and program administrators who hoped to use the pensions as a way to encourage poor and immigrant mothers to reform their motherhood practices could not help but make judgments about "proper" home life that sometimes hindered rather than helped. Yet the stinginess of the pensions made it difficult for women to live up to the high standards demanded: women struggling to survive on inadequate pensions often sought a relationship with another man who would help support the family, while the employment that became necessary for most pension recipients made it impossible to supervise children as carefully as caseworkers might have wished.

One of the most ironic outcomes of the mothers' pension programs was that, despite all the appeals to children's need for full-time mothering, and arguments about the damaging effects of maternal employment, the pensions did not eliminate the need for mothers to work. In fact, maternal wage-earning was encouraged as demonstration of a mother's worthiness and respectability. Although middle-class women's efforts to push the pension legislation through had depended on arguing for the universal value of full-time motherhood, in practice the distinction between prosperous and poor mothers remained. Poor mothers could not simply be mothers—they also had to be breadwinners. In Massachusetts, the policy of the State Board of Charity, which administered the pensions, was to encourage mothers to work: "To insist that the mother shall not work, regardless of home conditions, would tend to discourage that desire for thrift and independence which is an essential element in society. The policy should be stimulative, and constructive rather than destructive."[35] Addressing the Orphans Guardians Society in 1925, Evelyn Cavin, the director of the MAF for Philadelphia County, "spoke of the desirability of some mothers doing part time work in order, as she expressed it, 'to keep their economic muscles in trim.' "[36] A Children's Bureau study of pension programs in nine communities across the country found that over half the pensioned mothers worked to contribute to the family income. Investigator Florence Nesbit wrote,

> Some mothers were working because there was no other way to get an adequate income for the family, although the physical strain of work in addition to the care of the house and the children was probably more than they could long endure. . . . In many instances, how-

> ever, it was believed that some money-earning occupation on the part of the mother was a wholesome influence in the family life.[37]

In Philadelphia, the numbers were even higher, with 84% of mothers'-aid recipients working.[38] Mothers were encouraged to work, but not at full-time day jobs; rather, as with private charity cases, they were urged to take on part-time or seasonal work, such as scrubbing offices, domestic work by the day, or garment finishing. This work, one Children's Bureau study concluded, was often physically harder than factory work and less renumerative.[39] In the end, pensions did not enable women to devote all their time to mothering, as proponents had hoped, but rather supplemented their income while confining them to the most marginal position in the labor market.

Since mothers' wage work continued to be necessary, even among pension recipients, the need for day care persisted. A woman from Carthage, Missouri, wrote after reading about the Children's Bureau's opposition to day nurseries,

> Our last Legislature passed an excellent Mother's Pension Law but very thoughtfully refrained from providing any funds. . . . In our county, we now have a deficit of $19,500 in the "pauper fund" from which the mother's pension should be paid. . . . We have felt that a "day nursery" . . . would help solve our problems.[40]

Similarly, a nurse with the Butte, Montana, Board of Education wrote to the Children's Bureau about the many widows with children in her city who kept older children out of school to care for the younger ones while they went to work. "I have thought that since there is no chance of increasing the amount of the widows pension, the establishment of a few day nurseries would to some extent help to eliminate this evil."[41]

The gap between the ideals of the campaigns for mothers' pension legislation and the way in which the pensions were actually administered suggests the underlying tension between treating single mothers as breadwinners and treating them as mothers. The aim of the mothers' pension movement was to treat these women as mothers, dignifying their maternal work through state recognition and support, and enabling them to devote all their energies to mothering. Yet in practice, legislators balked at the demand that meeting this goal would make on state treasuries and feared that fully funding poor mothers would set a dangerous precedent of state responsibility for family support. Instead, they selected a very small number of women to support, and treated even these women as much like breadwinners as like mothers. Rather than seeing these women as mothers who should properly be dependent (whether on a husband or on the state), they saw them as heads of poor families who should not be allowed to become dependent on the public purse.

Taking on a Mother's Job: Day Nurseries

If the mothers' pension—at least in theory—emphasized the value of a mother's domesticity, the day nursery emphasized the value of her wage labor in keeping the family economically self-sufficient. On the spectrum of solutions to the poverty of women and children, the day nursery was in many ways a conservative choice, demanding nothing from the state or from employers, reinforcing the idea of the family's individual responsibility to support itself, and calling on the mother to demonstrate her worthiness to receive aid through her willingness to work. The day nursery became the woman's equivalent of the work test that many private charities used to see if the men they were helping were really worthy: just as a man would demonstrate his willingness to work by splitting stone, so a woman truly committed to supporting her children would be willing to leave them in a nursery during the day. Once again, the double standard in attitudes toward prosperous and poor mothers was reinforced: while the "good" middle-class mother stayed with her children at all times, ensuring their health and growth, the "good" poor mother left her children so that she could go to work.

Supporters of day nurseries frequently stressed the nursery's role in enabling self-sufficiency and preventing dependence and pauperism in poor families. In 1879, the Philadelphia Society for Organizing Charity called for establishing day nurseries in order to prevent dependence: "Many women, left suddenly widowed, are prevented for a time from earning their own living through the care of an infant on their hands. Some of them learn habits of dependence during this period which are not easily eradicated, and perhaps sink needlessly into the pauper class."[42] This line of thinking was also central to the Jane D. Kent Day Nursery's appeal for funds in 1888. Opening with the declaration, "Among the greatest blessings in life are ability and willingness to work," the appeal focused the reader's attention on the "many who are both willing and able to work, but are prevented from working to advantage by constant care of the little ones who make up the home circle." By freeing these mothers to work during the day, the argument went, "the earning power of the parents is increased to the maximum, and their income, fostered by sobriety and thrift, ere long secures comfort and self-support, the very ultimatum of all charitable assistance." This appeal was accompanied by a chart demonstrating that since its founding the nursery had cared for the children of 15,600 mothers at a cost of about $6,400. During those years, these mothers earned about $15,000. Printed on the back cover was the conclusion, "In a word, EVERY DOLLAR given to the poor through the Jane D. Kent Day Nursery has more than DOUBLED ITSELF."[43] Obviously the day nursery was a plan that made economic sense, saving the community money by setting the mothers free to fulfill their potential as wage-earners and supporters of families.

But economic rationality was not enough to counterbalance the strength of the ideology of full-time motherhood, especially by the Progressive era. Day nursery supporters, like advocates of mothers' pensions, were torn between the values of domesticity and self-support. Strongly committed to the idea of the family wage (despite the knowledge that such a wage was only a dream for many families), they were profoundly uneasy about encouraging mothers to go out to work. As we have seen, in order to combat their anxiety about enabling mothers to leave their children to earn wages, they emphasized that they served only those women who absolutely "had" to work to support their children, portrayed their service as a temporary stopgap in times of family crisis, and stressed the wholesome home they created for the children of wage-earning mothers, rather than the wage-earning itself. Cases where a woman worked to supplement her husband's inadequate income were troubling. In 1899, the Philadelphia Association of Day Nurseries (PADN) debated the question, "Shall children be admitted to day nurseries when both parents are working?" and concluded that "where it is possible, a mother should be encouraged to care for her children so that the unity of the family should be preserved."[44] While it was relatively easy to set policy in these general terms, however, day nursery boards often found it harder to carry out such policies when they knew that families would suffer.[45] In fact, in 40% of families applying to six day nurseries in Philadelphia during this period, mothers needed to work because of the inadequacy of their husbands' wages, unemployment, or illness.[46]

Just as some supporters of mothers' pensions held a radical vision of what mothers' aid might mean, there were a few people among the proponents of day nurseries who envisioned a broader future for nurseries. Helen Glenn Tyson, at the conclusion of a book describing the day nurseries' place in efforts for child welfare, wrote, "So much for the "poverty" nursery of today. . . . What of the nursery of tomorrow? Its organization should be democratic rather than philanthropic; it would be open to all children of the neighborhood, and located for the convenience of the mothers."[47] She then quoted from an article in which British nursery educator and Labor Party activist Margaret McMillan explained the Labor Party's demand for a system of public nurseries:

> "Why do you want nurseries?" asks the woman in the street. Why? "Why," we make answer, "is there a nursery in every rich man's house? . . . The rich man has a motor-car and we ride in trams and buses. The rich have great libraries, baths to every bedroom, tutors and governesses. The poor have public libraries, public baths, and Council Schools. But all have these things privately or publicly, because they *need* them. Well now, looking at our small and crowded homes, our ailing children, our dangerous and it may be dirty courts where little ones play, we say, "We want nurseries for all children because *they are badly needed*." . . . Just as, in 1870, it became law that every area should have a school, so it will be law soon that every Mother can have a nursery. We shall have to put up not one or twenty, but four or five thousand. [48]

Although the women who debated welfare policy in the United States never voiced such an eloquent demand for day care, a similar vision of day nurseries as a general need was laid out by Helen Brenton of the Chicago Association of Day Nurseries. In a letter to Children's Bureau chief Julia Lathrop, Brenton referred to a Fabian tract, *The Case for School Nurseries*, and suggested that the day nursery might become "a place where children may be left at the wish of the parents, regardless of economic need or status, an institution comparable to the public school, which the public education or health authorities might conceivably take over."[49] Indeed, the Los Angeles public schools sponsored day nurseries in the schools: by 1928, there were twenty-eight such nurseries serving thirteen hundred children in a year.[50] There was also a short-lived experiment in which a nursery was opened in a public school in Baltimore during World War I, but the idea never spread. While a handful of people imagined a permanent role for nurseries, filling a need as legitimate and as universal as that of the public schools, the majority of day nursery supporters continued to see the nurseries as charitable institutions providing a temporary and necessarily flawed solution for families in crisis.

Both mothers' pensions and day nurseries sought to work "for the interests of the home," the first by enabling women's domesticity, the second by enabling their wage-earning. In different ways, both mothers' pensions and day nurseries were conservative solutions to the problems faced by breadwinning mothers. Neither a woman who received a state pension nor a woman who worked for wages and brought her children to a day nursery was able to support her children comfortably and with dignity. Neither solution challenged the pay differential between male and female wages that was a fundamental cause of poverty for female-headed households. While mothers' pension programs represented a radical new claim on the state, they were grounded in a conservative assumption that mothers were naturally dependent and domestic, and that the state must step in to take over the absent husband's role. Conversely, day nurseries were based on the potentially radical idea that single women could be wage-earners and support their children without depending on a man, yet they avoided making any claims on the state or arguing that families had a right to publicly provided day care. Mothers' pension programs locked poor women into closely supervised domesticity; day nurseries "allowed" women to work long hours at tedious jobs for low pay.

"Not to Be Encouraged": Day Nurseries on the Defensive

Ultimately, mothers' pensions won the debate: the idea of state aid for domesticity was much more popular than the idea of enabling maternal employment, and reformers and social workers came to see mothers' pensions as the best solution to the problem of the single mother. Florence Kelley expressed the dominant opinion among reformers when she said in 1909, "There is no subject concerning which we are more foolish than this . . . idea of establishing institutions to take little children away from good mothers during their working hours, insisting that widowed mothers shall perform the tasks of fathers while some hired person pretends to be mother to their little ones."[51] Kelley, who spent her life fighting for better conditions for women workers, was no conservative, but she felt that working-class mothers who went out to work were carrying an impossible burden. (Her own experiences as a single working mother, boarding her children with friends in the Chicago suburbs while she worked and lived at Hull House, must also have affected her thoughts on this issue.)[52] Kelley's friend and Hull House colleague Jane Addams shared her poor opinion of day nurseries. Although she had originally supported the creation of a day nursery at Hull House, by 1905 Addams had changed her mind, writing that the day nursery was a "double-edged implement" which tempted poor mothers "to attempt the impossible," being "both wife and mother and supporter of the family."[53]

This attitude toward mothers' wage work was typical among Progressive reformers: while they were very sympathetic toward working mothers and their struggles, they also saw these women as a symptom of a larger maladjustment in American society. They proposed a variety of reforms that they hoped would reduce mothers' need to go out to work by making it more possible to depend on a male wage: raising men's wages; eliminating tuberculosis, industrial disease, and accidents that deprived families of their male breadwinner; and strengthening laws relating to desertion and nonsupport. When all these failed, they urged increasing support from public and private agencies rather than expecting mothers to take up the job of breadwinning in addition to the job of housekeeping and child care.[54] Day nurseries were an inadequate solution, many reformers felt; given inferior wages and jobs, it was cruel to expect mothers to earn for their children as well as to take care of them. Rather, insisting on higher male wages and expanding governmental support for the welfare of working families would ultimately produce greater results.

The federal Children's Bureau's advocacy of this position was influential in shaping debates about how to improve the lives of poor women and children. The bureau, established in 1912, played a central role as a clearinghouse of information and advice for states, local communities, and private agencies to draw on in shaping child welfare programs. A "female dominion" within the federal government of professional women reformers concerned with child welfare, the bureau stood as the most authoritative and up-to-date source of information about how best to serve mothers and children. The bureau had been established and was sustained partly through the efforts of hundreds of women's organizations, who depended on the agency to represent the interests of the nation's mothers and children in Washington.[55] Staffed by women who had invented professions for themselves in the field of child welfare and social work, the bureau was the center of what historian Molly Ladd-Taylor has called "progressive maternalism," which stressed the importance of mothering to the nation but also the values of expertise and professionalism. Through campaigns to halt alarming rates of infant mortality and improve the health of children and mothers, the bureau made a name for itself and earned the support of women across the country.

As maternalists, Children's Bureau staffers believed in full-time motherhood supported by a man's family wage; as expert reformers, they wanted to eliminate the conditions of poverty that sent mothers into the workplace rather than make it any easier for women to take on a "double burden." Because most of them had chosen to pursue professional work instead of living a conventional family life, they saw motherhood as incompatible with full-time work and pursued policies based on the assumption that most women (unlike themselves) needed to be dependent on a male wage.[56] If the Children's Bureau had embraced day nurseries, the nurseries would have multiplied, especially in the years before and after World War I, when people across the country wrote to the agency for information about establishing day nurseries.

The bureau's policy, however, was to discourage the creation of nurseries and encourage local communities to fund mothers to stay at home, rather than encouraging them to go into industry. Like Florence Kelley, the Children's Bureau believed that day nurseries were a dangerous solution that encouraged women to carry an impossible burden, and therefore threatened their health and the safety of their children. Studies of infant mortality conducted by bureau investigators showed a dramatically higher mortality rate for infants whose mothers were employed in industry than for those who were not employed. Rather than imagine the possibility that well-run day nurseries could provide safe care for children, the bureau staff concluded that the only way to avoid higher rates of infant mortality was to insist that mothers of young children remain in the home, devoting all their energies to child-rearing. In a memorandum prepared in 1918 in response to requests for advice about day nurseries, the Children's Bureau noted the high mortality rate for infants of employed mothers and decreed, "The most important measures for safeguarding young children are those which insure the care of the young child by a healthy mother in her own home." Mothers of young children should be the last group to be called on to work in war industries, and day nurseries, when and if they became necessary, should be held to "irreproachable standards of care" and carefully supervised. The memorandum concluded by reminding the reader that "if mothers of children of school age are forced into industrial life a peril to health and morals is created which can be overcome only by the efforts of the community."[57]

This policy of discouraging the establishment of day nurseries was effectively communicated to the Children's Bureau's broad constituency. Clara Savage, *Good Housekeep-*

ing's Washington correspondent, was somewhat surprised to learn of the Children's Bureau's lack of enthusiasm for the idea of day nurseries, but dutifully communicated the bureau's insistence on the need for women to stay home and take care of their own babies, supported by mothers' pensions when necessary.[58] In response to a woman in Auburn, New York, where the local day nursery was being pressured by manufacturers to take more children in order to free their mothers for wage work during World War I, Julia Lathrop wrote,

> Your letter came in the other day and I confess I hardly know how to answer it . . . the studies which the Bureau has made show that a little baby whose mother goes away to work has about half the chance of life that he has if she can remain at home and take care of him. In times like these, it does appear as if the wages of the father of a family ought to be sufficient to let the wife stay at home and take care of the young children.[59]

In response to a question about the ultimate place of day nurseries, Julia Lathrop wrote, "Personally, of course, I can not bear to face the social condition in which poverty requiring the mother to work outside of her home in order to support her children is a settled element in industrial life."[60] When one woman wrote to say that she felt that day nurseries were "a palliative measure," a representative of the bureau readily agreed, writing, "Undoubtedly in some instances they have to be tolerated, but in general they are not to be encouraged, and where they are established they need to be licensed and under supervision."[61] Other progressive maternalists concurred, calling for increased funding for mothers' pensions rather than establishing day nurseries. In an address before the National Federation of Day Nurseries in 1918, Jane Addams "was most sincere in her plea to keep the mothers out of the factories so that they could take care of their children in their own homes"; she called for pension funds to be increased so that mothers would not need to put their children in nurseries.[62]

The position of reformers like Lathrop and Addams posed a false choice between state-supported domesticity and wage-earning. While they spoke as if it were possible to choose between pensions that really allowed women to be full-time mothers, and daytime care for children that allowed women to be breadwinners, mothers' pensions were never implemented in such a way as to eradicate the need for wage-earning. Mothers continued to need to work to support their children. In Pennsylvania, for example, the need for day nurseries was as great as ever: in the ten years following the creation of Pennsylvania's Mothers' Assistance Fund, the number of day nurseries in the state rose from thirty-seven to sixty-one.[63] Reformers' commitment to the family wage and their enthusiasm for the idea of mothers' pensions blinded them to the continuing need for child care. Hoping that funding for pensions would improve, they continued to see day nurseries and support for mothers at home as mutually exclusive solutions, and seem to have preferred not to think about the fact that despite the legislative victory of mothers' pensions, poor mothers continued to work.

The idea of mothers' pensions had easily won the debate on an ideological level; nearly everyone agreed that it was better to support mothers at home with their children than to send them out into the work force, that it was better for the public to take on the father's job rather than the mother's. This consensus for mothers' pensions put supporters of day nurseries on the defensive. Although the need for nurseries did not abate, their ideological justification was knocked out from under them by the creation of a more appealing answer to the problem of the poor single mother. As historian Sonya Michel has written, "The existence of an alternative policy . . . threw into question the raison d'être of the entire day-nursery project."[64] The fact that the more appealing solution was not yet a reality provided a safe, but ultimately weak, justification for the continued existence of day nurseries.

Conceding that a system of mothers' pensions was preferable to mothers working and putting their children in nurseries, day nursery leaders could only point to the inadequacies of mothers' pensions in order to justify their own efforts. They spoke of nurseries as a temporary expedient and of their desire to ultimately eliminate their work altogether. For instance, a 1912 report of the Baldwin Day Nursery opened by saying, "Until mothers' pensions are adequate and universal, we must consider the continued existence of day nurseries as one form of charity suitable to meet the obligations which the community owes towards the children who are daily deprived of a mother's care."[65] While advocates of mothers' pensions were often critical of day nurseries, most day nursery leaders supported mothers' pensions. In 1921, for example, the PADN passed a resolution endorsing the work of the Mothers' Assistance Fund and its campaign for an increased appropriation.[66]

Indeed, many day nursery reports urged the funding of mothers' pension legislation as a better alternative to nursery care. In 1914, one year after the passage of the Pennsylvania mothers' aid bill, the Baldwin Day Nursery's report explained that in the families it served, "It was the father, the provider, who should have been supplied, but only the State could properly have taken his place, and in our country, as yet, the State is not willing to undertake this function, except in a limited way." Instead, "the mothers of these children took the fathers' places, and the Nursery took the mothers' places during ten hours of each work day."[67] Marion Kohn, the headworker at the Young Women's Union, was also very committed to the idea of mothers' pensions. In 1916 she wrote, "If the home is the highest and finest product of civilization, let not philanthropy take from the child or the mother their rightful heritage, let us look upon the day nursery not as a permanent factor in the community, but as a temporary resource, and while it must serve us, let it serve in its highest efficiency."[68] Echoing the words of the 1909 White House conference which had first put mothers' pensions on the national agenda (the home as "the highest and finest product of civilization"), Kohn looked forward to the day when the nursery would no longer be necessary.

Nurseries could be justified only as a stopgap measure until pensions were fully funded, and for families who could not be helped by the mothers' aid law. Kohn wrote in 1918, "I feel that the day nursery does not promote family life but is an expedient necessary only because of our present social maladjustment."[69] However, she argued, day nurseries had a place in meeting the needs of families where the earnings of both husband and wife were necessary to support the family, and also for cases of desertion, illness, or temporary incapacity of the mother.[70] Similarly, Helen Glenn Tyson argued that the nursery fulfilled a need by helping women who were automatically excluded from Pennsylvania's mothers' aid programs—deserted or unmarried mothers, and women with only one child.[71]

Accepting the view that a mother's care in the home was preferable to nursery care, nursery supporters adopted an apologetic tone in describing their services, and never felt sure enough of their cause to push for the expansion, or public support, of day care.

Working-class mothers often had to work to support their children as well as caring for them. Above, a woman works in the Frankford Arsenal during World War I. World War I Collection (Women in Industry), Historical Society of Pennsylvania.

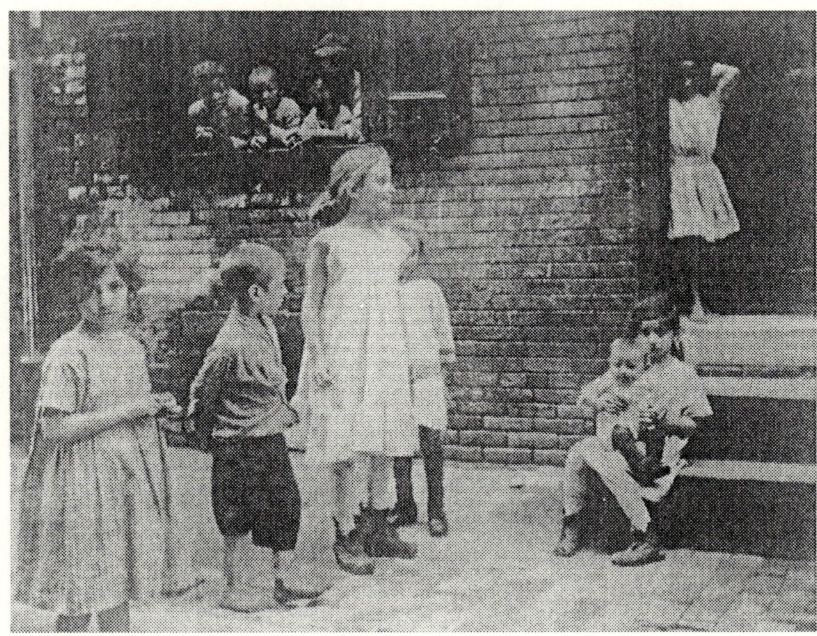

The women who founded Philadelphia's day nurseries wanted to take children like these off the streets, where they played and cared for their younger siblings. Urban Archives, Temple University, Philadelphia, Pennsylvania.

Day nursery managers were proud of the order and discipline that children experienced in the charitable nurseries. This picture, used in the annual report of the First Day Nursery in 1898, shows children bowing their heads in silence before dinner. Many nurseries, like orphanages of the time, prohibited children from talking during meals. Urban Archives, Temple University, Philadelphia, Pennsylvania.

This photograph of healthy and well-dressed but unsmiling children attending the Young Women's Union nursery was entitled "The Result of Our Care." The fact that this rather dismal picture was used for publicity indicates that nursery managers saw children's physical well-being as their primary aim. Neighborhood Centre Collection, Philadelphia Jewish Archives Center.

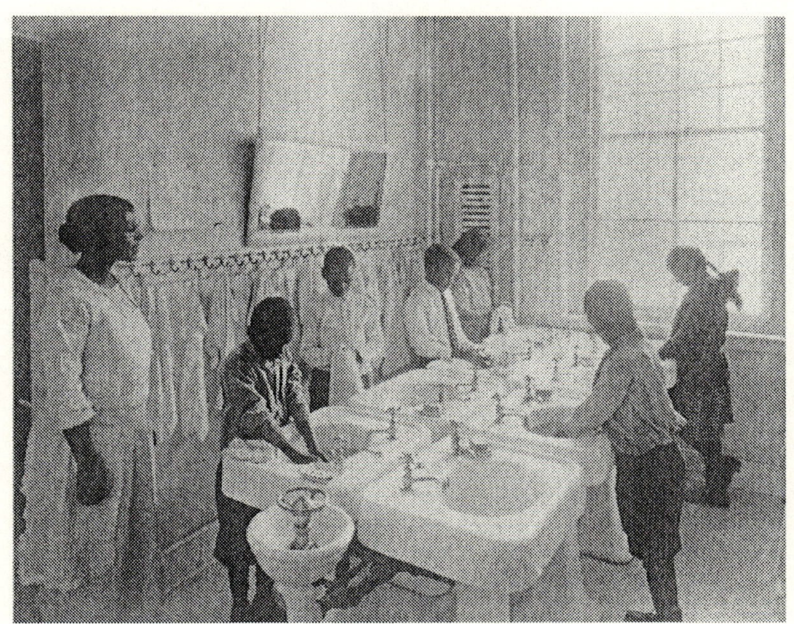

Day Nurseries sought to teach immigrant and African-American children hygiene, order, discipline, and patriotism. Above, handwashing was an important part of the daily routine at the Lincoln Day Nursery, which served African-American children. Urban Archives, Temple University, Philadelphia, Pennsylvania. Below, the Jewish immigrant children who attended the Young Women's Union were surrounded by American flags. Neighborhood Centre Collection, Philadelphia Jewish Archives Center.

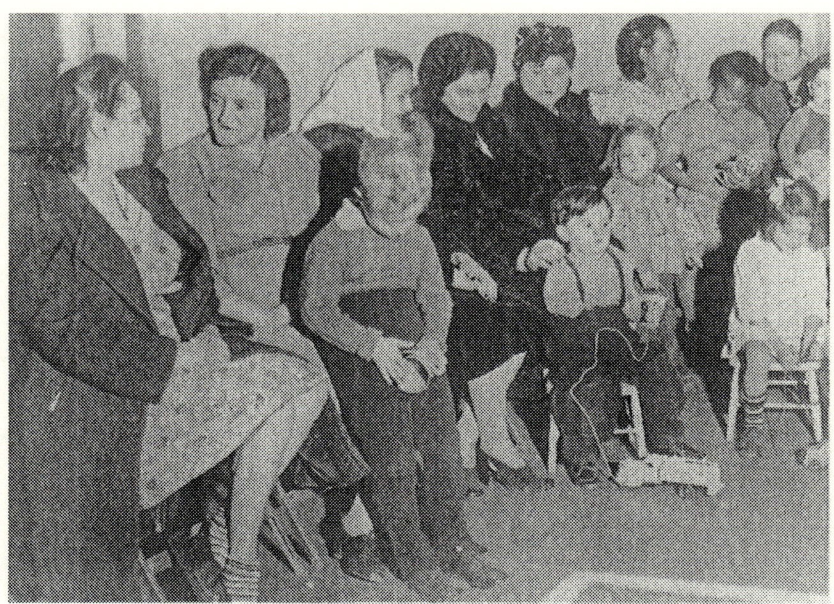

The demand for women's labor during World War II led to the opening of public day care centers in Philadelphia. In this picture, women and children wait in line to apply for spaces in the city's first public day care center, which opened in 1942 at the Tasker Home housing project. Urban Archives, Temple University, Philadelphia, Pennsylvania.

No longer objects of charity, working mothers and children demonstrate at City Hall in 1945. Demonstrations such as these were ultimately successful in keeping the city's public day care centers open after the end of the war. Urban Archives, Temple University, Philadelphia, Pennsylvania.

Religion continued to be an important part of day care provision in Philadelphia in the 1950s. This photograph was part of a United Fund fundraising campaign in 1953, featuring children at the Salvation Army Day Nursery. Urban Archives, Temple University, Philadelphia, Pennsylvania.

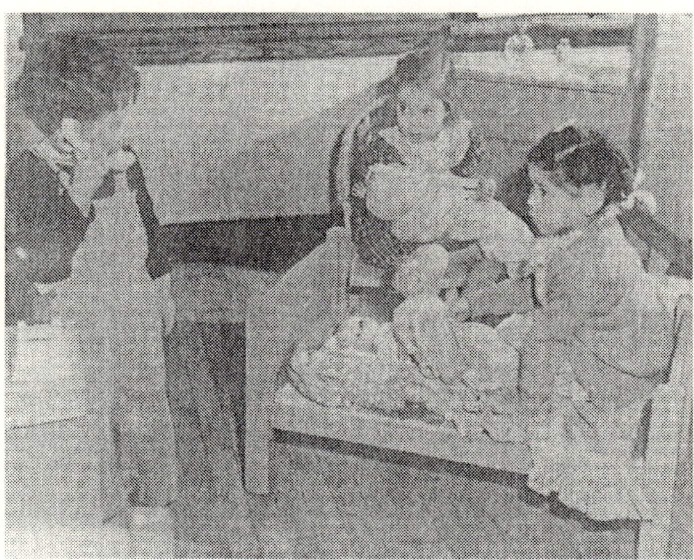

By the 1950s day care centers had adopted nursery school techniques, and provided an array of activities and toys to enrich children's development. Publicity for day care no longer pictured well-disciplined children in large groups, but rather showed children playing in small, family-like settings. In the 1954 picture above, children at the public day care center at the McDaniel School "play house." Urban Archives, Temple University, Philadelphia, Pennsylvania.

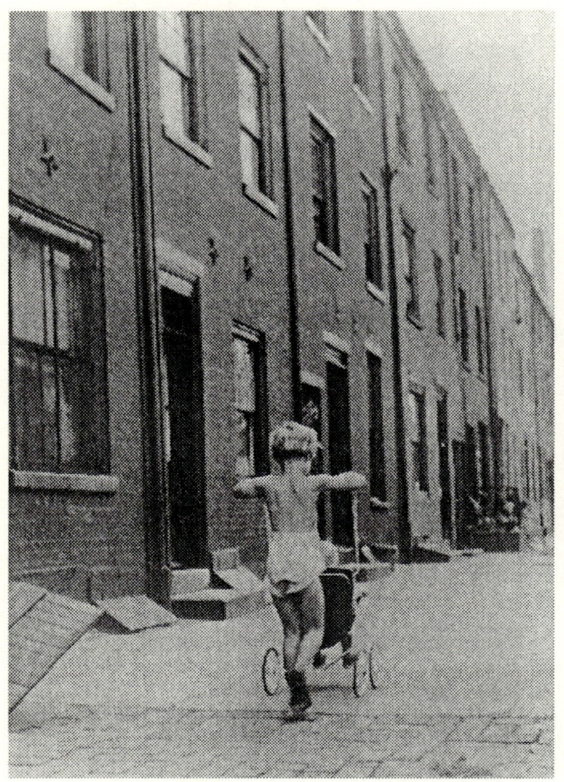

While children attending day care centers had adequate play equipment and supervision, many children in Philadelphia continued to spend their days on the streets. The child pictured at left, for a 1957 story on the need for more day care centers, was apparently caring for a younger sibling—much like the immigrant children who had inspired the founding of the city's first day nurseries in the late 19th century. Urban Archives, Temple University, Philadelphia, Pennsylvania.

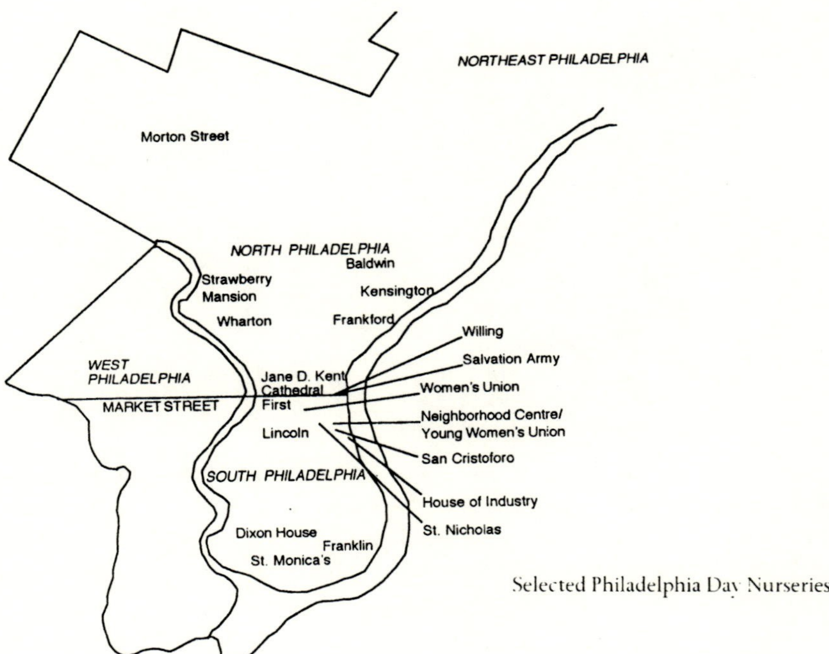

Selected Philadelphia Day Nurseries

The newsletter of the National Federation of Day Nurseries described a day nursery in California in the following terms: "Only children who cannot possibly be cared for otherwise are admitted, and the weakness in the family which makes day nursery care necessary, is remedied as quickly as possible."[72] When Marion Kohn described the process by which a family applied for admission to Neighborhood Centre's Day Nursery, she explained that cases were accepted only "when there is no other better provision for the children."[73] Addressing the PADN in 1922, the chief of the Children's Bureau of the Pennsylvania State Department of Public Welfare said that the day nursery's "ultimate aim should be the gradual prevention of its own work, by a constant effort to keep very young children with their mothers in the home."[74] The impact of mothers' pensions on the PADN is evident in the difference between the association's aggressive campaign to create new day nurseries in the period from 1903 to 1910 and the defensive position taken after the institution of mothers' pensions. Only three PADN nurseries were founded after mothers' pension legislation was passed in Pennsylvania in 1913, and none of these were founded directly by PADN members.

The PADN's retreat was echoed at the national level. At the 1918 conference of the National Federation of Day Nurseries, when Jane Addams criticized the idea of establishing nurseries so that women could work in war industries, Josephine Dodge, president of the federation, "said that in her thirty years of Day Nursery service she had never urged the starting of Day Nurseries, nor had she gone anywhere to give consultation about starting Day Nurseries unless she had been asked."[75] More interesting than the fact that this statement was false is that Dodge, the leader of the day nursery movement for decades, felt compelled to make it. In Boston, the Tyler Street Day Nursery closed in 1910 because "its promoters became convinced that it was doing more harm than good."[76] Similarly, a day nursery board in Lynn, Massachusetts, shut down their nursery, deciding it would be more worthwhile to pay the mothers to stay at home with their children.[77]

With such attitudes, nursery supporters could hardly persuade others of the rightness of their cause. In 1925, Helen Glenn Tyson noted that the day nurseries were one of the few child welfare groups that had not petitioned the legislature for state aid.[78] Part of the day nursery movement's reluctance to seek public support may have been linked to National Federation of Day Nurseries leader Josephine Dodge's belief that the government should stay out of social welfare and that women should stay out of politics.[79] But Dodge's political convictions are not enough to explain day nursery supporters' failure to seek public aid, for the national organization did not control its members, and day nursery leaders in Philadelphia spoke favorably of working to increase state involvement in other areas of social welfare, such as mothers' pensions, child labor legislation, and pure milk laws. Up until World War II, however, the members of the PADN never even mentioned the possibility of trying to gain public funding for day care, nor did they ever conduct a major campaign to increase the number of nurseries caring for children in the city. This failure to place day care on the public agenda has had long-term consequences: as historian Sonya Michel argues, mothers' aid became, "for good or for ill, a social right of American women," while publicly supported child care did not.[80]

Ultimately, both day nurseries and mothers' pensions were harmed by the tension in the minds of reformers and the American public between the values of domesticity and self-support, and by a widespread reluctance to treat poor mothers as "real" mothers.

This tension produced a major gap between the theory and practice of mothers' pensions, and also shaped the policy debate between mothers' pensions and day nurseries, posing a false choice between domesticity and breadwinning. In the long run, the terms of the debate and the reluctance to really take on *either* the father's or the mother's job meant that neither solution was given the chance to work, leaving women to struggle to both support and care for their families.

Since pensions won the ideological victory, day nurseries were shorn of their emotional and moral appeal: the upstanding widow struggling to support her children was now supposed to have somewhere else to turn. But in fact, she often ended up back at the nursery's door, like Leah Nadel. Since pensions did not win the political and fiscal victory they needed, the need for the day nurseries was not dramatically lessened. The result of the campaign for mothers' pensions was that day nursery supporters could only talk about the need for nurseries in defensive, even apologetic, terms, while social commentators and policymakers went on assuming that the family-wage system was basically functional, since mothers' pensions existed as a safety net. They were thus able to ignore the substantial numbers of women who fell through this safety net, did not have an adequate male wage to rely on, and suffered from a wage system that was constructed on the assumption of female dependence.

Foster Day Care: A Compromise Solution?

In 1928, Philadelphia's First Day Nursery came up with an innovative plan that addressed some of the problems of day nurseries and mothers' pensions. Rather than buying a new building, the nursery board decided to sell their property and start a "foster day care" program, whereby working mothers would place their children with foster mothers by the day. The "nursery," now consisting of an office staffed by a trained social worker, served as an intermediary, carefully selecting the foster homes, subsidizing the mothers' payments, and advising the foster mothers on standards of child care. The *Philadelphia Bulletin* explained, "The plan is intended to take the day nurseries to the children, rather than taking children to the day nurseries"; under this new plan, day nursery leaders hoped to increase the number of children cared for in Philadelphia from one thousand to fifty thousand.[81] Foster mothers could be more flexible than day nurseries, taking care of sick children, keeping children beyond the regular hours of the nursery, and even providing a home for the mother herself when necessary.

By switching from regular nursery care to this type of service, the First Day Nursery signaled dissatisfaction with group care and replaced it with a mother's care in the home, just as mothers' pensions did. By holding the child's own mother responsible for supporting her family while providing a substitute mother figure to care for the child in a substitute home, foster day care neatly resolved the contradiction inherent in mothers' pensions programs between promoting maternal care and encouraging self-sufficiency. And this substitute mother, unlike mothers receiving pensions, could be carefully selected and influenced, for she was an employee of the nursery.[82] In 1929, for instance, the nursery was able to select 20 foster mothers from a pool of 146 applicants. In presenting the foster day care idea at a conference of the National Federation of Day Nurseries, social worker Helen LaGrange described a case in which the foster mother's mothering skills clearly outshone those of the mother seeking day care. The working mother's children had "never been taught obedience" and showed their lack of training by throwing temper tantrums and wetting their pants; all three "had dirty little bodies because they came from a filthy home." The foster mother, by contrast, had a "very homey home, up on a little terrace, a front door yard of grass and flowers well kept and trim, and a large backyard." Her own children showed "rugged health and cleanliness in appearance and have contentment and happiness in their faces." Since being cared for by this foster mother, the working mother's children were transformed from "unattractive drab little mites, into youngsters with sparkling eyes, happy faces, and controlled behavior," and "best of all, the working mother has cleaned up her home, has learned control of the children, and is earning enough slowly to pay her debts."[83] Like the day nursery, then, foster day care could help transform both children and mothers; unlike the day nursery, the foster day care home really was a "home" and could provide individual attention to the children in its care.

The nursery's experiment with foster day care generated considerable interest, and requests for more information about the plan came from all over the country. Both Helen LaGrange, the social worker hired to institute the plan, and her successor, Luna Kenney, urged other nurseries to establish similar programs. Indeed, at a time when the other day nurseries, unsure of their legitimacy and apologetic about the services they offered, seem to have hesitated to draw attention to themselves at all, the energetic efforts of LaGrange and Kenney, who were clearly enthusiastic about the service they were providing, stand out. They wrote articles for the Child Welfare League's magazine; corresponded with people in Chicago, Cleveland, San Francisco, New Orleans, and Atlanta; spoke at child welfare, social work, and day nursery conferences across the country; met with an attorney from Chile interested in carrying the plan back to her country; prepared charts showing comparative costs of foster and institutional day care; and offered "consultative services" to nurseries in other parts of the country who were considering foster day care. With its emphasis on home care for children and supervision by social workers, the foster day care idea was attractive to social workers and child welfare experts, and the First Day Nursery became the only nursery admitted to membership in the Child Welfare League of America.[84]

But despite all of LaGrange's and Kenney's efforts, very few nurseries adopted the foster day care plan.[85] Most nursery boards were unwilling to give up the institutions they had created in order to subsidize what was basically a glorified system of boarding children. And other welfare agencies, which might have taken up the idea, saw in the foster day care plan simply another reason to put more money into mothers' aid programs. Indeed, even the First Day Nursery realized that the amount paid to board three or more children with a foster mother was more than many mothers earned in a week, and in several cases they decided to give the money they would have spent on the children's board directly to the mothers. This practice reaffirmed the idea that mothers' aid was preferable to day care, especially in large families.[86] While trying not to antagonize the other day nurseries, First Day Nursery board members repeatedly pointed out the savings achieved by foster day care, which did not require income for a building and equipment, and urged day nurseries to subsidize mothers of large families at home. Those who heard about the nursery's work, however, were more interested in subsidizing families than in promoting foster day care. In 1929, the nursery received a letter from a woman in Orange, New Jersey, "who said that their three nurseries had all asked for more money and after looking at our reports decided that what was needed was more relief to the Family Society rather than to the nurseries. The work of the First DN proved that Family Society work accomplishes more lasting benefit than institutional nursery work."[87]

Foster day care's failure to expand suggests that it was not only the low standard of care in day nurseries that made them unpopular with reformers, but the very fact that they enabled mothers to work for wages. Providing a surrogate mother was not as popular as trying to make sure that actual mothers could stay home with their children. Although the foster day care plan solved many of the day nurseries' real problems and may have been preferred by mothers seeking day care, welfare leaders had a strong preference for supporting mothers at home, and continued to promote mothers' aid rather than develop more flexible day care programs. Given the many limitations of mothers' aid programs during this period, the failure to explore options such as foster day care blocked off promising avenues for improving the kind of care available to children whose mothers went out to work.

The Emergence of Social Work

Along with the challenge of mothers' pensions, day nurseries also faced criticism from a new breed of professional social workers. Social work had been developing as a profession since 1874, when workers at charity organization societies throughout the country organized the National Conference of Charities and Corrections, later renamed the National Association of Social Work. The charity workers who spurred the creation of the profession of social work denounced the "sentimentality" of indiscriminate giving and urged the creation of a "scientific charity" that would eradicate, not just ameliorate, poverty. By 1921, the National Association of Social Work had four thousand professional members, and from 1898 to 1928, forty schools of social work were created in the U.S. and Canada. By the 1920s, social work was understood as a largely female profession, one which somewhat uneasily wed women's presumed compassion for the poor with the objectivity and rationality of professional culture. The new generation of social workers were to be efficient social investigators rather than old-fashioned Ladies Bountiful.[88]

If scientific charity was the goal of the new social work, casework was its methodology. As historian Linda Gordon explains, "Casework began with the collection of the most complete information possible about any individual or family, with the aim of long-term independence, not merely immediate survival, and the conviction that each case required an individual approach." While casework enabled reform-minded social workers to identify environmental causes of social problems and to seek public remedies, it also served to prevent the undeserving from receiving relief, and to keep clients from "working the charities" by getting help from more than one agency at a time.[89] Casework individualized social problems, calling attention to personal problems rather than the broader social or economic roots of poverty, and finding solutions in changing people's attitudes and behaviors. Social workers supervised their "cases" closely in order to try to change not only their economic situation but their immoral or destructive behavior patterns; social workers' language and professionalism gave scientific status to their sometimes narrow judgments about what consituted undesirable patterns of living.

As the field of social work became more professionalized, day nurseries increasingly fell into disrepute, becoming "the 'poor relation' in the field of child care."[90] Day nurseries were often left out of textbooks, conferences, and other arenas in which professional social workers discussed child welfare work. At a 1925 meeting of the PADN, members were outraged to discover that one of the textbooks used in the Philadelphia School for Social Work, a comprehensive directory of agencies caring for children in Pennsylvania, did not even mention the PADN.[91] Not only did this "exhaustive study of child-caring institutions and agencies" compiled by the influential Russell Sage Foundation neglect the nursery association, but it did not include even a single sentence about day nurseries.[92] Day nurseries were not included in the program of the National Conference of Social Work until 1919, and as late as 1939, the PADN advised the National Association of Day Nurseries against holding regional day nursery conferences, fearing that they "would further segregate the day nursery from other community agencies." Instead, they wanted to work to include day nurseries in state social work conferences.[93]

Social workers ignored day nurseries because the day nurseries seemed to ignore the importance of social work, as Helen Tyson explained in 1919: "It is chiefly because of their sins of omission in the casework field that social workers as a group do not think highly of day nurseries. The nursery too often has been content with giving the children protection and physical care and has ignored the dingy background of poverty and social maladjustment from which the children come."[94] Intent on "rehabilitating" the families who sought nursery care (who were defined as "maladjusted" by virtue of having a wage-earning mother needing charitable assistance), social workers criticized nurseries for being too liberal in their admissions policies and for not exercising more control over how clients used the nursery service.

In response to criticism and exclusion from the growing social work establishment, many day nurseries hired social workers to bring casework, outreach, and detailed investigations into the nurseries, increased their contact with other social welfare agencies, and drew up careful policies about what types of cases were eligible for day nursery care. Social workers came to play a major role within the nurseries, taking power and responsibilities away from board members and matrons; when charity federations centralized fund-raising, board members became even less involved in the routine operation of the nurseries. Social workers articulated a new goal for day nurseries: no longer satisfied with providing a good home for the children of working mothers and giving them training in healthful habits, they sought family rehabilitation, a change in circumstances and attitudes that would enable poor mothers to do without charitable assistance, preferably by returning to a "normal" family structure of breadwinning father and at-home mother. This was not a radical departure from earlier understandings of day nurseries: the elite women who founded day nurseries had also seen families as devastated by a mother's employment and had tried to encourage mothers to use the nurseries only as a temporary measure. But the incorporation of social work in the nurseries strengthened the more conservative elements of day nursery ideology, limited the nurseries' scope and mission, and amplified the charitable stigma attached to using day nurseries.

Criticism of day nurseries' practice of indiscriminate admission was not new in the 1920s; nineteenth-century charity workers had repeatedly urged nurseries to investigate parents' respectability before accepting their children to make sure that they were serving the worthy poor. One day nursery leader announced at a conference in 1897 that lack of investigation was "one of the weakest points in the day nursery work of the country."[95] Most nurseries agreed that investigation was necessary and wanted to be sure that only deserving families were helped. The Baldwin Day Nursery's rule, "No children are to be received until the character and home of the parents be known" was typical of many Philadelphia nurseries.[96] Investigation was typically done by the matron or by board members. One day nursery contemporary wrote that the matron had to "be a sufficiently keen observer to detect ordinary fraud, and experience has proved that the right kind of matron is the best possible investigator."[97] At the Franklin Day Nursery, for instance, the matron was praised for visiting each family regularly so that she could dismiss a child whose mother was no longer working, or help a family suffering from a new misfortune. According to the president of the nursery's board, the matron was "the personal friend of each mother on her list."[98] Matrons, busy with other duties, however, did not always have time for investigating new families or visiting old ones, and their judgments about what constituted a worthy case may have differed from those of board members.

Concern with the need for more careful investigation grew throughout the 1900s. By 1916, when the Child Federation issued its report on Philadelphia day nurseries, the concern had gone beyond establishing the "worthiness" of families applying for care, to emphasizing the need for detailed social investigation. The Child Federation report found that record-keeping in most nurseries was minimal and strongly urged nurseries to fill out case records on each family, including information about parents' employment, education, citizenship, marital status, and "diseases which may taint child"; reports of home visits on living conditions, including poverty, neglect, cruelty, and unemployment, number of people sleeping in each room, and distance to nearest water faucet; and reports from other welfare agencies that had contact with the family.[99] Three years later, Helen Tyson found that "the inadequacy of the records and the lack of knowledge on the part of the matrons as to the economic status of the families was most surprising." While two-thirds of the PADN-affiliated nurseries made visits to a child's home before admission, only three employed a trained visitor for this purpose, and only three or four of the nurseries gathered complete information about a family's economic need. Tyson wrote, "There is little doubt that if [the matrons] had seen any real value in record-keeping, most of them would have applied to it the same faithfulness and devotion that they gave to the actual care of the children."[100] But the matrons "consider home visiting as more or less of an 'extra' service—one of the things that can be sacrificed without much loss during press of work."[101] The nurseries' lack of interest in modern social work techniques was demonstrated by the fact that very few nurseries made regular use of the Social Service Exchange, a central registry of families applying for help to various charitable agencies, which Tyson described as "the hub of the wheel of social service activities in the community today," used by more than a hundred social agencies in the city.[102]

Spurred by the criticism in these two reports, as well as by ongoing criticism from social work leaders, nurseries that tried to keep up with trends in social welfare began to consider hiring someone especially for the tasks of investigation, visiting, and record-keeping. For instance, the Jane D. Kent Nursery reported in 1913 that it had hired a "trained visitor to visit the children and the mothers in their homes, thereby coming in direct contact with the environments of our little ones and in this way being able to assist financially and help in other ways the homes of our children."[103] From 1908 to 1931, nineteen out of the twenty-nine day nurseries that ever joined the PADN reported hiring social workers, mostly after 1920.

By hiring social workers to investigate and visit day nursery families, nursery boards sought to bring the latest in modern social welfare practice to the nurseries. Social workers brought the day nurseries into closer contact with other social agencies, conducted more rigorous investigations of families than had been done by matrons and board members in the past, and instituted careful record-keeping. Anna Frigond recalled that before the Strawberry Mansion Day Nursery incorporated the services of a social worker into its program, "Intake was done by board people who had a basic desire to help and an ear for a tale of woe; and the better the story was told, the quicker the child was admitted."[104] Social workers, by contrast, would conduct a thorough investigation of each applicant's story, visiting her home and talking with her neighbors, employers, and relatives before admitting her children. As Marion Kohn explained in 1914, "An admission means the most careful investigation not only of the parental home, but often of relatives and family acquaintances."[105] In order to get further information about a family and prevent "cheating," social workers typically checked with the city's Social Service Exchange to see if other agencies had had contact with a family. Social workers also brought the nurseries into closer touch with other welfare agencies in the city, referring families to other agencies for help and getting referrals from other agencies. At the Neighborhood Centre Nursery, for example, Marion Kohn was constantly in touch with other social workers at Jewish welfare agencies, the Mothers' Assistance Fund, the Juvenile Court, the Court of Domestic Relations, and the social service departments of various hospitals in the city. Bringing nurseries into greater contact with the web of social agencies in the city could enable clients to get help from different sources, but it also increased the social worker's power over her clients. For good or for ill, a family using a day nursery no longer entered simply that nursery, but the entire urban welfare system.[106]

Social workers, intent on uplifting the families who came into contact with the day nursery, also placed great emphasis on transforming these families by encouraging them to adopt nursery standards of hygiene, order, nutrition, and discipline at home. Most nurseries placed great emphasis on teaching their children habits of personal hygiene and providing each child with his or her own towel, brush, comb, washcloth, and toothbrush. Almost every nursery report included a reference to the belief that merely spending time in the orderly and healthful atmosphere of the nursery would improve the lives of children and their families. Several social workers claimed that this broad-based education was in fact the larger purpose of their work. A 1926 report of the Franklin Day Nursery praised "the patient training in obedience, honesty and cleanliness which is as important a part in Nursery work as the nourishing diet and rest."[107] Similarly, a 1928 Neighborhood Centre report explained, "The physical care we furnish in the Nursery for our children is but a small part of our program. Our larger purpose is the projection of Nursery ideals into the home." The report went on to say that the "lessons in hygiene, proper feeding, social habits and the like that are acquired in the Nursery" had to be learned by parents as well as children in order to be of lasting influence. In 1928, the Jewish Welfare Society (JWS) asked the Neighborhood Centre Day Nursery to continue working with two children who had originally come to the nursery because of the family's economic situation. The purpose of nursery care now was to continue the nursery's good influence on the whole family: the JWS social worker wrote that the children "have become fastidious about their appearance and also the type of food the mother offers them, and we think that the children are setting a higher standard for the parents."[108]

Day nursery workers did not rely only on children pressuring their mothers at home to get their message across. They tried to teach the mothers directly, "lest the web which is so carefully woven by day be unraveled each night" by uneducated mothers.[109] Nearly every nursery belonging to the PADN found that, along with visiting the children's homes, mothers' clubs were an effective way to reach out to day nursery mothers. A typical day nursery mothers' club alternated between social events, handiwork projects, and "instructive talks" given by day nursery workers or local doctors, nurses, and nutritionists, for one of the long-term goals of these mothers' meetings was to train nursery mothers to listen to experts.[110] For instance, Neighborhood Centre's house physician organized special health meetings for the centre's day nursery mothers, recruiting other physicians and dieticians as speakers. "The response of the mothers," reported the social worker, "has been most gratifying. They ask many questions of the doctors and discuss the meetings with us on many other occasions."[111] Topics discussed at these meetings over the years included infant mortality, first aid to the injured, "The Province of the Home," "Women in the World of Industry," children's behavior problems, and selecting toys for children. Although there was some variety, day nursery mothers' clubs tended to focus on practical tips for mothering and housekeeping, areas in which day nursery mothers were presumed to need instruction. For instance, the Sunnyside Nursery sponsored "a very successful supper in which we tried to demonstrate a simple and nutritious meal, not hard to prepare."[112]

Mothers' meetings at the Baldwin Nursery had a different tone—and seem to have been better attended than those at the other nurseries. These were "women's temperance socials," Gospel meetings that always included an opportunity to take the total abstinence pledge, which women often did "with babies in their arms or clinging to their skirts." The managers of the nursery felt "that this work is having a great influence over the homes in the neighborhood," a mill district in which many of the applications for day nursery care read simply, "drink," in the space where the applicant was to explain the cause of marital conflict. Although nursery workers at Baldwin sometimes organized a health talk for the mothers, the women seemed to prefer the regular abstinence meetings, with their "short, practical Bible lessons, and much hymn singing."[113]

In addition to strengthening the nurseries' attempts to reshape the homes of day nursery families, conducting more rigorous investigations, and linking the nurseries to other social welfare agencies, the presence of social workers in the day nurseries also shifted relationships and responsibilities for the nurseries' operation, as social workers took on the tasks of both matrons and board members. At some nurseries, a new figure emerged: a day nursery director, or superintendent, with professional training in social work or child welfare. Like Marion Kohn at Neighborhood Centre or Helen Lockwood at St. Nicholas, these women not only took on the matron's task of maintaining daily contact with the nursery families and overseeing the daily operation of the nursery, but also provided leadership and advice on nursery policy to the board. They gradually came to have greater power in determining what happened at the nursery than the members of the board. Even at nurseries that maintained a traditional role for the matron, the presence of a social worker on the staff altered dynamics, for although she was an employee of the nursery like the matron and cook, she was also a professional whose training and specialized knowledge conferred high status, and board members generally followed her lead.

Another factor diminishing the power and involvement of board members was the growing strength of charity federations, which combined the fund-raising efforts of a variety of charitable organizations. These umbrella groups simultaneously removed board members' responsibility for fund-raising and their freedom to decide how to spend their money; they also developed standards of how welfare agencies should operate, encouraging reliance on social workers, careful record-keeping, and coordination among agencies. Charity federations emerged just as professional social work was taking hold, and they were part of the same impulse to rationalize and centralize welfare. Several historians have suggested that they also encouraged conservatism and discouraged social activism.[114] In Philadelphia, charities dominated by Jews of German descent were the first to join forces, forming the Federation of Jewish Charities in 1901, and the Protestant charities eventually followed suit, creating the Welfare Federation in 1921. Most of the day nurseries that belonged to the PADN had joined one of these charity federations by the 1920s, giving up both the work of raising money and the power to decide how to spend it.[115]

In making this exchange, female nursery boards ceded power to charity federations led by men. Looking back in 1945, Strawberry Mansion Day Nursery director Anna Frigond used family metaphors to describe her nursery's decision to join the Federation of Jewish Charities:

> Our financial situation was a difficult one. . . . We put ourselves up for adoption. Fortunately, by then we were a rather "cute baby" with some forty-odd charges, and the [Federation of Jewish Charities] agreed to "father us" while allowing us to remain under our "mother's" (the board's) care. Of course our new father did not always have sufficient funds to be generous with us, and we have had to make things do on low minimums.[116]

While female nursery boards had been fully responsible for both operating and supporting the nurseries in their early years, the emergence of charity federations split the labor along gender lines. Just as day nursery managers, in visiting the homes of their clients, urged them to create families where the father supported the children financially while the mother nurtured them, so dependence on charity federations enabled the managers to carry out this division of labor in their day nursery work. Perhaps the earlier day nursery boards felt, like many breadwinning mothers, that the "double burden" of support and daily care was too heavy a load. With their primary function of fund-raising taken away, however, day nursery managers became less actively involved in the nurseries, transferring many of their "mothering" responsibilities to the social worker and other staff.

The combination of professional social workers taking over the visiting and charity federations taking over the fund-raising left little space for the involvement of elite board members. Looking back in 1940, a First Day Nursery board member expressed her feeling that "something was the matter with board members." In the past, she observed, women served on the board of only one charity, for which they did "a great deal of work," but things had changed. "Today, with the necessary money handed to board members, responsibility ends at coming to meetings. . . . Boards are too dependent on the social service workers for general information."[117] Indeed, when Mrs. Harrison, a board member of the First Day Nursery, and Helen LaGrange, the social worker hired by the nursery, fielded questions about the new foster day care plan at a 1929 conference, the shift in authority was clear. While Harrison, as a board member, was theoretically responsible for interpreting the nursery's work to outsiders, it was LaGrange, the social worker, who knew the answers to the audience's questions, whether they concerned details about the daily operation of the program or broader issues about the program's goals.[118] Having given up direct involvement and personal investment in the work of the nurseries, many board members reduced their participation to the minimum needed to carry on board membership as a social obligation and family tradition. No longer the "one charity" by which an elite woman would be known, day nurseries were increasingly governed by the budget dictated by the charity federations, and on a daily basis by the matron and social worker.

A parallel process of centralization and professionalization occurred within the PADN. In 1916, the organization's executive board discussed the idea of hiring an executive secretary in order to standardize records kept by individual nurseries, cooperate with organized social agencies, and implement the recommendations of the 1916 Child Federation report, as well as the day nursery standards drawn up by the PADN itself. In 1920 they hired Frances Colbourne, a social worker who had worked closely with Helen Glenn Tyson for many years in the Social Service Department of the University Hospital, and in the office of the Mothers' Assistance Fund.[119] Colbourne worked out of a downtown office alongside offices of other charitable agencies, corresponded with day nursery directors and social workers across the country, attended professional conferences, and kept PADN board members up to date with the latest trends in child welfare work.

"Is It Necessary to Know All My Business?"

Under the guidance of new professionals like Colbourne, and under pressure from charity federations and social workers to limit the scope of their work, day nursery women affiliated with the PADN came up with new guidelines dictating who would be eligible to send their children to nurseries. Nurseries had always been intended primarily for single mothers who worked out of clear financial necessity, although they were also used by married women seeking to supplement their husbands' insufficient wages. During the 1910s and 1920s, an even more limited vision of the proper nursery mother emerged. The Child Federation report recommended in 1916 "that it be uniformly understood that children are not to be accepted so that both parents may go to work." Social worker Helen Tyson urged day nurseries to avoid taking children whose fathers had deserted or whose parents were separated, unless every possible effort had been made to force the father to pay for the children's support. She wrote, "Until every possible means has been exhausted to place this legitimate responsibility on the father, no nursery has a moral right to act as his substitute, especially where the help it offers may not be fully adequate."[120]

Although this rule made sense from the viewpoint of the social planner, it often conflicted with women's own strategies for supporting their children. For instance, when Mrs. Solomon applied to place her two children at the Neighborhood Centre Day Nursery, she "stated that she and her husband were no longer living together, that she was unwilling to go the court for support order as she saw no good of so doing, and that others she knew had gone to court and their husbands had paid for a short time and had stopped. She did not care for the notoriety of court proceedings, and preferred to support herself and the children. She had secured shirt waists from a factory and was going out to sell them for a few hours of each day." Since she refused to go to court, however, the nursery refused to help her. Finally, when the aunt with whom she had been living died, leaving her no place to leave the children, she consented to swear out a warrant for her husband's arrest. The children, "undernourished and anemic," were promptly admitted to the nursery.[121] In its desire to enforce a husband's duty to provide, the nursery thus made Mrs. Solomon's predicament worse, until she was desperate enough to agree to cooperate. Other rules codified by the PADN in 1920 similarly limited working mothers' flexibility: at the urging of Frances Colbourne, the Medical Regulations Committee resolved that nurseries should refuse to accept any babies younger than nine months; mothers of young infants applying for day nursery care should be referred to a charitable agency that could support them at home.[122] Similarly, mothers with more than two children were to be discouraged from using nurseries: Tyson wrote, "The granting of service to a large family of little children should not be a source of pride to a nursery—it but marks another failure on the part of society to recognize the real value of a mother's service to her children."[123]

Social casework, with its emphasis on individual diagnosis and treatment, also moved the nurseries away from an emphasis on serving large numbers of families. Rather, social workers urged day nursery managers to serve fewer families more intensively. In 1912, Marion Kohn asked her board to lower the number of children attending the nursery in order "to afford more individual care." A year later, she complained of being unable to keep closely enough in touch with all the families using the nursery. Gradually the numbers of children attending the nursery did decrease dramatically, from an average of about a hundred children daily during the 1910s to an average of about fifty-five from the 1920s on. This preference for intensive service to fewer numbers of families was reflected in many day nursery reports during this period, as the aggregate statistics about the number of children cared for during the year—the thousands of baths given, meals served, and bottles prepared that had filled the reports in the nurseries' earlier years—gave way to detailed information about the social conditions that gave rise to the need for day care. These reports listed parents' occupations, nationalities, marital status, and the reasons they gave for seeking day care; analyzed the causes of deaths of fathers and the frequency of debilitating illness or insanity; and detailed contacts with other agencies in order to show that nurseries were attempting not only to provide a service but to diagnose the root causes of the need for day care.

Social workers intent on rehabilitating families often saw the day nursery as a stopgap solution, and did what they could to discourage women from going out to work. Helen Glenn Tyson, who had served as the executive secretary of the PADN, articulated clearly many day nursery social workers' vision of their role when she wrote in 1919, "The nursery's obligation is not discharged until to every family under its care has been restored, as nearly as possible, that normal home life on which our modern society was founded."[124] Many social workers were even more convinced than board members that the nursery was a second-best solution, and counseled women accordingly. Frances Colbourne announced at a conference of the National Federation of Day Nurseries, "We prefer to have trained social workers make visits and investigations. The visitor should try to get the mother to take care of the children in the home; if she cannot, the children are admitted to the nursery."[125] Looking back in 1949, Anna Frigond remembered, "25 years ago the mother's expressed need to work was the sole criterion for admission. No other possibility of meeting her problem was considered, and no evaluation of how constructive or destructive the experience would be, was made."[126] In other words, the mother's own decision to seek paid work was likely to be respected. Following the institution of case work, however, a mother's strategy of going out to work was much more likely to be challenged, and the social worker likely to dwell on the "destructive" aspects of her employment and her child's presence in the nursery. For instance, when Vera Moskowitz applied for care for her two children, explaining that she did not get along with her husband and wanted to place the children in a nursery so she could work, the Neighborhood Centre social worker strongly discouraged her. She "discussed with Mrs. Moskowitz her duty to her children, that is, that it is far better for her to remain at home and care for them, also that it was rather late for her to think that she no longer cared for her husband; that she must realize that her children were his children and they have a right to have both parents all the time."[127]

Social workers were often at least as proud of cases where they successfully discouraged a woman from working and using the nursery as they were of cases where they helped a woman to use the nursery well. This was especially true at the First Day Nursery following its switch from group care to foster day care. In 1928, the social worker reported that she had had investigated twelve new cases of which only one would be accepted, "but in the other cases she has aided in adjustments so that nursery care was unnecessary." She explained, "The work now really consists more of a Bureau for Working Mothers than a day nursery, as nearly as much work is done on cases not taken as those that are."[128] A few months later, board members were told that in about half the applications that came to the social worker, "some other plan more suitable than nursery care has been found."[129]

For the women who brought their children to charitable day nurseries, the emergence of case work meant closer supervision over almost every aspect of their lives, and less respect for their own judgment about everything from the decision to go out to work to what they were cooking for dinner. Social worker Rosetta Stang of Neighborhood Centre explained in 1928, "Proper diet, the forming of definite health habits, discipline of children and such matters can not be stressed too strongly. It is only when the mother has definite ideas about these things that case work is actually taking place."[130] (Of course, the problem was not usually that mothers did not have "definite ideas" about these issues, but that they did not always have the *right* definite ideas.) One mother who used the nursery was visited by a home economist twice a week; the home economist was distressed to learn that the mother did not plan or systematize her housework; she reported that Mrs. Grossman "was in the habit of using delicatessen food and that the children drank tea and coffee instead of milk. She had little knowledge of how to prepare vegetables and cereals and knew nothing of their value." Although the home economist "had quite a difficult time convincing woman that her ideas were wrong," she continued to visit, instructing Mrs. Grossman in cooking and in managing her children, who were disobedient. The home economist "tried to explain to the woman that the fault lay within her and that she must be more careful and use better disciplinary measures with the children." The Jewish Welfare Society, which had sent the home economist on the day nursery's request, wrote that the visits were "helping Mrs. Grossman to become a home-maker."[131] Another mother told Marion Kohn she was trying to follow her instructions about proper care of her baby: "as you have sent word with my daughter I should not rock the baby and hold it in my hands I have tryed to do my best not to do so."[132]

Mothers responded differently to this new involvement of social workers in their lives. Some objected outright, like Mrs. Whittaker, who was trying to get her daughter back into the First Day Nursery after some absence. When the social worker started asking her all the questions necessary for the new admissions card, Whittaker "asked what new nonsense this was," saying, "Is it necessary to know all my business just because you take care of my child a few hours a day?"[133] Other mothers sought to use the social worker's involvement to their advantage, either in their struggles to get obedience and respect from their children, or in their efforts to get more help from the nursery. Thus Mrs. Singer told the Neighborhood Centre social worker that she "could not manage" her nine-year-old daughter Isabelle, who played with friends in the neighborhood until ten or eleven at night. While the social worker talked with Isabelle about the need for an early bedtime, Mrs. Singer "frequently interrupted with threats that worker would place Isabelle in an orphanage." Again, when the social worker visited the home to instruct Mrs. Singer "in how to obtain obedience" from her children, Mrs. Singer "threatened them with 'placement in a home if they did not obey her,' and said worker had called regarding their behavior and to discuss the matter of 'placement' with her." After the social worker had given her many different "lessons" in how to discipline and control her children, Singer finally lost patience. When she returned home one evening and found a note from the social worker telling her to come see her, she stormed into the office. "She was very excited and said 'Youse have my children all day so why can't you train them? I am too nervous and they don't mind me.' She went on in this train for almost a half hour," speaking "at the top of her voice." Of course the social worker was not willing to accept this division of labor, and she "tried to impress on [Mrs. Singer's] mind the fact that the children belong to her and that it is her duty to train them."[134] The boundary between the nursery's and the mother's responsibility had been crossed by the social worker herself, with her involvement in many different aspects of Isabelle's home training—but she would not accept Mrs. Singer's demand that since she knew so much more about children, she should take over the responsibility.

Social work did not immediately become pervasive in all day nurseries, and nurseries that did not do in-depth investigations or visiting continued to flourish. A report made in 1920 of Jewish day nurseries in Philadelphia was full of praise for Neighborhood Centre, yet it concluded that the city's two other Jewish nurseries were "institutions of the older type, which have not kept pace with modern standards." The report explained that these nurseries, although they treated children "with motherly concern," limited their work "almost entirely to providing food and shelter to the children while under care. No attempt is made to discover the background of family life and to carry higher standards into the homes, without which effort, the influence of the Nursery may be vitiated."[135] Similarly, the *Catholic Charities Yearbook* explained in 1923 that in most of the nurseries, the nuns "restrict their work to the shelter"; the efforts of the Sisters of St. John's Nursery, who "visit the homes and carefully investigate each case and give whatever help and advice that is in their power," were rare enough to be worthy of special mention.[136] Most children were referred to the Catholic nurseries by their parish priests, who presumably knew the family situation, and further investigation or counseling, beyond that done informally by the nuns, did not seem to be necessary.[137] But social work and careful record-keeping had become a central part of the PADN's definition of a good day nursery. When PADN members visited the Forty-ninth Street Station Day Nursery in 1928 and found that the nursery's matron received applications in addition to all her other work, did not use the Social Service Exchange or record any social history, and kept all the children's medical cards together whether or not the child was still attending, they insisted that the nursery institute better record-keeping and conduct more thorough investigations of children's families before they would accept the nursery back into the association.[138]

When PADN member Ruth Weaver sought to codify the basic principles of the day nursery movement in 1931, she demonstrated the way in which the influence of social work had limited the scope of the day nurseries. She explained that nurseries should confine themselves to "families which are genuinely dependent," and should not be regarded as appropriate for all such families, but "as a place of last resort." Large families; families who could be helped by relatives, friends, or other agencies; and families with mothers who were not competent wage earners or good homemakers were all to be excluded. Families that could get by without the mother's wages were clearly infringing on "nursery hospitality," and Weaver reported "a shocking indifference to the ethics of the situation," as "the parents seem to think that the nursery is under an obligation to care for any children which are sent to it."[139] Family counseling was part of the day nursery's responsibility: by admitting children from "broken homes," she wrote, day nurseries were obligated "to make a far reaching plan for each family and each child," in order to reestablish "family integrity at the earliest possible date."[140]

Weaver described the nursery's overall goal as "to re-unite the disorganized or disrupted members of the family, to correct health problems, augment the family income, raise the standard of living and bring about a secure social adaptation of the children."[141] This description of the work of day nurseries shows to what extent nurseries were trying to ally themselves with other family casework agencies and downplay the fact that they enabled mothers to go out to work; nowhere in this description of the day nursery's purpose do we hear the simple phrase "care for the children of working mothers." The nurseries' longstanding ambivalence about enabling mothers to go out to work had found expression in the language of professional social work, which could define the nursery as a tool for family rehabilitation rather than a way to provide good care for children while their mothers were at work.

Throughout the 1910s and 1920s, then, ideas about how best to help poor mothers and their children shifted, leaving day nurseries with no popular rationale for their work. The spread of mothers' pension programs did not eliminate the need for day nurseries, but by offering a more attractive solution to the problem of the single mother, it did invalidate the nurseries' moral appeal. At the same time, nurseries were sharply criticized by leaders of the new profession of social work and excluded from professional conferences and courses of training. Challenging these developments would have taken a confidence and positive vision of day care that the day nursery leaders did not possess. Their response was rather to retrench, admitting their faults and positioning themselves as a limited, flawed, and temporary expedient to serve families in times of crisis. The end result of the challenges posed by mothers' pensions and the growth of professional social work was to limit the scope, mission, and ambition of day nursery leaders, discouraging them from placing day care on the public agenda next to other legitimate needs of women and children.

4

Day Care as Education

The Emergence of the Nursery School

While the charitable day nurseries were falling into disfavor in the 1920s, nursery schools emerged, offering a new understanding of the purpose and meaning of day care. Taking as their model the school rather than the orphanage, nursery schools defined day care as an experience intended to benefit children, not their mothers. Designed to provide an educational experience for middle-class children in an era when childhood seemed increasingly complicated, nursery schools convinced some affluent parents that they needed the help of trained experts to raise happy, well-adjusted, independent children. Day care in the nursery schools was not a matter of charity, but of privilege: parents were willing to pay in order to give their children the benefit of nursery school training. Thus a two-track system of care for young children took shape: affluent children would receive carefully designed educational care in nursery schools, while working-class children would receive only custodial care in charitable day nurseries.

Both nursery schools and day nurseries assumed that the mothers they served were incompetent to raise their children without expert guidance, but the problems of the mothers as well as the remedies offered were different. Middle-class children seemed to be "overmothered," and needed the nursery school to establish independence and learn social skills that would fit them for the business world of the future. Working-class children, on the other hand, apparently did not receive enough mothering and needed the physical care as well as the discipline of the day nursery. The help that both kinds of child care programs offered to mothers came at the cost of women's confidence in their ability to rear their children; yet many mothers welcomed their new dependence on experts, even finding in it a measure of class status and modernity. Some day nurseries tried to incorporate nursery schools into their programs in order to gain status and attention, but had trouble finding the resources necessary to replicate the nursery-school environment. In time, however, the challenging notion that group care for children was beneficial, even preferable to maternal care, would transform attitudes toward day care. By focusing on enhancing children's development rather than enabling mothers to earn, nursery schools developed an attractive rationale for providing care for children.

A Mother's Job or the State's Job?

The boundary separating education from child care, public from family responsibility for the care and training of children, has shifted throughout U.S. history. For instance, in the three decades before the Civil War, elementary education—previously the domain of parents, employers, tutors, "dame schools," church, and charity schools—became a government responsibility in many northern states. After an experiment with "infant schools" failed in the 1830s, however, these state and local governments decided not to accept responsibility for the education of very young children and limited public schooling to children over the age of five.[1] As this example suggests, the American public has been much more willing to support educational programs for children than to provide physical and emotional care, properly seen as the province of mothers.[2] While taking on the "intellectual" part of a mother's job—the education and training of children—has been legitimized as a proper duty of the state, taking on the messier job of physical care and nurturing has not.

In the late nineteenth century, the kindergarten movement again questioned the boundary dividing child care from education. The widespread public adoption of kindergartens by the turn of the century offers a sharp contrast to the marginalization of day nurseries, suggesting the difference in public interest between programs defined as educational and those that took on a mother's work of child care.

The kindergarten idea originated in Germany with Fredrich Froebel, a rural schoolmaster inspired by the Romantic poets as well as by the educational philosophies of Rousseau and Pestalozzi. Critiquing the way children grew up in middle-class families, Froebel sought to create an environment that would center on children's innate desire to explore the world through play. Instead of hornbooks and catechisms, his "child garden" was to be filled with simple toys designed to teach complex ideas.[3] Froebel's ideas gained widespread public attention in the United States in the 1870s and 1880s as a technique of fostering the development of both rich and poor children. While mothers of means sought kindergarten training for their children, others began to push for free kindergartens for poor urban children.

These free kindergartens took on a broader mission than Froebel had envisioned; many kindergarten adherents sought to transform poor families and neighborhoods suffering from the economic crises of the 1870s and 1880s. The free kindergarten's mission of social uplift is suggested by a description given by kindergarten director Constance MacKenzie of the changes wrought in one Philadelphia neighborhood:

> Chairs were cleaned when "teacher" was announced, and by and by the rooms were kept brushed up to greet her unexpected coming. . . . Lessons of cleanliness, thrift, and trust were learned through experience and communicated to the homes through the insistence of the children and the friendly home talks of the kindergartners. . . . Then followed . . . a shamefaced determination to do as "the kindergarten teacher did," until a new atmosphere pervaded many a home which at first sight had seemed irredeemable.[4]

A typical "kindergartner" spent her mornings actually conducting the kindergarten and her afternoons and evenings visiting families, organizing classes for mothers, and generally doing social work in the neighborhood. Instead of Froebel's emphasis on freeing children from the restrictions of middle-class family life, the kindergartners focused on teaching slum children habits of cleanliness and discipline at an early age (many took children as young as three years old), while preparing them for primary school. These kindergartens functioned as "child-saving stations," providing hot meals, clothing, and baths to the children and offering guidance to mothers through the kindergartner's visits to children's homes and through evening classes for mothers. The zeal of many kindergarten advocates is evident in the words of Elizabeth Peabody, who wrote that kindergartning should not "be regarded as a business, but as a religion."[5] By 1890, more than one thousand free kindergartens had sprung up in orphanages, churches, factories, missions, and other locations across the country.[6]

Reformers' confidence in the redemptive powers of kindergartens quickly led them to seek public funding. In Philadelphia, the effort was spearheaded by Anna Hallowell, a descendant of a prominent Quaker family.[7] The first woman to be elected to the Philadelphia Board of Public Education, Hallowell successfully used her position there to campaign for free kindergartens. In 1882, the city school board agreed to help support kindergartens organized by reformers like Hallowell, and five years later, the kindergartens were officially made part of the public school system. By 1910, Philadelphia had 271 public kindergartens.[8]

In many ways, these early kindergartens were indistinguishable from the day nurseries that were established around the same time. Both were seen primarily as child-welfare institutions, both were aimed at the children of the city's poorest neighborhoods, and both emphasized providing a safe, clean environment that would not only protect children from the dangers of the streets, but also train them in good habits at an early age and inspire their mothers to adopt "modern" ideas about child-rearing and hygiene. Indeed, a description of a free kindergarten in Boston could almost have been used to describe a day nursery: in an neighborhood "filled with the poorest and most degraded classes," immigrant working parents were forced to "turn their children out into the streets in the morning to care for themselves"; the kindergarten teachers brought these "neglected waifs and strays" into "home-like Kindergartens" where their faces were washed and lunches of bread and milk were served daily at ten o'clock.[9] Day nurseries and kindergartens served similar aims in these years: several Philadelphia day nurseries hired trained kindergarten teachers to conduct classes within the nursery, and kindergartens enabled mothers to work part-time while older siblings took young children to school with them.[10]

But despite the similarities between the free kindergartens and the day nurseries, there was a key difference: the kindergartens were part of a broader pedagogical movement that was seen as beneficial for *all* children, while day nurseries were restricted to the children of working mothers. According to the founders of the kindergarten movement, the children of the rich were just as badly trained as the children of the poor, and thus just as much in need of the opportunities offered by the kindergarten. Kindergarten methods—the Froebelian toys, the circle games, the songs—were as much in vogue among affluent parents as they were among urban reformers, and the growth of free kindergartens in the 1880s was paralleled by the growth of private, tuition-charging kindergartens.[11] Although the free kindergartners tended to emphasize the social welfare functions of the kindergartens, the kindergarten's identity as primarily an educational movement gained it greater legitimacy and a much broader appeal than the day nursery movement ever had. As time went on, kindergartens became even more identified with education and less with social welfare, since the school administrators who came to control the kindergartens were more interested in preparing children academically to enter the primary grades than in engaging in social reform.[12]

By emphasizing education and avoiding the question of maternal employment, kindergartens elicited broad support. They were promoted by the National Education Association (which established a special division on kindergartens), the National Congress of Mothers, the Women's Christian Temperance Union, and the General Federation of Women's Clubs, as well as by organizations formed specifically to lobby for kindergartens.[13] The federal Bureau of Education also worked to expand kindergartens, setting up a special division to distribute letters, articles, and films to further the kindergarten cause. (By contrast, the federal bureau responsible for child welfare, the Children's Bureau, opposed day nurseries and actively worked against them.) Several influential men of letters, including the editors of liberal New York journals such as *Scribner's, The Century*, and *The Forum*, joined the campaign for public adoption of kindergartens, publishing articles describing the squalor of the slums and the salvation offered by free kindergartens.[14] At the same time, universities and normal schools established programs to train kindergarten teachers, and thus formed another bloc of support for the expansion of kindergartens. In the end, the kindergartens flourished where the nurseries did not because they emphasized the education of children rather than the relief of mothers' burdens; took over the job of educating, not nurturing, children; sought to supplement, not substitute for, a mother's care; won the full strength of professional educators' organizations; and were able to appeal across class lines.

The history of kindergartens is important for understanding the history of day care, for it demonstrates that it was not the group care of children per se that made day nurseries controversial or unpopular. Instead, because day nurseries were designed primarily to serve wage-earning mothers they were condemned to second-class status. Education was justified as a universal need of all children, while the needs of working mothers seemed particular, limited, unfortunate, and (many hoped) temporary. Day nursery supporters, who were themselves ambivalent about their work, did not share the kindergartners' quasi-religious enthusiasm and conviction that providing good care for children would uplift the whole society. So perhaps it is not surprising that day nursery supporters never even discussed trying to pursue the path kindergartens had followed to making day nurseries a public responsiblity.

Nursery Schools: Education for the Affluent

Shortly after kindergartens were firmly established in urban public school systems, another educational experiment appeared on the American scene: the nursery school. The nursery school offered a different understanding of day care: not a charitable effort to bring poor children in off the streets, but an educational, enriching experience for the children of well-educated, affluent families. If child care was offered as a gift to the poor in the day nurseries, in the nursery schools it was *sold* to parents who had other choices. Nursery schools, typically aimed at prosperous middle-class families, grew out of the conviction that even educated, well-intentioned mothers with resources were unable to rear emotionally healthy children without the guidance of experts. By paying to send her child to a nursery school, a mother gained both advice about training her child and some time off from the full-time task of mothering. In exchange, she often had to be willing to change her mothering practice according to the advice of nursery school teachers. For like the day nursery, the nursery school could only justify taking on "a mother's job" by defining mothers as inadequate. But because the nursery school was intended primarily to benefit the child, not to free the mother, and because it was self-supporting, it carried none of the stigma attached to the charitable day nurseries.

The nursery school was part of a new anxiety about child-rearing that emerged in the 1920s. As advice to mothers shifted from a focus on physical health, nutrition, and hygiene to matters of children's mental health and emotional adjustment,[15] the tasks of motherhood became more complex. For instance, while the Children's Bureau's popular 1914 booklet *Infant Care* had given detailed instructions for keeping children healthy, clean, and well-fed, by 1928, a new pamphlet asked, *Are You Training Your Child To Be Happy?* In order to meet these new demands, mothers needed the help of experts, for maternal instinct and the advice of older and wiser women were no longer sufficient guides. Scientifically oriented advice spilled forth from public health and social work agencies, schools, women's clubs, magazines, pulpits, newspapers, and the federal government, especially the U.S. Children's Bureau—and mothers energetically consumed it, eager to benefit from the knowledge that science could provide.

Even affluent, highly educated mothers who could afford to devote all their time to mothering worried about their inadequate parenting skills. In their classic study of a small midwestern city in the 1920s, sociologists Robert and Helen Lynd noted that both working-class and "business class" parents felt "that child-rearing is something not be taken for granted but to be studied."[16] One Middleton mother confessed: "Life was simpler for my mother. In those days one did not realize that there was so much to be known about the care of children. I realize that I ought to be half a dozen experts, but I am afraid of making mistakes and usually do not know where to go for advice." Mothers expressed need for help in bringing up children, a sympathetic forum for their concerns, and guidance in "learning what it is we are doing when we are mothers," as one mother's letter to a researcher phrased it. Another woman writing to the Children's Bureau from Montana voiced the new assumption that motherhood required training, writing, "It may be that I don't understand children. . . . I have had no such training and am at a loss what to do with my baby." White middle-class mothers were more likely than others to seek the guidance of experts to solve child-rearing dilemmas, while mothers from working-class and minority backgrounds tended to be more distrustful of expert advice. For instance, one African-American mother told an interviewer in Nashville in 1933, "I don't need nobody to tell me anything. All I need is a place to leave my William when I go to work. I used to go to that Mothers Club, but shucks, it ain't nothing. White folks just naturally can't tell you nothing about raising children."[17]

Professionals—home economists, doctors, psychologists, parent educators, and child development experts—and lay organizations were happy to oblige mothers looking for guidance. The Laura Spelman Rockefeller Memorial spent over $7 million dollars in the 1920s to achieve its vision of expert, scientific child-rearing by funding university research stations, bringing together experts from different disciplines, and training teachers and home economists as parent educators.[18] Child development became part of the curriculum at many universities, high schools, and even grade schools, and centers for research on child development emerged at several public and private universities, as well as at special schools like the Merrill Palmer Motherhood and Homemaking School in Detroit.[19] The National Congress of Mothers and the Child Study Association of America joined with the American Association of University Women in a campaign to educate women for motherhood. They encouraged the formation of child study groups, in which a small number of mothers came together regularly to discuss the latest literature on child development and training and to analyze their own children's behavior. The child study movement offered women help with the work of mothering: for instance, parent-educator Sidonie Gruenberg wrote, "In this complex age, it takes more than any one human being can know to take charge of a child's full development. Every mother should avail herself of all the assistance obtainable."[20] But it simultaneously shook women's confidence in their ability to raise healthy children, invalidated the advice that they received from their female elders, and created a new set of anxieties about their competence as mothers that could never be fully allayed.

Mother-love, previously seen as the source of all social good and the rallying point for maternalist reformers, was no longer enough—indeed, it could even be dangerous. As historian Nancy Cott has remarked, the only common ground of the child study movement was its "redefinition of the parent-child relation as a *problem*."[21] And the mother was generally at the root of the problem. Much of the new child study literature assumed that mothers were incompetent, and that untrained mothers were likely to inflict great psychological damage on their children. Speaking at a White House conference in 1930, the president of Stanford University explained, "It is beyond the capacity of the individual parent to train her child to fit into the intricate, interwoven and interdependent social and economic system we have developed."[22] Significantly, all mothers (not just poor or immigrant mothers) were now seen to be ignorant and possibly dangerous. Behaviorist psychologist John Watson felt that no one knew enough to raise a child: "The world would be considerably better off if we were to stop having children for twenty years (except for experimental purposes) and were then to start again with enough facts to do the job with some degree of skill and accuracy." Watson, who dedicated his book on child-rearing to "the first mother who brings up a happy child," only carried to an extreme the general mistrust of mothers pervasive in the child-study literature. Like many other experts writing in these years, he saw maternal love as a dangerous force, leading to "smothering" a young child's will, destroying the child's independence, and impeding the development of a healthy personality.[23] He urged mothers to stop caressing their babies and advised treating children as young adults, with objective and kindly but firm behavior. "Never hug and kiss them. Never let them sit in your lap. If you must, kiss them once on the forehead when they say goodnight. Shake hands with them in the morning." It was a mother's duty to keep away from her child for a large part of each day; if a mother was too tender-hearted to avoid watching her baby as he played in the yard, Watson advised using a periscope.[24] While most advice books did not go to such extremes, they shared Watson's concern with promoting a child's independence and separation from his or her mother.

One way in which middle-class mothers could improve their mothering skills and ensure their children's healthy development was to send their children to one of the new nursery schools that were established during the 1920s, typically either as part of a university research center or as a private school. In effect, the nursery school placed both child and mother under the supervision of experts, while providing researchers with an ideal laboratory in which to study child development. Nursery schools promised to help children develop social skills, play in a group, and learn to control both emotions and bodily functions. The schools were also to be "laboratories for parents"; some schools had mothers take notes on the teachers' techniques and later discuss them with the nursery director, and most required mothers to spend time observing the classroom on a regular basis.[25] The director of the nursery school at Vassar College explained in 1929, "The nursery school is fundamentally a training school for parents to teach them how to train the child."[26]

Nursery schools were aimed at well-educated, affluent professional families, often centered around universities; one nursery educator referred to nursery schools as serving "the children of the intellectual classes."[27] Faculty wives at the University of Chicago established the first nursery school in the United States in 1916; it was soon followed by laboratory nursery schools at other universities across the country.[28] By 1931, seventy-four American colleges and universities sponsored nursery schools, in conjunction with teacher training programs, home economics departments, or child development institutes.[29] Other nursery schools were established by child guidance clinics, social service agencies, and private schools, as well as parent cooperatives and private individuals.[30] Although the British nursery school which had been the inspiration for some of these early schools was aimed at poor children, in the United States nursery schools were associated with relatively privileged families. At the Merrill-Palmer School in Detroit, for instance, the laboratory nursery school was reserved for "the cream of the crop parents, the best," who represented the "wide variety of elements found in what is called the 'great middle class.'"[31] Most nursery schools were either subsidized by the university or college with which they were associated, or supported through parents' tuition payments.

Families turned to nursery schools because they had been convinced that mothers alone could no longer perform the complicated task of fostering children's emotional and social development. Nursery schools were necessary, as one chapter of the Child Study Association agreed in 1930, because "very few homes could be normal in this complicated age in which we are living."[32] Whereas earlier commentators had reserved the word "abnormal" for families disrupted by death, desertion, poverty, abuse, and mothers' wage work, comments like this suggested that even educated, middle-class, two-parent families with some resources could not be trusted to bring up their children without help. Supporters of nursery schools frequently argued that the nursery school was a necessary institution for the "modern family." Cramped apartments, smaller families living far from their relatives, and the isolation of mother and child were all seen as adding to the handicaps of modern family life that made the nursery school necessary. Smiley Blanton of the Vassar Nursery School told the National Federation of Day Nurseries in 1929 that the nursery school was a necessary part of "modern" life:

> Just as the luncheon clubs have come in to take the place of the old corner grocery store . . . just as the golf club has come in to take the place of the farm and the demand to get out and exercise, so the nursery school has become an absolute necessity in modern life. It takes the place of the old home, commodious, full of children, with aunts and uncles and grandparents about with whom the child might associate.

In talking about modernity, Blanton also signaled the social class of nursery school families. The nursery school as he described it was intended to serve people who ate in luncheon clubs and frequented golf courses—a very different group of people from those who sent their children to day nurseries.

The nursery school's promise of producing children who were "well-adjusted," could get along in a group, and had learned self-control (of emotions as well as of excretion) at an early age was particularly attractive to middle-class parents who worried how their children would fare in the new business world that was taking shape in the 1920s. If this new world judged people based on "personality" and their ability to work well with others, then children who developed these skills early would have an advantage. Smiley Blanton explained, "The successful person is the person who has learned to adjust himself and his wishes and desires to other people, to find an outlet for his desires in a way that is satisfactory to other people." Creating children who got along well with others was crucial, for "competition is so fierce in modern life that we can hardly afford to overlook any one factor that may make for success." Blanton asserted that children who were timid, anxious, grouchy, ill-tempered, moody, irritable, overaggressive, or oversensitive were just as worrisome as those with crooked feet or curvature of the spine. The nursery school could fix these emotional maladjustments before they turned children into people that "you wouldn't want as sons-in-law, you wouldn't want as secretaries, you wouldn't want to work with them in an office."[33] Other nursery schools shared Blanton's concern, focusing on "habit training" and "mental hygiene." For instance, a 1929 guide for nursery school teachers explained that the nursery school's purpose was "to rid growing boys and girls of undesirable physiological habits, of unsocial attitudes and of perverted values." The good habits to be inculcated ranged from routines of personal hygiene, eating, and sleeping to learning to take turns, stand up for oneself, and exercise emotional control.[34]

Some of the more progressive nursery schools were less concerned about habits and put more emphasis on giving children the freedom to express themselves and develop their individuality within carefully constructed limits. Harriet Johnson, whose nursery school serving the children of writers and artists in Greenwich Village became a center of child development research, explained that the aim of her school was "to avoid dictation, to let the children learn by self-initiated experience and experimenting." She objected to the common emphasis on "habit training"; instead of toilet training and learning manners, she spoke of wanting to inculcate in children "a readiness to get to work on the material at hand, persistence of interest, the tendency to investigate and experiment in constructive ways."[35] At the Vassar Nursery School, Smiley Blanton also spoke of treating children like individuals, granting them freedom from unnecessary restrictions and allowing them to choose how to spend their time. He explained his attempt to "individualize" the child by allowing children "to be perfectly free" except for a few basic rules. "There is no program that makes the child do this or this or this. If one child wants to read a book . . . and another child wants to listen to music and another wants to ride a tricycle, they are all perfectly free to do so." The contrast between this description and the highly regimented life of a day nursery child, who might have been considered lucky to have one toy or activity, is echoed today in ethnographer Sally Lubeck's contrast between a middle-class preschool and a Head Start program. Children in the preschool that Lubeck observed were encouraged to make individual decisions about how to spend their time and urged to act on their environment, whether by painting at the easel or playing with sand. Children in the Head Start program, however, were treated as a group, taught to take responsibility for each other, and spent as much time in group activity as the preschool children did in individual play.[36]

The ideal nursery school also encouraged children's individuality by employing different techniques to enhance each child's development. If day nursery staff tended to treat the children in their care as an undifferentiated group with similar needs, nursery school teachers, who typically worked with much smaller groups of children, could afford to pay individual attention to each child.[37] Blanton described the Vassar Nursery School's technique of intensively studying each child, then arranging situations in the nursery school that would help the child with his or her specific needs. A shy child was urged to play the leading part in certain games and encouraged to fight when other children tried to take toys from her; a child who had had no contact with other children was gradually taught to play in the right way; a child weeping at being separated from his mother was left alone out of respect for his grief.[38]

Nursery educators promoted the idea that this kind of skillful nurturing of children's personalities and social development was beyond the capability of most ordinary mothers in the home. For instance, Smiley Blanton argued that the trained nursery school teacher was more adept than the modern mother at teaching children fundamental habits of eating, sleeping, dressing themselves, and controlling their excretory functions. He alluded to the inadequacy of maternal instinct for teaching these important lessons by pointing out that few parents had any formal training in child-rearing and that, furthermore, "the average mother doesn't know how to give the child a bath or what kind of soap to use or how many clothes to put on the child unless she is specifically told by some doctor or unless she reads it out of a book."[39] If mothers needed to rely on the knowledge of experts for such simple matters, Blanton implied, then surely expert knowledge was required for the more challenging, psychologically fraught tasks of child training. Similarly, in the *Women's Home Companion*, Ethel Puffer Howes answered the question, "But is it not better for mothers to train their own little children?" by saying, "No doubt, when they know enough of what experts know about the mental and physical hygiene of little children, are wise and patient, and have plenty of time for patience!"[40] As child development emerged as a profession, young college women seeking a "feminine" profession came to fill positions in nursery schools. For instance, Cornelia Minsinger, who came to the Neighborhood Centre Nursery School in Philadelphia in 1929, was described in a letter of recommendation as "an altogether fine type of college young woman"; her credentials included a B.S. degree in "Professional Home Economics" with a major in child care from Oregon State Agricultural College, work in the college's nursery school, and a term of study at the Merrill-Palmer School in Detroit.[41] Teachers could point to such academic training in child development to further their authority as experts; professional parents who themselves valued educational credentials were likely to be convinced.

Like the day nurseries, nursery schools did not think that taking on a mother's job was enough: their larger purpose was to improve the ways in which women mothered their children. While both day nurseries and nursery schools emphasized parent education as part of their mission, they meant quite different things. Day nursery workers tended to assume that the mothers they served did not know how to take adequate physical care of their children; thus parent education was largely concerned with hygiene, nutrition, and housekeeping skills. The same term in the nursery schools, however, was meant to address maternal *over*involvement, and meant training in child development and psychology, teaching mothers how to manage a child's emotions and how to train children to be self-sufficient, independent, and well-adjusted. Many nursery educators felt that mothers needed thorough retraining: nursery school director Caroline Pratt stated confidently that there were "no bad children, only bad parents" and confessed that she sometimes believed that children would be better off without their parents altogether.[42] Both day nurseries and nursery schools assumed that mothers were incompetent to raise their children successfully without guidance, but the nursery school mother seemed more promising than the day nursery mother, for she was seeking out help from professionals, while day nursery mothers had to be trained, if not coerced, to listen to expert advice.[43]

Their mistrust of women's mothering skills led nursery school advocates to develop more positive attitudes toward group care for children. By claiming that it was good for children to be separated from their mothers, they turned earlier arguments about the dangers of taking on a mother's job on their head. Nursery school director Caroline Pratt, for example, saw the nursery schools as the first step in the child's "emancipation from the home."[44] If mothers were domineering, overanxious, unhappy, or too wrapped up in their child, their children would flourish only when they were released from the emotional intensity of the home. Another nursery educator wrote,

> By four, the child . . . trained [by nursery school methods] has acquired spontaneously and unconsciously many of the habits that the isolated child in the home is still struggling and fighting over. Spinach, for instance, eaten in a group, is rarely either as distasteful or as interesting for dramatic purposes as when a devoted mother and nurse make it and the child the daily center of a thrilling emotional scene.[45]

The need for separation was typically seen as a need of the *child*, although some did note that mothers had just as great a need to be liberated from their children. Smiley Blanton of the Vassar Nursery School explained why it was acceptable, even beneficial, for a mother to take her child to a nursery school:

> No business man, would act as a night watchman in his business all night and work at his business all day, and that is exactly what the average parent has to do with the young child. . . . The result is that the average mother is too tired; she is so tired that she has not that resiliency nor that background which will enable her to do the best for the child when she is with him. The nursery school . . . gives the parent time to get rested, to get a new perspective.[46]

Although nursery school supporters did not generally advocate nursery schools as a form of day care, many did mention, as an additional selling point, the fact that the nursery school freed the mother for part-time employment or other activities outside the home. Paul Klapper wrote that to an "intelligent" mother who had a profession before marriage, the nursery school might be "an avenue of escape from a regimen of housekeeping that is physically exhausting and mentally stupefying."[47] According to this line of thinking, the mother's needs for activity outside the home dovetailed nicely with the child's needs for companionship and play outside the home; it was healthy for both to be separated temporarily. Because the nursery school was justified primarily as a beneficial experience for children, not as a convenience for mothers, and because families paid for the service, nursery educators seem to have seen mothers' work in somewhat more positive terms than did most day nursery social workers. Discussion about combining a professional career with marriage in the 1920s sometimes mentioned nursery schools as a good way to meet both children's and mothers' needs. Liberating children from the home could also liberate women; nursery school director Harriet Johnson (who was herself a mother) wrote that it was normal for a mother, like a father, "to have interests which absorb her" and to want to pursue them. She suggested that mothers as well as children would find the hours spent at home "more precious because of the nursery school, more precious because they are less a matter of routine."[48] But Johnson's argument was rare; most nursery educators wanted mothers to focus more on their child-rearing, not less, and even most career-marriage advocates were wary of encouraging women to combine full-time work with motherhood.[49] Nursery school advocates writing in the 1920s often felt they needed to defend mothers from the charge that they were "shirking" their duty to their children by using a nursery school.[50]

The mother-child separation envisioned by nursery educators was to be brief—many nursery schools ran for only three or four hours and also required mothers to spend time observing and helping in the school. Whatever "outside interests", including work, a mother wanted to pursue had to be fitted around this schedule. Clearly a mother working a full-time job could not rely on the nursery school to care for her children, unless arrangements were made to combine nursery school with other forms of child care. But although nursery schools were not designed to provide day care for mothers who worked full-time to support their families, they did offer a much-needed respite to the mothers who used them. Nursery schools released mothers from constant responsibility for their children and, perhaps more important, widened the circle of adults interested in a individual child beyond the confines of the family. As "training schools for parents," they also offered mothers expert guidance at a time when motherhood was a source of great anxiety. Of course, this help came at the price of mothers' confidence in their ability to raise their children wisely. Ironically, as historian Kathleen Jones has argued in another context,[51] mothers may have welcomed the experts' diagnosis of their incompetence, for this opened the door to the nursery school, justified their need for respite from full-time motherhood, and also gave them a chance to talk about some of their most intimate problems.

The nursery school was ultimately successful in creating a form of child care for middle- and upper-class children that did not carry the stigma associated with day nurseries, was understood as an educational experience for the child rather than as a convenience for the mother (although in fact it could be both), and was associated with scientific research and the most modern ideas about training children. Nursery educators who felt that they had proved the worth of their experiment hoped that nursery schools might be universalized and incorporated into public schools systems, as kindergartens had been. But although the nursery school idea was widely accepted by the late 1920s, the number of nursery schools across the country remained relatively small, and resistance to the idea of dramatically expanding their numbers was significant.[52]

By showing that group care for children could be beneficial and educational, nursery schools seemed to offer the beleaguered day nursery movement a new way of thinking about its mission and place in American society. Nursery educators challenged the assumption held by many day nursery leaders that maternal care was always better, argued that mothers and children of all social classes could benefit from a good nursery experience, and suggested a path by which day care could gain greater respect and legitimacy. Given the constraints on the charitable day nurseries, however, it would be some time before they could take up the challenge.

Day Nurseries: Education or Welfare?

Day nursery leaders welcomed the nursery school, for it seemed to confer value and legitimacy on the idea of providing group care for children. Indeed, the assumptions behind the nursery school movement had the power to transform understandings of day care. To nursery educators, a mother's temporary absence was not an unfortunate necessity but a positive step promoting her child's independence; care for children went beyond providing for their health and keeping them busy to creating a beneficial, educational experience. Although most nursery schools aimed their curricula at middle-class or elite families, the idea behind the nursery school—that children needed to be trained in good habits at a young age in order to succeed later in life—was appealing to those who worked with poorer children as well. In fact, the nursery school's emphasis on "habit training" and parent education meshed quite nicely with the educational mission of the day nursery. If the children of the affluent needed nursery school training, some day nursery leaders reasoned, how much more so did the poorer children who made up the day nursery's population? As the idea of the nursery school became more popular, day nursery leaders sought to ally themselves with the nursery school movement by creating nursery schools within or alongside their day nurseries. In the long run, however, most of these nursery schools did not succeed, for day nurseries did not have the resources of tuition-supported private nursery schools, and many charitable agencies saw nursery education as a luxury that poor children could do without.

In the late 1920s, the National Federation of Day Nurseries (NFDN) encouraged its members to expand their work by creating nursery schools in conjunction with, or instead of, day nurseries. In the pages of the NFDN's newsletter, nursery schools were discussed as an exciting and fashionable new trend. For instance, a 1927 article explained that virtually every mother would find the nursery school appealing:

> Any mother, who for one reason or another must delegate most of her child's hours to the supervision of nurses, governesses or any one other than herself, will find a nursery school offering the most satisfactory solution of her problem. . . . For a mother who lives in a section of the city that makes the city streets her child's daily playground . . . again the nursery school is ideal. . . . Mothers who work from either necessity or choice, those whose daily household routine is absorbing, those who are nervous or impatient or who find themselves unable to struggle with the ceaseless energy of the toddler, will ultimately find the nursery school a haven of peace.[53]

Clearly the restrictive terms in which day nursery advocates had learned to talk about day care did not apply to the nursery school. One article announced breathlessly, "The child of properly enlightened parents has had a place in the nursery school reserved for him even before his birth. . . . Nursery schools are being established all over the country

... these do not resemble the old-fashioned day nurseries in which children of working mothers received only physical care."[54] A month later, another article announced, "All over the country, the nursery schools continue to record long waiting lists. Parents, of course, cannot praise them enough."[55]

The nursery school was the center of attention at the NFDN's national conference in 1929. The president of the organization proclaimed her sympathy "with the educated, wide-awake mother who longs for something more than a humdrum life." She continued, "Yes, I believe absolutely in the girl who desires to perfect herself in more ways than one and who feels the need of outside interests and companionships and wants her children to have contacts and advantages with other children."[56] She declared, "Already the so-called privileged classes are clamoring for their children to have the daily opportunities, contacts, education and supervision of the nursery school," and she urged members to visit the model nursery school that was conducted at the conference in order to encourage them to establish nursery schools in their day nurseries.[57] Delegates watched children at the model nursery school as they dressed themselves, set up cots for napping, and "moved freely, choosing their own work or play from the cabinets, singing and chatting as they busily moved about, putting the materials back when they were through." Staff were on hand to answer questions about converting day nurseries into nursery schools and to explain the many charts and records kept on each child: "An Aims and Purposes Chart, a Montessori Materials Chart, a Health Care, Sleep Chart, and Bowel Record Chart were posted on the Bulletin Board."[58] Delegates to the conference also heard from prominent nursery educators like Smiley Blanton, Lois Meek, and Patty Hill of Teachers College, who urged the day nursery women to "introduce more education into our philanthropy." Finally, a representative of the New York Welfare Council concluded that day nurseries were "ceasing to be charitable institutions and they are becoming educational institutions."[59]

Some day nurseries did in fact transform themselves completely into nursery schools. One of the most influential nursery educators in the country, Abigail Eliot, began her career in this way. In 1921, the Women's Education Association in Boston sent Eliot to observe a pioneering nursery school in England, with the understanding that on her return, she would change the organization's own day nursery into a nursery school. She remembered walking into the day nursery on her return, and finding it, like others she had visited in Boston, "spotlessly clean but oh! so dull and uninteresting." She saw her main task as transforming the environment into one that would stimulate the children's interest: rather than "rows of white-faced listless children sitting, doing nothing," she wanted children to be "active ... alive ... choosing ... gay, busy, happy."[60] With the full support of her funders, she changed the physical setup, stopped serving babies, and shortened the hours slightly. She was very successful at promoting parent involvement because of the unusually positive attitude she took toward parents, encouraging her teachers to feel "that every mother loves her child and truly wants to do her best for him." Ruggles Street, serving a poor neighborhood in the Roxbury section of Boston, soon became a nationally prominent nursery school and developed into a training center for nursery teachers.[61]

But other day nurseries that adopted the nursery school plan did not find it so easy to transform themselves, for they were pulled back and forth between their educational and their charitable missions. Several day nurseries in Philadelphia set up a nursery school program as part of their nursery in the 1920s.[62] Most of these day nursery–nursery schools, however, did not have a long life, for day nursery boards found it difficult to pay a specially trained nursery school teacher who expected to work only limited hours and who did not expect to take on other duties within the nursery (especially the more menial ones typically performed by the matron). Locating a nursery school within a day nursery caused other problems as well: children attended irregularly (as they did in the day nursery as a whole), and mothers working at outside jobs had little time for the participation and observation that was so important in the private nursery schools.

Neighborhood Centre: A Nursery School for the Working Class?

One of the earliest—and longest-lived—day nursery–nursery schools in Philadelphia was at Neighborhood Centre, the city's Jewish settlement house. Looking at its history illuminates the tensions surrounding different ideas about taking on "a mother's job." Neighborhood Centre had initially been established by Jewish women of German heritage for the purpose of Americanizing new Jewish immigrants from Eastern Europe. In addition to offering classes in English and citizenship, clubs and playgrounds, the settlement established a day nursery in 1885 to serve poor children whose immigrant parents worked in nearby sweatshops, laundries, factories, and small stores. The day nursery at Neighborhood Centre was one of the larger and more professionally run day nurseries in the city; it was among the first to integrate the services of social workers, psychologists, nutritionists, and other professionals into the work of the nursery. So it is not surprising that when nursery schools became a frequent topic of conversation in child welfare circles, Neighborhood Centre would again become a pioneer in expanding the functions of the day nursery.

When the nursery school was first established in 1924, it seemed attractive to both settlement workers and local families. Neighborhood Centre staff were clearly excited to be part of an educational experiment linked to the new science of child development, and one which carried more status than the work of the day nursery. The nursery school was also embraced by local families whose class position was gradually shifting. As the immigrant Jews who were Neighborhood Centre's main clientele achieved a degree of social mobility, they seem to have welcomed the chance to define their need for child care on educational rather than economic grounds. The families who sent their children to Neighborhood Centre were working-class people aspiring to middle-class status; they experienced both economic stress and concerns about their children's healthy development. But the existence of the nursery school enabled them to find help with child care by highlighting their children's educational needs rather than the precariousness of their economic stability. Many mothers, seeking the status that went along with middle-class American motherhood, seem to have preferred to claim that they were unable to properly manage their children than to admit that they needed to work, for embracing the identity of an incompetent mother was more appealling than claiming poverty. Although the nursery school's approach toward taking on "a mother's job" appealed to both staff and parents, however, the agency that funded the program ultimately proved unwilling to bridge the gap between education and welfare.

When the Neighborhood Centre Nursery School first opened, the agency's staff were enthusiastic. The head worker of the settlement house emphasized the contribution that the school would make to scientific inquiry into early childhood development. In a monthly report in 1925, she wrote,

> The Nursery School continues daily to delight us as we note the response of the children to scientific care. It has been the subject of interesting articles in "Progressive Education" and in the "Day Nursery Bulletin." . . . Much attention is being focused on the Nursery School in educational circles—and if we are to do our share in offering correct, full and continuous observations on the work, to be pooled with similar observations now being made in other places, we must give the Nursery School every opportunity to develop.[63]

While educators and scientists ignored day nurseries except to criticize them, nursery schools were an exciting new trend in a growing field. A press release announcing the opening of the nursery school at Neighborhood Centre explained that one of the purposes of the school was "a scientific investigation of the pre-school child, his capabilities, his development and his needs," requiring careful observations of the children's actions and vocabularies, as well as regular testing by a staff psychologist.[64]

The nursery school staff not only expected to contribute to the new science of child development, but they also placed great faith in new scientific tools for measuring, diagnosing, and treating children's problems. Every child who attended the school went through a battery of intelligence tests, and each was labeled according to his or her "mental age" depending on the numerical score they received on the test. Children whose parents or siblings were defined as "feebleminded" were watched especially carefully, and a social worker's decision about how much could be expected of a particular parent or child was often based on the outcome of these tests. Psychological testing was another important part of the nursery school's program; the school had close ties to the psychiatric department of the Community Health Center, a medical clinic that was itself an outgrowth of Neighborhood Centre. Every child who attended the school was tested by staff psychologists, while particularly difficult children and their parents were referred to the psychiatric clinic for counseling. The advice they received there would almost always coincide with the suggestions given by the nursery school teacher, thus giving her advice the weight of male medical opinion.

Like other nursery schools, the Neighborhood Centre school sought to train children in good habits and to teach parents how to manage their children at home. For both of these goals, creating the proper environment in the nursery school was important. The executive director reported, "The room has been newly decorated and everything in the furnishings and accessories suggests purposeful activity and the formation of good habits."[65] During the first meeting of the Mothers' Child Study Group, the social worker reported, "We visited the Nursery School room and showed the mothers the gay curtains and other means which had been used to improve and brighten the children's environment, encouraging them to come to us for suggestions if they too wished to improve their home environment in small ways, so that the children would not feel the contrast too much."[66] The annual report for 1927 proudly announced that the nursery school children "for at least eight hours in the day are living in a child's world which is directed through a simple educational program to create the most desirable physical, mental and social development."[67] But the training received at the nursery school would not have been sufficient without training mothers to continue the work at home. Thelma Day, the nursery school teacher, wrote in 1928, "When we can be assured that our work has carried over into the homes of our children so that the child receives the same type of care while he is at home as he has received while he is with us, our work will have real value."[68]

Transforming mothers' child-rearing methods was thus as important a part of the nursery school's work as instilling good habits and independence in the children who attended the school. Descriptions of nursery school "success stories" suggest the central role that parent education played in the mission of the nursery school. For instance, in a case of two children who had many behavior problems,

> work in the Nursery and in the home . . . brought the mother to a better understanding of her children. . . . It is very touching indeed to hear the appreciation of both the mother and father and to see their willingness to carry out the Nursery School program into the home. Literature on child training has been furnished them by the Nursery School teacher. The mother is constantly coming here for advice and suggestions. The father, while out of work for a half a day not long ago, spent that time observing in the Nursery School.[69]

It was not only the transformation of the child that the social worker celebrated, but the change that had taken place in the parents, especially their willingness to follow expert advice in training their children.

Knowledge of the educational mission of the nursery school quickly spread among neighborhood families, altering the grounds on which they could legitimately ask for help with their children—and changing the script they used with day nursery social workers. Instead of presenting themselves as forced by poverty to go out to work, mothers talked about the more intangible needs of their children. Day care was now not only for the children of poor working mothers, but for children who misbehaved, had eating problems, lacked playmates or adequate play space, or needed more attention than parents could provide. Clearly, this shift in understanding the purpose of day care could widen the range of people who saw themselves as potential clients of a day care agency.[70] Families that social workers would consider "normal" (i.e., with two living parents, an employed father and an unemployed mother) could now get help with their children.

Some women turned to the Neighborhood Centre Nursery School for the same reasons that their more affluent counterparts turned to private nursery schools: they felt that they needed help carrying out the complex duties of modern motherhood and believed that the nursery school would be good for them and their children. For instance, Ethel Roszcuk became terribly jealous when her baby brother was born in 1926, and her mother, a single woman who supported herself sewing coats, became concerned. The Family Society, which helped Ethel's mother, wrote to Neighborhood Centre, "We thought it would be a good idea if Ethel could be admitted to the nursery school for a time, at least until she has gotten over to some extent being so tied up with her mother." It is hard to imagine a social worker, before the advent of the nursery school, suggesting that it would be *good* for a two-year-old child to be separated from her mother, unless the mother was decidedly immoral.[71] In a similar case, Faye Levinstein, who was worried about her four-year-old daughter Linda's eating habits and was at the same time "much occupied" with the care of a new baby, told a visitor from Neighborhood Centre that "we could do her as well as child a great deal of good if we could take her into our nursery school." She explained that Linda almost "drove her crazy" during her pregnancy; the child was so disobedient that Mrs. Levinstein would lose patience and whip her, leaving both mother and child "in a state of exhaustion." Now, she explained, she was trying hard to train the baby to "avoid mistakes she made with Linda." The family doctor also thought the nursery might help; remembering Linda as the child who always upset things when she came to his office, he said, "If a nursery could take her for a week or two and 'give her a piece of your mind,' it would do both the mother and child a great deal of good."[72]

The anxiety of "modern" motherhood also brought Anna Kelman to the nursery school, hoping for help with three-year-old Herbie's temper tantrums and disobedience. Herbie obeyed his aunt because she "has him scared out of his wits," but Anna sought a more scientific solution. In the words of the social worker who kept Herbie's records, his mother "has tried everything with Herbie, consulted physicians at Babies Hospital, she has read books, she has spoken to others about their children, trying to find some points of similarity so that perhaps she might learn what others did with their children. . . . Told us she tried to find 'psychological reasons' for Herbie's behavior." Unable to find answers either from doctors or from other mothers, "Mrs. Kelman said that she was on the verge of a collapse from worry because of her ineffectual treatment and because of strained relations between herself and husband. Mr. Kelman cannot understand why Herbie should be behaving as he does and feels that Mrs. Kelman is somehow to blame." Caught between her inability to control her son and her husband's insistence that she do so, Mrs. Kelman turned to the nursery school.[73]

Mothers such as these now had a place to go when they needed help with the work of mothering. But accepting the help of the nursery school often meant accepting one's own inadequacy as a mother and agreeing to change. Some mothers were perplexed by the new demands placed on them. Lena Kleinfelt, a substitute teacher who started bringing her daughter to the nursery school in 1928, worried about the child's emotional and psychological development. She confessed to the Neighborhood Centre social worker that the child "is a great problem to her. W has no control over her and consequently child is accustomed to getting her own way in everything. . . . W is anxious for child to receive a psychological in order to ascertain her IQ." Kleinfelt, who was the only Neighborhood Centre mother with a professional job during these years in the case records sampled, was more aware of intellectual trends in psychology and child-rearing that most nursery mothers. Social worker Helen Landis noted that Kleinfelt was "very proud of the fact that she has read many books on child training, however, it seems evident that she does not apply this reading in the case of her own child." Concerned with her daughter's thumb-sucking and worried that the child was developing an "inferiority complex," she took Pearl to the child guidance clinic. The social worker there recorded that she was "very anxious to know child's IQ, also to find out whether her methods of training child are correct." Lena Kleinfelt was eager to be a modern mother, using the tools of science to diagnose and correct her child's behavioral problems.

The psychiatrist at the child guidance clinic, however, decided that the problem was not with Pearl, but with her mother. Dr. Pearson reported that in their first appointment, Kleinfelt said that she did not understand "just what kind of work the clinic did. Was there anything wrong in the way she handled Pearl. She thought the clinic could do something with Pearl and apparently the object was to treat her instead." The next time Kleinfelt saw social worker Helen Landis, she called out, "say[,] what are you folks trying to do to me. You sent me up for a psycho-analysis and I never expected it." She had disliked Dr. Pearson at first, but she now appreciated what he was trying to do. "I never thought when I sent Pearl to the clinic that it would have anything to do with me, but he seemed to make me feel that I had many problems." Although she tried to get some direct suggestions regarding her daughter's behavior, "he did not seem to want to talk about her but only about myself."[74]

Not every mother was willing to transform her mothering style in exchange for child care and professional advice. In some cases, nursery school staff found that training the mother was more difficult than training the child. Beatrice Cook, who was described as being "disturbed over her inability to handle" her son Mitchell, ran into conflict with the nursery school staff when she came to observe one day. Against the wishes of the teacher, she sat down and started to feed Mitchell his lunch, spoonful by spoonful, "commenting all the time how awful the food was and said she could not blame the child for not eating it." When the angry teacher, confronting her, asked what her reasons were for bringing the child to nursery school, she responded, "I would never have brought him had I been able to manage him myself."[75] The idea that mothers had a right to some relief from caring for their children could be empowering, and mothers sometimes turned social workers' words to their own purposes. Mrs. Meltz, whose two sons attended the nursery school, came into frequent conflict with the Neighborhood Centre social worker, who was frustrated with Meltz's lack of interest in improving her child-rearing methods. One day, the exasperated social worker asked Meltz "what she thought was being accomplished by keeping Isaac in school. 'I get a little rest,' she said promptly, 'you yourself say that is important.' Triumphantly, she said that."[76] For these mothers, whether or not they decided to cooperate with the teachers, the nursery school provided a welcome respite from, and help with, children they felt were beyond their control.

Even when women fully accepted the idea that they needed expert guidance, other family members did not always share the view of professionals that mothers had the right to have help with the complex task of child-rearing. It was a mother's job to raise her children without relying on outside help of any kind. For instance, when Anna Kelman brought her Herbie to the nursery school, she faced opposition from her husband, who said "that it was Mrs. Kelman's duty to raise Herbie." Mr. Kelman blamed his wife for the child's misbehavior and thought she should not rely on others to help her "fix" it. Anna, who feared that the boy's problems were putting a dangerous strain on her marriage, continued to send Herbie to the nursery school, and her husband eventually became reconciled to the plan, although he always refused to talk with the social worker himself.[77]

Eva Weiss struggled with similar opposition as she tried to negotiate conflicting definitions of a mother's responsibility—even years after the nursery school had become a familiar part of the neighborhood landscape. When she first came to apply for care for her two-year-old son Joseph in 1941, Weiss explained that she wanted him to attend the nursery school for both economic and educational reasons: she wanted to work to supplement her husband's salary, and at the same time wanted to provide companionship for Joseph and enable him to learn "how to eat." Her image of the nursery school as a place where children "have companionship of other children, and a place to play away from traffic," appealed to her, but the social worker noted that she seemed to fear the service as much as she wanted it. When asked how her husband felt about enrolling Joseph in the nursery school, "she told us that he felt that she should be able to take care of him herself. That she might use such a service, only if she went out to work, but not to be rid of him." She seemed to accept this idea that day care was acceptable for working mothers, but not for anyone else, and once she gave up finding a job, she was consequently plagued with guilt at the idea (constantly reinforced by her in-laws) that she was trying to get rid of her son. The social worker noted, "Her guilt seemed so overpowering about the fourth week Joseph had been in school, we stopped her, and asked . . . whether NS was serving the purpose she wanted it to, and whether she felt that Joseph was getting something out of the experience. She burst into tears, and sobbed out that she was a bad mother." When she got control of herself, she explained that her in-laws had been "expressing their disapproval in strong language" and that she herself was confused about what she was doing. The social worker made a case for the educational value of the nursery school, trying to convince Mrs. Weiss that part of a modern mother's responsibility was to provide a nursery school experience for her child: "We suggested that she think about it, in terms of education rather than of 'putting him away.' Could she duplicate the Nursery School environment in her own home? . . . She seemed to need help in recognizing the school as such, and not as a place to hide children by the day." But the conflict continued, and after much vacillation she finally decided to withdraw Joseph. She explained that she knew "she should be grateful for the opportunity of this service which is generally available only to the very wealthy," but that she realized the only time she had not felt guilty about it was during a brief period when she was employed. "The rest of the time she has been quite miserable and unhappy because she felt that everyone was critical of her."

Although Eva Weiss's problems clearly originated in a conflict between her family's ideas about total maternal responsibility and a more "modern" assumption that nursery schools were good for children, the social worker summarized the case by blaming her. "Although Joseph was making progress in the Day Nursery and benefitting from the program," she wrote, "his progress was blocked by his mother's conflict about his separation from her and her need to have him dependent on her."[78] Eva Weiss faced a no-win situation: while her family saw her as neglectful, the social worker saw her as smothering. No matter what she did, she could be condemned as a bad mother. In the end, however, her family's condemnation mattered more to her than the diagnosis of nursery school social workers.

By combining education with welfare, the nursery school allowed the families who used it to strengthen their identity as middle-class Americans. Many of these second-generation immigrant families were on the road toward upward mobility, owning small stores or businesses and sending their children to high school and even college, but they still often required a mother's labor (either in the family business or as an additional wage earner) to carry them through. The transition in class status that many of these families were hoping to make is reflected in the words of one child, who was questioned about his plans for the future during a psychological exam in 1937. First he told the examiner that "of course he was going to be a doctor." When she "suggested that this was a difficult profession to enter, he casually stated, 'Well, maybe I'll be a hosiery worker. Just like my father.'"[79] The nursery school at once gave families like this boy's a "respectable" way to justify seeking day care so that mothers could work, and at the same time offered them the comfort of knowing that their children were receiving the benefits of nursery school training, which was usually only available to more affluent families.

Indeed, calling on the help of psychologists and trained nursery school teachers may have become a symbol of middle-class American motherhood for these women, like relying on pediatricians for advice about the physical care of their children rather than turning to their own mothers for advice. One Jewish woman who raised her children in Philadelphia during the 1930s remembered, "Just because your mother and your grandmother did it, I didn't think that was the best thing. I was a modern mother and the modern way was to go to a specialist." Another recalled her conflict with her mother about when she would feed her baby. As "a perfect mother," she remembered, she followed the advice of the time and would only feed the baby on a strict schedule: "if the doctor said every four hours, every four hours." While she watched the clock and followed the doctor's instructions, her mother banged on the door and called her a murderer, begging her to feed the child. (Her pleas were ineffective, however, as her daughter simply locked the door.) For these women, expert medical advice on mothering was absolutely essential, part of their definition as American, modern mothers.[80] Ideas about how to discipline children had changed just as much as ideas about how to feed them, and modern mothers needed scientific expertise from professionals, not old-fashioned advice. Although the nursery school teacher did not have the cultural authority of the medical doctor, the psychological and behavioral advice she offered might play a similar role, especially if it were seconded by a psychiatrist. In this way, the nursery school could become an emblem of modern, progressive, American mothering, unlike the day nursery with its taint of charity and poverty.

Some mothers self-consciously distinguished themselves from others who did not seek out professional advice. Shirley Rivers, a Jewish woman whose family business was in an Italian, Irish, and African-American neighborhood in Philadelphia, never talked to her neighbors about child-rearing or child health issues. Another explained that she did not talk with her Catholic neighbors about doctors because "maybe I thought they didn't know as much." Similarly, Selma Cohen explained why she did not discuss her child with her next-door neighbor: "[She] was not like I was. I mean, she didn't believe. She took her children to a doctor occasionally when they were sick. . . . She didn't do the reading that I did. She didn't teach her children like I did."[81] Just as some mothers distinguished themselves from their lower-status neighbors by their approach to health care for their children, so others used the nursery school to draw a line. For instance, one mother explained that her child needed the freedom to run around in the nursery school, for he could not play in his neighborhood: "He is not allowed out because they live in a very poor neighborhood where the children are left on the street unkempt and ill while parents are working or in taprooms."[82] So seeking professional help with the work of mothering, although it involved an admission of failure, may have also been a sign of status. Indeed, women seem to have felt less shame about explaining their failures with their children than about explaining why they needed to go out to work.

By the time the mission of nursery school training and of parent education in general had become well-known in the late 1930s, it was rare to find a family who defined their need for day care solely on financial grounds, even if financial reasons were in fact paramount. For example, Clara Varshay applied to place her daughter in the nursery school primarily because she was "extremely anxious to seek employment." Although her motives for making day care arrangements for her daughter were financial, when asked specifically why she wanted nursery care for Sylvia, she referred to the inadequate play space available to the child in their home.[83] Nearly every request for day care came to include some special need for the nursery school, whether because of behavior problems, inadequate play space, or the need for group association. An analysis done by Neighborhood Centre staff in 1932 of forty-six families who applied to the nursery school shows that the most common reasons for applying were the need for "habit training" (including social, emotional, eating, and physical habits) and the need for the companionship of other children. But in most of these cases, these psychological reasons were accompanied by financial pressures making it necessary for the mother either to help her husband in his business, or to work at an outside job.

Both mothers and staff seem to have preferred the nursery school's approach to taking on a mother's job to the more restrictive and less "modern" approach of the day nursery. Ultimately, however, the charitable agency that funded the settlement house was not willing to devote community resources to taking on the job of at-home mothers. The tension between the educational and the welfare purposes of the nursery school had become more prominent as the families who used Neighborhood Centre became more prosperous. As time went on, it became even more difficult to reconcile the school's dual mission of education and welfare. In 1938, the Day Nursery Committee tried to clarify the educative as opposed to the social work mission of the nursery school. The committee discussed thorny issues such as setting a maximum family income for admitting children on an economic basis and ways of avoiding casework for familes who applied to the nursery school for purely educational reasons.[84] A year later, a report focused on the difference between the Neighborhood Centre school and private nursery schools, and concluded that the difference lay largely in its clientele: unlike other schools, Neighborhood Centre "offered its services to families in the community who need it and primarily [to] those who are unable to pay the fees in other nursery schools." The staff and board members clearly believed in the educative value of the nursery school and were committed to making the school available to those who wanted it; on the other hand, they could not ignore that the settlement house was a social welfare agency. In 1941, they were forced to limit access to the nursery school when a study done by the Jewish Welfare Society concluded that community funds should not be spent serving families who used the nursery school only for its educational value. That year's annual report stated bluntly, "The nursery does not accept children primarily on an educational basis."[85]

Later that year, the Federation of Jewish Agencies, which funded Neighborhood Centre, decided to eliminate the nursery school entirely and replace it with a day nursery program to serve the wartime needs of local families. In making this decision, they referred to another outside study that had concluded that the program "had no right to function as a purely education unit." Like Eva Weiss's relatives, Federation officials had decided to support day care for working mothers, but not for anyone else. Nursery school parents did not agree; they protested the closing and the thinking behind it. They formed a Committee to Save the Nursery School, argued with representatives of the funding agency that nursery school service was not a charity and should be available to everyone in the community, and discussed running a nursery school themselves on a cooperative basis. At a meeting held by these parents, "The general feeling of the group was unanimous in preferring a N.S. to a Day Nursery if it was possible to have a preference."[86] The parents' efforts to save the nursery school, however, were not successful, and Neighborhood Centre returned to providing day care only to the children of working mothers. A 1942 guide to prioritizing needs for admittance to the day nursery put family needs before the emotional needs of the child, and put a family's economic needs before other types of needs.[87]

The resolution of Neighborhood Centre Nursery School's dilemma in favor of custodial day care suggests the continuing force behind defining day care for poor children as a welfare measure, and separating that care from the educationally oriented programs available to children of other classes. The distinction between day care and education remained significant as a marker of class: while affluent children attended nursery school for their own benefit, poorer children attended day nurseries so that their mothers could work. Nursery education would remain a luxury available only to those who could afford it.

But while the emergence of the nursery school did not immediately benefit the charitable day nurseries, in the long run the idea that group care could be educational and desirable for children would alter attitudes toward day care, changing the grounds on which women could seek help with their children and widening the circle of women who would consider using it. The nursery schools shifted the terms of the debate about taking on a mother's job by redrawing the boundaries separating child care from education and private from public responsibility for children. Like the day nurseries, they could only justify helping women with their children by arguing that mothers were inadequate to the task of child-rearing and needed expert guidance. By claiming that even middle-class mothers needed help in raising their children, and by creating a group of professionals to provide that help, the nursery school movement simultaneously increased women's anxieties about their ability to mother their children, offered them respite from full-time motherhood, and lay the groundwork for public support of educational programs for young children in the future.

II

TRANSFORMING DAY CARE, 1930–1960

5

Day Care and Depression

From the 1890s through the 1920s, certain fundamental assumptions shaped the provision of day care: that a mother's employment was an evil to be avoided whenever possible, that day care was a second-class welfare measure for poor women and not a proper province of the state, and that day care's purpose was essentially custodial rather than educational. After 1930, changes in both women's wage work and social welfare began to challenge these assumptions, gradually altering the meaning of day care.

Most significantly, as married women's employment became more widespread, the assumption that day care was a welfare service for desperately poor single mothers gave way to a broader conception of day care as a legitimate need, even a right, of mothers who worked in order to improve their children's lives. As more middle-class mothers entered or returned to the paid labor force, the class-based distinction between educational and custodial day care grew fuzzy, and the idea that day care programs should only serve dysfunctional poor families became harder to sustain. As Americans' ideas about the role of government expanded, government involvement in day care became more legitimate. Slowly, a new definition of day care emerged: a need of normal families, an educational experience for children, and a legitimate responsibility of the state.

This transformation in the meaning and practice of day care was just beginning to take shape during the second half of the period of this study, and would not have its full impact until after 1960. Yet its seeds were planted in the responses of individuals, families, day care agencies, and local and federal government to the national crises of the Great Depression, World War II, and the Cold War. Each of these crises forced revisions in ideas about women's labor and family responsibility, calling into question the idea that a mother's job was always in the home. This chapter looks at the responses of all these various actors to the economic crisis of the depression, while the following chapters examine the fate of day care during the transformations of the 1940s and 1950s.

During the 1930s, widespread male unemployment forced a fundamental reconsideration of the nature and purposes of day care. In previous chapters, we have seen how strongly the idea that a father's wages should support a family shaped debates about women's work and welfare policy. During the depression, however, those ideas were challenged by men's inability to provide for their families. Many women became breadwinners, supporting their families when their husbands could not and unleashing deep anxiety about overturning gender roles within the family. The meaning of these experiences, of course, varied according to class and race: whites who had been suddenly precipitated into poverty seemed to experience more of an identity crisis than African-Americans who had been accustomed to living with unemployment. The economic crisis not only forced families to send mothers into the workplace, but it also prompted charitable day nurseries and the federal government to revise their attitudes toward day care, albeit temporarily. Private day nurseries expanded their scope, throwing aside earlier understandings of their mission. The federal government, displaying a new willingness to take on a mother's job and bringing to a much wider audience the idea that group care for children could be desirable, sponsored public nursery schools throughout the country. Although no one intended these changes to become permanent, the experiences of the 1930s shook many of the assumptions that lay behind the provision of day care, setting the stage for further changes in the 1940s and 1950s.

Switching Places? Unemployed Fathers and Working Mothers

The women who ran day nurseries, like most other Americans, assumed that under normal circumstances a husband's wages would support his family; thus only women who had lost access to a man's wages would need to work. Like other maternalist reformers, day nursery managers sought to support the women and children who fell through the cracks of the family wage system, not to question or challenge that system. And they assumed that the number of families who would fall through those cracks would be small, especially after reforms like mothers' pensions, workman's compensation, and strict laws punishing nonsupporting husbands had been put in place.[1] During the depression, however, the "abnormal" family that had to send a wife out to work became more common, forcing day nursery workers to revise their expectations. In 1933, 11.5% of native-born whites, 16.2% of African-Americans, and 19.1% of foreign-born whites in Philadelphia were unemployed; women who could find work often became the primary support of their families.[2] In response to this new situation, Philadelphia's day nurseries opened their doors to a wide range of families, taking in children with unemployed fathers, children whose parents both spent their days looking for work, and children who simply needed nutritious food and a cheerful environment away from apartments crowded with worried adults. Neither day nursery workers nor the families they served, however, were completely comfortable with the idea of mothers replacing fathers as breadwinners, and just as wage-earning mothers looked forward to the day when their husbands would again support them, day nurseries quickly sought to return to their earlier, narrower, sense of purpose.

In the early years of the depression, day nursery workers observed that women seemed to have an easier time finding work—low-paid and irregular though it was—than men. Their observations coincide with those of recent historians, who argue that the gender segregation of the labor market, which had long depressed women's wages and restricted their work options, kept women employed during this time of economic crisis. Because women were concentrated in areas of the economy (such as light industry, domestic and service work) that rebounded relatively quickly from the depression, and because many employers decided to cut costs by replacing male with female workers, women often found it possible to get work when their husbands could not.[3] In the Kensington mill district of the city, the Baldwin Day Nursery noted, "There has been more work for the women than for the men. This has never happened before."[4] Willa May Gaskill of the House of Industry noted the progression by which the Italian women in the settlement's neighborhood became breadwinners for their families:

> The first step is the influx of applications from families where both parents must take jobs—in lines of work where employment is so irregular that only by both working when there *is* work can they make both ends meet. . . . Then we find that only the mother has a job, prices have been lowered in the shop until the men are forced out and only women employed.[5]

The St. Nicholas Day Nursery also reported that African-American women were replacing men as breadwinners, since domestic work was easier to come by than work for men. In 1931, Neville Barry reported, "Since it is so difficult for men to get work of any kind, mothers who have never had to leave home before have been forced to find employment."[6] This pattern was not confined to day nursery families, nor to African-Americans, but was part of an overall trend: a government study of workers on relief in seventy-nine cities found that in all but one, men were out of work longer than women.[7] Despite public hostility toward women's work, the percentage of women gainfully employed during the decade inched up slightly, and a significant proportion of new workers during the 1930s were women. Statistics show that, compared to previous decades, wage-earning women were increasingly married women with children.[8]

Such shifts in gender roles represented a nightmare for many Americans in the 1930s. A writer in *Harper's* magazine in 1933 declared that the prospect of husbands becoming dependent and wives becoming providers was a problem "vastly more terrifying than the economic wolves howling at the apartment door."[9] Prolonged unemployment shook the foundation of many men's identity as breadwinner and family provider. After interviewing many unemployed families, one contemporary investigator concluded, "In his own estimation, [the unemployed father] was failing to fulfill the central duty of his life—the very touchstone of his manhood—the role of family provider. . . . Every purchase of the family—the radio, his wife's new hat, the children's skates, the meal set before him—all were symbols of their dependence on him. Unemployment changed all that."[10] When unemployment threatened to rob men of their dignity as breadwinners, women could become heroines by playing the role of the self-sacrificing mother whose resourceful homemaking skills and emotional strength helped their families weather the economic crisis. In John Steinbeck's *The Grapes of Wrath*, for instance, Ma Joad sustains her family through the sheer force of her love; the strength of this powerful character lies in her determination to keep the family together, not in her willingness to take on "a man's work."[11]

Women who tried to improve their families' material conditions by entering the paid labor force themselves, however, were not seen in such positive terms.[12] Literary scholar Laura Hapke argues that most of the fiction of the 1930s embraced the "widespread conviction that women were intruders in the workplace," either ignoring breadwinning women or downplaying the importance of work in their lives and those of their families. The same was true of visual representation. Dorothea Lange's famous photograph of migrant Florence Thompson with her three children captured the desperation of a farmworker who was the sole support of six people. At the time the picture was taken, with no work available in the migrant camp, she had sold her possessions for food and did not know where to turn next. Yet Lange's photograph, which came to be one of the most celebrated images of the depression, was almost never identified as a picture of an anxious unemployed breadwinner. Instead it was interpreted as a depression-era version of the Madonna-with-child image and a vivid reminder of the helplessness of mothers and children amid the social upheaval of the economic crisis. The dominant cultural impulse, Hapke argues, "was to remove woman from the labor landscape and sanctify her as a maternal figure." The exception to this impulse is the work of African-American writers like Langston Hughes and Richard Wright, who portrayed women's work and wages as the bedrock of their families—whether they depicted mothers with fondness or with rage. But for most writers and observers, the story of the depression was primarily about male unemployment, male frustration and despair, with woman cast as a "nurturer rather than productive worker, a consoler rather than a producer, a helpmeet rather than an independent entity."[13]

These attitudes about women's proper place translated into resentment and hostility toward women who did become breadwinners. As work became difficult to come by, the popular hostility toward married women's employment that was always in the air became more focused and vigorous. Married women workers were now accused not only of neglecting their children and their homes, but of taking jobs away from male providers. PADN member Ruth Weaver wrote, "The man on the streets loudly condemns working women, especially married women, for taking jobs from men and food from babes. The minister from his pulpit exhorts the mothers of his flocks to confine their activities to the supervision of their homes and instruction of their children. . . . Vaudeville artists, cartoonists and radio announcers ridicule the husband of the working wife."[14] Since jobs were scarce, many felt they should be distributed among those who had a real need for them. Women were by definition not providers, and therefore did not need jobs; they were commonly portrayed as working for "pin money" and luxuries. An article in the liberal magazine *Forum* called "Pin-Money Slaves," for instance, deplored married women who forsook family responsiblities for a little extra cash.[15]

The same idea was behind popular campaigns to ban married women from public employment at local, state, and federal levels. Public opinion on this issue was unusually strong: when 82% of respondents answered "no" to a 1936 poll asking if wives should work when their husbands had jobs, George Gallup observed that he had "discovered an issue on which voters are about as solidly united as on any subject imaginable—including sin and hay fever."[16] Both public and private employers restricted hiring married women: Texas, for example, instituted a means test for women in state transportation jobs, dismissing women whose husbands earned more than $50 a month.[17] In Philadelphia, Dora Lipman was only kept on at the cigar factory where she had been working when a day nursery social worker persuaded the foreman there that she really deserved the job. The foreman "was opposed to taking on a married woman, . . . but we asked him to give her a chance since she was so much in need of the money."[18] In another Neighborhood Centre case, Eva Kramer, who had gotten her husband a job at the dress manufacturing place where she worked, hid her marital status from her workmates.

> W uses her maiden name at factory. No one knows that she is married to M but she told the people she works for that he is a man living in her neighborhood. . . . She feels that to keep her maiden name and go along as unmarried has been a help to her because most employers do not like married women. Strange as it may seem, Mr. and Mrs. K seldom come from work together, but whenever it has been necessary for them to call for both chn [children] we have found that one of them always comes before the other one.[19]

As these cases suggest, hostility toward married women who did not absolutely "have to work" made life difficult for women who did become breadwinners. Lorena Hicock lamented that businessmen "won't believe there are any women who are absolutely self-supporting," yet more than a third of all American working women were the sole support of their families, and four million homemakers doubled as wage-earners during this period.[20]

The male breadwinner paradigm was particularly important to white men and women who were striving for (or clinging to) middle-class status, like many of the immigrant clients of Neighborhood Centre. A 1931 report explained that despite wretchedness and squalor, the neighborhood surrounding the settlement house was marked by the hope of upward mobility: "The parents may be sweat-shop workers, factory laborers or peddlers, but their children are destined for greater things—for the law, for medicine, for banking or teaching."[21] Women applying for day care at Neighborhood Centre in the 1930s often expressed hopes that their sojourn in the work force would be temporary. For instance, after explaining all the steps she took to hide her marriage in order to keep her job, Eva Kramer told the Neighborhood Centre social worker that "it will be a happy day for the family" when she would no longer have to work in order "to keep things going."[22]

Men in these families especially suffered from their loss of status as the family's chief breadwinner and seemed to experience their failure as breadwinners as a challenge to their very identity. For instance, Leo Weiss was pushed over the brink of sanity by his inability to make a living for his family. According to his wife, Weiss had become so despondent over his string of business failures and his inability to secure work, "and finally the necessity for her to go to work," that he suffered a nervous breakdown and had to be committed to a mental hospital.[23] Most men did not react so dramatically, but the crisis was profound nevertheless. When Mollie Steinberg went to work in the hosiery mill after a long period in which the family had no income, her husband "resented the fact that it was his wife who was the wage-earner, and not he." Later on, in speaking with the social worker, he explained his "insecurity and unhappiness" by saying "that if a man is able-bodied and in his right senses, there is no reason why his wife has 'to wear the pants.'" Still later, he affirmed his desire to return to a "normal" arrangement of gender roles: "Mr. S's chief desire is for him to earn enough so that his wife would not have to continue working, but could remain home and care for the children in a normal fashion." The role of the family breadwinner was important enough to Steinberg that he "still left [home] in the morning, so that everyone would think that he was working."[24] Bernie Kelner also went to some pains to conceal the extent to which "normal" gender roles in his family had shifted. When social worker Sara Glantz called at his home, she "encountered M who was out of doors supervising Joseph. He said that W had gone to the store for a 'few minutes.'" Only later, after the social worker had waited a while for the mother to reappear, did he "mention . . . that she is at work and he takes care of

Joseph during day."[25] The title of family provider also seemed important to Isadore Kolowsky, a contractor. During a discussion with the nursery's social worker,

> [H]e began to cry, . . . Until 2 yrs ago he was very comfortably fixed. His wife and child had known every luxury that money could buy. . . . He blamed his present circumstances entirely upon unemployment. . . . It hurt him very much when his wife had to go to work. He respects her desire to do her share and is indeed grateful for the brave way that she has carried on during this period of his unemployment. He knows of nothing to do but commit suicide.

When Isadore was called in for a meeting with the social worker a year later, he offered a similar defense, saying that "he never dreamed that the day would come when he would have to depend on the few pennies his wife makes."[26]

African-American women, whose employment was common long before the depression, were largely excluded from the national debate about the propriety of married women's work, just as they had historically been excluded from being seen as "good" mothers. African-American women had always been identified by whites as workers more than as mothers, so their employment did not seem as disturbing as did that of white women. As Jacqueline Jones comments, "Few congressmen or labor leaders evinced much concern over the baneful effects of economic dependence on the male ego when the ego in question was that of a black husband."[27] How did African-American women and men themselves feel about mothers as breadwinners? Recent scholars have suggested that African-American women's own conceptions of motherhood encompass wage-earning and economic support of children to a much greater degree than those of white women.[28] Evidence from the case records of the the Women's Union Day Nursery seems to support this idea: the African-American families who used the nursery during the depression talked in a matter-of-fact way about women's need to go out to work. Most clients did not present themselves as experiencing the kind of profound personal crisis that the more prosperous Jewish families who used the Neighborhood Centre nursery described. While the Neighborhood Centre case records are filled with accounts of the tension wrought by reversing the male breadwinner/female caretaker roles, the case records written by social workers at the Women's Union Nursery are almost silent on the subject.

But for African-Americans as well as for white immigrants, the male breadwinner/female homemaker paradigm was an ideal that symbolized middle-class status and comfort. Interviews with African-American women who were domestic workers in New York during the 1930s suggest that although "it was a near impossibility for a black family to make it during the Depression on one salary," many husbands did not want their wives to work. "These men felt the woman's place was in the home and they wanted to be able to 'sit her down' so that she could fully attend to her duties as a wife and mother." Many of the women went to work anyway, although some worked part-time so they could arrive home before their husbands and appear to play by his rules.[29] Although few of the poor African-American families who show up in the Women's Union Day Nursery case records could afford to do without a mother's wages, the hope of a male wage that would enable a woman to stay at home remained a vivid dream. Sometimes this dream was even realized: Irene Johnson, a widow who had lived with her mother while working in a restaurant and as a domestic, made plans to remarry in

1937. She proudly told the Women's Union social worker that her fiancé was employed regularly, making twenty-seven dollars a week, a salary far above the combined income of most nursery families. They were planning to settle in a more affluent African-American neighborhood in West Philadelphia and were buying furniture and looking for a home. In keeping with her new status, Irene would not work for wages: "They have decided that W will not work out, but remain at home and care for her house and child."[30] Failure to attain this ideal sometimes caused conflict among Women's Union families as much as among the immigrant families of Neighborhood Centre. Thomas Cooper, who had been unemployed for two years after losing a good job at the Belmont Iron Company, left his wife in 1932 and moved in with another woman three doors down the street. "When he left home in May," the social worker noted, "it was because he was unwilling to stay home and care for his own child while his wife went out to work." Clearly there were other tensions in the marriage, for Mrs. Cooper later learned that her husband was taking care of his new girlfriend's children, but the fact that he would give the reversal of gender roles as a legitimate reason to leave his wife suggests the power of the ideal.[31]

The work that most women could get during the Depression was not much to be jealous of; indeed, one of the ironies of the controversy about women taking men's jobs was that most women worked at jobs that men would not consider taking. As one writer reminded the public, "a coal miner or steel worker cannot very well fill the jobs of our nursemaids, cleaning women, or the factory and clerical occupations now occupied by women."[32] Women who desperately needed jobs found themselves putting up with exploitative working conditions. Women factory workers, for instance, were often required to come to work when there was no work to do, and thus no pay. Willa May Gaskill of the House of Industry described a common pattern:

> For the past year, even the little bit of tailoring is for the most part worthless—a woman reports each day at the factory and waits for work. Perhaps she makes a dozen buttonholes, perhaps the pockets on four coats, earning about enough for carfare, but there is always the hope that business will improve, and those "on the job" will have an opportunity to earn.[33]

The Neighborhood Centre Day Nursery Committee, meeting in 1935, expressed concern about this "problem of women sitting around in factories waiting for work."[34] Factory workers also suffered from speed-ups, stretch-outs, exploitative piece-work rates, and the ever-present fear of lay-offs. Yet they were not as badly off as domestic workers.

Domestic work had long been unpleasant and underpaid, but during the depression exploitation reached new heights. African-American women, who had previously monopolized the field, now had to compete with white women who could not find jobs in clerical or factory work and who benefited from employers' preference for white servants. Nevertheless, African-American women in Philadelphia remained overwhelmingly concentrated in domestic service: 80% of the women in the Women's Union case records reporting an occupation and twenty-five out of the twenty-seven women who brought their children to the St. Nicholas nursery worked as domestics in private homes, hotels, stores, or institutions. Most of these women were day workers, not live-in servants; while this gave them flexibility and the right to have a life separate from their employers, it also meant that work could be very irregular and wages low, and there was no guarantee of room and board. The long hours required of domestic workers, even of day workers, made it difficult for mothers to spend any time with their children. Virginia Wilson, for instance, eventually left her job as a domestic in a drug store, "stating that it was to[o] confining since it kept her until 8 and 9 o'clock in the evenings, preventing her from giving her children proper attention."[35] Vera Walker worked irregularly throughout the 1930s, visiting an employment agency daily in search of more work. When she finally got a full-time job in 1938, working six days a week, she felt that she had to work as late as seven or eight o'clock without extra pay several days a week in order to keep her position.[36]

All domestic servants during the depression found their wages driven down while their hours were extended, and one person was often expected to do the work performed in the past by several servants.[37] Some women received only carfare, clothing, or lunch for a day's work, and live-in servants were suddenly charged for their room and board. Helen Remer of the PADN reported in 1933,

> There are those in our city, who like to exploit their neighbors. . . . Selfish advantage is taken particularly of colored women in domestic work. These slave-driven women are some of our nursery mothers, who are employed for eight hours a day, by women who cannot afford to have their housework done for them. So wages varying from twenty-five and fifty cents to $1.50 are paid for eight hours of house-cleaning, with or without lunch and carfare. . . . The need of these colored women for their children is so great and the competition so keen, that they are driven to accept these pittances for self-respecting work.[38]

As Remer noted, during the depression new groups of housewives, many of them working-class women themselves, took advantage of the depressed labor market to hire household workers for the first time. In order to get work, African-American women had to suffer the indignities of the "slave market": women needing work congregated on certain street corners early in the morning and employers drove by and offered work to those who would sell their labor at the lowest rate.[39] Helen Satterwhite, a Philadelphia domestic worker, remembered: "It wasn't easy to get jobs. You would go and stand on the corner and people would come out and pick you up. Everybody in North Philly was standing on corners to get work. . . . It was very hard housework. They wanted you to scrub floors and windows and all kinds of stuff."[40] Employers abused the system, lying about the kind of work they needed, turning the hands of the clock back to keep from paying their workers, or demanding that a woman do additional work for their friends and relatives for no extra pay.[41]

Both African-American and white working-class women found it difficult to earn enough to support their families, especially when husbands were unemployed. But white families often had more resources to draw on in facing the economic crisis of the 1930s. In her study of working-class women during the depression, Lois Helmbold describes different sets of strategies that families used to survive hard times: subsistence strategies, including replacing consumption with home production such as canning, gardening, or sewing; financial strategies, such as liquidating resources and going into debt; and personal strategies such as moving, sharing housing, going on relief, or taking help from relatives and friends. She finds that families used subsistence strategies first and continuously, financial strategies when necessary until money resources were depleted, and personal strategies when no other methods were available.[42] These strategies are all evident in the stories of Philadelphia day nursery families, but African-American and white families had different access to them. African-American families in the Women's Union case records tended to already be struggling for daily survival before the depression ever hit. Already sharing housing and reducing cash outlay, these families had no assets to liquidate and therefore had nothing to fall back on but the "personal strategies" of seeking help from friends and kin and going on relief.

Indeed, for the African-American families who used day nurseries in Philadelphia, the struggle for daily survival during the 1930s was not a new experience. Economic conditions in the city deteriorated more quickly for African-Americans: as early as the mid-1920s, many of the African-American women and men who had come north in search of a better future were finding it difficult to get by. Although they were hardly strangers to poverty or hard work, these migrants may still have been shaken by the failure of their dreams for a better life in Philadelphia and may have experienced a mother's need to go out to work as a devastating blow.[43] These families certainly suffered during these years, with high rates of unemployment, unusually exploitative working conditions, and financial strain taking its toll on family relationships. But the Women's Union families did not talk about the depression as an unusual time. This may reflect their actual feelings, the questions that social workers asked, or the clients' perceptions of what they needed to say to get help; because women's wage work was more common and accepted among African-Americans, they probably did not feel the same need to prove that they were in desperate straits in order to get help with their children. These women went on relief when they needed to, complaining about how hard it was to get by on small wages or relief checks, but did not tend to blame their situation on "hard times" or to compare it to how things had been for them five or ten years earlier.

By contrast, for many Neighborhood Centre families, the depression represented a sudden reversal of fortunes, a traumatic fall from lower middle-class status to real poverty. One day nursery mother described her father, whose business had failed in the depression, "as having gone from 'rags to riches and then back to pickles.'"[44] For many of the men in these families, who had worked as skilled factory hands, artisans, salesmen, or in their own businesses, the depression meant their first bout with extended unemployment, the first time that their wives had to work to support the family, and the first time they became dependent on relatives or charity to provide their basic needs. Men and women who had spent their childhoods watching their immigrant parents trying to climb out of poverty were particularly alarmed when they found themselves without money for rent, grocery bills, or children's clothes. They frequently compared their situations to the better times they had experienced before the depression, often trying to impress the social worker with some measure of their previous affluence to prove that they were "respectable" people who had fallen on hard times. One woman told how her husband had presented her with a hundred dollar bill when she returned home from the hospital after the birth of their first child, and said that she never used to do her own washing before her husband lost his job.[45] Benjamin Kolchick, a pharmacist who had lost his store, described his fall from status and comfort by saying that at one time he had paid as much as $35 for an apartment and had had full-time help for his wife.[46] These people had a hard time accepting their changed status and were particularly reluctant to apply for charitable relief; many even found dependence on relatives hard to get used to.

In both African-American and white families, the breakdown of "normal" roles of support and dependency could cause a great deal of tension. The pressure on men to provide, and their inability to do so, affected many relationships, and men who could not provide were often seen as worthless husbands and fathers. In one case, this pressure ended a relationship even before it had really begun. Esther Kohlberg, a divorced and unemployed garment worker with one child, met a man at a friend's party who seemed interested in her. After a few weeks, however, the relationship ended abruptly, due to the intervention of her well-intentioned landlords:

> One evening when her friend called, the landlord and landlady saw him and told him that if he was interested in W, he would make an attempt to meet the rent for her and in W's words, "they threw him out and told him not to come back until he could do something for me." According to her own statements, from that time on, he was so humiliated, he never returned.[47]

Similarly, the expectation that a good man was a good provider forced African-American domestic worker Jennie Bell to keep her marriage a secret, "because most of her friends have criticised her choice as M is not employed."[48] In many families, men's inability to provide provoked conflict and separation. Several women refused to stay with men who were not supporting them, expressing their view that economic support was the primary purpose of marriage. Leah Ross explained to the Neighborhood Centre social worker that "she no longer loved her husband and therefore, did not want to go on living with him, especially since he was unable to provide for her adequately." Her husband, in turn, explained to the social worker that his inability to support the family would prevent his wife from taking him back: "He does not believe that they can be reconciled at this time, in view of the fact that he is unable to earn sufficient to care for his family."[49] Likewise, when Anna Kolowsky left her husband after a long and stressful period when he was unemployed and she worked at a series of waitress jobs, she explained to the Neighborhood Centre social worker that she "does not feel particularly bad about leaving him. . . . They can not live together again until M is able to support W and child."[50]

Male unemployment also affected relationships with extended families, a crucial source of support for struggling couples. One of the most common steps that families took when times got hard was to move in with relatives; 34% of Neighborhood Centre families and 39% of Women's Union families were living with relatives when they applied for nursery care. When this dependence on relatives was unexpected, it often caused great stress. Neighborhood Centre clients Dora and Charlie Lipman moved in with her mother in 1931 when his earnings began to decline. From the time they made this move, Dora said, "it has been hot," for tension between Charlie and Dora's mother grew unbearable. Dora told a social worker that her mother "began to be meddlesome to the extent that M and W quarrelled and did not speak for days at a time. Then another woman came into M's life." The tension between Dora's mother and Charlie apparently arose out of Charlie's inability to maintain his wife and children independently. Charlie told the social worker that his mother-in-law had not been critical of him when his earnings were good (in fact, according to Dora, she had urged the marriage), but "as soon as he stopped earning because of economic conditions, his mother-in-law started accusing him of spending his money on someone else and not caring for wife and children." When social worker Helen Bennett talked with Dora's mother, "she cried and sighed heavily. She wanted us to know that 'he,' her son-in-law, has been the 'ruin of my life.' He has darkened her door from the moment he first met her daughter. He has never made an attempt to earn a living nor is he interested in the children." Ultimately the couple separated, Dora and her children staying in her mother's house while Charlie went to live elsewhere, threatening to seek a divorce on the grounds of "cruel and barbarous treatment and nagging."[51] Moving in with relatives also caused problems in the marriage of Women's Union clients Virginia and William Wilson. Virginia explained to social worker Susie Watson that William's unemployment had disrupted their life together, making it "necessary to live with his relatives and be partially dependent upon them." The couple separated and were not reunited for another three years.[52] Generally, however, Women's Union Nursery clients, unlike Neighborhood Centre families, did not point to their need to move in with relatives as the cause of the breakup of their marriages. Indeed, perhaps because living with relatives was *more* common among African-Americans (especially those who had recently migrated to the city), it was not experienced as a crisis or as a departure from the norm that threatened the integrity of the couple. This does not mean that African-Americans did not come into conflict with their relatives. But perhaps because dependence on relatives, and living in close quarters with them, was an expected part of life, it did not become the focal point of explanations for marital problems.

Relying on kin for child care became another source of conflict, as women's need to earn wages created demands that relatives could or would not meet. For instance, domestic worker Virginia Wilson lived with her husband's parents, but they "refused to allow the children in the house," so the children stayed with an uncle instead. The uncle refused to keep the children when the Wilsons failed to pay their board, and Virginia moved in with her sister, who supported her and her two children for several months. The sister, however, was only able to provide limited help: "[she] has two children of her own and refused to mind Mrs. Wilson's children, which created an unemployment situation."[53] In other families, female kin who might have been willing to care for their grandchildren, nieces, and nephews were drawn into the labor force themselves. The help of kin was crucial to most of the families who came to both the Women's Union and the Neighborhood Centre nurseries; social workers and clients alike assumed that female relatives would naturally take care of children during a mother's absence. But female kin were often reluctant to take on major new responsibilities when they themselves were struggling.

Depending on relatives for child care could create further tension when different ideas about child rearing were at stake. For instance, Morton Polsky did not want his mother to take care of his son Edward, because, as he told the Neighborhood Centre social worker,

> she [is not] the type to train Edward. It is her opinion that Edward could be brought up in the way that he and his brother and sister were reared, but M would not like this. He did not say this in a criticizing way but explained that a woman like his mother, having lived the greater part of her life in Russia, would not be familiar with child training.[54]

Such tensions were not limited to immigrant families: William Jefferson told the Women's Union social worker that he refused to allow his mother-in-law to care for his son, "as she is a firm believer in severe corporal punishment for children for the slightest offense."[55] In both these cases, fathers may have been trying to appeal to a social worker who could be expected to sympathize with their own more "modern" approach, but they also indicated broader family tensions.

When kin could not help, mothers who had to spend long hours looking for work often had to scramble to make sure their children would be cared for. Anna Kolowsky, who was living apart from her unemployed husband, spent many days looking for work as a waitress. In August 1929, she called the Neighborhood Centre social worker, explaining that she had a chance to obtain a steady job if she worked two evenings the first week. She asked if the nursery could make an exception to its regular hours and take care of her daughter these evenings, but the answer was no. A few weeks later, "a strange woman" brought Anna's daughter to the nursery, explaining that the child had slept at her house all night because her mother had to get up very early to look for work. This happened several times, and when the social worker inquired, Anna "stated that child has been staying at home nights but that friends in the neighborhood volunteer to bring her to [the] day nursery because W has to go out before 7 o'clock in order to follow ads."[56]

Male unemployment disrupted conventional patterns of family life in several different ways: creating tensions within marriages, forcing a sometimes uncomfortable dependence on relatives, and pushing mothers into the work force. But despite popular fears that unemployment would overturn the traditional division of labor within the family, the shift in roles was never complete. Although many women temporarily took over their husbands' breadwinning role, few men seem to have been willing to take over child-care responsibilities. Fathers may have performed certain specific tasks while their wives worked (such as picking up children from the day nursery or from relatives, doing the laundry, shopping, or feeding the children), but in 127 cases from three day nurseries, it was rare to find a father who assumed full responsibility for the daily care of his children.[57] Only one father in the Neighborhood Centre records really took on this responsibility, and the social worker clearly saw him as an unusual case. She observed,

> While M is not working steadily, he takes the responsibilities in the home. He brings the children back and forth from the d[ay] n[ursery], takes them for any medical refers, and straightens the apartment. He does this very willingly and we have never heard him voice any discouragement about the times. . . . [Visitor] found M at home caring for the children. . . . W had been going to work during all this time. We also made a visit to the home on our return and found the children receiving excellent care. On this visit, we found M washing a tub full of clothes, and there was no indication on his part that he objected to doing this.

Golda Hernandez, who along with her husband was a politically active socialist, felt "that a woman should share in [the] family's support when advisable"; the social worker saw this as "part of her general philosophy of greater equality in the entire social system." Significantly, she was the only woman in all the day nursery cases from the 1930s to express positive feelings about working: when her two children returned to the nursery after having been ill at home, "she confidentially told us that even if she were well off financially, she would prefer to go out to work and have the chn attend a nursery."[58]

Examples of fathers taking on child care and housework were also relatively rare among Women's Union families, despite African-Americans' higher rates of long-term male unemployment and female employment. The comments of southern-born Isetta Peters, who worked as a domestic in Washington, D.C., during this period, may be to the point here: "Now, the father of the childrens never minded nobody. No, in them days a man didn't do no mindin' for no child. Maybe a half hour or so, but somebody's be over there quick 'cause he wasn't staying in there with childrens long. No sir."[59] A few men did take on more responsibility. Taylor Smith, a chef whose wages and hours had been cut, was described as caring for his two children while his wife worked as a domestic; even when he did have work, he was the one who picked up the boys at the nursery. During his wife's illness in 1935, he did the housework, cooking, and caring for the children, who remained at home. A few years later, when Women's Union worker Susie Watson visited the home, she found Taylor at home washing clothes.[60] But a newspaper article featuring a father whose children attended the African-American St. Nicholas nursery suggests by its tone just how novel it seemed for fathers to take over responsibility for their children. Entitled "Father Is Mother For Day Nursery," the article explained, "One of the best 'mothers' on the St. Nicholas lists is a father. He is a widower and a longshoreman with three children under nine years who does all his own housework and cooking. His kitchen is always spotless and there is never so much as a wrinkle on his bed sheets. And his children are well behaved youngsters. . . . He takes his youngsters regularly to the clinic and does everything the social workers suggest."[61] Since his wife was dead, he had to take full responsibility for his children or else place them in foster care or an institution. The fact that he kept the family together at all already marked him as an unusual father, and the meticulous care he gave the children and the house singled him out as truly exceptional at a time when jokes about husbands taking on housework often touched a nerve.

Aside from these few cases, none of the families from Neighborhood Centre, Women's Union, and St. Nicholas nurseries who described an alternative to day nursery care (i.e., day care arrangements that were made either before a child was admitted to the nursery, after the child was discharged, or during illness or times that the nursery was closed) mentioned a father's care. Female kin, neighbors, or friends, women who "boarded" children for a fee, landladies, and hired help were all more likely options. While men performed certain discrete tasks or took care of children on a temporary basis, very few couples were willing to accept a permanent reversal of the traditional division of labor within the family.[62] Some women did not seem to want their husbands to take on child care responsibilities. When the Jewish Welfare Society's employment department offered Jennie Leibesky work as a night nurse, she refused it, saying that she "did not want to give M the resp[onsibility] of caring for chn at night, alone." The social worker chided her, saying "she should be willing that he learn to take care of the chn since in her financial condition she can not expect to do things as formerly." In response, Jennie claimed that "she does not blame M, but . . . she has never wanted him to do for the chn what she has always done."[63] For women like Leibesky, as well as for most of the men who appear in these records, maintaining a traditional division of labor within the home carried deep significance, even when women were taking over the role of family provider outside the home.

The economic crisis of the 1930s, then, called into question the male breadwinner/

female caretaker paradigm by which most families structured their lives. Men's inability to earn wages during the depression pushed more married women into the labor force, sometimes prompting identity crises and family tension along with economic hardship. The reversal of gender roles, which caused such anxiety to many Americans, however, was generally understood by men and women alike as a temporary answer to an emergency, not a permanent rearrangement of family roles.

Expanding the Mission of Day Nurseries

While women went out to work, day nurseries expanded their mission in the early 1930s, supplementing public relief with material assistance and breaking all the rules that social workers had worked to implement in better times. During these years of crisis, a broader view of the benefits of day care prevailed; day nurseries were seen as appropriate not only for children of working mothers, but for any child whose family was experiencing hardship. Day nurseries found themselves serving children whose parents were both looking for work, children whose mothers were supporting an able-bodied but unemployed husband, and children who simply needed good food and an escape from crowded homes. Annual day nursery reports from the early 1930s are filled with accounts of these changes. In Kensington, for instance, the Baldwin Day Nursery "had to set aside former standards of admission in order to meet the present situation" and accepted children whose mothers were not employed and children whose parents were both at home.[64] The rules that these nurseries were violating had been intended to make sure that able-bodied men would not have an excuse for failing to support their families; in the context of the depression, however, such concerns seemed irrelevant. The Frankford Day Nursery reported, "Until recently the Nursery only admitted children of one parent, usually widowed or forsaken mothers. On account of present financial conditions, however, all former rules which limited the Nursery's service were suspended, and children are being taken whenever it seems advisable."[65] Indeed, PADN president Helen Remer noted that in 1933 the percentage of nursery children with unemployed parents had gone from 25% to 50%.[66] Several nurseries also broke rules established in better times by allowing children whose parents were out of work to attend without paying the usual daily fee. The House of Industry Nursery spoke for many nurseries in its report: "So many of the points for which we worked in other years have just gone by the board—but if we can ease the mother's mind from part of her worry by providing for the child a happy environment and proper food, are we not justified?"[67]

Nurseries not only admitted children they would have rejected before, but they also engaged in creative relief efforts in order to help families weather the storm. Helen Remer summarized these efforts in 1932: "Some superintendents taught unemployed mothers sewing, laundry and housework and obtained employment for them. . . . Rent in small amounts was paid to avoid eviction, and where there was desperate need, coal, milk, clothing, cans of hot food, food orders, and even a set of false teeth, were given!"[68] Many nurseries sent food, clothing, and fuel into the homes of nursery families, and several nursery boards created special emergency funds to aid families in particular distress. The Salvation Army Nursery kept children and even some mothers overnight when families ran out of fuel to heat their homes. The Kensington Day Nursery provided food for mothers who only had part-time work and advertised for positions for mothers who could not find work.[69] St. Nicholas also advertised for work for its mothers and estimated that these advertisements enabled a group of mothers to earn over a thousand dollars.[70] Neighborhood Centre provided "made work" for unemployed nursery mothers in a sewing room, as well as employing needy parents throughout the settlement.[71] Helen Remer reported in 1932 that several nurseries had undertaken the task of subsidizing unemployed families in their own homes; the Sunnyside Day Nursery, which had switched to the foster day care plan, reported attempts to hold families together when mothers lost their jobs by paying directly to the mother the amount usually paid to care for her children in foster homes.[72]

In response to the overwhelming need of day nursery families, many nurseries came to see their purpose as providing a form of direct relief, not just care for children. Food was often the most tangible benefit of day nursery care, and several nurseries justified keeping the children of unemployed parents on the nursery rolls in order to ensure that they were adequately fed.[73] In 1932, when one Neighborhood Centre mother was asked to "discuss her financial situation in more detail," she replied "that she could sum it all up in one statement by telling us that if Eva were not eating at the nursery, 'she would starve like I am.'" Later, social worker Helen Landis Bennett was able to persuade the recalcitrant Eva to stay at the nursery by reminding her that her mother could not afford to give her the food she needed at home.[74] Anna Kolowsky "was moved almost so that she could not express herself, by the food that child gets here. [She] stated that she would be happy if she could have one meal like ch[ild] gets."[75] When the Hernandez children continued to attend the nursery faithfully despite the fact that their unemployed father was home every day, Bennett concluded that "nursery care is necessary as a relief measure."[76] And when a Women's Union worker discussed with Mary Frederickson the possibility of discontinuing nursery care, she said "that she does not see how she could possibly manage without nursery care at this time as she could not feed her family on the maximum allowance for food in her budget."[77]

Despite their best efforts, however, these Philadelphia day nurseries realized how little a handful of charitable nurseries could do to alleviate the national economic crisis. Philadelphia's energetic attempts to meet the needs of its citizens through private charity had proven inadequate by 1932, when Horatio Lloyd's Committee on Unemployment Relief disbanded and organized relief in the city stopped.[78] In general, Americans were starting to turn to the federal government rather than to private charities like day nurseries to alleviate the distress of unemployed families. And as policymakers in Washington drew up plans to combat poverty and promote economic security for families, it became clear that the idea of day care as an antipoverty tool had vanished.

While day nurseries had been discussed alongside mothers' pensions in the Progressive era, by the 1930s the idea of mothers as providers was so distant that the shapers of the New Deal welfare state did not even discuss day care as a policy option. Instead, the welfare system they created was based on the assumption that male breadwinners supported women and children. The Social Security Act of 1935 provided contributory social insurance for male wage-earners and their dependents, but if a woman's husband deserted, divorced, or separated from her, if she never married, or if her husband worked in a sector of the economy not included under the social insurance plan, she would have to seek benefits from the Aid to Dependent Children (ADC) program, a federal expansion of the old state mothers' pension programs.[79] Feminist scholars have critiqued the way in which this division between contributory social insurance for male workers and categorical, needs-based relief for mothers, embedded in the Social Security Act, institutionalized an unequal two-track welfare system divided along gender lines.[80] The new system also made a clear distinction between different groups of women. "Unworthy mothers"—African-American women and deserted, divorced, and unmarried women—who had been channeled away from mothers' pensions and into domestic relations courts before the depression, would now be channeled into ADC and away from the more respectable and better-paying social insurance program.

The exclusion of day care from the welfare system established by the 1935 legislation and its subsequent amendments is not surprising, for both social insurance and ADC programs were based on a vision of women as dependent mothers, not as workers who might support families. Mothers' pensions had already gained recognition as the social policy of choice for poor women and children, overshadowing day care, so it was the mothers' pension idea that was written into federal law. As in the Progressive era, the state was willing to fill in for a missing father by providing economic support to children, but not for a mother who wanted to support those children through wage-earning. At the same time, New Deal labor legislation, which did try to improve conditions for female as well as male workers, did not try to address the needs of working women's children. The assumption that the problem of the depression was essentially one of male unemployment, and that woman's role was as the self-sacrificing mother of *The Grapes of Wrath*, not as a worker, thus shaped public policy and individuals' options. Even relief efforts such as the WPA work projects sent the message that it was the unemployment of male breadwinners that was the important problem; women often found it difficult to prove their eligibility for these jobs, and the majority of the projects were intended to employ men.[81]

As the government took on more responsibility for public welfare, private welfare agencies had to rethink their role: since government was providing direct relief, private agencies increasingly defined their purpose as providing specific kinds of help to families with specialized problems.[82] Developing clear guidelines and adhering to rules developed by professional social workers was an important part of this effort. Centralized funding agencies, dominated by professionals, played an increasingly important role in defining the role of private welfare agencies, and in controlling their budgets and policies. As part of an effort to make sure private welfare agencies were following their specified purpose, the Philadelphia Welfare Federation and the Federation of Jewish Charities thus pressured day nurseries to come back into line with their more narrow predepression mission of providing day care for the children of employed mothers.

Retreating from the idea that day care could benefit a wide range of children, Philadelphia day nurseries returned to their original role of providing day care only in very specific circumstances. In 1933, the Welfare Federation forbade nurseries from accepting children from families that were receiving other forms of relief. Aiding unemployed families was the job of public agencies; day nurseries should not care for children unless mothers were employed. Although several day nursery advocates objected to this directive from the Welfare Federation, they had to comply or else face further cuts in their budgets.[83] In subsequent reports, Helen Remer of the PADN presented this decision as a positive one, although it clearly had circumscribed the nurseries' role. In 1934, she noted approvingly, "Nineteen day nurseries of the Philadelphia Association busily and conscientiously worked last year to fulfill the purpose for which they were started many years ago in Philadelphia—namely, to care for children of mothers who had to work." She then called on day nurseries to think "from the standpoint that the normal place for a child is his home" and not to admit children simply to provide food or a more positive environment.[84] Similarly, in 1935, PADN executive secretary Lillian Kensil commented on nursery efforts in the early years of the depression to relieve the strain on unemployed families.

> As time went on it became clear that such attempts were futile. . . . Taking from a mother her right and responsibility to care for her own children when she was able to be at home was socially unsound. Economically it was unsound because supplementing public relief in this way was too expensive.[85]

By 1936, the Strawberry Mansion Day Nursery's annual report felt a need to justify providing day care when there was an able-bodied man in the house. After noting that a third of their cases were families in which the father was unemployed, the report explained, "It is important to note that in most of the cases the woman earns more than the man *so that we feel justified in giving her the opportunity to continue working*" [emphasis added]. The report continued by explaining that it was important to check up on these cases periodically to make sure that the women still needed to work.[86]

Day nursery workers, adjusting to a new world of welfare, walked a fine line between encouraging families to use public relief when it was necessary and urging them to maintain their independence and pride. Like their clients, they often seemed unsure whether public relief was an entitlement of citizenship or a badge of shame. Some, echoing their nineteenth-century predecessors' fears that providing direct relief would result in dependence and "pauperization," emphasized the day nursery's efforts to keep families independent and self-respecting. The Willing Day Nursery reported its efforts to "watch each case carefully in order not to overstep the very delicate line between pauperizing, and giving relief where it will really help." One way to encourage "independence" was the universal practice of charging a small fee for nursery care, and making sure parents paid it. For instance, the San Cristoforo Nursery reported proudly in 1931 that no child had attended that year without paying a fee, no matter how small, and credited the nursery superintendent's efforts "to budget the families, teaching them to pay even a little toward every obligation." In addition to this, many day nursery workers worked to keep families off public relief. For instance, Ada Lewis of the Franklin Day Nursery reported, "Careful budgeting of the incomes of the parents has kept the number of our nursery families asking for relief down to the irreducible minimum."[87] Neville Barry of the St. Nicholas Nursery wrote approvingly, "Many families, when in difficulty for the first time, apply to the nursery before going to any other social agency: for their thought is to help themselves rather than ask for actual financial aid."[88]

The clients of the Neighborhood Centre Nursery were just as apt as social workers to distinguish between day nurseries and other forms of charity. Because coming to a day nursery was usually part of a strategy that involved finding work rather than depending on a relief order, clients often felt that, rather than treated like charity cases, they should be given credit for trying to be self-supporting. May Milstein expressed her feeling "that it was bad enough to have to look for work and not coming to JWS [the Jewish

Welfare Society] for aid was an asset on her part." After her attempts to get her daughter admitted to the nursery and to secure free clothing for her met with repeated failure, Mrs. Milstein told the Neighborhood Centre social worker "that she does not think it is fair for an agency to allow a family who want to get ahead by themselves, who want to work, to starve because they refuse to arrange DN placement." She was not looking for assistance, she claimed repeatedly, "but just to place the baby."[89] Knowing the nursery workers' desire to keep them off relief, some clients tried to use this as leverage in their dealings with nursery social workers: the Neighborhood Centre worker noted that when Clara Kelner found out that she could no longer send her son to the nursery, "she remarked in a tone suggestive of threat, 'Well, I guess the only thing for us to do will be to go on relief.'"[90] Many Neighborhood Centre clients were distressed when they learned that, in order to get their children into the day nursery, they had to apply through the Jewish Welfare Society; several people walked out the door when they found this out. Clearly, these people made a distinction between enrolling a child in a day nursery and becoming a client of a relief agency. People who used the nursery but refused food orders from the JWS or the County Relief Board also insisted that there was a difference between the two forms of help.[91] Anna Kolowsky, who was acutely aware of the benefit that her daughter received from the food she got at the nursery, refused a food basket that a local charity offered for Hanukkah, saying that "she would not accept relief."[92]

In the face of this sort of attitude, social workers struggled to explain that despite the fee, the day nursery was a form of charity. When Golda Hernandez came to apply to place her children at Neighborhood Centre, social worker Helen Landis explained that nursery care cost the agency about $1.50 a day. If Golda could pay twenty-five or fifty cents a day, Landis explained, she would be accepting the difference in relief. Landis noted,

> The above statements seemed to make W rather uncomfortable. She has hesitated to come to an agency to ask for any form of relief and so she wishes to consider the problem in the light of what she already knows. . . . She can not see her way out of this at present because if it were not for the fact that she was going to work, she might have to go to the JWS for assistance.[93]

Despite her hesitation, Hernandez clearly preferred accepting the charity of the nursery to becoming completely dependent on JWS handouts. Similarly, when May Milstein insisted that she was "not asking assistance, merely clothes and a day nursery placement," the social worker "tried to explain this as relief in kind," but Milstein "refused to listen to our explanation." Instead, she continued talking about "the way the welfare [agencies] assist individuals who do not need it, and allow the worthy to go neglected."[94] In fact, most day nursery clients were quite aware of the charitable status of the nursery; they simply identified it as a more honorable form of charity than accepting direct relief. Some Neighborhood Centre clients carefully calculated the benefit of a certain type of help against the loss in independence and pride. For example, although Freda Marcus used the day nursery for her son Bernie, she did not want the nursery social worker to arrange for her to get help from the city's Bureau for Unemployment Relief, "as she does not feel that their grocery order is of sufficient help for her to warrant her losing her independence entirely."[95] The distinction between day nursery care and other forms of relief may have been parallel to the distinction many people drew between work relief (such as that offered by the WPA) and direct relief; although they knew that it was still a charity, it was of a kind that enabled them to go out to work, thus maintaining a sense of independence and integrity.[96]

Some felt shame about the need to come to any kind of charitable agency, even a day nursery, for help. Gertrude Polsky's sister "cried during our entire visit. . . . She could not help but bewail her sister's fate and the fact that the family must come to a federated agency."[97] Harry Shapiro would not meet with the nursery social worker, Helen Landis, because "he did not wish to appear in the building of a charitable organization"; when she called at his home, he stayed in another room while his wife explained that he "tried to avoid meeting anyone who had anything to do with social agencies." Both he and his wife expressed shame about taking help from the nursery and feared that their neighbors would find out. Mr. Shapiro (when he finally consented to talk with Landis) "said that his wife is doing and has been doing a noble thing by keeping a job and supporting the family" and wanted to be sure the social worker knew that "she never had to work before." "As soon as I get any kind of work," he told her, "I hope to take the children out of the DN."

Second-generation immigrants like these may well have grown up hearing tales of conflict between poor immigrants and the German Jews who controlled most of the major Jewish welfare agencies in the city, so their reluctance to accept help from such agencies ran deep. Having risen above the economic struggles of their parents' generation, many were particularly determined to avoid the humiliation of depending on "strangers" for assistance. If they could not avoid turning to an agency for help, however, they could at least prevent their neighbors and relatives from finding out. Just as men pretended to go to work in the morning, or said their wives were "just around the corner," women often pretended that they were managing without charitable assistance. Mrs. Shapiro told Landis that the fact that her neighbors knew that the family was not paying the rent was "worse than starving," and when she asked Landis to look over a new apartment for her, she was anxious that Landis not identify herself to the new landlady as being from the day nursery.[98] Anna Kolowsky refused to give the Neighborhood Centre social worker addresses for her father or sisters, as "she did not want them to know that she was coming to an agency to help her in her problems." Her husband told the worker that "he was sorry that the child had to have DN care since he was so able bodied. . . . He has never in his life had to come to any form of charity." (Mr. Kolowsky had some unique ideas for cutting down the family's expenses so they would be less reliant on the charity of the nursery. Helen Landis Bennett recalled, "He asked us outright whether as a representative of the community we feel that it is right for a man such as he . . . to have to get his 'sex out of the house.' He became very excited when he told us that he has to spend money to get what 'naturally comes to a man.' *In his opinion it is little short of a crime to spend thusly when we have to take Shirley into the DN*" [emphasis added]).[99]

Like employment patterns and child care arrangements, clients' attitudes toward charity and relief varied, depending on how many options and resources they had. Thus the people who expressed the greatest reluctance to accept relief tended to be those Neighborhood Centre clients who had previously thought of themselves as "middle class"; conversely, the African-American families represented in the Women's Union case records seemed to apply for relief in a matter-of-fact sort of way, without appearing to agonize over it. For these families, going on relief did not connote a major drop in status and did not represent a major departure from life in better economic times; it was a way to get the support they needed for their families when other means had been exhausted. When these women talked about relief, it was usually to report some problem with getting it, or to express their resentment with social workers' attempts to use relief to dictate their family relationships. For instance, Blanche Gray, who received a grocery order and a quart of milk when she was separated from her husband, lost this support when her husband moved back in with her. She angrily reported that the social worker from the relief agency had told her that "since she took her husband back, she can take care of him."[100] Similarly, Evelyn Jeffrey's food order was cut off until her teenage daughter Beverly agreed to file a court complaint against the father of her child, and Rosemary Wynn's order was cut in half when her son refused to go to camp.[101] In the same way, the Women's Union clients did not seem to make distinctions between day nurseries and other forms of relief; the day nursery was simply an available resource to use when other child care arrangements did not work out. Several families expressed remorse when they could not pay their nursery fees—at least one family kept their children at home rather than continue to bring them to the nursery when they could not pay the fee—but none expressed shame at having to come to the nursery in the first place.[102] The fee itself may have made these mothers more comfortable; since many African-American mothers paid a small fee to board their children with a neighboring woman while they went out to work, a nursery which charged a fee might not have seemed like charity at all.

The depression forced day nurseries and the families who used them to consider what kind of help was legitimate in the face of the disruption caused by widespread unemployment. Who could or would take on a mother's job while mothers became breadwinners? Men's inability to support their families not only forced families to reconsider the way they divided their labor, but it also forced day nurseries to question the purpose and meaning of day care. Although the responses of both families and day nurseries to the economic crisis were temporary, they had long-term implications. During the early years of the depression, day nurseries defined day care as potentially beneficial to a range of children, and different types of families came into contact with these nurseries. The typical day nursery client was now less likely to be a widowed or deserted mother, and more likely to be a married woman working to help keep her family together. In the long run, this shift would contribute to the lessening of stigma attached to using the day nurseries, opening the way for a broader understanding of the purpose of day care.

Mixing Welfare and Education: The Federal Nursery Schools

While private day nurseries were returning to their narrower mission and New Dealers were constructing a welfare state around the figure of the male breadwinner, the federal government launched the first public day care program in U.S. history. The nursery schools that were established in every state as part of the government's work relief program were not intended to serve working mothers, but rather to provide work for unemployed teachers and food for underprivileged children. Administered by the Federal Emergency Relief Administration (FERA) and later by the Works Projects Administration (WPA), the main purpose of the program was always to provide work for unemployed teachers. In keeping with this primary goal of work relief, 95% of the federal funds for the nursery schools were earmarked for wages.[103] At the same time, however, the nursery schools were also meant to help children whose families were "on relief or near relief," by providing an educational experience as well nutritious meals and medical care. Although the government nursery schools suffered from contradictory goals and erratic funding, they set an important precedent for governmental involvement in child care, began to blur the lines between education and custodial care for young children, and introduced the nursery school concept to thousands of families who would never have had access to the private nursery schools of the 1920s.

In Philadelphia, the federal program, established in 1933, encouraged the expansion or continuation of previously existing child care programs. Four nursery schools, all located in settlement houses, were initially established in cooperation with the Board of Education, with each school serving about twenty-five children; two more schools were added later, bringing the total number of children to between 150 and 200.[104] The Wharton Centre school, for instance, started as a small project run by settlement workers who had noticed how "the heavy hand of the depression" fell on preschoolers in this poor African-American neighborhood; federal funding enabled the settlement to expand its program.[105] The Morton Street Day Nursery, which had been in existence since 1884, had just recently closed down and renamed itself the Germantown Settlement when it was able to start a government nursery school. Similarly, the House of Industry settlement, which had operated a day nursery since 1896 for the Italian children in its South Philadelphia neighborhood, used federal funds to replace the day nursery with a nursery school in 1934.[106] WPA teachers also staffed a nursery school at the Carl Mackley Houses, a low-rent housing development in Kensington sponsored by the American Federation of Hosiery Workers and built with Public Works Administration funds in 1935.[107]

Significantly, the government program provided money for nursery schools, not for day nurseries. As we saw in the last chapter, nursery schools represented an exciting new frontier of education, while day nurseries had been largely discredited as offering only custodial care to poor families who had no better options. Federal administrators, committed to creating a program that would gain support in states and localities, insisted that their nursery schools, unlike day nurseries, were primarily educational. Administrators vigilantly rejected applications from local communities for programs that were for day nurseries rather than nursery schools. One memo stated tersely that two projects were being rejected because they were intended to establish day nurseries, and "day nurseries are not education projects." Another raised concern about nursery school projects that were not conducted under educational auspices, stating "[I] am sure that it is not the intention that the standards which we have maintained for the nursery schools shall be broken down."[108] In response to a 1933 letter from Nebraska questioning whether day nurseries could be funded by federal relief, the director of the Emergency Educational Program wrote that "nursery schools, as contrasted with the old type of day nursery which has come into disrepute among social workers, may be financed from the educational grant."[109] And during a 1939 meeting held between WPA administrator Grace Langdon and representatives of the Philadelphia nursery schools, it was explained that one factor shaping the definition of WPA programs for preschoolers was the "feeling against going into a Day Nursery situation."[110]

The early childhood educators who administered the government nursery school program insisted on its educational purpose because they saw it as an opportunity to dramatically expand nursery education in America. From its inception, the federal nursery school program was closely linked to the field of early childhood education and supervised by experts in that field. Preschool educators proposed the idea of government nursery schools, helped raise private funds to pay the salary of the program's first director (who was borrowed from the U.S. Office of Education), and served as regional supervisors for the schools.[111] Nursery educators, who felt that they had proved the value of nursery schools by the late 1920s, had been looking for a way to create publicly funded nursery schools several years before the federal program was announced. For instance, in 1931, the president-elect of the National Association of Nursery Educators, George Stoddard, proclaimed, "We must be prepared to recommend expenditure of possibly half a billion dollars per year on the systematic education of five million preschool children." Educators thus welcomed the federal program, which enabled the kind of expansion of nursery schools in the United States that they could only have dreamed of before the depression. By 1935, there were about nineteen hundred emergency nursery schools serving some seventy-five thousand children across the country, whereas surveys a few years earlier counted fewer than five hundred nursery schools in the nation.[112]

By stressing the educational nature of the public nursery schools, administrators hoped not only to justify hiring thousands of unemployed teachers, but also to inspire local school districts to adopt nursery schools on a permanent basis. Program director (and nursery educator) Grace Langdon often spoke of continuing the nursery schools indefinitely, explaining that it was her goal "to carry on a program of such high caliber that school superintendents in time may wish to take it over."[113] Other nursery educators shared this goal of making nursery schools a permanent, universal part of school systems across the country. Christine Heinig, a professor of child development at Teachers College, saw the government nursery schools as "a powerful statement to the country—a very dramatic statement—that the early years in a child's life are important educationally."[114] George Stoddard announced in 1935 that since the government nursery schools had proven successful, it was time to take on "the hard task of welding, once and for all, the needs of five million preschool children to the great body of education."[115]

To this end, program officials sought to identify the nursery schools as much as possible with the public schools. Conducting nursery schools in public school buildings was an important part of this strategy: a list of guidelines for nursery schools in Pennsylvania stated, "If possible, emergency nursery schools will be organized in school buildings. If settlement houses or other places are used, they will be approved by the local superintendent of schools."[116] Running the nursery schools on the same schedule as the public schools was another way to associate the two. In a letter to the Pennsylvania WPA administrator, Grace Langdon expressed her disapproval of a proposal to operate the nursery schools in Philadelphia only four days a week by saying, "We have all worked throughout the operation of the program to keep the nursery schools on a sound educational basis and to identify them in the minds of the public with the public school program. Operating on a schedule of fewer days a week than the public school operates at once differentiates between the two programs in the minds of people."[117]

Yet the educational aspect of the federal nursery school program was precarious from the outset. Administrators committed to making the program an educational one found themselves caught between professional educators' concerns about maintaining educational standards, and the fears of state and local education officials, who rebelled at any suggestion that they would be expected to permanently absorb the government nursery schools into their school systems. This conflict was evident in choosing a name for the program: while national nursery educators "were emphatic that the name indicate that the program be educational and not custodial," school superintendents who feared the expansion of their school systems wished to stress the emergency nature of the program and its status as a welfare measure.[118] The name finally chosen, the Emergency Nursery School Program, was an attempt to address the concerns of both groups. But ultimately it proved easier to find a suitable name for the program than to maintain the delicate balance between its different goals of providing jobs for the unemployed, nutrition and health services for disadvantaged children, and an educational preschool program in line with the latest nursery school techniques.

Nursery educators' fears about educational standards in the government nursery schools were well-founded. Some teachers employed in the government schools had no prior teaching experience. Although they attended training workshops conducted by preschool specialists, even teachers accustomed to working with elementary or secondary students often did not understand nursery educators' emphasis on play and informal pedagogy. Even if they embraced nursery school pedagogy, an overall teacher-child ratio of one to nineteen, high teacher turnover, and inadequate space and equipment made it difficult to carry out the careful educational program of private nursery schools. After visiting government nursery schools around the country, Grace Langdon concluded that despite the hard work of preschool specialists and state administrators, "many units probably exist under the name of emergency nursery schools which in no way even approximate a good nursery school."[119] A study comparing the techniques of nursery school teachers in a WPA nursery school in California with those of the more highly trained teachers in a university nursery school found a similar gap between the atmosphere of WPA and private nursery schools. In interacting with the children in their care, the WPA teachers used physical handling and imperative commands three times as often as teachers in the university nursery school and were less likely to explain the reasons behind the rules they enforced. Physical compulsion was used more often, as were physical demonstrations of affection. The questions that WPA teachers asked the children tended to be very basic (i.e., "Where are your mittens?"), while those that the university nursery school teachers asked were designed to stimulate the children's curiosity and interest (i.e., "Do you know what tree this leaf came from?") The authors of the study, who were educators associated with the university nursery school, concluded, "All this would seem to indicate a more authoritarian attitude on the part of the [WPA] teachers . . . and perhaps more concern with having orders carried out and routines followed through than with the educational possibilities of these experiences for the children." They also suggested that this emphasis on making sure children complied with the rules was partly a product of the WPA nursery school's limited staffing and awkward physical setup.[120]

Not only did the government nursery schools sometimes fall short of the standards of private nursery schools, but despite the efforts of program administrators to portray the nursery schools as educational, in practice the schools served multiple purposes. Government nursery schools often served as both nursery schools and as day nurseries, combining educational with custodial care. For instance, the nursery at the Carl Mackley housing project in Philadelphia, which was partially staffed by WPA teachers, was described in a 1941 newspaper article as both a day nursery for the children of working mothers and as a nursery school that sought to "develop each child to his fullest potentialities as a well-adjusted personality and useful member of his group." Although it seems to have been clearly intended to provide day care for mothers who worked in nearby hosiery mills, the Carl Mackley Nursery resembled a private nursery school in some respects: it was only open from nine in the morning until three in the afternoon, it only served children between the ages of two and five, and it was well-equipped with toys and art materials.[121] A handful of case records from the Wharton Centre Nursery School suggests that its WPA program also served as a mix of a day nursery and a nursery school. While the nursery school was intended to teach children social skills and good "habits" while training mothers in appropriate child-rearing techniques, families also used the school to provide care for their children when mothers went out to work. In Wharton Centre's African-American neighborhood, mothers' need for day care often overlapped with their desire to give their young children an educational experience. For instance, Sarah Adams applied to place her son Howard in the nursery school after she heard about it from the settlement house's cook. "She heard Miss Griffin talk so much about it that she decided that she didn't know how to teach her child all the things she had been told." Howard refused to drink any milk, and his doctor wrote that the discipline of the school would be as helpful to him as the milk. Howard was admitted to the nursery school to improve his physical health and give him the opportunity to play with other children, but further down on the application form, the social worker noted another reason: "need for mother to help support family."[122] The nursery school was used not only by children like Alberta Packer, whose doctor said she was "very rebellious, needs disaplain!" but also by children like Virginia Atkinson, whose mother sought to place her in the nursery school so she could help support the family by supplementing her relief check.[123]

The government nursery schools in Philadelphia seemed to have had more in common with the charitable day nurseries than with the most progressive private nursery schools. At the House of Industry, a 1935 report commented on the continuity between the nursery school and the older day nursery program it replaced: "The habit-training functions of the day nursery, with additional educational work with the mothers, was developed on a much more intensive scale for a group of sixty children."[124] The type of parental education that was offered as part of federally funded nursery schools in Philadelphia was closer to that of the day nursery mothers' club, with its emphasis on physical care and rudimentary child management, than to the more sophisticated instruction in child psychology and development advocated by private nursery school educators in the 1920s. For instance, the Italian mothers whose children attended the Dixon House nursery school heard talks on scarlet fever, tonsils, healthy diets for children, and "The Dinner That Saves the Day"; no psychologists or child development experts appear to have been invited to address the group.[125] Similarly, the African-American mothers whose children attended the nursery school at Wharton Centre were informed about nursery procedures including "the importance of button on overalls, shoe laces and change of underwear"; they also heard lectures on birth control and other health issues, "the things that go to make a good home," and how to buy a dress. The child-rearing advice they received from a doctor included keeping nails trimmed, ears clean, and not picking one's nose in the presence of a child. (It is difficult to imagine the latter instruction being given with a straight face to the more educated, middle-class white parents who paid to send their children to private nursery schools.) While there were a few discussions focusing on such issues as managing children's eating, sleeping, and toilet habits, temper tantrums, and children's need for attention, the vast majority of these meetings focused on the basic physical care of children, not on their social, emotional, or cognitive development.[126]

Even descriptions of the federal nursery school program by WPA administrators often emphasized welfare over education. In an article in *Progressive Education* in 1938 (a venue where one might expect educational goals to be given top priority), Grace Langdon wrote, "By its very nature, the nursery school under the relief set-up is essentially a community service agency."[127] The article went on to stress the vital importance of the food and health care that underprivileged children received in these nursery schools; while emotional and social growth was also described, it was not given as much attention. Similarly, a 1935 memo listing the purposes of the federal program put educational goals toward the bottom of the list, after providing nutritious meals, rest, health care, and opportunities for play.[128]

In Philadelphia as elsewhere, the government nursery schools suffered from the contradiction between the program's work relief goals and its other goals. Two particular problems made it difficult to maintain a consistently high educational standard: the WPA rule stipulating that no worker could be kept on a relief project for more than eighteen months, and the need to hire untrained teachers. There were only a handful of institutions in the country that offered training for nursery school teachers in the 1930s, and most of the graduates of these schools did not have trouble finding employment. Since teachers had to be eligible for work relief in order to work in the federal nursery schools, most of the teachers who were hired had not been trained for nursery work. They tended to be either young college graduates who had not been able to find work as teachers or older kindergarten and primary teachers who had been dismissed from public schools when budgets were cut.[129] Standards for WPA nursery school employees in Philadelphia required that teachers have two years of post-high school training, preferably in a normal school, but did not specify any other requirements.[130] Few localities were able to fulfill the suggestion of federal administrators that teachers be provided with 160 hours of training before beginning work in the nursery schools.[131] When the head worker of the Wharton Settlement evaluated the settlement house's nursery school program in 1943, she commented, "My overall criticism of the project was the inefficiency of the teachers we were forced to use, because they had to have relief status in order to be employed."[132] But it was the WPA's eighteen-month rule that caused the greatest problems for the nursery schools, creating constant turnover among experienced staff and ensuring a lack of continuity in the program. The records of the WPA nursery school at South Philadelphia's Dixon House Settlement are filled with protests against this rule and attempts to get exemptions for particularly gifted teachers.[133] A summary of the Wharton Settlement's experience describes how "eminently qualified workers were constantly dropped from the rolls and thus withdrawn from the program, often to be replaced by far less competent and skilled assignees." This report notes that the initial frustrations of uncertain funding were gradually replaced with "an annoying lack of continuity of staff assigned to the program."[134]

The Philadelphia nursery schools suffered throughout the 1930s not only from problems securing qualified teachers from the relief rolls, but also from tenuous and erratic funding by different government agencies; programs were rarely secure enough about their future to plan more than a few months ahead. A 1934 letter informing the Wharton Settlement that the nursery school could be extended for another month, apologized: "I regret very much this constant indecision which must be annoying to you as well as to the nursery school workers. We are, unfortunately, working from week to week on this program."[135] Another letter a few months later stated that "very serious" budget cuts for each of the nursery schools had delayed opening the schools and referred to "our inability to proceed without further clarification of terms and purposes with Harrisburg."[136] Several months after that, the settlement's newsletter reported that the school had closed and had not yet reopened, "due to delays in the State administration."[137] Wharton was not the only program to have these problems: at the House of Industry, a 1935 report noted the impact of erratic funding on that settlement's nursery school, stating, "It has been a most valuable extension of our program in spite of the fact it has been intermittent. We must hope at some time that such a program with trained teachers . . . can become a stabilized feature of our program."[138] Two years later, the annual report again noted the instability of the nursery program: "The nursery school . . . program now provided through WPA has meant the development of a second group of mothers, young, interested and active. Here in lies a great responsibility for us. Will the government continue? If not how can we find ways and means of continuing?"[139]

Federal nursery schools were again endangered in the late 1930s when a conservative coalition in Congress began to threaten New Deal programs, including the WPA. By September 1939, nursery school mothers at Wharton were being urged to attend a meeting on the closing of the nursery schools and to write letters to Eleanor Roosevelt protesting this possibility. A few months later, Wharton mothers were told that they would have to raise additional money in order to keep the nursery school open, as the WPA would no longer cover all the costs. The mothers made plans to raise money for the school through a neighborhood committee made up of clergy, schoolteachers, an undertaker, "a colored newspaper," and several neighborhood clubs; mothers also contributed to the cause by preparing lunch for the teachers at cost.[140] Similar efforts were required at other federally sponsored nursery schools in the city, as the WPA cut funding. At Dixon House, a sponsoring committee made up of nursery parents and neighborhood leaders (including a butcher, grocer, and public health nurse) took on the responsibility for raising money to cover food and other operating costs for the nursery school. Drawing on the resources of the settlement's Italian neighborhood, the committee was quite successful at raising money through "coffee clutches" and neighborhood parties. Yet in the summer of 1941 the nursery school program again appeared to be in jeopardy. Settlement staff organized parents and community members, including businessmen and union leaders, to write letters of protest to WPA administrators and congressmen. This strategy was ultimately successful, and in July three state representatives wrote to the settlement's headworker that they had succeeded in convincing WPA officials to continue the program.[141] Similar sponsoring committees were active at other WPA nursery schools in the city, raising money through newspaper publicity and by soliciting from private schools, churches, and neighborhood clubs.[142] The nursery school at the Kensington High School, for instance, urged local businesses and other groups to "adopt" a nursery school child by contributing thirty dollars a year to feed that child at the school. The *Philadelphia Inquirer* helped publicize this campaign, telling the story of Mrs. Margaret Cameron, a mother of five living on a $12.40 weekly relief allowance, who "at first misunderstood when she was told that Mrs. Franklin Roosevelt had 'adopted' her daughter, Joan. . . . 'Why,' exclaimed Mrs. Cameron, 'that sort of makes us related to the president, doesn't it?'"[143]

The uncertain funding for nursery schools after 1939, and the need to coordinate the work of the individual sponsoring committees, spurred the formation of a WPA Early Childhood Education Committee in Philadelphia. This committee spent most of its time discussing ways to publicize the work of the nursery schools to gain public support and facilitate fund-raising efforts. They talked about seeking support through radio broadcasts, appealing to public school teachers, encouraging the development of nursery schools in housing projects, and showcasing the fund-raising successes of different sponsoring committees.[144] By 1941, members were discussing the place of the nursery schools in the national defense program and seeking ways to ensure that the schools would continue in the next decade.[145] Despite many attempts to define nursery schools as an essential part of national defense efforts, however, all government-sponsored nursery schools were closed down when the WPA was liquidated in 1943; the only way to continue was to apply for Lanham Act funds to establish day care facilities for mothers working in war industry.[146]

Ultimately, parents, nursery school staff, and professional nursery educators were faced with the fact that the federal nursery school program had been designed as a temporary measure whose first priority was to provide employment for teachers. Unlike mothers' pensions, unemployment insurance, and other Progressive-era solutions to working-class poverty, day care was not to become part of the permanent welfare system established by the New Deal. Nor—despite the hopes of preschool educators—would it become part of the nation's system of public education. Local school boards did not adopt the nursery schools, which were seen as a temporary relief measure, not a universal educational program. Without a concerted campaign for public school adoption, similar to the campaign taken up on behalf of kindergartens at the turn of the century, the public nursery schools were fated to have a short life.

During their short life, however, the government nursery schools in Philadelphia and across the country set some important precedents. First, and most obviously, by sponsoring the nursery schools, the federal goverment sent the message to the public and local governments that the care and education of young children was a legitimate public responsibility. Just as Eleanor Roosevelt's "adoption" of Joan Cameron symbolized the government's new interest in child welfare, so government funding of the nursery school that Joan attended suggested that nursery education was a positive social good, an experience that could be beneficial to children. Second, the program made nursery schools, previously the near-exclusive domain of the affluent, available to a much wider range of families. For instance, the WPA program at Wharton Centre was the first to offer a nursery school program for African-American children in Philadelphia. By making nursery schools more accessible, the WPA program spread the idea that day care could be beneficial and educational for children, not just convenient for mothers, and that mothers deserved help and guidance in the task of child-rearing. Shortly before the Kensington Nursery School closed in 1943, the president of the school's mothers' group reflected this idea when she told a reporter, "We all think the group play the children get is very good for them and we'd be heart-broken if the nursery school should have to close during the summer. But besides wanting to help keep the school going, I think we're really learning a lot about child care."[147] Finally, by combining education and welfare, the government nursery schools helped blur the class distinctions between nursery schools and day nurseries that had been so sharp in the 1920s.

In all the areas this chapter has addressed—the division of labor within the family, the place of day nurseries in the welfare system, and the government-sponsored nursery schools—temporary solutions to the crisis of the depression challenged the status quo. Middle-class mothers joined the labor force, male breadwinners became dependent on their wives' wages, day nurseries functioned as relief agencies for two-parent families, and the government funded a significant child care program. These challenges were circumscribed by their very status as emergency responses to crisis, and several of them did not outlast the depression. Yet even those that did not last—for instance, the widened relief mission of day nurseries—contributed to a gradual shifting of attitudes toward maternal employment and day care by at least temporarily exposing new segments of the population to the problems long faced by day nursery clients. Although change would not become evident immediately, in the long run these haphazard and uncertain responses to the economic emergency of the 1930s undermined some common understandings of what constituted "normal" patterns of paid and unpaid work for women and men, and public and private responsibility for children.

6

Battling for Mothers' Labor

Day Care During World War II

Although the depression started to change the ways that Americans thought about day care, it was World War II that made day care into a full-fledged public issue. As the nation recognized its need for women to work in defense plants during the war, government officials, social workers, employers, and ordinary people had to weigh the value of women's paid labor against the value of their work as mothers. The conflicting solutions that different people reached led to a confused national debate and an inadequate national response to the problem. But despite the inadequacies and temporary nature of the day care provided during the war, the war years represented a sort of watershed in *attitudes* toward day care and women's paid labor. By the end of the war, there had been a fundamental shift in thinking about day care and the people who used it.

Taking advantage of the new legitimacy of women's wage work, women in Philadelphia began to redefine the meaning of day care. No longer the last resort of the desperately poor single mother, day care was increasingly used by married couples, including middle-class people and professionals. The boundary between educational and custodial care blurred even further than it had in the 1930s, as clients expressed their growing conviction that day care was educational and beneficial to children, a tool that the modern mother might use in raising her children. The opening of federally funded day care centers in Philadelphia's public schools furthered the dawning perception that day care could be seen as a public service for ordinary families, not a charity for those who had nowhere else to turn.

Where Is a Mother's Job? The Debate Over Public Day Care

Throughout the war years, child welfare professionals in the Children's Bureau fought with representatives of war industries over whether a mother's job was in a defense plant or caring for her children at home. These battles over day care raised larger questions about the relationship between motherhood and citizenship: did women, like men, have a direct obligation to the state, or was motherhood itself a civic duty that overshadowed all others? Did women's private obligations to children and families override their public, civic obligations?

Child welfare advocates, like their predecessors in the 1910s, made the maternalist argument that bearing and rearing children was a civic service that should be valued and given national priority. But while earlier maternalists had faced little opposition when they argued that a mother's place was at home caring for her children, the demands of the war and changes in patterns of women's wage work had altered the ideological landscape, so that maternalists were no longer the only ones with a legitimate claim to mothers' labor. While child welfare advocates pushed for a government policy that would define mothering as a patriotic service and would not require (or encourage) mothers to join the paid labor force, those concerned primarily with meeting the needs of defense industries urged the creation of day care facilities in order to encourage mothers to take up defense work, thus helping the war effort.

Although their voices were no longer the only ones to be heard, child welfare advocates and social workers who opposed day care played a major role in shaping government policy. Their conviction that encouraging mothers to be workers would harm family life led them to resist expanding day care in the early years of the war, and then to insist on limiting and controlling it. By resisting the creation of easily accessible group day care facilities for the children of employed mothers, child welfare advocates in the Children's Bureau effectively worsened the situation, leaving no influential voice to speak in moral terms of the needs of mothers and children. Day care was thus left to the mercies of those concerned with increasing war production, who in turn created programs that many working mothers were reluctant to use.

As we have seen in previous chapters, the Children's Bureau had developed an anti–day care policy early in its existence. In the 1910s, Children's Bureau staffers argued that day nurseries encouraged women to take on impossible burdens by combining paid work and mothering, and instead urged state and local governments to support mothers in their homes through mothers' pensions. The bureau's hostility toward day nurseries also grew out of the conviction that most day nurseries offered substandard care and were organized with mothers' convenience rather than children's welfare in mind. These were legitimate and serious concerns, but rather than trying to improve the quality of day nurseries, the Children's Bureau ignored them, hoping that expanding welfare benefits would ultimately solve the problems of wage-earning mothers and render day care unnecessary. As historian Gwendolyn Mink has argued, because these maternalist reformers felt that wage earning and motherhood were inevitably in conflict, they were not inclined to push for measures like day care that would help women reconcile paid work with family life.[1]

Children's Bureau staff carried these prejudices against day care with them into the war years and were never able to support day care with genuine enthusiasm. Perhaps they could hardly be expected to, since even most day care advocates at this time saw day care more as a necessary evil than as a positive social good. Instead of establishing easily accessible day care centers during the war, child welfare professionals urged the creation of networks of foster day care providers along with after-school programs for older children and advocated providing counseling to mothers in the hopes of dissuading them from going out to work. While they did insist on high standards of child care and a variety of services, and recognized that day care was going to be a long-term issue, their vision of mothers' employment as an unfortunate necessity prevented them from becoming strong advocates for quality day care during the war.

From their earliest discussions about wartime day care, child welfare advocates displayed their ambivalence. As the nation geared up for war production, the Children's Bureau, worried about encouraging substandard programs, discouraged local efforts to start day nurseries. In 1940, the executive director of the National Association of Day Nurseries wrote to Katharine Lenroot, chief of the Children's Bureau, to express her concern that factories would establish day nurseries when they hired women to meet defense orders. Rather than applauding this extension of the day nursery, she worried, "The possibilities of weakening family responsibility, and of inadequate care for the children in this situation are great," and wondered what could be done to protect the children and their families. In response, Lenroot assured her that the government "has never promoted and is not now promoting day nurseries."[2]

As early as 1941, however, Children's Bureau staff realized that warning against inadequate care was no longer enough. Seeing themselves as spokeswomen for children, whose interests conflicted with those of industrialists and military leaders, they urged the nation to put children first. Grace Abbott, an earlier chief of the bureau, explained in a 1931 speech how she saw her role:

> Sometimes when I get home at night in Washington I feel as though I had been in a great traffic jam [of vehicles representing the different demands of government agencies]. . . . I stand on the sidewalk watching it become more congested and more difficult, and then because the responsibility is mine and I must, I take a very firm hold on the handles of the baby carriage and I wheel it into the traffic.[3]

During the war, Children's Bureau staffers were convinced that the best way to look out for children's interests was to keep mothers at home. A conference sponsored by the bureau in July 1941 called on policymakers to give "consideration to mother and child welfare when developing employment policies relating to national defense," keeping in mind that "mothers who remain at home to provide care for children are performing an essential patriotic service in the defense program." In the face of calls for women to work in defense industries, the bureau reminded the American public that mothering was work and a contribution to the nation. Only after priority had been given to mothering work over defense work did the conference recommend developing nursery schools and day care centers to meet local needs.[4]

Even the federal Women's Bureau, the primary advocate of working women's rights, took a similar position. Although she defended women's right to work, bureau chief Mary Anderson seemed to share the Children's Bureau's negative feelings about wage-earning mothers: she explained in 1942 that mothers of small children should not be recruited for war work "unless there is a much more serious labor shortage than is now envisioned," for even if day care were provided, these women would be forced to carry a double burden. While acknowledging that some mothers needed to work and could make adequate provision for their children's care, she concluded, "Most mothers prefer to remain at home to look after their children. In this time of crisis there is no finer contribution such women can make."[5]

A range of influential voices echoed these sentiments. Child development expert Arnold Gessell, for instance, argued in a 1944 speech that increased child care facilities were not the answer to the problems of working mothers. Rather, he argued, women must "be practical enough to hold to what was most important—the *family*." Gessell "referred to Germany, Japan and Russia (in part), where the family is secondary to the State. He stressed that where there is conflict between the values of the family and the values of industry, family values must prevail, that nothing must jeopardize the family unit."[6] Parenting advice columnist Angelo Patri also urged mothers to stay home with their children rather than taking up war work. After painting a scene featuring a little girl whose mother was always "too busy or tired or something" from her defense job to play with her, Patri concluded that mothers who could choose to stay home "should do so with a free conscience," for "rearing children is the greatest service any woman can render her country now or at any other time." He concluded the column by pleading, "Let any mother who can, stay by her little children so that none of them can know the grief of not being loved by their own mothers, who are so busy with the world's affairs as to leave no time for the one special duty they owe their children."[7] J. Edgar Hoover, director of the Federal Bureau of Investigation, agreed with these child development experts that mothers should be discouraged from working in defense industries. In a 1944 article entitled, "Mothers . . . Our Only Hope," Hoover wrote, "She already has her war job. Her patriotism consists in not letting quite understandable desires to escape for a few months from a household routine or to get a little money of her own tempt her to quit it. *There must be no absenteeism among mothers.*"[8] The National Catholic Welfare Conference joined Hoover in emphasizing the vital importance of full-time motherhood. In 1942, Emma Lundberg of the Children's Bureau reported getting pressure from Catholic welfare groups to encourage "preservation of home life and care of children by their own mothers, etc."[9] Journalist Susan Anthony reported that Catholic leaders were active in opposing day care and blamed "the hostility to group care on the part of a few highly placed members of the Catholic hierarchy, ignoring or overriding the obvious needs of their own Catholic working mothers" for halting government efforts to provide day care.[10]

Some offered an even stronger link between mothering and patriotic service by calling on mothers to nurture democracy within the family. At the 1940 White House Conference on Children in a Democracy, President Franklin Roosevelt explained, "A succession of world events has shown us that our democracy must be strengthened at every point of strain or weakness," and the family was the place to start. Participants in the conference resolved that the family could be "the threshold of democracy, . . . a school for democratic life." Sociologists who had been tracing the emergence of a more democratic family structure, which presumably would replace the patriarchal patterns of the past, heralded this new American family as a bulwark against fascism, and called for parent education programs to bring about more democratic family relationships.[11] The Children's Bureau's pamphlet "Children's Charter in Wartime" built on this idea of the family as the cradle of democracy, explaining, "The American home has emerged from the search for freedom. Within it the child lives and learns through his own efforts the meaning and responsibilities of freedom."[12] This vital task of instilling democratic values in the next generation could clearly not be sacrificed while mothers took up defense work.

By insisting that motherhood was a patriotic service as valuable as producing ammunition, child welfare advocates revived an eighteenth-century concept that historians have called "republican motherhood." Invented in the aftermath of the American Revolution to define a role for women in the new republic without overturning male privilege, republican motherhood held that women expressed their citizenship not by voting, governing, or serving in the military, but by raising their children, especially sons, to become good citizens.[13] Women's private obligations as wives and mothers thus substituted for the public obligations of full citizenship. This idea that women fulfill their civic obligations by serving their husbands and children has been influential throughout American history, excluding women from the obligation to perform military service or serve on juries. But while republican motherhood conferred social and political value on women's work as mothers, it was always a double-edged sword; for without the public obligations of citizenship, women could not claim the rights of full citizens.[14] Futhermore, the idea that all women fulfilled their political duties through their families left little room for women to choose other paths to citizenship. In the 1940s, arguing that women fulfilled their civic responsibilities through motherhood enabled child welfare advocates to claim some space for children's needs as war industries sought to draw mothers into defense factories. But it ignored the fact that mothers made different choices about how to divide and prioritize their labor, meet their children's needs, and fulfill their duties as citizens.

The Children's Bureau was especially intent on discouraging the employment of mothers with children under the age of two, since child welfare experts generally felt that group care was harmful to these very young children. Late in 1943, bureau chief Katharine Lenroot wrote to the secretary of labor to protest the decision by defense manufacturers Curtiss Wright in Buffalo and Kaiser in Portland to establish day care centers for their workers that cared for children under two years of age, which was "contrary to accepted principles of child care. These children," she wrote, "should be cared for in individual homes."[15] A special Children's Bureau conference on the topic of day care for children under two concluded that foster day care—a system by which a few children were cared for during the day by a woman in her own home, supervised by a social worker—was greatly preferable to group care, since it provided a homelike environment and the opportunity for "mothering" that was absent in group care situations. Even when foster day care was an option, however, mothers were to be discouraged from taking up work. Conference attendees heard Dr. Benjamin Spock urge that the nation not "sacrifice the children" to its need for war manpower, and resolved, "Every effort should be made to preserve for the young child his right to have care from his mother."[16] This rhetoric of "children's rights," which child welfare advocates often employed, was effective in linking the needs of children to American political discourse about rights. But it did not leave room for an argument about mothers' rights—whether their right to a certain kind of care for their children or their right to make their own decisions about how to divide their labor. The idea that children had a right to full-time care from their mothers also ignored the wide variety of child-rearing styles that families across the country used in nurturing their children and assumed that there was only one way to meet children's needs.

To encourage women to stay at home with their children, the bureau urged day care agencies to provide counseling to women seeking day care. Such counseling was based on the premise that women were rushing headlong into paid work without considering their duty to their children, and that they should not be allowed to take up employment without proving to a social worker's satisfaction the soundness both of their reasons for going to work and of their plan for their children's care. Advocates of counseling services clearly did not trust mothers to make adequate arrangements for their children, or understand the implications of their decision to go out to work. A Children's Bureau policy paper issued early in the war explained the need for counseling by saying, "The mother must be helped to think through her problem and to make plans that will safeguard the health and welfare of her children."[17] Advocates of counseling for mothers requesting day care were almost always those who most opposed mothers' employment; they often assumed that if mothers really "thought through" the situation, under the guidance of a trained social worker, they would decide to stay at home with their children. In practice, mothers often did not want this type of help; a 1943 study of applicants to a Baltimore family agency found that half the applicants rejected offers of counseling, as they "wanted to use the agency for the purpose of receiving immediate and business-like direction in the matter of effecting a specific type of child-care plan."[18]

Because she feared that it would become another way of setting up barriers to employing women, Women's Bureau chief Mary Anderson also raised objections to counseling. She reminded government planners at a 1941 conference that women work "for the same reason that men work. They work to live. They work to get bread and butter not only for themselves but for dependents." Thus Anderson only supported counseling if it could be done in a nonthreatening and helpful way.[19] After Anderson voiced her objections, however, Elizabeth Clark of the National Association of Day Nurseries reiterated her support for counseling, explaining that "we do want to make sure we are not creating a lot of emotionally ill and neglected children" by encouraging mothers to go out to work. Although she recognized that asking potential workers whether they had children and what plans they were making for their care was "a very delicate question," she insisted that it was necessary. Moreover, "asking the question isn't enough, we feel, for mothers with children under 2. It is a very serious situation to take those mothers out of the home."[20]

Urging mothers to stay at home was not the only way to speak for children's interests during the war. Although child welfare professionals were focusing on keeping mothers out of the work force, nursery school leaders realized that the war presented an opportunity to extend nursery education to all children. Day care advocates meeting in Harrisburg in 1942 spoke of the need to persuade government officials and the public that "nursery education should be considered as much a priority as steel and automobile tires."[21] By providing children with "the opportunity to live with their peers," the National Association for Nursery Education proclaimed, nursery schools could ensure that the new generation "will be a healthy, wholesome, and better adjusted one than we have had until this time."[22] Although both the Children's Bureau and nursery educators sought to put the needs of children first, they differed significantly in their vision of what those needs were and how to meet them. While the Children's Bureau assumed that a mother's care was always preferable, nursery educators believed that every child should have the opportunity to benefit from a nursery school experience. At a forum on day care sponsored by the Child Welfare League of America in June 1945, these differences became clear when social workers and nursery educators argued about how to define day care programs for children. While the social workers at the meeting wanted to make a clear distinction between care given because of children's educational needs and care given because of parents' need to work, the nursery educators insisted that nursery education was a way of meeting children's needs regardless of how many hours they were under care. Because they had a more positive vision of day care in general, the nursery educators "objected to any negative phrasing on the part of social workers (referring to mother as 'confused' about wanting to work, etc)."[23] Ultimately, however, it was the Children's Bureau's more conventional vision of children's needs that had the greatest impact on national policy.

The Children's Bureau's policy of discouraging mothers from taking up employment, on the grounds that mothering itself was an essential patriotic activity, was instrumental in shaping government policy. The resolution adopted at the bureau's 1941 conference, "The first responsibility of women with young children, in war as in peace, is to give suitable care in their own homes to their children," was declared official War Manpower Commission policy in August 1942 and again in 1943.[24] Although the War Manpower Commission officially forbade discrimination against mothers seeking work (and the Women's Bureau especially stressed that such discrimination was "not to be tolerated"), some public officials and private individuals urged job discrimination against mothers as an easier and more effective policy than establishing child care services.[25] Even in the absence of formal discrimination, some branches of government clearly wanted to discourage mothers from taking up paid work: one government pamphlet addressed to employers urged that job applicants with children under fourteen be questioned closely about provisions for their children's care.[26]

The Children's Bureau's position against encouraging mothers to take up defense work was also influential among day care planners in Philadelphia, where ambivalence about mothers working in industry surfaced early. At a meeting held in January 1942, planners expressed the fear that women taking training courses for defense jobs would neglect their mothering duties and questioned whether day care agencies had the "right to subsidize industries at the risk of the welfare of children." Planners agreed that "the primary principle we are concerned with is the preservation of family life and that women should be encouraged to remain at home with their families." A representative from the Children's Bureau declared that "working mothers will need counseling service before they have a right to determine what kind of service they ought to participate in." Both the "rights" of mothers to go out to work, and the "rights" of day care agencies to provide care for children were tenuous, dependent on the approval of social welfare workers. Maud Morlock of the Children's Bureau described the mistake that England had made by allowing mothers unfettered access to industry; this had resulted in a high delinquency rate among children, which "might have been avoided had England realized that the first base of defense lies in the home."[27]

Although child welfare advocates feared inadequate day care and encouraged mothers to stay home, the war did force them to recognize that day care had become a long-term issue. The needs of children would continue when defense plants no longer needed women workers, and Children's Bureau staffers as well as nursery educators and others saw that meeting children's needs would require some redefinition of older attitudes toward day care. Emma Lundberg, the head of the Children's Bureau's Day Care Unit, tried to disentangle day care from its historic association with charity, noting that mothers who could afford to pay the entire cost of care for their children, and whose work was vital to defense efforts, often could not find good quality care.[28] Lundberg also called for community support of day care, pointing out that "facilities such as public school education, certain health services, and opportunities for various forms of recreation are commonly furnished without charge by the community for all who wish to avail themselves of these services," and arguing that the public schools should take on responsibility for nursery education and after-school activities for children of working mothers.[29]

While acknowledging that day care was going to be a long-term problem and proposing that the public take responsibility for it, the bureau's vision remained strongly biased against easily accessible group care for children. The agency's proposal for a long-term system of day care, outlined in a 1944 memo, included school-sponsored services for older children (including nursery schools and after-school programs), foster day care programs for younger children, and counseling services for mothers. While the schools were to provide an educationally oriented program (for instance, the length of the care provided each day "should be determined by educational criteria, not by the home needs of the child"), the welfare department was to be in charge of services for younger children. The goal of welfare departments, the memo directed, should be to reduce and ultimately eliminate the need for day care centers, by replacing them with foster day care and homemaker services, which would provide care to children in private homes.[30]

In Philadelphia, the Children's Bureau's push for both foster day care and counseling for mothers was taken up most vigorously by the First and Sunnyside Day Nursery (FSDN). This agency, founded in 1863 as the first day nursery in the city, switched to providing foster day care in 1928 and became an energetic national advocate for foster day care.[31] Since the beginning of its experiment with foster day care, First and Sunnyside had insisted on the importance of counseling mothers,[32] and during the war, the agency emphasized the importance of its counseling service in encouraging mothers to stay home. In a 1942 report, executive secretary Dorothy Patterson explained that many families withdrew their applications because they "realized after discussion that their children were better served by them remaining at home." She seemed to be proud of the fact that, partly due to counseling, only half of the 183 families who inquired about the agency's services that year actually continued their applications. She reminded her board that the U.S. Children's Bureau was "still emphasizing the need of women to remain in their homes," and reported that "we have also followed that policy of urging women with children to remain at home where they can offer most in stabilizing the unrest and insecurity that their children are exposed to."[33] She even cast the delays the agency experienced in finding foster homes for children as a benefit, for it gave the mother more time to reconsider her decision to go out to work.[34]

Agency staff frequently described women's desire to work for wages as a psychologically unhealthy product of wartime insecurity. Social worker Mary Rogers, for instance, blamed the government's "repeated appeals to aid the war effort" for encouraging mothers to sacrifice their children's needs to those of the country. In her 1945 report, Rogers emphasized the psychological instability of the women who came seeking day care. "Sometimes she is bored with her fairly recent role of mother and child's nurse and she mobilizes external reasons, which are often real enough, of debts and friction in the home in which she is living to cover this feeling toward the child."[35] Rogers expressed sympathy for these mothers' uncertainty, referring to the difficulty of carrying the burden of a full-time paying job, the job of motherhood, and housekeeping duties as well. Yet the language in which she referred to these women—as "emotionally immature, undecided" mothers who were covering up unhealthy feelings toward their children and who needed expert help—reinforced the idea that counseling was necessary because the mothers were unstable and not able to make decisions in the best interest of their children.[36] In explaining her agency's budget to the executive director of the Community Fund, Rogers stated, "Actually, our work may be counted as more successful when the mother decides that with some assistance from another agency in budgeting, or in some other problem, she can remain at home."[37]

Other day care agencies in Philadelphia, however, had more positive feelings about providing day care. Social workers and directors of most of the city's private day nurseries were not as determined as the FSDN staff to discourage mothers from going out to work, and PADN board members readily agreed to support the efforts of the Philadelphia Council of Defense's Committee on Day Care, which operated public day care centers in the city before federal funding was secured. The PADN board justified their support on two grounds: day care represented an opportunity to contribute to the war effort, and it also offered a way to prevent juvenile delinquency among the children of working mothers. One member spoke of the urgent need for day care "brought about by the pressure and opportunities for mothers to go into defense and other work." A statement from the Day Care Committee referred to figures showing the increase in the proportion of women workers in Philadelphia and warned that "as these numbers increase, without proper care and forehanded action, juvenile delinquency will increase. This happened in England and it can happen here." The committee asked for the PADN's help in "helping to guard a future adult generation" and explained that by providing day care the organization "would be making it possible for the trained or potentially skilled worker to do what we are unable to do, in factory and workroom."[38] While the mostly upper-class women of the PADN were unlikely to take up work in a defense factory, by providing day care they could enable another woman to do so, thus helping the war effort.

In Washington, as in Philadelphia, many people both inside and outside the government disagreed with the Children's Bureau's position that women's labor was better spent in the unpaid work of mothering than in paid work in industry. Although the War Manpower Commission adopted this position as official policy, it conflicted with the needs and desires of employers, other government agencies seeking to intensify war production, and many mothers who saw new wartime employment opportunities as a chance to provide their children with a secure future. Popular support for day care emerged as attitudes about married women's wage work changed abruptly during the war: while 82% of Americans surveyed in 1936 had disapproved of married women working, by 1942, 60% of respondents in a National Opinion Research Center poll believed that married women should work in war industries.[39] Convinced that day care was an effective tool for recruiting women, defense contractors like Curtiss-Wright in Buffalo and Kaiser Industries in Portland, Oregon, opened day care centers for their employees, although most other defense plants did not follow their lead.[40] Recruiting and retaining women workers was the motivation behind Henry Kaiser's support for day care, and day care staff at the Kaiser shipyards were constantly reminded that their work was valuable as long as it improved war production. For instance, the manager of the Kaiser day care centers told his staff that their work had made available for war production "the impressive total of 1,246,773 woman hours of labor."[41] Employers and government agencies who did advocate providing day care during the war thus did so out of a concern with war production, seeing day care as an aid to defense industries, not necessarily as a good in itself. Day nursery activist Ethel Beer reflected the ambivalence that many day care advocates felt as they argued for day care: "It may not be ideal for mothers to leave their homes to earn a living," she wrote. "But they do. That is why the day nursery exists. . . . [It] is as sure a weapon as the gun on the battlefield."[42]

Despite the official policy of encouraging mothers to stay with their children, the government's campaign to recruit women workers targeted mothers as well as other women, publicizing the availability of employer-sponsored and public day care centers. Women workers were encouraged to see themselves as patriots, contributing directly to the war effort on the home front just as their men contributed on the front lines of military service. War work was women's form of civic obligation, their brand of wartime sacrifice. Indeed, the white middle-class woman who took up war work out of patriotism was pictured as a heroine in women's magazines and wartime propaganda. She became a symbol of a broader message: the need for civilians to sacrifice their personal interests for the larger national good, just as soldiers on the front lines were sacrificing their lives. Women who stayed at home, on the other hand, were seen as shirking their duty to their country.[43] Like men, these recruitment campaigns suggested, women owed the nation direct service in a time of crisis. Recruiters did not depend on women's abstract patriotism, however: in encouraging women to become defense workers, they appealed to women's desire to bring husbands and sweethearts home faster, just as men in the military were urged to think of their service as a way of protecting their women and children. Americans of both sexes were thus urged to join the war effort to fight for the family.[44] In wartime advertisements picturing new homes and consumer goods as the reward for the sacrifices of war, both men and women were also urged to fight in order to secure a better and more comfortable future.[45]

To encourage women to take up war work, the Office of War Information (OWI) asked popular magazines to present positive images of married women workers. Attacking the idea that the employed woman was an aberration in American life, writers and magazine editors sought to place her at the forefront of the public mind. Marriage and family responsibilities were not to be portrayed as a full-time career, but as fully compatible with the wartime duty to work.[46] But even the magazines that made a particular effort to help the government's recruitment campaign conveyed mixed messages about motherhood and wartime sacrifice. Magazines such as the *Saturday Evening Post* carried images of the heroic woman war worker gracefully managing her home responsibilities, but they also contained advertisements and stories that pictured mothers and young children in a more passive light, as symbols of what men were fighting to protect. The message of these images was that women's most important war job was maintaining the home, the centerpiece of American values—not in making an individual contribution to defense production.[47]

The message of wartime propagandists was that women were supposed to take jobs out of duty, not out of a desire to better themselves, and not because women had a right to work.[48] But most of the women who worked for wages during the war were not new to the work force, and most went to work to benefit their families and themselves rather than out of patriotic duty.[49] This view of war work as a new opportunity for women, rather than a measure of patriotic self-sacrifice, was particularly typical of African-American women, who were able to earn higher wages and work in better jobs during the war than ever before. One African-American woman told an interviewer, "My sister always said that Hitler was the one that got us out of the white folks' kitchen."[50] Many white working-class women also saw the war as an opportunity. For instance, Madeline Karpowitz told a Philadelphia newspaper reporter in 1942 that she was eager to get a job, although she had not worked in the six years since her marriage.

> The way I feel is, here's a chance for women like me to learn something that's interesting. But we haven't been able to do it on account of the children. . . . Not that I'd swap the children for 50 jobs. But it would be nice to work and know that they're in good safe hands. . . . And I could use the money.[51]

Defining women's war work as an expression of patriotic heroism served to recruit women, give them a wartime role equal to that of their men, and define women's wage-earning work as a temporary aberration necessitated by national crisis—not a normal state of affairs. It thus ignored the real benefits that some women gained from their employment and the reasons they went out to work in the first place. By ignoring these aspects of women's work, the public could avoid thinking about the long-term challenge to gender roles that women's wartime employment might pose.

The OWI addressed the specific concerns of working mothers by putting out broadcasts, newsreels, and traveling exhibits of photographs about the Kaiser day care centers, and asked the editors of women's magazines to portray child care centers in a favorable light.[52] Historian Maureen Honey reports that fiction writers responded to OWI's request for positive images of day care centers by setting romances and comedies against the backdrop of centers. In one story, a romance develops between a shell-shocked veteran and the head of a child care center; he helps her with her duties at the center while recovering from his wounds. Another story features two "fun-loving debutantes" who take jobs in the welfare department of an aircraft factory and encourage the workers to raise money to establish a nursery at the factory (they especially encourage one worker to focus on this project to heal her broken heart). Their project is so successful that they are swamped with requests from defense plants all across the country for information on how to set up similar facilities.[53] But even this propaganda campaign reflected the ambivalence that many Americans felt about the idea of mothers going out to work. The fact that both these stories feature women as staff of day care centers, not as clients, suggests the difficulty writers had picturing day care in positive terms. Positive portrayals of day care were much more common in middle-class magazines like the *Saturday Evening Post*, whose readers might see themselves as directors or volunteer workers at day care centers than in working-class magazines such as *True Story*, whose readers were more likely to be the working mothers who used the day care centers. Maureen Honey observes that although motherhood was central to the fiction published in *True Story*, and heroines in these stories were likely to be mothers, the magazine gave little support to the government's child care program, never featuring a single mother who used a day care center.[54]

One way to bridge the gap between the need for women's war work and the conviction that mothers should be at home with their children was to focus on recruiting women as "foster mothers" to care for the children of defense workers. Social workers and child welfare experts had long preferred foster day care to group care in day nurseries, for it provided a substitute mother figure to care for the child in a substitute home while the child's mother was at work. Nevertheless, foster day care programs were relatively rare. To recruit more women to serve as foster mothers through the First and Sunnyside Day Nursery's program, the Philadelphia United War Chest launched a publicity campaign. "As Wacs and Waves are releasing men for active service on the battle fronts," a press release started, "Philadelphia foster mothers are making it possible for other women to do necessary war-plant work." The press release featured a woman who, with a son in the army and a husband in the navy, spent her days taking care of four young children whose mothers were employed. "Because of her," the text announced, "three other women are able to help the war effort in industry and business, serene in the knowledge that their children are being competently and lovingly looked after while they work." Mundane tasks of child care were newly defined as a patriotic duty: pictures showing children playing and eating lunch in Mrs. Stoever's house were accompanied by a caption reading, "Milk goes down in a big way for four contented youngsters, and Mrs. Stoever's hands are full with this important war-job."[55] Mrs. Stoever's efforts on the home front, like those of defense workers themselves, were presented as an example of how patriotic mothers could join their sons and husbands in winning the war. Her story may have been particularly appealing because it showed a woman contributing to the war without leaving her home or violating conventional gender roles in any way.

While the popular press and the government sent mixed messages about mothers' patriotic responsibilities, union women offered strong and unambivalent support for day care during the war years. Indeed, the war was the first time that working-class women really made themselves heard in national debates on the subject of day care. The Children's Bureau recognized that unions were important players on the day care issue and sought to include both AFL and CIO union leadership in conferences about day care.[56] The United Auto Workers (UAW), one of the leading unions to speak out on the issue, urged its affiliates in 1943 to take responsibility for "the care and solicitude of the children of these soldiers and working mothers," by working for "the planning, the establishment and the continuation of this much needed venture."[57] In the struggles over providing public day care in Philadelphia, unions were among the strongest consistent voices supporting the idea: over the years that the School Board and City Council were debating the city's day care program, the two bodies heard from the Central Labor Union of Philadelphia, the Philadelphia Joint Council United Retail Wholesale and Department Store Employees, the Regional Council of the United Federal Workers, the Philadelphia Industrial Union Council, and the International Workers Order.

Although unions were among the few organizations that could speak for working mothers, the loudest demand for accessible day care came not from the union leadership, but from the CIO women's auxiliaries. Male union leaders generally viewed women's employment as a temporary product of the war and were not committed to working for increased day care facilities or other steps which suggested that women were in the labor force to stay. The disinterest of most union leadership in working for day care so angered reporter Susan Anthony, who generally presented herself as a friend of the labor movement, that she wrote, "It has often been believed that the labor movement itself is not free of the directive influence of the Church. This might explain the strange backwardness of some of our national labor leaders to fight for the nurseries that their members' children need so urgently." She contrasted the hesitancy of labor leaders and the hostility of the Catholic leadership with the "vast majority of Catholic workers" who were in favor of day care and referred to the large numbers of Catholic workers in the United Automobile Workers, who "made their position clear at the UAW Convention in Chicago last year when they passed a unanimous resolution urging the establishment of child-care centers."[58]

Despite a lack of support from union leadership, however, the CIO women's auxiliaries vigorously campaigned for day care. At a conference held in Philadelphia in 1943, the women's auxiliaries drafted a complete program for day care "based on the experiences of working mothers themselves."[59] They resolved that "an adequate child care program must be made available to every child of working mothers" and urged that nurseries be established "in every neighborhood where working mothers live," administered by boards of education, and located in the public schools or in buildings close to elementary schools. The auxiliary women also demanded that nurseries serve nutritious meals and operate for long hours to accommodate working women's schedules.[60] On the local level, CIO women's auxiliaries initiated local child care committees and lobbied for government funding for day care.[61] As historian Susan Hartmann has argued, while elite advocates for day care (such as the members of the PADN) tended to talk about day care in terms of preventing child neglect and juvenile delinquency, union women emphasized working mothers' anxiety over the security of their children.[62] In order to gain support for day care, union women could not just speak about mothers' peace of mind, however; they had to appeal to the government's need for women's labor. Eleanor Fowler, head of the Congress of Women's Auxiliaries, testified before Congress that "[t]he establishment of child-care centers [would] enable women to make their maximum contribution to the defense of our country."[63]

Feminist journalist Susan B. Anthony (niece of the famous suffrage leader) also based her arguments for day care on the government's need to mobilize women for war production. Anthony's book *Out of the Kitchen—And Into the War* was a passionate argument for the government to take the necessary steps to enable women to contribute fully to the war effort. She did not accept the maternalist argument that motherhood was women's only contribution to the state: rather, she argued that women's civic obligations were similar to men's. She clearly saw the war as a chance to increase opportunities for women and promote equality between the sexes, and felt that women could only claim equal rights if they made an equal contribution to the nation. Her contempt for the claims of domesticity was particularly evident when she spoke of the need to bring housewives "*and other irrelevantly occupied women* [emphasis added] out into the open of direct war production."[64] Rather than contributing to the state indirectly by raising good citizens, Anthony argued, women must lend their labor directly to the war effort. In this way, she implied, women would prove their worth as full citizens, as well as take advantage of expanded opportunities after the war. If women had a direct obligation to the state, however, the state also had an obligation to them: "to provide a vast network of approved, low-cost nursery schools . . . , so that the children we cherish will not be among the growing list of war casualities."[65]

The arguments of most day care advocates were thus completely dependent on the need for women's labor caused by the war emergency. Although advocates of day care such as Anthony and the CIO auxiliary women referred to the idea that quality day care programs could be educational for children, their main justification for why the government should provide day care always rested on women's work in war production. This was a compelling claim in the midst of a labor crisis, but it could not speak to the long-term needs of children and working parents. For instance, a spokesman for the federal agency entrusted with the government's day care program explained that approval of the program "was predicated exclusively on a war-connected emergency need."[66] The focus on women's war work left no voice for mothers who would continue to earn wages after the war, for mothers who worried about the quality of care their children received in government-funded day care centers, or for the children themselves. While CIO women and feminists like Anthony may have envisioned a broader future for women's wage work and day care, their core argument about the nation's need for women's labor during the war did not provide the basis for any kind of ongoing claim to day care.

The federal child care program that grew out of this need to mobilize women's labor was never able to fully meet the needs of employed mothers and their children. Federal funding for day care was established by a 1942 amendment to the Community Facilities Act, known as the Lanham Act. Originally passed in 1941, this legislation was intended to help construct schools, sewers, streets, and other necessary facilities in areas experiencing heavy migration due to the growth of defense industries. The agency entrusted with the government's day care program was the Federal Works Agency (FWA), a successor to the WPA, which was primarily concerned with construction projects. None of the federal agencies responsible for children's welfare, women's work, or public education were intially involved. The Lanham Act day care program had many shortcomings: funds were not made available until well into the war, when it became apparent that married women would have to be recruited into defense industries; money was only available for group care, despite the varying needs of working women and their children; and little effort was made to assure that the day care centers would be held to high standards. Local groups complained that funds were slow and insufficient, the application process was cumbersome, and the centers were often inconveniently located, with short hours, high fees, and inadequately trained staff. Even at its peak in July 1944, when there were more than three thousand nurseries, the Lanham program served less than 3% of the children under fourteen whom the Census Bureau estimated had employed mothers.[67] This was a great disappointment to day care advocates such as the National Commission for Young Children, which dissolved itself in October 1943 in order to create a more effective structure for leadership on the day care issue. The commission's final report read in part, "Here we have a great opportunity to build an efficient program of child care and we are letting it fail."[68]

In Philadelphia, day care advocates turned to Lanham funds after the Philadelphia Council of Defense realized that it needed a broader base of support for its city-funded day care centers. The Council of Defense's eleven day care centers had begun operation in December 1942, but were only able to provide care for a tiny fraction of the children who needed it. Although Philadelphia's school superintendent and teachers' union had been pushing the school district to adopt the day care centers for more than a year,[69] it was not until December 1943, when the Council of Defense explained that the school district could apply for federal funds to expand the city's day care program, that the Board of Education was willing to take on responsibility for the day care centers. Even then, some board members were hesitant. Leon Obermayer, who steadfastly opposed the public day care centers throughout the war and postwar period, voted against the resolution, saying, "Mothers should be sent home to look after their children. The idea of day care centers is copied directly from Russia, where children are brought up in similar centers." But school superintendent Dr. Alexander Stoddard pointed out that nationally about twenty school systems had taken on this kind of project. He did not express enthusiasm about the idea, but cast it as a wartime duty: "Most of them wish they didn't have to do it, but they recognize it as a war measure which, as a Board of Public Education, they must undertake."[70] The wording of the Board of Education's resolution to accept responsibility for administering the day care centers reflected its hesitation: the program was accepted "as a temporary emergency program," and with the provision that the Board of Education receive the funding to cover the operating costs of the centers.[71] The board quickly applied for federal funding from the Federal Works Agency, and in April 1944 received a grant, which was renewed in 1945. The grant must have been smaller than planners had expected, for the total number of day care centers in the city never reached the original goal of thirty (at the program's peak, there were twenty centers), and the city continued to appropriate money to supplement the program's budget.[72]

Federal funding for day care in Philadelphia was clearly based on the need to recruit more women into war industries. A newspaper story about the first public day care center in the city opened by referring to "the reservoir of potential industrial workers which must be tapped in 1943 to keep the wheels of war production moving." The story focused on the difficulties women who wanted to go out to work had in finding good care for their children. Mrs. Mary Kolb, for instance, was a sheetmetal worker at the Navy Yard who had gone to work to help make ends meet after her husband enlisted. She worked on the night shift so she could care for her three children, but was worn out and ill from the strain and lack of sleep. "My, it will be a relief," she said, "if I can get my kids in the nursery!"[73]

As the need for women workers increased, so did support for day care. In the summer of 1944, Philadelphia's labor shortage was so critical that the War Manpower Commission (WMC) ordered a forty-eight hour week for workers in certain industries, and froze almost half a million men and women in their jobs, while the Selective Service threatened to immediately draft all men between thirty and thirty-eight who left work in a defense plant. Despite these measures, the Quartermaster Corps was so shorthanded at one point that German prisoners were put to work in its depot.[74] Under these circumstances, day care was clearly seen as an attractive way to recruit and retain workers. When Federal Works administrator Major General Fleming announced an increase and expansion in federal funds for day care that summer, he referred to the shortage of women workers in Philadelphia and to the finding of the WMC that "additional child care facilities will assist materially in freeing women for jobs, and reducing absenteeism and turnover."[75] Similarly, renewed funding in January 1945 was intended to "check the downward trend in the employment of women in war work." Philadelphia had recently been classified as a critical labor shortage area, needing an additional twelve thousand women workers in its war industries. The number of women in principal war industries in the city had fallen off 4% during the fall, and "worry over their children was given as a contributory cause for wholesale resignations."[76]

In Philadelphia as across the country, public day care centers met only a fraction of the demand for day care services. When the Board of Education took over the day care program from the Council on Defense, the total enrollment in eleven centers was 434; a year later it jumped to 1,051 in nineteen centers, reaching a peak in April 1945 of 1,262 children in twenty centers.[77] This was impressive growth (far outstripping the number of children ever cared for by the private day nurseries), but it still did not cover the 3,000 children that the Navy Department's investigator estimated were in need of care in 1943 and did not begin to accommodate the children of the additional twelve thousand women workers the War Manpower Commission hoped to recruit. Not only did the public centers serve a limited number of children, but the rearrangement, closing, and moving of centers once the School Board took over suggests that the original centers were not conveniently or rationally located.[78] The city's entire public day care program remained disorganized until near the end of the war; the full program of twenty centers was only put into operation eight months before the war ended.[79]

While the disorganization of the government's day care program may have been one factor in the reluctance of working mothers across the country to use the public centers, the long-standing equation of day care with welfare and poor women was also a deterrent. Historian Karen Anderson notes that many working parents, fearing the warehousing of their children and inadequate and impersonal care, were suspicious or hostile toward public day care centers.[80] When asked in a Gallup poll in 1943 whether they would accept a job in a war plant if their children were to receive child care free of charge, 29% of mothers replied yes while 56% replied no. One mother asked, "Why should I put my children in a place where they're lined up from morning till night?" Another commented, "Child care centers are all right for charity cases; but my children belong at home." The historical association between day care and charity steered many families away from using day care centers. In ten cities studied by the Children's Bureau, only 5% of mothers sampled decided to place their children in a day nursery while 71% made arrangements with a relative or neighbor.[81] Even the Kaiser Child Service Centers suffered from this association between day care and charitable institutions. James Hymes, the educator who managed the centers, remembered, "[Al]though our set-up was excellent, some of the women workers pegged our centers as being like the county orphanages back home. They didn't want to have anything to do with us at first."[82] Only when women realized that "it was not a 'charity thing'" were they willing to consider using the centers.[83] Day care planners were aware that they had to revise the popular image of the day nursery as a sort of dreary orphanage for neglected children: a poster-sized fact sheet produced by the Family Welfare Association of America to encourage the use of day care centers declared, "This is a war program, not a charity."[84] But overcoming the historic definition of day care as a charity would take more than this.

Despite the inadequacies of the government-sponsored day care centers in Philadelphia, their status as a public service rather than a private charity represented a turning point in attitudes toward day care. While private day nurseries were clearly seen as welfare agencies, the public centers presented themselves as a service for which parents paid a fee, and which the government helped support because of the war. The centers were explicitly geared toward serving the children of working mothers, and unlike the private nurseries, did not accept children who needed day care for health or psychological reasons. Since mothers' employment was the only criteria for admission, the public centers did not employ social workers to investigate and screen applicants, nor did they admit any child whose parents could not pay the fee.[85] (Charitable day nurseries also charged a fee, but it was often waived on the social worker's recommendation, and parents often did not perceive it as a real obligation.) The public day care centers also differed from the private day nurseries in their link to the public schools. Like the WPA nursery schools, the wartime day care centers were located in public school buildings. Not only did this make the centers easily accessible, but it also reinforced their identity as a public service similar to public education, available to all, and suggested that they were providing education as well as custodial care. If day care was equated with public education, it could be defined as a right of all citizens rather than as a gift to poor mothers. Perhaps this is what the CIO women's auxiliaries had in mind when they stipulated that day care centers be run by boards of education and located in public school buildings.

The Lanham program came under fire from child welfare professionals in the Children's Bureau and the Office of Education, as well as from state officials who resented the intrusion of the federal government into the domain of welfare and education, areas typically controlled by the individual states. Competition among different federal agencies exacerbated philosophical disagreements about how to administer a good day care program. The Federal Security Agency, which sided with the Children's Bureau, used money from President Roosevelt's emergency fund to tell local communities not to apply for Lanham Act funds, since they were sure that the Children's Bureau and the Office of Education would soon have a superior child care program that could be properly administered by state officials.[86] The Children's Bureau was particularly disturbed by the FWA's refusal to allow Lanham Act funds to be used for foster day care programs. Relying on states to initiate day care programs was risky, however; in Philadelphia, day care advocate Emma Johnson reported that the regional director of Defense, Health, and Welfare had held up the public funding of day care centers because he felt that day care projects should not be applying for federal funds. She concluded that "the avenues through which a community project must pass" to become established and receive federal funding, "are too devious, and too likely to be held pending, [while] certain individuals in key positions get over personal biases."[87]

Conflict among government agencies came to the fore when Senate hearings were held in 1943 to debate a child care bill proposed by Senator Elbert Thomas of Oklahoma. The Thomas Bill, which proposed transfering jurisdiction over the federal child care program from the FWA to the Children's Bureau, the Office of Education, and their state counterparts, also supported the Children's Bureau's vision of day care by emphasizing foster day care and counseling services for mothers. It was supported by child welfare advocates who felt that the move would ensure a comprehensive high-quality program administered by experts in child development and lay the groundwork for a long-term child care program in the postwar period. The bill was opposed, however, by those more concerned with the quantity and accessibility of day care services, who feared limiting appropriations for day care and dismantling the existing program no matter what its problems. Susan Anthony described the Thomas Bill as an effort to destroy the Lanham day care program, putting in its place a program with limited funds that would place the entire burden of initiative for establishing day care services on the states.[88] Her fears may have been confirmed when during hearings on the bill, Senator Robert Taft explained that it would not only save the government money by limiting the total federal appropriation for day care, but it would create a program that would be more easily dismantled at the end of the war than the Lanham program. Thomasina Johnson of the African-American sorority Alpha Kappa Alpha testified against the bill, noting that a program administered through state governments would exclude large numbers of blacks, and contrasting the FWA's good racial record with the historic "lack of concern" for African-Americans demonstrated by the Office of Education and the Children's Bureau.[89] Labor union women also tended to oppose the Thomas Bill, fearing that it would dismantle the only existing day care program and replace it with one that would be less accessible to working women. They could point to the disorganization following the dismantling of the WPA nursery schools as evidence of the problems that could be caused by replacing a program in midstream. Critics of the Thomas Bill were right when they argued that the legislation, by limiting federal investment in day care and by putting responsibility for day care in the hands of the states, would curtail the scope of the wartime program. But they did not have a strategy for continuing public support for day care once the national emergency of the war was over.

The Thomas Bill was ultimately defeated in the House—perhaps as much because of legislators' wariness of funding any long-term child care program as because of the opposition of labor and African-American groups—but competition and hostility between the different federal agencies involved in child care continued. Although some of the conflict between the FWA and the Children's Bureau can be attributed to bureaucratic infighting over control of programs and money, this was more than a battle over turf. The two agencies had fundamentally different approaches to the problem of day care, although both were equally grounded in the public's hesitation about supporting paid work for mothers and day care for children. The FWA program and its supporters were primarily concerned with facilitating war production; day care was seen as a way to encourage women to work, and was not meant to continue past the wartime emergency. Child welfare experts in the Children's Bureau, on the other hand, saw their role as standing up for the interests of children in the face of demands from industrial and military leaders to sacrifice all for defense production. A 1944 press release entitled, "Mothers and Children Come First in Good Community Day Care Programs," stated point-blank that "No community day-care program which is concerned solely with increasing the labor force can be sure of success."[90]

Thus while the Lanham program expressed public ambivalence about day care by defining it as a temporary need created by the national emergency, the Children's Bureau expressed another side of that ambivalence by asserting that day care, and mothers' employment generally, was bad for children. By resisting the expansion of day care and seeking to define it as a welfare measure, Children's Bureau staffers sought to advance the interests of children by protecting their mothers from the government's demands for their labor. But the bureau's opposition to day care ended up worsening the day care situation, leaving a void where what was needed was a strong voice speaking of the needs of mothers and children for quality day care. With lukewarm support from the child welfare establishment and from union leaders, the issue was left to the vagaries of industry's need for women's labor. No one enthusiastically advocated day care as beneficial for children or advanced the view that mothers' wage work could improve a family's quality of life—as the mothers who used day care in Philadelphia were increasingly suggesting.

Mothers Redefine Day Care

While politicians, bureaucrats, and child welfare professionals argued about providing public day care, working mothers in Philadelphia made their own decisions—and ultimately redefined the debate by asserting that both mothers' wage work and day care could be beneficial for children. Most of these women did not see themselves as patriotic heroines; they went out to work because they needed to support their families or because the war created new opportunities, not because they were called on to sacrifice their own interests for the good of the nation. Like the child welfare professionals, these women may have believed that family obligations were more vital than civic duty, or that motherhood was a way of contributing to the war effort. But their view of how they could best fulfill their family obligations differed from that of Children's Bureau staffers, for they saw their wage-earning as the best way to ensure their families' interests and their children's future.

The war not only drew unprecedented attention to the issue of day care and created new public day care programs, but it also shaped the provision of day care by private day nurseries. The war particularly affected day care at Wharton Centre and Neighborhood Centre, two settlement houses that had offered nursery school programs during the 1930s. In the case of Wharton, a settlement house serving an African-American neighborhood in North Philadelphia, the war provided an opportunity to meet a long-standing need for day care. In 1942, the settlement's report explained that day care "was not a new need but one which existed long before the rise in employment. The war accented this need. We were again overwhelmed with demands from our community to do something about this problem."[91] The settlement had conducted a WPA nursery school during the 1930s, but the war created even greater need and provided new opportunities to meet that need. Noting that applications from the Wharton area were more numerous than from any other part of the city, the head of the city-operated day care program recommended Wharton as a site, and Wharton began to operate a day care center in March 1943, with costs split between the settlement and the city. The day care program at Wharton was thus a mixture of private day nursery and public child care center; while the settlement employed a social worker (unlike other public centers), guidelines for eligibility and rates were governed by the Board of Education. Former WPA nursery schools at Dixon House, the House of Industry, and the Germantown Settlement, as well as Wharton, also became public day care centers. Neighborhood Centre, the Jewish settlement house sponsored by the Federation of Jewish Charities, also transformed its day care program to meet wartime needs; in 1941, it closed the nursery school and replaced it with a day nursery. Nursery school techniques for training children and encouraging independence were still used in the day nursery (as they were in many day nurseries), but the overall purpose of the program was now to provide day care to the children of working mothers, rather than providing nursery education.[92]

As the war progressed, nursery workers and board members at private day nurseries throughout the city prepared themselves to start taking in the children of defense workers. In 1945, the president of the Strawberry Mansion Nursery recalled that in the early war years, she "had to be flexible enough to accept children whose mothers might not have needed work because of financial distress, but rather because of some mothers' desire to do something to help the war effort by taking a job in a defense plant."[93] Dorothy Patterson of the First and Sunnyside Day Nursery explained in her 1942 report that potential foster mothers "also have been influenced in this present crisis and many of them are considering going out to work themselves." Some apparently decided that volunteering for Civilian Defense work was more important than taking care of other women's children during the day, while "some of them . . . have lost the perspective of the need for them in their own homes."[94]

But, while policymakers debated providing day care to encourage women to take up defense work, and day nursery boards prepared themselves for applications from defense workers, the women whose applications to Philadelphia's private day nurseries have survived were not primarily defense workers. Defense workers made up only one out of seventeen mothers applying for day care at Neighborhood Centre, two out of nine whose applying for day care at the First and Sunnyside, and none of the seven people applying for care at St. Nicholas during the war years. Defense work was more common among the Wharton Centre's African-American clients, who were eager to leave domestic service jobs. Even at Wharton, however, only 19% of the mothers were employed in defense industries, while 29% were employed in other factories and 30% worked as domestics.[95] Defense work was often not the most attractive choice for women with young children, for workers in defense plants changed schedules frequently and often had long commutes, making child care arrangements difficult. Defense work seems to have been more important for the fathers in the Wharton families, for 40% of the men were working at defense jobs, the highest percentage of any one category of work.

So while public attention focused on women working in defense factories, the reality of women's wage work was often less dramatic and had more in common with their work before the war. In 1941, the Strawberry Mansion Day Nursery reported that "the largest proportion of our parents have not even been affected to any great extent by the greatly publicized employment opportunities, a result of the National Defense Program."[96] In June 1942, the director of the First and Sunnyside Day Nursery reported that the reasons clients gave for applying for day care were essentially the same as in other years: broken homes, emotional and financial difficulties. While there were a few cases of women who worked because their skills were valuable to the war effort, most were working out of financial need.[97] Again in 1943, she noted, "The types of families coming to us have been, on the whole, the same as we have met in the past except that they are more numerous and situations in them change with rapidity."[98] Neighborhood Centre reported that in 1943, the majority needed day care either because of a father's insufficient earnings or because the mother was needed to help in the family business. As the war progressed, the center saw more families in which a mother was working while a father served in the military, but very few of these women actually became defense workers.[99] This pattern of day care centers serving women who were not defense workers was a national one, for day nurseries were typically established in older neighborhoods that were often distant from defense plants.

Indeed, while day care advocates like Susan Anthony relied on arguments about the contribution women workers were making to the cause of the war, mothers themselves described their wage work in terms of family needs, not on the grounds of service to the nation. Many of these mothers seem to have agreed with the Children's Bureau's sense of priorities, portraying their struggles to support their children as more worthy of recognition than their defense work. Yet their solution was not to stay home with their children (as many child welfare advocates might have wished), but rather to find good day care so they could go out to work. One woman wrote to the Wharton Center in 1943, "Why is it that getting your children into a 'Day care Centre' is such a difficult matter.... I'm not just a worker in wartimes, but a lone mother trying hard to make a living for a family of three."[100] To this woman, her struggles as a mother trying to support her children were more important—or more likely to help her get assistance—than her status as a war worker. In requesting day care, other women cited concerns for their children's safety, their conviction that private arrangements were inadequate, and their fears of encouraging juvenile delinquency. Mothers were much more likely to request day care "for the welfare of my child," as one Wharton mother put it, than on the grounds of their contribution to the war effort.[101] For instance, Gloria Farley came into the Wharton social worker's office in 1943 waving a piece of paper with the name and address of the day care center on it. She talked rapidly about finding someone to make her nine-year-old son go to school. Apparently Earl "had recently been associating with an older group of boys who were leading him astray," skipping school, and stealing money from the landlord. Since she had to work, she explained, "she has to 'find someplace where he can stay and be made to go to school.'"[102] Mothers often mentioned inadequate supervision by neighbors, friends, and relatives as a reason for seeking formal day care for their children. The anxiety that wage-earning mothers carried with them about their children's care and physical safety was a frequent theme in the Wharton case records. When social worker M.S. Toombs explained that she was leaving her job in order to take better care of her sick son, several mothers expressed their empathy. One mother seemed to be speaking from her own experience when she said, "This will be a good thing for you as it will rest your mind."[103]

Although they were not primarily defense workers who left their homes to further the war effort, these women's decisions to seek employment were influenced by the war. Wartime migration, new opportunities for work, and the requirements of military service made for new patterns of work within families and new needs for child care. Many families migrated to areas where defense jobs were available, or where they could be near a family member on a military base, separating themselves from support networks and extended family who might have cared for the children. Even families who did not move often had problems finding adequate care for their children, as women—including family members, neighbors, and friends who might have taken care of children in the past—were increasingly drawn into wage work. For instance, Janie Matthews, a packer at Campbell's Soup, wrote on her application, "Sister take[s] care of the child, but she is going to work next week, and I have no one to take care of her."[104]

Women who had not worked since marriage found themselves unable to get by on their military allotments, so they decided to look for paid work. For instance, three months after her husband went into the navy, Florence Levin found it difficult to manage on her hundred-dollar-a-month allotment and decided to go out to work rather than continuing to deplete her savings. Having married at the age of sixteen (she listed her occupation on the application form as "housewife"), she had never held a job before and, according to the Neighborhood Centre social worker, was "somewhat frightened by all that it involves."[105] Similarly, one Wharton mother applying for day care "explained that her husband has been in the navy for quite a while and since it was not possible for her to get along on the allotment, she has taken a job at the Naval Aviation Supply Depot."[106] Indeed, the problem of getting by on the allotment provided by the military was so widespread that it was featured in a 1943 newspaper article entitled, "How Mom Pays the Rent When Pop Goes Off To War."[107] Some women had to help maintain businesses for a missing breadwinner, making it necessary to find someone else to take up their child-caring work. For instance, Aaron and Mollie Miller applied for day nursery care for their child because they were taking over a grocery store for a cousin who was in the army.[108]

Wartime migration from the South made it particularly difficult for many African-American families to arrange for day care. Recently detached from their support networks at home, these families often had trouble finding someone to care for their children, and many turned to day nurseries or public day care centers. Of the 138 families applying for day care at Wharton who listed birthplaces, only 28% were natives of Philadelphia; most were migrants from Virginia, North Carolina, South Carolina, and Georgia.[109] More significantly, most of these people had migrated recently; the average length of time they had been in Philadelphia was only 2.1 years. Several mothers who had recently migrated to Philadelphia explained that they could not make trustworthy child care arrangements in the neighborhood since they did not know their neighbors. For instance, domestic worker Beatrice Reamon had been leaving her son in an unsatisfactory situation because as "a stranger in Phila[delphia] knew nothing else to do."[110] Many mothers relied on relatives "back home" to keep their children, but these arrangements were often temporary. For instance, when Betty Briggs applied at Wharton, she explained that she had recently come to work in Philadelphia with her husband, leaving their son Elisha in South Carolina with her mother. But Betty's mother had recently died, and Betty needed to find care for Elisha in Philadelphia.[111] In another family, a grandmother was caring for eight other children and was unwilling to take on any more.[112]

The women who used Philadelphia day nurseries saw their wage work not as an act of patriotism, but as a way of contributing to their families. Increasingly, women justified working outside the home not on the grounds of dire economic straits, nor on patriotic grounds, but because through this work, they could improve their families' quality of life. Although many mothers applying for day care were, as in the past, single mothers who were the sole support of their children, a growing number of applicants were married women who worked to supplement their husbands' income. They saw their wage work not as a temporary response to an emergency, but as a long-term solution to family needs. Many Neighborhood Centre families were small business owners who found that running small stores or restaurants required the labor of both husband and wife, making child care difficult. For instance, when Leon and Naomi Gardiner bought a house and storefront in North Philadelphia with the intention of opening a dress shop, Naomi explained to the Neighborhood Centre social worker that "they have a very good chance to make a success of the business in this locality if both of them are free to devote their time to the store."[113] African-American mothers applying to Wharton for day care also explained that their wage work was necessary to improve their families' standard of living, not just for sheer survival. In one case, where the man had found it "somewhat difficult to manage on his income," he and his wife decided that she would go to work "so that they could help each other and get ahead."[114] When questioned whether she absolutely needed to work, given her son's apparent need for attention, another woman "said she had been thinking a lot about it. Frankly, she did have to work. They were buying their house and her earnings were greatly needed."[115]

These explanations signal an important departure from the way women's wage work and day care were discussed during the 1930s, when male unemployment or dire economic necessity seemed to be the only acceptable reasons for mothers to enter the labor force. While women in both periods explained their wage work in terms of helping their families, the anxiety about and hostility toward women's employment that was so evident in day nursery case records during the depression was absent during the war. Husbands who felt threatened by their wives' going out to work were rare in the case records from the war years; indeed, most fathers seem to have fully supported their wives' plans to work in order to contribute to the family's ultimate well-being. This shift in attitude is complicated, attributable in part to differences among nurseries and their clients. Case records exist for Wharton only from the 1940s, so we cannot know what families in this neighborhood were saying about women's wage work during the depression—although records from St. Nicholas and Women's Union nurseries for the 1930s document African-American families in other parts of the city. During the 1930s, the more affluent Jewish families using the Neighborhood Centre nursery were more likely to be disturbed by a mother's employment than the African-American families using the St. Nicholas and Women's Union nurseries; perhaps Neighborhood Centre fathers did not object to their wives' working during the 1940s because the women were increasingly working in family stores rather than in factories. Immigrant families had long made a distinction between "inside" work, which was respectable for married women, and "outside" work, which was less so.

But although the differences in how clients talked about their work is partly due to different attitudes toward women's work among African-Americans and white ethnic groups, it is also a result of more open attitudes toward mothers' wage work that resulted from the war. While most of the mothers using day nurseries were not actually defense workers, they were affected by the way in which the campaign for women defense workers changed public attitudes toward married women's employment. This campaign encouraged women to go out to work to help the war effort, which in turn was presented as a collective sacrifice to improve life at home. Women applying for day care no longer felt the need to justify their work on the basis of getting their families through an economic crisis, but explained it in terms of improving their families' standard of living and ensuring a better future for their children. Whether or not they worked in a defense plant, their reasons for working were thus filtered through messages about the meaning of the war. Just as men went to war and women went to ammunition factories to ensure their families' future safety and prosperity, so women who went to work in nondefense jobs could define their work as a way to ensure a better future for their children, an "American" standard of living.

As it became more common for women to work to supplement their husband's wages, the "reason for applying" section on the application forms used by day nurseries began to change. The new category that social workers began to use—"both working"

—is significant because it did not assume that a mother's wage work needed explanation or justification, as it always had in earlier sets of case records, when acceptable reasons for applying for day care included "widow," "man deserted," "father ill," "insufficient income," and so on. This new category, a creation of the war years, became a common explanation of a need for day care; during these years, it was second only to "single mother" as a reason for applying to a day nursery among the private nurseries for which there are records. (For the people applying to Wharton, it was the single most common explanation.)

Another significant change in the case records during the war years involved the marital status of mothers applying for day care. Originally, the charitable day nurseries had been intended to serve single mothers—women who had lost their male provider through death, desertion, illness, or failure to marry. This began to change during the depression, as we saw in the last chapter. By the 1940s, 56% of the families applying to Neighborhood Centre, Wharton, First and Sunnyside, and St. Nicholas day nurseries were headed by married couples with both parents present, and another 11% were married couples with the husband in the military. Of the families applying to Neighborhood Centre, a full 88% consisted of married couples living together. This represented a major shift in the day nursery population; taken together with the changes in reasons given for applying for day care, it suggests that day nurseries were no longer being used primarily by single mothers who were "forced" to work out of extreme economic stress, but by two-parent families who made the decision to use a mother's labor in wage work rather than exclusively in unpaid household work.

As day nurseries became more respectable, their clientele expanded to include professional and relatively affluent families. Dorothy Patterson of the First and Sunnyside Nursery commented in 1943 that "many women whose children receive care come from an economic and cultural background quite different from many we knew during the depression. Now that the supply of domestic help is at a minimum, many people who have never been aware of social agencies before have turned to them for help in caring for their children."[116] This observation is borne out by the case records; only 6% of 286 families applying for day care at Neighborhood Centre, Wharton, First and Sunnyside, and St. Nicholas during the war years had contact with another welfare agency, compared with 30% during the 1930s.[117] The war exposed a long-standing divide in how people of different social classes provided care for their children. While affluent families had often relied on domestic help, this type of child care was often invisible and rarely entered into public debates about day care and mothers' obligations. But with the war making all women's labor more visible, affluent women's dependence on domestic servants as well as on nursery schools for child care became more of a public issue, and some of these women started to turn to day care centers as another source of help. The fact that wartime day care was serving a new and more affluent population, accustomed to using domestic help in raising their children, became evident at a 1944 conference of the United Federal Workers of America. Representatives from Philadelphia and other locals spoke about their problems as working mothers, stressing the difficulty of finding maids and complaining about not being allowed to deduct maid service from their income tax. Child care was a major topic of discussion, and the delegates called for preference from employment agencies in securing maids as well as "more and better nursery schools."[118]

Professional families were especially common at the First and Sunnyside Day Nursery during the war. Families applying to the agency during these years included a man who commuted to a job with the consulate in New York, while his wife taught at the University of Pennsylvania; a psychiatric social worker working on a master's degree whose wife worked at the Friends Service Committee; a woman who had worked intermittently for the government "on secret stuff," and was "evidently a very valuable worker"; a couple described as "middle-class, well-to-do," who owned a farm and house; and a couple who both served on the Social Security Board, while the husband attended law school at night.[119] Several Neighborhood Centre families had incomes high enough from their businesses to consider hiring private nurses or signing their children up for private nursery schools as an alternative to using the day nursery.[120] Indeed, the high incomes of these families created a dilemma for social workers who knew their mission was to serve poor and working-class families. Even at the Wharton Centre, where most of the African-American parents worked in factories or as domestics, professionals and small-business owners were represented. Professional people using Wharton for day care for their children included social workers, public school teachers, a policeman, a commercial artist, a former nursery school teacher, a doctor, and a druggist.

Another crucial aspect of day care's increasing respectability was the growing conviction that it was educational and thus benefited children, not just their mothers. Both Wharton Centre and Neighborhood Centre had operated nursery schools during the 1930s, which had been transformed into day care centers in order to meet wartime needs; thus both staff and clients at these centers were particularly aware of the educational aspect of day care services. Staff at both centers saw their work as serving children's developmental needs as well as employed mothers' needs for custodial care for their children. Some parents did not understand or share the nursery's educational goals: a Wharton social worker recounted her discussion on the subject with one client: "I said that perhaps he did not understand that we did a little more for a child than feed her and keep her until the parent returned. . . . We did seek to encourage a child's growth and development and to help with a child's adjustment in the group. . . . Mr. S said that he could give his child all the necessary training she needed. It was just that he needed someone to look after her when he is working. She is not a difficult child."[121] Similarly, the vision of nurseries as "sad places for neglected children" (the phrase of one applicant to Neighborhood Centre) did not completely disappear.[122] One Wharton mother had earlier expressed shame about her son born out of wedlock, asking if the center "took people like her." The social worker noted, "From time to time she showed a lot of guilt about putting the child here; she kept saying, 'Oh, I hate to put him out, I hate to put him out' and very frequently there were tears in her eyes. I could see that she was greatly disturbed about having had the child and now to put him 'away' with strangers seemed unbearable to her."[123]

But many Wharton parents felt that the day care center at the settlement provided superior care to what they could get elsewhere. One mother told the social worker, "Having the Center care for her Louise is much more satisfactory than leaving Louise in the care of irresponsible neighbors."[124] Several mothers felt that day care was so beneficial to their children that they would bring them whether or not they needed to work. For these women, the day care center was a tool of modern motherhood, like the nursery school in the 1920s and 1930s, a way of teaching children important lessons in getting along with others. Mrs. Kingston "realized whether or not it was necessary for her to work, Beatrice had to learn how to get along with other children and she felt it would be much simpler for other children to teach her this to her than for an adult."[125] Similarly, Jessie Low "said, laughingly, that she could not explain this part to her mother but had said she was coming over here . . . because she is anxious for her [daughter] to be able to get along with other children."[126] In making their applications for day care, parents increasingly mentioned their belief that the experience would benefit their children. Forty percent of the families applying to Neighborhood Centre cited "educational value" as their primary reason for seeking day care; by contrast, only 6% of the Wharton families put this first, but it was often one of several reasons given. Clara Cohen brought her son Herbie to Neighborhood Centre in 1941, explaining that she and her husband, both university-educated professionals in Germany, had come to Philadelphia as refugees three years earlier. The social worker noted that three-year old Herbie "looks angelic but rules his mother so firmly that she is completely overwhelmed by his resistance to her. . . . She is completely unable to discipline him . . . [She] recognizes that she must have help in controlling him. She appears high-strung, easily tearful and seems to stand in fear of Herbie." Mrs. Cohen was "extremely interested in NS [Nursery School] for Herbie so that she may learn better how to handle him both for her sake and for his."[127]

While a few families, especially at Neighborhood Centre, sought day care purely for educational reasons, most families were looking for day care for both educational and economic reasons. For instance, Jennie Lobofsky, who needed day care so she could help her husband with the family's dress shop, also felt that her daughter would benefit from attending the nursery. In their current situation she had no playmates, "and being a gregarious youngster, has manifested a need for group association that the family cannot supply. The mother feels that the child can gain a great deal from NS group experience, learn social amenities and get a chance to develop."[128] Similarly, the Wharton social worker felt that Mrs. King was not only looking to go out to work to supplement her husband's declining earnings but "was asking that we take her child and give her the sort of training which she had not been able to give her herself. . . . She said she finds it difficult to discipline the child and generally gives in to her. Her husband had heard of the Center and felt that Helen needed to be some place where she would have a little more strict training than she gets at home."[129]

Several mothers sought day care at Wharton who apparently would not have considered other child care arrangements; living out the worst fears of day care opponents, they explained that they made plans to go to work only because they knew quality child care was available. One mother, who worried that both she and her husband were spoiling their adopted son, explained to the social worker that "she thought it would be best for all of them if she were able to go to work and leave Harry in a place where he could be associated with other children and where the adults around him would not have such a tendency to spoil him." She also mentioned her hopes that Harry would learn to read and learn his ABCs at the nursery.[130] Perhaps the status of the settlement house in the local African-American community also played an important role in establishing the respectability of the day care center. Many applicants mentioned that they were completely comfortable sending their children to a day care program at Wharton because of their own long connection to the settlement house.

Several parents who sought upward mobility for their families applied for day care at Wharton in order to prevent their children from being influenced by other children in their neighborhoods. One mother expressed her resistance to using a different day care center: "She feels her children will come in contact with a good many children from whose group she tries to exclude her own children during the evenings when they are home. She said she has tried very hard to bring her children up with a certain standard of behavior and she does not want to expose them to these children. . . . She went on to discuss some of the things which the children in her neighborhood have been doing and how she forbade them even to sit on her front steps."[131] The Maxwells, a professional couple, explained that "what concerned them most was the laxity of supervision of Calvin in their present neighborhood. . . . The neighborhood is conducive to delinquency and they believe they would be more responsible for Calvin by providing a better kind of care for him."[132]

Concerns about children's physical well-being mingled with the conviction that day care was socially and developmentally beneficial for children. In a reversal of earlier attitudes, parents seem to have assumed that the care provided at the center was clearly superior to what neighborhood women or relatives could provide. Many husbands, exhibiting a new involvement in child care decisions, made it clear that their wives had to find quality care for their children. One woman explained that her husband would prefer to have her stay home with their daughter, Jessica, but that he could "trust the supervision of the teachers at the centre" more than that offered by neighbors. Later, when Jessica's mother withdrew her from the center, her father "said that he was going to see that Jessica returned. He went on to say that she was his only child and he wanted her to have the best of everything. He had told her mother that he didn't like this haphazard way of caring for her."[133] Such statements suggest that these African-American parents had embraced ideas about modern child-rearing: that trained teachers in a formal program could provide the best guidance for young children, that children needed to learn to get along with other children in a group, and that children could benefit from being separated from their mothers.

As they explained their reasons for using day care, parents such as these indicated the ways in which the status and meaning of day care had changed by the mid-1940s. Day nursery social workers were increasingly willing to admit children for reasons other than extreme financial need, validating an expansion of the role that day care could play in a family's life. No longer only the refuge of single mothers with no choice but to turn to charity, private day nurseries were being used increasingly by married couples with some resources. The idea that day care was beneficial to children as well as to parents gained new currency as the boundaries between nursery schools and custodial day care began to fade. But these changes in the meaning of day care were not yet reflected in national debates about women's paid and unpaid labor. Continued ambivalence toward employed mothers shaped day care policy, ensuring that day care would be provided in a limited and haphazard way.

World War II brought new attention to day care, forcing government officials and child welfare advocates to weigh the benefits of women's work in industry against that of their work as mothers. The possibility of shaping a coherent national policy on day care that would meet the multiple needs of women and children was lost as child welfare professionals, union women, and those concerned with war production struggled to implement their different visions of how women should prioritize demands on their labor and balance private with patriotic obligations. But the increasing acceptance of women's wage work that was a result of the war also had its impact, making it socially permissible for women to work in order to improve their families' quality of life.

Examining day care thus enables us to understand the ways in which World War II affected ideas about women's roles. While some historians have asserted that the war was a vital turning-point, a watershed in ideas about women's place in society, others have convincingly pointed out the ways in which the challenges to conventional gender roles posed by the war were carefully contained and limited.[134] The story of wartime day care suggests that both conclusions are correct. Deep ambivalence about the idea of mothers becoming paid workers ensured that the war itself would not threaten traditional ideas about maternal responsiblity for children or about women's role. Policymakers' reluctance to take on a mother's job and to challenge the division of labor between men and women prevented the war from becoming a reason to invest heavily in child care. Indeed, it ensured that the day care that was provided would be inadequate to meet the needs of working mothers, and that day care would be understood, like women's presence in the workplace, as a temporary response to an emergency.

But when we look at the ways in which women in Philadelphia explained their attitudes toward day care, we see that there are more dimensions to the story. While public debate swirled around them, mothers made their own decisions about how best to fulfill their family obligations. Although they did not speak in terms of patriotic sacrifice, their attitudes were shaped by the way in which government campaigns to recruit women as defense workers helped legitimize maternal wage-earning. As wage work became more legitimate, day care gained legitimacy as well. Both the establishment of public, government-funded day care centers and the ways in which the older day nurseries were used distanced day care from its old association with charity and desperate poverty. All of these changes in the meaning of day care set the stage for struggles over public day care in the immediate postwar period.

7

From Charity to Legitimate Need

The Postwar Years

The postwar period was a time of transition in ideas about women's work and family responsibilities—and in ideas about day care. Encouraged by a new ethos of consumption and by a growing demand for their labor, mothers increasingly took up wage work in order to improve their families' lives. Women's claims about how wage work and day care could benefit families became more widely accepted in the postwar period, lending new legitimacy to day care. As more women began to see wage work as a part of their adult lives, the recognition of day care as a permanent need of normal families grew, the gap between custodial and educational modes of child care narrowed, and women started to speak of day care as a right rather than a charity. Although many voices still linked day care to poverty and family pathology in the 1950s, changes in conceptions of women's work, children's needs, and public responsibility for families were gradually transforming day care's meaning.

The most striking change in the postwar years was the way in which working mothers began to insist that they had a *right* to day care. Rather than quietly retreating to their homes at the end of the war, mothers in Philadelphia challenged politicians and policymakers, lobbying and demonstrating in the streets to keep wartime day care centers open. A mother's place was thus not only in the home, or in the workplace, but also in the realm of politics, where she might gain attention for her children's needs. By claiming a right to day care, these mothers helped redefine it as a legitimate need of many families, not just a charity for a few.

Several historians have recently urged us to question popular conceptions of the 1950s as a time of the baby boom, the "feminine mystique," and women withdrawing from the public sphere to devote themselves to suburban domesticity. Instead, they argue, we need to pay careful attention to the complexities of changing identities during this apparently conservative era.[1] The history of day care told in this chapter supports the contention that the postwar period was indeed a time of change, when new ideas about "a mother's job" would emerge to challenge the assumptions on which day care provision had previously been based.

"Indignant Mothers' Marches": Struggles Over Public Day Care

Looking back in 1948, the *Philadelphia Bulletin* described the city's public day care program as having a "stormy history, punctuated by indignant mothers' marches on City Council, skirmishes with the police, political recriminations and repercussions, and the like."[2] The need for women's labor during the war had politicized the issue of day care, and energetic protests by local mothers meant that day care would continue to be a serious public issue in Philadelphia well after the war came to an end. The voices of wage-earning mothers, which had been difficult to hear during the war, now took center stage, as women insisted that the city had a responsibility to provide care for their children. Drawing on arguments about the state's obligation to soldiers' families, the dangers of juvenile delinquency, and the virtues of women's wage work, these women successfully pressured city officials into extending a wartime measure into a permanent obligation of local government. This victory meant that instead of closing their doors when the soldiers came home, Philadelphia's public day care centers continued to operate for more than twenty years. The women's victory, however, was limited by the very arguments they used. By focusing on women who were compelled to work to support their children, and playing up fears of juvenile crime, they reaffirmed the connection between day care and poverty, ignored the idea that day care could be beneficial to children, and lost an opportunity to make a larger claim about public responsibility for all children.

Although the public day care centers had been clearly defined as a temporary wartime measure, the cutoff of federal funds in 1945 brought waves of protest. Members of the Philadelphia Association of Day Nurseries (PADN) met in the summer and fall of 1945 to address the emergency that would be created by the sudden closing of the centers in September. They planned to ask the Federal Works Agency for more funding and urged the Board of Education and the City Council to make an interim plan to maintain the public centers.[3] Members of the city's social service agencies also discussed how to secure more funding for the short term and how to develop a long-term plan "which would provide for day care services over and above those available prior to the war."[4]

The most effective protests over the closing of the public day care centers came not from day nursery leaders, however, but from mothers who used the centers.[5] Several Philadelphia mothers wrote angry or pleading letters to government officials in 1945, demanding that the centers be kept open. They also organized public protests and lobbying efforts. On August 30, 1945, a delegation of six servicemen's wives who had children in the Feltonville Child Care Center carried a petition to the mayor, urging that the twenty centers be kept open. The women also asked the City Council for an emergency appropriation to operate the centers until Congress had a chance to act to continue funding.[6] A week later, thirty-five protesting mothers met with the mayor, demanding that the city's centers be continued as a peacetime activity. Twenty protesting women attended the City Council session where their request for an emergency appropriation was introduced. "If something isn't done by next Thursday," one woman said, "we will have 200 women, with the children, in the balconies of City Council's chamber on that day."[7]

Although she did not make good on this threat, the newspaper reported that sixty wives of servicemen did attend the next council meeting, providing the council "with its liveliest session of the year." The women filled the gallery during the session, and when the meeting adjourned without discussing the day care centers, Mrs. Rose Bloomfield rose and asked, "What about the child welfare centers? We want a reply." When told that the meeting had adjourned, several of the women insisted that they wanted action. The council members were obviously taken aback and tried to leave the room quickly. But twenty of the women followed the council president to his office, insisting "on an assurance of prompt Councilmanic action." The women seemed to be satisfied when council president Garman announced that he had asked Councilman Louis Schwartz, together with five of the women, to talk to the secretary of the Board of Education about keeping the centers open.[8] The next day's paper reported that Schwartz was planning to request additional city funds to keep the centers operating until January. But the protesters had broader aims: Rose Bloomfield, speaking for the mothers, said, "We want the centers to stay open permanently and eventually became [sic] a part of the school system."[9]

Over the next several days, however, it became unclear whether the City Council would even be willing to find the money necessary for the short-term fix. Wallace Eagan, chair of the council's Finance Committee, maintained that city officials had "scraped the bottom of the barrel" and could do no more; continuation of the centers was dependent on federal funds. Louis Schwartz, however, insisted that the centers be continued and called for seeking other ways, including appealing to the governor, "to see that these children and others are cared for so they may develop into good citizens."[10] The *Philadelphia Bulletin* was on the mothers' side; its reporter described the protesting mothers in favorable terms, somewhat bemusedly describing how their presence upset politicians on the City Council. The day after the women demanded action at a City Council meeting, the paper carried an editorial favoring the extension of the centers. It explained, "City Council has reason to feel that the baby is on its doorstep. The City has been sharing with the Federal Government the cost of operating the Centers, but the Federal Government has walked out, at least for a time." Rather than debating whose responsibility this baby was, the editor continued, the City Council must "tide over the situation" until a more permanent arrangement could be made.[11]

The mothers continued their efforts to pressure the council, attending council sessions and meeting with the mayor. In October, a group of fifty mothers and fifteen children demonstrated in front of City Hall. They carried placards reading "Child Care Centers vs. Orphanages," and detailing cases of servicemen's families who depended on the centers. The protesters not only wanted to secure funding for the centers for the coming year, but were also demanding that the centers be made permanent for all working mothers. Pressure on the national level saved the day, at least for a while, for the demonstrating mothers were told that Congress was expected to extend federal aid until March 1, 1946.[12] Councilman Wallace Eagan affirmed that the city would appropriate the money to continue the centers so long as they were needed for servicemen's children "but not beyond that, so far as I am concerned."[13]

This issue of limiting the centers to servicemen's children became the next topic of controversy. Was day care only a wartime emergency, or would it continue into peacetime? Did the city have a responsibility only to those whose husbands had not yet returned from war, or could other families also claim a right to public day care? After heated debate, on November 16 the City Council approved a motion to limit the centers to the children of servicemen. Wallace Eagan argued that day care was only a wartime obligation, but Mrs. Albert Nalle, the chair of the Day Care Planning Committee, contended that the city had an ongoing responsibility to care for the children of working mothers, widows, and crippled men. Nalle pointed out that the children of servicemen were too scattered to make efficient use of the centers, that limiting the centers in this way would eliminate two-thirds of the children they served, and that women "forced to help support their families" would probably resort to unsafe and unsatisfactory methods of care for their children if good day care was not available.[14] Mrs. Sally Spizer, one of the mothers who had been demonstrating on behalf of the centers throughout the fall, "pleaded for the care of all children whose parents are forced to go out to work," and one councilman asserted that "there is a tendency in our government to continue this wartime project as a peacetime agency."[15] According to the *Bulletin* reporter, however, it was the testimony of Juvenile Court judge Charles Brown of the Municipal Court that swayed the council. After Brown "made a strong plea . . . declaring that children of working mothers should be given this protection" in order to prevent juvenile delinquency, the council voted to remove the proposed restriction.[16]

All the participants in the Philadelphia day care debate were aware that federal funding was a temporary phenomenon (indeed the total period during which the centers were ever even partially supported with federal funds was about two years), and when that funding ran out, the Board of Education was ready with a new plan. The board announced that it was willing to operate the centers for another four months, by using the remainder of the City Council's appropriation, raising the fees that parents paid, and closing three of the centers.[17]

Although this new plan was intended as a stop-gap measure, it set a precedent for continuing the public day care centers as a peacetime program. Many members of the Board of Education were not happy with this responsibility and feared meeting the protesting mothers' demands that the day care centers become a permanent part of the public school system. In May 1946, the board requested an additional appropriation from the City Council to continue the centers through the end of December, but also recommended to the mayor the formation of a committee "to determine when the temporary emergency has terminated and to make recommendations for the financing and administration of child care centers thereafter."[18] This committee was not actually formed until December 1946, and the Board of Education was already getting restless. Before the mayor's committee had even met, the board was threatening to close the remaining centers unless the City Council appropriated special funds. The council did fund the centers through June 1947, but at an April meeting, school board member Leon Obermayer, who had voted against the day care program at every opportunity, pressed for an end to the program. Obermayer "expressed sharp criticism, declaring the care of children below school age never was the function of the public schools and that the child care centers should have been dropped by the schools long before this."[19] In June 1947, the board voted to terminate its operation of the child care centers.

The protesting mothers, however, did not accept the Board of Education's verdict. Twenty working mothers who used the public day care centers walked in on City Council committee meetings to lobby for the continuation of the centers. The "surprised Councilmen" ushered the women into an adjoining chamber, and told them that the question was beyond the council's jurisdiction. The mayor had told previous delegations of mothers that he supported them and was trying to determine if the centers could be operated by another city agency, but the women were skeptical. Spokeswoman Mildred Buehler said, "Every place we go, we get a different answer." Another mother replied, "Well, we'll keep going until we see the Governor." They continued on to the Board of Education building, where Add Anderson met with them, explaining that "the time had now come to decide by whom [the centers] were to be operated as a non-emergency service." After meeting with Anderson, spokeswoman Buehler said that the City Council appeared indifferent to the importance of the problem, and that the mothers felt that the Board of Education was better qualified than any other agency to continue the centers. Finally, the board decided to honor Mayor Samuel's request to continue operation of the centers until June 1948 in order to give the mayor's child care committee time to study the situation and give a report.[20]

In April 1948 (just before the mayor's committee's report was expected), "a report gained circulation" that the City Council would not allot the money necessary to keep the centers open. In response, more than 150 angry mothers "besieged City Hall," carrying placards protesting the closings. Police ousted the women from the City Hall courtyard, but they quickly applied for a permit and reassembled, buttonholing every councilman "or anyone who looked like a councilman." The protesters won a promise that the council would consider appropriating funds for the day care centers, but not until the mayor's committee made a recommendation as to whether the centers should be continued.[21] When the committee finally issued its report in May, it hedged its bets, recommending that the centers be continued until the end of 1948 and that a detailed survey be made "to see if other means are available for caring for the children now using the centers."[22] The School Board subsequently extended its deadline for closing down the centers from August 1948 to December 1948, and then to June 1949.[23] At that point, the mayor's committee finally decided not to ask the City Council for any more money for the child care centers and passed a resolution requesting the Community Chest (the umbrella organization of private welfare agencies in the city) to assume responsibility for the financing of the centers; if the chest did not agree to do this, the child care centers would be discontinued in December 1949.[24]

Once again, protesting mothers blocked the closing of the day care centers, insisting that day care remain a public responsibility rather than a matter of private charity. Although the City Council was no longer receptive to their demands, they were able to secure support from the mayor.[25] Starting in 1949, the centers were funded through appropriations from the mayor's budget, which included items such as salaries for his secretaries and chauffeur, official entertainment expenses, special scholarships, and miscellaneous contributions.[26] The fact that the mayor chose to fund the day care centers in this way suggests that he had given up convincing other city officials that day care should be a long-term responsibility of government. The women had won an immediate victory in securing funding for the centers, but they were not able to persuade most city officials of the worthiness of their cause.

Who were these women whose protests and demonstrations succeeded in keeping Philadelphia's public day care centers open? They always identified themselves as working mothers who used the child care centers, never as members of any organization, and none of their leaders seem to have been publicly prominent in Philadelphia in subsequent years. Yet their actions were clearly well-organized and carefully planned, and they moved with confidence through the offices of city officials. Available accounts do not indicate how the protests were organized, but mothers who met each other every day while dropping off and picking up their children may well have organized through parents' associations linked to the centers.[27] Perhaps some of them drew on experience in local labor unions, or came from politically active working-class families.

These women may also have been influenced by other protests led by working-class women in Philadelphia and across the nation during the immediate postwar years, when cost-of-living issues sparked a housewives' movement similar to that of the depression years. Immediately following the end of the war, women in Philadelphia organized to picket and boycott food markets and to conduct rent strikes.[28] Housewives from Philadelphia were among the more than six hundred women who poured into Washington in 1947, demanding that Congress enact price controls on food and housing, and they also played a significant role in a nationwide meat boycott in the winter of 1951.[29] The day care protesters may also have been inspired (whether or not they were directly associated with) the efforts of the Congress of American Women, which in addition to organizing campaigns for fair food prices and affordable housing, fought for funding for day care and services for working mothers. Under the slogan, "Ten women anywhere can organize anything," local chapters of this Communist-linked organization were established in most of the nation's large industrial cities to work on a wide variety of issues, from organizing women workers to fighting local loan sharks.[30] Whatever the specific organizational experiences or connections of the women who conducted the day care protests in Philadelphia, their activism was part of a larger context in which women—as mothers, workers, housewives, and citizens—were increasingly making demands on government.

The protesting women seemed to have the support of the public. When the mayor's committee issued its first report in May 1948, the *Philadelphia Bulletin* took the opportunity to feature the child care issue in its Sunday Forum. Reminding readers of the public day care centers' "stormy history," the paper quoted advocates and critics of day care, and asked for readers' opinions.[31] The response was overwhelmingly positive; the paper noted, "Never before have readers exhibited such overwhelmingly strong support for a measure." Ninety-seven percent of the readers who responded felt the public centers should be continued; 93% favored City Council funding of the centers; and 88% wanted the number of centers increased. The editor noted that a disproportionate number of the readers who responded to the poll were clients of the day care centers, and were thus particularly interested in supporting the program. Yet the fact that so few people who objected to the centers or felt they were used as "baby-parking stations" wrote in to express their views suggests a positive public opinion.[32]

With support from the mayor's budget, the school district continued to operate about ten day care centers with public funds throughout the 1950s and into the 1960s. This continued funding was a victory for the women who had organized protests throughout the late 1940s: it made Philadelphia one of the very few cities across the country that continued to fund its wartime day care centers for years after the end of the war.[33] But this victory was limited in some significant ways. Although the centers continued to exist, day care as a public issue did not. After 1949, the public day care centers became almost invisible in the public record. They did not appear again in the official proceedings of either the Board of Education or the City Council, except in the annual budgets or when the board was approving contracts for grocery and laundry service for the centers. From 1949 to 1960, no member of the City Council or of the Board of Education ever mentioned the day care program in a formal meeting. Records kept by the school district also made it clear that the day care program was not to be considered part of the school system: annual reports did not include the day care centers in its statistics about students or programs, nor did it include the day care program as part of the school district's normal budget.[34] The press, which had faithfully followed the mothers' protests throughout the late 1940s, was also nearly silent on day care after 1949. A note written in the margin of a clipping from the *Philadelphia Daily News* in 1958 suggests the difficulty of getting press coverage about day care. The clipping featured photographs of children playing in day care centers, and the note read, "Miss Gingrich [the director of the city's day care program] claims that it has taken her four years to get this in."[35]

The twelve centers, ten in public school buildings and two in housing projects, continued quietly throughout the 1950s, serving between eight hundred and twelve hundred children and charging fees set on a sliding scale according to family income. Preference was still given to the children of employed mothers, but the centers also took families who were referred by social agencies because of illness in the home or special needs of the child.[36] After a temporary decrease in enrollments in 1946, when federal funding and the number of centers were cut, enrollment in the centers rose steadily; from 1952 on, the number of children attending the thirteen centers was higher than in 1945 when there had been twenty centers.[37]

It soon became clear that the centers, which served approximately 1,000 children, were only reaching a small percentage of those families who could have benefited from their services.[38] A sympathetic series of articles in the *Bulletin* in 1957 noted that there were 54,000 working mothers in Philadelphia with children under six, an increase of 54.5% since 1950; there were also 222,000 working mothers with children aged six to seventeen.[39] By 1964, the number of employed mothers with children under eighteen in the city had grown to 292,000, and the number of mothers with children under six had almost tripled to 151,400. In her 1964 report, Gingrich lamented the fact that the day care program had not grown since 1950, despite "a continuous increase in the number of women employed throughout the country and in the Philadelphia area." The program had not expanded, Gingrich felt, because of "a lack of interest in its growth" on the part of the Board of Education and the city's Department of Welfare. In the meantime, parents were looking in vain for child care: "Daily calls are received in the central Child Care Center office regarding care either in areas where there are no centers or in areas where the centers are overcrowded."[40]

Despite its limitations and invisibility, however, the public day care program was significant because it presented day care in a different light than did the charitable day nurseries. While most of the private nurseries saw social work as part of their mission, the public centers saw themselves as straightforward providers of a service that many families needed. They did not "investigate" families applying for care, nor did they provide ongoing counseling and intervention. Another important difference was in fees. While both the public centers and the private nurseries charged fees, their meaning seems to have been different. Parents' fees made up a larger part of the budget of the public centers than of the private nurseries; at the centers, they ranged from 20% in 1944 to 47% in 1953, while at the nurseries they ranged from 16% in 1941 to 30% at the Strawberry Mansion Day Nursery in 1953.[41] Perhaps more important, the public centers presented themselves as a service for which one paid a fee, while the private nurseries were still clearly charities despite requiring a fee. In the public centers, the fee was set and could not be waived or reduced—making paying for child care similar to buying other goods and services—while in private nurseries the fees were negotiable depending on the family's situation.[42] The private day nursery case records are filled with endless negotiations between clients and social workers about the amount the family could afford to pay in fees, and about timely payment of these fees. These negotiations suggest that the mothers who used the day nurseries knew that the fee was more of a symbolic gesture toward parental responsibility than an absolute prerequisite for a child's care in the nursery.

The public day care centers, then, transformed the landscape of day care in Philadelphia. Not only did they double the number of children who were cared for in organized day care programs, but they also offered an alternative understanding of day care to that offered by the private day nurseries. While the private day nurseries were still predicated on the notion that day care was a welfare measure serving families in crisis, the public day care centers advanced the view that day care was a legitimate need of many families and a public responsibility. Public day care was something that could be fought for, something that women could argue they had a right to. Removed from the realm of private charity, day care became politicized, subject to what philosopher Nancy Fraser calls "needs-talk . . . a medium for the making and contesting of political claims."[43]

Through their protests, mothers started to translate their *need* for day care into a right. By contrast, the private day nurseries offered day care as a gift, and mothers could not object when it was taken away. When the Neighborhood Centre Nursery was closing in 1950, for instance (due to budgetary constraints and demographic changes in the settlement house's neighborhood), the only recorded protest came from one of the children who attended the nursery: "My mommie said she knew we just had to close, it just couldn't last."[44] This fatalistic statement makes a striking contrast with the vigorous and sophisticated protests conducted by the mothers using the public day care centers.

Arguing for Day Care

During these public debates and protests, day care advocates faced the difficult task of overcoming public ambivalence about working mothers and cultivating public support for child care at a time when private domesticity was celebrated as the highest social virtue. Day care, which had been justified during the war as a weapon in the defense effort, now had to be redefined as a legitimate responsibility of government in peacetime. No longer a means of serving the nation, day care was now defended as a means of serving the family. Protesting mothers and child welfare professionals based their arguments for day care on the state's obligation to the families of soldiers, the virtue of women's wage work when it arose from economic necessity, the wisdom of providing day care rather than public support for poor children, and the need to prevent juvenile deliquency. These arguments were effective in securing support for the city's day care centers, but because they did not challenge the assumptions underlying the provision of day care, they ultimately narrowed and restricted the demand for day care, limiting its potential clientele and diminishing the scope of its mission.

Women who sacrificed for the war effort expected to get some help in return, so when the federal government withdrew funding for the day care centers before the men had returned home from war, many expressed their righteous indignation. One Philadelphia mother, whose husband was not due back from overseas for some time, wrote to the Children's Bureau in 1945 that the closing of the centers was "so unfair it makes my blood boil." Similarly, a sailor still in the service expressed his anger on hearing that the day care centers were to be shut down, making it difficult for his wife to continue working:

> That, my good people, is what we in the service enjoy getting. We just love serving our country and giving our life and blood and just as soon as the skies look clear again, people just forget all that we gave up so that we could live in a peaceful world again. . . . Did you ever try to run a house and take care of two children on $100 a month? . . . We didn't kick about that either, instead our wives went out and worked so that they could have enough. Filling jobs in defense plants, donating blood, buying war bonds and doing everything they possibly could to help the war effort. So, now that it's all over, you say "Thanks a million sucker" and start kicking our families around.[45]

Another letter-writer also pointed out the government's obligation to help the wives of servicemen, who needed the centers until they could once again "become plain housewives as they desire." She pleaded for "a little consideration for these . . . mothers, who tried all they could, not [only] in giving up their husbands, but also the pleasures of taking care of their own children, so they could plan and hope for the future."[46] She thus cast women's wartime work as virtuous wartime sacrifice that should be rewarded by the government. Working for the future of one's family, she implied, was a central part of the war effort. Similarly, Daisy Glass, who was working to pay her children's medical expenses in her husband's absence, felt that she had earned the right to publicly funded day care: "I think our government owes us mothers a moral favor in return for the use of our husbands and I ask that money be appropriated to keep these centers open."[47] Women who had sacrificed for the war effort—whatever form that sacrifice took—felt they deserved something in return. Observing the ways in which their male relatives were honored for their wartime activities, they may have decided that the government owed them something, too.

Rose Bloomfield, who would soon become a leader in the day care protests in Philadelphia, took these appeals one step further. Instead of demanding support for day care only until the nation returned to normalcy, she closed her letter to the Children's Bureau with a broader claim—that day care should become a permanent right of American women. She urged Katharine Lenroot to "convince Congress how important it is to allocate funds immediately," writing, "We've won the bloodiest war in history, now let's win permanent Day Care for our children."[48]

The mothers who organized the public protests were obviously aware of the claim that servicemen's wives and children had on the state. Wives of soldiers were often the ones chosen to lobby city officials for the continuation of the centers, and during the October 1945 demonstrations, protesters carried placards describing cases of servicemen's families who depended on the centers. One read, "Husband Killed in Action. Has Two-

Year Old Child!" Demonstrators also sought to make a patriotic claim by carrying signs reading "Our fathers sacrificed themselves to save America," referring to children as "war orphans," and putting young children waving American flags at the front of the demonstration. They also called on the American Legion to support their cause, furthering the idea that servicemen's families were particularly in need of child care centers.[49]

As the mothers who protested the closings of the day care centers were well aware, however, arguments about the public's obligation to the families of servicemen could only be effective for a limited period of time. To "win permanent day care for our children," the protesters would have to make the more difficult argument that the state had an obligation to provide care for children even in peacetime. Slogans such as "Why Sacrifice Our Children, America's Future?" and "We Are Future Citizens" suggested that the state had an interest in providing for children. To claim their right to day care, protesting mothers also threatened to use their power as voters: during demonstrations in 1948, they carried signs such as "Remember Working Mothers Also Vote!" and "No Funds, No Votes."

But arguments for permanent day care could only garner broad support if mothers' wage work was portrayed as legitimate means of meeting their private obligations to their families. Day care could thus be cast as a way for the government to help women serve their families better, just as it had helped them serve the nation during the war. Supporters of day care often sought to make mothers' employment legitimate by stressing that women worked from economic necessity, not from choice. Their claims to day care thus arose from needs, not from an argument about women's right to work. For example, the demonstrators at a 1945 protest carried signs such as "Mrs G. Husband is Low-Paid Worker, Have Many Debts—Wife Must Work! Needs Child-Care Center!" and "Being a Widow, Must Work." Such women, the protesters implied, were equally as deserving of government aid as those whose husbands had been killed in action during the war. The *Philadelphia Bulletin*'s 1948 forum on day care also highlighted women who needed to work to support their families. One woman wrote simply, "Who will help me if I don't work? Nobody. I could write all day and night and you couldn't understand what this means to me." And Mrs. M.A. explained that she was working only because she was separated from her husband; without her wages, her children "would have had to be put away." In response to those who worried that public day care centers would encourage women to work and abandon their children, she wrote, "So that's how I am working. No mother would want to work to leave her children."[50]

This emphasis on justifying women's work as an economic necessity was particularly strong among elite child welfare advocates, who saw wage work as an unfortunate necessity, not as a noble attempt to provide for the future. While the protesting mothers asserted a *right* to day care, child welfare advocates focused on the *needs* of widows and children. Such advocates often spoke of mothers who "must work," or who were "forced to help" support their families, and grouped together working mothers with widows and women with crippled husbands.[51]

Child welfare advocates' mixed feelings about mothers' paid work made for half-hearted advocacy. In comparison with the persistent protests by mothers, the efforts of the PADN to lobby for the continuation of the centers were quite weak. In 1949, when it was reported that the mayor's committee was not going to request funding for the public centers, Ella Harris of the PADN urged the group to "do all they can in getting the funds for the day care centers into the city budget" and suggested calling on city councilmen to lobby for continued funding. Others present at the meeting, however, brought up instructions the PADN had received from the Community Chest, cautioning its member agencies "to be careful of maintaining their non-tax status and not to become too active in propaganda and politics."[52] This reminder seems to have killed discussion about actively working for the public day care centers. But it was the organization's continued ambivalence about the value of day care, not only fear of losing its tax-exempt status, that kept the PADN from effective advocacy for public day care. During a discussion at a 1951 meeting about the need to gain more public support for day care, Mary Rogers of the FFDCA "suggested that if you do too much publicity, it looks as if we are encouraging mothers to work."[53] In contrast, protesting mothers like Rose Bloomfield and Sally Spizer saw wage work as a laudable effort to ensure a better future for their children and used a triumphant tone in talking about "winning permanent day care for our children" and "making day care permanent for all working mothers." During the 1945 protest in front of City Hall, for instance, two children held up a sign which declared, "Because there will always be a need for them! We want them as a permanent part of our school system!"

In addition to casting mothers' wage work as a means of serving the family, day care proponents argued that day care furthered government interests by helping poor mothers avoid dependence on public welfare. By arguing that providing day care was preferable to encouraging reliance on welfare or charity, day care advocates revived the national debate of the 1910s and 1920s about mothers' pensions and day care as solutions to women's poverty. Many experts continued to prefer expanding public aid to mothers. For instance, the 1945 edition of Benjamin Spock's *Baby and Child Care* included a plea for public support to mothers:

> It would save money in the end if government paid a comfortable allowance to all mothers of young children who would otherwise be compelled to work. . . . Useful, well-adjusted citizens are the most valuable possessions a country has, and good mother care during early childhood is the surest way to produce them.[54]

The Children's Bureau continued to share this view, although it was increasingly coming to recognize that the answers were not so simple.[55]

During the debates over continuing public day care centers in Philadelphia, however, very few voices embraced the idea of increasing aid to mothers at home. The exception was the Blue Star Mothers of America, a group that seems to have operated at the fringes of the day care debate. Agnes Lewis of that organization explained in writing to the *Bulletin*'s 1948 forum on day care,

> While we have opposed these child care centers as communistic, we have pleaded with our public officials that, inasmuch as billions of dollars find their way into foreign countries, they should see to it that the widows' pension and mothers' assistance funds are adequate to allow mothers to stay in their own homes to care for their children. This would greatly decrease juvenile delinquency.

In Lewis's formulation, day care centers were un-American, while full-time motherhood was the foundation of the nation's values. She declared, "America is built on the bedrock of family ties and we refuse to imitate the Soviet Union, where 6,000,000 children are in such centers while the mothers are in forced labor camps." But most of those who wrote to the *Bulletin* objecting to providing public day care did not endorse alternative solutions like expanding mothers' aid. Indeed, the tone of their arguments suggests that they would not have been receptive to any step that increased public responsibility for mothers and children. Kenneth Roth wrote, "No public agency should ever be obligated to raise children so mothers can work." Similarly, Mathilde Christman wrote, "A child is each parent's responsibility, not the state's. Let's keep him in the home until kindergarten age."[56]

Most of the letter-writers, however, felt that day care was more honorable, and a better deal for the general public, than charity or public assistance. Ann Halliday of the League of Women Voters pointed out that closing the centers would result in greater spending on public assistance to provide for women who gave up work. And Mrs. John Kotzian wrote, "God bless the child care centers. They enable us to maintain our dignity and pride by using the two hands God gave us, instead of crawling and begging for charity."[57]

Like Mrs. Kotzian, many of the women applying for private day nursery care for their children also expressed their preference for working over relying on public assistance. For instance, although Viola Jackson agreed with the Wharton social worker's judgment that her son was having trouble adjusting to day care, "she quickly added that she could not accept relief and stay home. She is accustomed to being responsible and wants to provide for her family in her own way."[58] Similarly, Emma Hawkins, who received a mothers' pension while she took a vocational course at an evening high school, explained that she "prefers employment to continued dependence on State Funds," and later "expressed the feeling that she would be failing [her children] if she did not now take over the role of chief supporter."[59] Although these women knew that day care was linked to charity and public funds, they all saw the nurseries as part of a strategy of self-reliance that preserved their dignity in a way that direct public aid did not.

In addition to justifying their need to work and their desire to avoid relying on charity or welfare, mothers pushing for the continuation of the public centers also spoke about their children's needs. Some defended the day care centers merely on the grounds that they kept children safe, just as the elite women who established day nurseries in the 1890s had emphasized getting children off the streets. For instance, truck driver Charles Stokley wrote to the *Bulletin*'s forum on day care to say that he saw "so many children running the streets and I don't want my truck to hit any of them." Knowing the dangers of the streets, he was grateful for the good care that his little girl received in one of the public day care centers.[60] Women protesting in front of City Hall in 1948 also suggested the need to protect children from the streets, with signs reading "Give our children back their chance for a safe and happy childhood. Keep our centers open" and "Animals Can Roam the Streets—Children Can't."[61]

Protecting children was not only a matter of physical safety, however. Concern over juvenile delinquency ran high during this period, and wage-earning mothers were often blamed for adding to the problem by neglecting their children. The protesting mothers turned the common conviction that working mothers created juvenile delinquency to their advantage. For if mothers' employment raised the specter of juvenile delinquency, then day care centers could be justified as a means of prevention. At the 1945 demonstration, a school-aged girl carried a sign reading, "Door-Key Children [Need] Protection."

In 1948, mothers picketed City Hall carrying signs asking city officials to "Help Keep Our Children Off the Streets," "Prevent Juvenile Delinquency—keep centers open!" and arguing that if the centers closed, their children "will have no refuge but the streets while their mothers are working."[62] Indeed, the connection between working mothers and juvenile delinquency was so strong that at one point during the 1950s, the city's day care director asked the Juvenile Aid Division of the police department to check the police records of school-age children who had left the centers. When investigators found such a small incidence of arrests that they decided to drop the study half-way through, Leah Gingrich reported proudly, "It is hoped that the experience of these children in the center was one of the prime factors in this very low record of delinquency."[63]

Only a few women went beyond talking about children's needs for safe shelter to argue that day care provided a positive experience for children. Rose Bloomfield, for instance, based her appeal to Katharine Lenroot partly on the high quality of the Philadelphia child care centers. "And the centers, Miss Lenroot, have you ever visited one? Do you know just how wonderful they are? . . . The Centers will close their doors and the lovely toys and tools of the children will gather dust. It's not fair! I want you to do something about it."[64] Tregua Mack also made a broader argument for day care centers, writing, "It is of greater benefit to the children to live together, and have supervised play and instruction, than to rely on questionable help who may or may not contribute to the possible child delinquency of tomorrow."[65] Although they talked about their children's needs for safety and protection, and positioned children strategically at the front of their marches and demonstrations, however, most of the protesting mothers did not make claims based on their children's educational, developmental, and social needs. Given how frequently mothers applying to place their children at Wharton and Neighborhood Centre day nurseries cited these types of explanations, their absence from public debates and demonstrations is striking.

The main arguments that the "indignant mothers" made in favor of the public day care centers—that they prevented juvenile delinquency, provided a safe haven for children, and permitted women in dire financial straits to work rather than rely on public assistance—were fundamentally similar to those made by the elite founders of private charitable day nurseries at the turn of the century. Most of the women fighting for the extension of day care centers did not challenge the belief that maternal employment was only justifiable in terms of financial necessity or unusual family needs; they certainly did not suggest that mothers had a right to work. Nor did they use the newer explanations of women's wage work and day care that had emerged since the 1930s: that mothers' employment could raise a family's standard of living and improve the quality of children's lives, and that day care was educationally and socially beneficial to children. Perhaps organizers and day care proponents felt that these types of arguments would not convince politicians and taxpayers of the need to pay for day care centers; or perhaps they did not feel secure enough themselves about these justifications for wage work to use them in making a case for public support of day care centers.

The result of this strategy was to narrow and diminish the demand for day care. By focusing on women who were compelled to work to support their children, day care advocates reaffirmed the connection between day care and poverty, charity, and welfare. By relying on the connection between employed mothers and juvenile delinquency to gain attention for their cause, they reinforced the idea that the children of working mothers were by definition neglected and in need of public protection. Although they called for the day care centers to become a permanent part of the public school system, they did not advance the idea that day care was a positive educational experience that could benefit all children. Their attempts to translate needs into rights thus remained incomplete: although they claimed day care as a right, their rhetoric emphasized particular needs rather than universal entitlement. While casting day care as a special need of mothers who worked out of financial necessity enabled the protesters to appeal to city officials, it ultimately limited the scope of their victory. Protesters were successful in pressuring local government to recognize some responsibility for the children of wage-earning mothers, but the very claims they made served to undermine the idea that day care might be defined as a widespread need, provided without question as part of the state's responsibility to its citizens.

Mixed Messages About Women's Work

These struggles over public day care showed both a new recognition of mothers' wage work and the persistence of old attitudes. Mothers could claim a right to day care and pressure city officials into funding it, but only if they justified their employment as an unfortunate necessity and emphasized their children's need for protection. Ideas about married women's wage work were in transition in the postwar period, as a glorification of domesticity and full-time motherhood coexisted with a growing recognition that employment would be part of many women's adult lives. Attitudes toward day care were caught up in this transition and reflected the ambivalence that many Americans felt about how to define a mother's job.

On the one hand, the postwar period saw the invention of new ideas about motherhood that seemed to require full-time devotion to child-rearing. As Americans turned their energies to their homes and families after the war, full-time motherhood gained new importance as the ultimate source of meaning and fulfillment in a woman's life. Popular culture trumpeted the message that motherhood—not paid work, politics, or friendship—was to be the center of women's lives. Historian Elaine Tyler May notes that the widespread assumption that women were naturally fulfilled in motherhood was so powerful that some doctors saw any anxiety or ambivalence surrounding pregnancy as a pathological condition. The editor of *Better Homes and Gardens* wrote, "Perhaps there is not much more needed in a recipe for happiness . . . we become complete only thru our children."[66] Similarly, a 1962 *Saturday Evening Post* article explained that "the chief purpose of [a woman's] life is motherhood."[67]

This glorification of domesticity meant that motherhood was invested with broad social and political significance. Writers such as journalist Agnes Meyer wrote, "It is for woman as mother . . . to restore security in our insecure world—not the economic security on which we now lean far too much, but the emotional security for which the world longs as much as it longs for its daily bread." And presidential candidate Adlai Stevenson charged the graduates of Smith College in 1955 with helping to win the Cold War by "making homes and whole human beings in whom the rational values of freedom, tolerance, charity and free inquiry can take root."[68]

New advice about *how* to be a mother also seemed to require that women make child-rearing their only occupation. Mothers were no longer to raise their children according to a strict schedule to encourage regular habits and self-discipline; they were now to let the children set the agenda and be constantly available to meet their children's emotional as well as physical needs. The "permissive" mothering style, popularized in the postwar period by Dr. Benjamin Spock, required more time from the mother than the earlier strict-schedule approach. Permissive mothering also took a greater emotional toll on the mother, for her job was no longer measurable in concrete terms. While the physical work of mothering was reduced by greater access to household technology, the psychological work spiraled as the child's path to adulthood was portrayed as fraught with psychological dangers and neuroses that mothers could induce. Historian Nancy Weiss writes that in Dr. Spock's manual "an emotional workday is superimposed on the mother's physical workday, in part devoted to monitoring her own behavior so as to provide the proper environment for her offspring's 'self-realization' through 'self-discovery' and 'self-motivated behavior.'"[69] Mothers were expected to doubt themselves and were urged to turn to experts—pediatricians, child psychologists, and early childhood educators—rather than relying on their own instincts or their own mothers' advice for help in rearing their children.

Mainstream advice for mothers stressed that child-rearing was a full-time job. Popular magazines that had encouraged women to go out to work during the war now emphasized children's need for full-time mothering. Even before the war ended, government guidelines suggested that magazines turn their attention away from day care centers to concentrate on the "new national problem" of juvenile delinquency. Advertisements started to picture the unhappiness and instability of children whose mothers went out to work: one showed a factory worker pleading before a juvenile court judge for her teenage son, who had been accused of vandalism, while another showed a girl being carted away to a foster home because her mother had to work.[70] Parenting advice often drew on the work of British psychologist John Bowlby, who studied children raised in hospitals and orphanages and concluded that "deprivation of mother-love in early childhood can have a far-reaching effect on the mental health and personality development of human beings." He called for "the provision of constant attention day and night, seven days a week and 365 in the year" and referred to children who did not have their mothers' full-time care as victims of "maternal deprivation." As historian Lynn Weiner writes, "The working mother was now labeled a neurotic or, worse, a cause of neurosis in her children." A popular textbook on child development published in 1948 placed the discussion of working mothers in a chapter entitled "Families Under Stress," and cited "lonely, neglected, and unsupervised children" as among the social costs of a mother's decision to work.[71] Similarly, Dr. Spock's enormously popular *Baby and Child Care* sandwiched a small section on working mothers between premature babies and handicapped children in a section on "Special Problems" at the end of the book. Spock's portrayal of motherhood throughout the book clearly defined it as an all-consuming job, with paid work nowhere in the picture.[72] In popular media, motherhood and career were often portrayed as mutually exclusive; many women's magazines wrote approvingly of women who had given up careers in order to devote their time to their children, and stories about Hollywood celebrities emphasized their devotion to motherhood.[73] Such stories rarely articulated the idea that supporting children economically was part of a mother's job.

But the postwar period carried more than one message about women's work and family responsibilities. Alongside the glorification of motherhood and domesticity that we commonly associate with the 1950s emerged a new legitimation of women's paid work. If the Cold War spurred some Americans to seek security in traditional gender roles, it simultaneously provided a reason for some business leaders and government officials to encourage women's employment. Problems with manpower during the Korean War led government planners to focus on day care as a means of recruiting workers to crucial defense areas.[74] The war in Korea, however, seemed to be only the beginning. A 1951 Children's Bureau memo warned that the situation was not merely an emergency war crisis, but a problem of "partial preparedness for a long time to come."[75] This concern with mobilizing women's labor power on a long-term basis required increased attention to day care.

Concerned that the nation was "losing out in a race [with the Soviet Union] for highly trained manpower," the government officials and civic leaders who made up the National Manpower Council sought to facilitate women's participation in the paid labor force and change popular attitudes toward women's public roles. While the experts associated with the council did not directly challenge women's domestic responsibilities, they suggested that children could be separated from their mothers "for substantial periods during the day, if adequate substitute care is provided" without causing juvenile delinquency or maladjustment. The council decried the inadequacy of existing arrangements for child care and pointed to benefits resulting from the employment of mothers outside the home: higher standards of living, greater partnership between parents, and mothers who were more satisfied with their lives. They even prefigured the "quality time" debate of recent years by asserting, "it is not the amount of time spent with the child but what happens during that time that really matters."[76]

This desire to increase "the effectiveness of our woman power" led to the 1955 White House Conference on Effective Uses of Womanpower, which inaugurated a new government policy of encouraging women to move into the labor market, not just to meet the demands of a temporary emergency, but as a long-term strategy for meeting labor needs.[77] Skilled workers were especially encouraged to combine motherhood with paid work. A shortage of nurses during the 1950s led some hospitals to offer part-time hours and on-site day care in order to encourage women with children to come back to work.[78] Similarly, in a 1952 letter to the Women's Bureau, a former stenographer responded to a news article about the shortage of stenographers by saying that like hundreds of other young mothers she knew, she would be glad to return to work if she could find good care for her child, since "with prices as they are today an added income in a family is always welcome." She suggested that the bureau would have more luck bringing those "good stenos" back to work if sufficient low-cost nurseries could be found.[79]

Congress also took a step toward legitimating day care and mothers' employment in 1954 when it approved President Eisenhower's proposal to make child-care expenses tax deductible. The measure received broad support, although many legislators made it clear that they intended it to help only those women who truly "needed" to work. Proponents of the bill argued that women's labor was necessary to the nation's economic and security interests, claimed that the deduction would help promote rapid mobilization in a wartime emergency, and insisted that child care was as legitimate a business expense as entertainment, travel, and country club membership. All parties to the debate recognized that mothers' employment was a fact of life and sought to accommodate public policy to that new reality.[80]

Like public policy, popular culture also promoted mixed messages about women's place in postwar America. Looking again at the popular magazines of the 1950s, we see that they did more than simply promote the "feminine mystique" of women's fulfillment through full-time domesticity. After surveying mass-circulation monthly magazines from 1946 to 1958, historian Joanne Meyerowitz concludes that in their nonfiction writing, postwar journalists offered an alternative to the "feminine mystique," often expressing "overt admiration for women whose individual striving moved them beyond the home." These writers insisted that women worked for wages because they needed to and also advanced the view that employment could bring personal satisfaction. While magazine writers might have argued for a woman's right to work, however, by placing women's work within the context of individual striving and achievement, they made it difficult to envision collective solutions to the problems encountered by wage-earning women—such as finding good child care.[81] Magazine writers were, like many Americans, ambivalent about working mothers, but the magazines reflected the distinction that women themselves were increasingly making between working at a career and at a job. While career women were often suspect, women who worked intermittently at low-status jobs in order to raise their families' standard of living were becoming increasingly normal.

Indeed, one of the central ironies of the postwar period is that despite prevailing images of full-time domesticity, women worked for wages in increasing numbers. By 1950 the number of employed women was slightly higher than it had been during the war, and it continued to grow after that.[82] The growth in the proportion of married women in the work force was particularly striking; while in 1950 wives earned wages in 21.6% of all families, ten years later the number had risen to 30.5%. Nor was wage work any longer the exclusive domain of poor families: whereas in earlier decades, there had been an inverse correlation between a husband's income and the likelihood of his wife's working, by 1950 that correlation was reversed for white women: the more a woman was capable of earning, because of increased education, the more likely she was to work.[83] The proportion of women with small children who sought to go out to work increased by one-third and that of those with children under six by more than a quarter.[84] In Philadelphia, the rate of growth was much higher: a newspaper article reported that from 1950 to 1957, the percentage of women with preschool children who were in the work force grew by more than 50%.[85]

These statistics reflected a trend, accelerated by the war, of women working in order to contribute to their families' budgets. The consumer-driven economy and materialism of the postwar years, when those Americans who could scrambled to buy the things they had lived without throughout years of depression and war, was a major force motivating women's wage work, and was in constant tension with the postwar ideology of domesticity. Historian Elaine Tyler May explains the general ambivalence toward married women's employment: "On the one hand, it was unfortunate if a wife had to hold a job; on the other hand, it was considered far worse if the family was unable to purchase what were believed to be necessities for the home." By enabling their families to participate in the new culture of consumption, wage-earning women helped achieve the "American standard of living," which was to prove America's superiority in the world, and it was hoped, would confer security and abundance on their children.[86]

Legitimizing Day Care

The war had changed some ideas about how women could best serve the family; employment was increasingly seen as a way to fulfill part of a mother's responsibility. The ways in which day nursery workers in Philadelphia explained the need for their services reflect this growing acceptance of mothers' employment. Without apology, nursery reports from these years described various legitimate family needs that a mother's wages could help meet and explained their mission as serving families who needed day care on an ongoing basis. For instance, the Neighborhood Centre Day Nursery's 1946 report stated: "The adjustment of the veteran to family life and the increased cost of living is compelling many young mothers to work. Economic trends being what they are today, in all likelihood there will be a persistent need for the service we are rendering."[87] In its report for that year, the First Family Day Care Association (FFDCA, formerly the First and Sunnyside Day Nursery) explained that the wives of men who decided to take advantage of the GI Bill to return to school also continued to work to supplement the family budget while their husbands were studying.[88] Another FFDCA report noted that mothers also explained their need to work by referring to "the desperate need for a home and the continued high cost of everything the family has to buy."[89] Similarly, among the top seven reasons given by families for using Philadelphia public day care centers in 1948 were the insufficiency of the father's income, the need to pay off accumulated debts, to support a husband going to school, and to purchase a home.[90] These patterns were part of a nationwide trend; when nine thousand female union members were surveyed in 1952, they explained their work by referring to their families' need to purchase a home, educate children, or meet specific goals such as paying medical bills, purchasing home furnishings, or keeping up automobiles.[91]

Day care workers found that their "typical" client was changing: no longer the poor single mother on relief, but families who were seeking a higher standard of living by sending mothers as well as fathers into the work force.[92] Married couples in which both spouses were working used Philadelphia's day nurseries in increasing numbers during the postwar period; at the three private nurseries for which we have case records, 59% of the families applying for day care were headed by married couples; at the First Family Day Care Association, 66% of the applications came from married couples.[93] The percentage of families applying for day care at the private day nurseries so that the woman could supplement her husband's income rose from 9% to 16%, and the percentage who wanted day care so the mother could work to help buy a house rose from 1% to 4%.[94] The trend is particularly evident at Wharton, where the proportion of applications from families where two parents were working increased, and more women explained that they were working in order to buy a home. Although the clientele at St. Nicholas Day Nursery was still heavily weighted toward single mothers and wives working to supplement an insufficient male wage, the "both working" category made an appearance for the first time during the postwar period. (Single-parent families were more common at the public day care centers. Still, single mothers were a minority at three of the public centers studied for a 1955 report, and the mothers in the two-parent families justified their work by explaining the need to improve their families' standard of living.)[95] The general shift away from day care as a welfare measure is suggested by the fact that only

5% of the families applying to the three Philadelphia day nurseries during this period had contact with another social welfare agency.

Mothers in the African-American neighborhood surrounding the Wharton Centre in North Philadelphia had always worked from economic necessity. Even at Wharton, however, many of the women who applied for day care in the postwar period did not speak of their work as the last bulwark standing between their families and dire poverty. Rather, they were working to help their husbands "get ahead," buy a house, or generally raise their families' standard of living. For instance, "Though Mr. Turner has a good job and works regularly they are buying their own home, and the cost of living is so high that Mrs. Turner has gone back to work to help out. She said they are very much in need of her salary at this time." Mrs. Turner mentioned that her daughter "frequently asks her why she does not stay home with her. She always gives her the explanation that she has to help her daddy."[96] Other children attending the Wharton day care also understood that their mothers were working so that the family could buy a house, the consummation of the American dream. One child came into the office where the social worker was talking to her mother one day. "After greeting her mother, [she] pleasantly asked her 'if she had bought a house.' Mrs. Sampson then said that she had explained to Arlene that she was going to work so they could get a home to themselves."[97] Many women explained their work not as a temporary response to an emergency situation, but as a long-term strategy for meeting family needs. LaBarbara Sewell, who was living with her in-laws, "wants to go to work so that she can help her husband save some money. . . . She expects to be working steadily so that she prefers to make a long-term plan for the two girls."[98]

For the families who used the Wharton Centre, dreams of a middle-class life-style depended on having two breadwinners. Thelma Jackson "wants to give her children the best care possible, but is ambitious and feels that it takes the two incomes, if the family is to get ahead."[99] Rebecca Roberson also felt "that now is the time to get ahead. She wants to get out and help, so that they can accumulate and get on their feet while they are still young."[100] "Getting ahead" was often an elusive goal. For instance, when Nellie Wilson first applied for day care, she "said that she had worked for many years only to help her husband attain their goal of a home of their own and having reached this, they both decided she would continue so that they could pay it faster and save toward Bobbie's education." Two months later, however, Mrs. Wilson's wages became the only income supporting the family when her husband lost his job.[101]

Like the mothers applying for day care at Wharton, those who sought day care at Neighborhood Centre after the war were also hoping to "help out" their husbands, typically by working in the family store. For instance, Sarah Spolsky applied for day care in 1947 so she could help her husband in her parents' second-hand furniture business. Her husband had been "actively engaged" in his in-laws' business for the past year, and the couple "want to develop the furniture shop along more modern lines since her parents are getting old and they feel eventually the business can be theirs."[102] Similarly, Jennie Kleinberg applied for Beatrice in 1949 because she wanted to help her husband in his business, a wholesale and retail plastic curtain concern; he had been in this business, in partnership with her father, for ten months. The social worker noted, "Because business did not net enough for two families Mr. & Mrs. K felt that they could make a living if Mrs. K took care of the customers, bills, etc while Mr. made the curtains and shades. This would mean a change in the family's plans since originally Mrs. K had not considered being active in the business."[103]

While women were expected to use their labor to improve conditions for their husbands and children, however, economic cooperation within an extended family was less legitimate. The strong emphasis on the nuclear family in postwar culture rendered extended family bonds and obligations suspect; films and television comedies like *Marty* and "I Remember Mama" featured stories of young people shifting allegiances from ethnic multigenerational families to the "emancipated nuclear family."[104] Thus women who were working in family businesses sometimes had a hard time convincing the Neighborhood Centre social worker to take their work seriously. Lillian Vilman applied for day care for her daughter Rhoda, explaining that "she felt it important to help her mother, who has a fruit and vegetable store on 4th Street, because her mother's sister who had formerly helped out in the store was taking a position on the outside." The worker wrote, "Despite the fact that Mrs. Vilman would be pretty much occupied during the day in her parents' business, she would be receiving no compensation, and there was real question about accepting Rhoda for admission since there were so many other requests from women who were working." The narrow definition of what constituted "working" here is striking, as is the rigid definition of "family" in the social worker's summary of the case. She wrote, "Since Mrs. Vilman would be receiving no compensation for helping her parents in their business, and we would be helping her assume responsibility for her parents rather than for her own family, admission was refused." When Lillian applied again a month later on the grounds of needing relief from caring for Rhoda because of her physical condition (she was pregnant and having trouble with varicose veins), the child was easily admitted. Living with relatives over a family store, as so many of these families did, was not considered real family life. When the Vilmans decided to move into a home of their own, the worker rejoiced. "The family are seriously looking for an apartment so that they can move, and finally be a family unit without maternal grandparents and uncles and aunts."[105]

The strong emphasis placed on the nuclear family in the postwar years made it difficult for families such as these to secure the recognition and help of day nursery social workers. The same nuclear family emphasis rendered the working mother nearly invisible in popular culture and in discussions of child-rearing and family life. Yet it was also during these years that mothers worked for wages in larger numbers than ever before, in the name of commitment to family and to providing a secure future for their children.

Both single and married women applying for day care frequently spoke about their work in hopeful terms, as contributing to a better future for their children. For instance, in a 1952 article, day care advocate Ethel Beer quoted a Sicilian woman who worked in a factory to supplement her husband's earnings, explaining, "I want my kids, they should have it better than I have."[106] In applying to the Wharton day care center, Lucille Hunter also spoke of her desire to make all her children's lives better than hers had been. By using the day care center, she could spare her oldest daughter the burden of being forced to skip school to care for younger siblings.

> She doesn't want this to happen to Gloria anymore. She, herself, had gone through this experience as a youngster and related how she had had to care for her six young brothers and sisters while her mother worked. Mrs. H said that she has always been unhappy over

> the fact that she only had three years of schooling in her life. . . . Before her mother took her out, Mrs. H had begged that she be allowed to finish because she had been anxious to become a teacher. Mrs. H says that she wants to make it possible for all her children to finish school even though she needs to work indefinitely.[107]

Lucy Broomer, another Wharton mother, saw her work as a way to provide "certain advantages she wanted the children to have. . . . We asked her just what advantages did she mean. She gave an example of wanting to give the children music lessons."[108] And Margaret Rawson, who worked on the city subway in order to pay off the mortgage on a farm that her husband had bought before his death, also saw her work as a way to improve her children's future: she told the Wharton social worker that she hoped the farm would be "some security for the children."[109]

No longer an act of desperation, a mother's paid work could now be seen as part of a family's plan for achieving a better life. Even publicity for the private day nurseries reflected this shift. Neighborhood Centre, whose early publicity had emphasized the dramatic plight of widows and deserted women, began to portray mothers' wage work in positive terms. Mrs. Irene Silversein, who sent her two daughters to the Neighborhood Centre Nursery School,[110] was interviewed on a public-service radio broadcast "Planned Parenthood on the Air," in 1950. The radio interviewer described Silversein's work in the beauty shop that she operated with her husband and commented, "You are both busy with additional matters beyond the moulding of good family relationships. You really have a double job!" Silversein responded, "Yes, and I enjoy doing two jobs, one in the shop, and one at home." Rather than pitying the working mother who was forced to carry a double burden, this piece of publicity expressed a new enthusiasm for women's paid work. Silversein was also very positive about her children's experiences with day care; she told the interviewer that the nursery school staff gave "wonderful physical care" and used "skilled techniques to develop character and ability." She explained, "It's terribly important to every mother who works to feel secure and know that her child is being well cared for."[111]

When working and using day care was perceived as a way for families to "get ahead," it became more attractive to professional couples and to families seeking middle-class status. Ten percent of the parents applying to Wharton during this period were employed as professionals, and St. Nicholas saw its first applications from professional families during these years. Parents applying to these two African-American nurseries from 1946 to 1952 included nurses, teachers, social workers, insurance agents, a Census Bureau statistician, a bookkeeper for the Internal Revenue Service, and the pastor of a Baptist church. Professional families also turned to day care agencies when mothers needed to work so that fathers could study for an advanced degree. This was particularly common at the First Family Day Care Association (FFDCA). The agency's 1950 report gave the example of the Whitlocks, who placed their son Bobby in a foster day care home while the mother worked as a teacher in order to put her husband through medical school. "Now the medical course is completed," the agency's social worker reported, "this very self-reliant couple have left for another city where Dr. Whitlock is to have his internship."[112] Although the majority of parents who sent their children to the FFDCA and other private day nurseries continued to be clerical workers, sales clerks, factory workers, domestics, and laborers, the increase in professional families using the nurseries suggests the fading of the charitable stigma attached to day nurseries throughout their earlier history.[113]

Clients had begun to redefine day care during World War II, but not until the postwar period did social workers and child welfare professionals began to reflect this shift by promoting the idea that mothers' paid work could be beneficial to families. In 1949, the magazine *Child Welfare* carried an article entitled "Why Day Care?" which suggested that day care agencies might serve women who worked for a variety of reasons—not just out of sheer economic need. The author noted that "an increasing number of women who have enjoyed the benefits of employment or the satisfactions of a career are not emotionally receptive to becoming housewives," and that professional and white collar families "are caught in the dilemma of cultivated tastes frustrated by inadequate income"; she argued that such women should be free to seek employment.[114] Strawberry Mansion Day Nursery's Anna Frigond wrote an enthusiastic letter to the editor of the magazine in response. "What we actually see at present," Frigond wrote, "is that the need for day care service in our culture is growing, not abating, and that the large volume of need, if we recognize it as such, is not entirely dependent on crises and wars."[115] In an annual report two years later, Frigond explained that the day nursery's emphasis on serving the broken family was preventing it from responding to the variety of other needs for nursery service that existed in the community. Families who were not poor also had legitimate reasons to seek day care so the mother could work: those who were squeezed by the high cost of living, those who lived with their in-laws because they were unable to establish their own home on the man's salary alone, those who needed to work so their husbands could acquire further training, and those who were not happy as homemakers and had some professional training "through which she is able to make a contribution to society and in pursuit of which she will become a less frustrated individual, consequently, being a better wife and mother."[116]

Other evidence also suggests that social service professionals were beginning to reevaluate some of their assumptions about day care, broadening their sense of whom day care was for. For instance, the Day Care Committee of the Philadelphia Health and Welfare Council somewhat reluctantly endorsed expanding day care:

> In our society we believe that children develop best if they can remain at home with their parents. Our economic and cultural pattern, however, shows a trend for increased employment of mothers of young children. . . . Day care should be available to those children who need it for reasons growing out of the family situation and should not be limited to children of working mothers.[117]

Participants at a 1952 Child Welfare League conference agreed that day nurseries should serve families of higher incomes as well as their traditional low-income clientele.[118] And Gertrude Binder wrote in the *Social Work Journal* in 1953 that day care should aim to promote "the well-being of an expanding circle of human beings rather than merely to mitigate the ill-being of the exceptionally unfortunate." She proposed that day care should shift from being seen as an emergency resource for poor women to being seen as a community-based educational resource for children.[119]

This more positive attitude toward day care was in part the result of experiences with public day care during the war. In a 1947 article, Ruth Koshuk suggested that the success of the wartime day care centers had created support for expanding nursery schools and day care. The centers had not only enabled women to work in war industries but had also strengthened family relationships in a time of stress and exposed mothers to up-to-date child-rearing techniques. Mothers who used centers in California reported that their children benefited from the experience, and 87% of those Koshuk surveyed believed that nursery schools should be established in all school districts and be open to the children of nonemployed as well as employed mothers.[120] In Philadelphia, the experiences of the war strengthened the commitment of several day care centers to provide day care services. Esther Frank Siegel of Neighborhood Centre wrote in 1946, "We face our first peacetime year as a day nursery . . . with the realization that need for day care has not abated and might concernably be increased. There has been an increasing public recognition and realization of the importance of good day time care for children." She concluded, "I believe we can be justifiedly proud of the roll [sic] we played during the war by supplying a measure of security to the family and stability for the child. However, the ending has brought additional problems and new uncertainties for both the family and child, and our roll [sic] in the post-war world will be equally vital."[121] Attention to day care was also growing on the national level. In 1954, the board of the Child Welfare League of America, earlier an opponent of day care, decided "to take aggressive action to arouse more widespread concern for day care problems."[122]

More people were voicing the conviction that day care was a responsibility of government, not a matter of private charity. A publication of the Child Welfare League argued, "It is hardly American to leave a mother, too often poorly paid for her work, to shift for her child without some minimum guarantee of community service and some subsidy for the child's care."[123] The idea that failure to provide day care for working mothers could be seen as "un-American" surely indicated a transformation in attitudes. Similarly, a speaker at a 1957 meeting of the National Conference on Social Welfare declared, "Tax-supported child care centers are essential to every large community," a statement that could not have been made prior to the experience of World War II.[124]

Educational Care

A crucial aspect of the growing legitimacy of day care was the conviction that day care was educational and thus benefited children, not just their mothers. The connection between the wartime day care centers and the public schools had helped strengthen the connection between day care and education. Rhoda Kellogg, a California day care advocate, told the Women's Bureau in 1951 that "nearly 100% of the thousands of women I have interviewed want *educational* and not *welfare* auspices to operate the child care centers." Kellogg urged the Women's Bureau to support an educationally oriented program, for this would "attract mothers, protect children from the stigma of relief, from case work investigation of homes, and the subordination of their educational needs to . . . custodial ones."[125]

As day nurseries and day care centers increasingly tried to model themselves on nursery schools (by using nursery school pedagogy and hiring trained nursery school teachers), the distinction between educational and custodial care for children began to fade. And as the program of nursery schools and day nurseries began to converge, so did their clientele. In 1952, the PADN discussed the question of serving "parents who have more money than they have ever had." The group linked this change in the clientele of day care centers to a change in the basic function of day care: originally a welfare service aimed at mothers, it was becoming an educational program aimed at children.[126] During another PADN meeting, a discussion about who should use day care centers included the recognition, "Some parents want the educational facilities of nurseries for their children. Some boards feel that only the most needy economically speaking should have it, but other needs do exist."[127]

When day care shifted from welfare for poor mothers to education for the middle class, its meaning changed significantly. A comparison between Neighborhood Centre's original day nursery and a nursery school operated by the agency in another section of the city suggests the implications of this shift. In 1950, after a fire in its main building, Neighborhood Centre followed its upwardly mobile clientele to one of the new Jewish neighborhoods in the north of the city. A few years later, in an attempt to serve a scattering population, the settlement house established branches in two other neighborhoods. In 1955, the Bustleton Avenue branch decided to open a nursery school. The differences between this nursery school and the nursery operated by Neighborhood Centre in its downtown location are striking and resulted from the primarily middle-class parents who used the Bustleton Avenue school being able to fully pay tuition, which covered the school's costs.

Publicity and registration materials for the Bustleton Avenue Nursery School suggested that the school was a community service open to all who could afford it, not a charitable enterprise. Any child between the ages of three and five could enroll and would be accepted on a first-come, first-serve basis. Publicity materials tried to "sell" the nursery school to parents, touting the creativity and high quality of the program, the training and experience of the teachers, and the educational and social value of the nursery school overall. Such an attempt at promoting the downtown day nursery to its clients would have seemed incongruous and was never attempted. But perhaps the most striking difference between the "uptown" and "downtown" nursery schools was captured in the forms that parents had to fill out to enroll their children. The "downtown" nursery school/day nursery application blank was long and complicated, almost identical to the application forms that were used for other forms of charity, such as mothers' pensions, family assistance, or foster care. These forms asked for detailed information about parents' marital status, employment and wages, housing conditions and rent, relatives and their financial resources, union or insurance benefits, and contact with other welfare agencies or hospitals. Furthermore, no child would be accepted by the nursery without a thorough investigation of the family by a staff social worker, which always included an inspection of the family's living quarters and often involved interviews with neighbors, employers, or relatives. The Bustleton Avenue form, by contrast, was short and simple. It put questions about the child before questions about the parents and asked no questions about the family's income. Instead, the form asked questions related to the needs of the school's program: could mothers accompany the group on trips? Did they have a car available? Could they assist on school projects?[128]

While the "downtown" nursery assumed that families needing day care were always troubled, the Bustleton Avenue Nursery School seemed to assume that its families were normal and healthy, for seeking a nursery school experience for children was a normal part of family life. The Bustleton Avenue school did not employ a social worker and did not engage in investigations or home visiting, although parent education programs were offered. Although the switch from "downtown" to "uptown" nursery schools represents a shift in funding and in the social class of the families using the service,[129] it also suggests the transformation that many day care programs were undergoing as they began to redefine their mission from welfare to education.

Day care programs increasingly presented themselves as being educational rather than merely custodial; during a discussion with one client, the Wharton social worker noted, "I said that we do not think of ourselves as a place in which children are left for day care alone, that our greatest interest is in a child's development."[130] Leah Gingrich described the Philadelphia public day care centers as offering "the same experiences as nursery and kindergarten education programs . . . based on knowledge and understanding of the fundamental needs, growth and development of children." Because of the educational value of the program, five-year-old children were kept in the centers rather than being sent to the public kindergartens.[131] When the "Planned Parenthood on the Air" radio show interviewed Irene Silversein about Neighborhood Centre, she not only mentioned the "wonderful lunches" and outdoor activity provided for the children but also emphasized the teachers' training and concern for child development. She stressed that her own parenting skills had improved as a result of the guidance offered by Neighborhood Centre, including discussions with teachers, round-table discussions led by psychiatrists, and "movies which help in child-rearing."[132] The growing convergence between day care and nursery education is further reflected by the fact that when the Philadelphia Association for Nursery Education held its third meeting in 1950, one of its officers was a teacher at one of the public day care centers.[133] Including day care center teachers among the officers of this organization marks a significant departure from earlier decades, when nursery educators worked hard to identify themselves as professionals and tried to distance themselves from day nursery workers, who were seen as providing only minimal physical care.

Parents applying to Wharton and Neighborhood Centre during the postwar period often mentioned the centers' educational, developmental, and social value for their children, suggesting that in some circles, at least, day care had come to be associated with modernity and middle-class status. Not only might a mother's work improve a family's future prospects, but the day care center itself would benefit children directly. Some Wharton parents expressed their confidence that attending the day care center would make their children more refined and cultured. Mary Bishop, who worked as a maid in a doctor's office, "gave as another reason for wanting Juanita to come to the nursery, her desire to have her in a good environment and in contact with the kind of people who can help her grow up to be a 'nice child.'"[134] One father "said that his only interest now is in raising his child according to the highest possible standards, making her as fine as he could."[135] Another father, who worked as a teacher, wrote to the nursery, "I understand that [my daughter] is a student there in the nursery again. I am very glad to know this because I feel that her past attendance there did much for her cultural background."[136]

Several parents looked to the nursery to provide social interaction for their children. For instance, one woman explained that her daughter "is in need of companionship. She is an only child and being alone is not able to come in contact often with other children. Frequently Mrs. C arranges contact with other children, but this is not always convenient."[137] Similarly, Lillian Vilman explained to the Neighborhood Centre worker that she was applying for her daughter Rhoda not only so that she could work in her parents' fruit and vegetable store, but because Rhoda "had no playmates." Mrs. Vilman may also have hoped that attending the nursery would help make her daughter more refined, for the social worker noted, "Her standards for Rhoda are quite high and there is indication that she feels 'better' than other people in the neighborhood."[138]

Other parents felt that the nursery's modern child-rearing techniques would help their children and reinforce their own attempts to raise their children to be well-adjusted and successful. Maryann Coleman "said that the nursery experience has been an excellent support for the kind of training she has been giving [her son] and expressed the feeling that . . . this might be the saving of him."[139] Lucille Hunter described herself as someone who "takes the problems of motherhood very seriously. She said that she cannot accept easily the advice of neighbors and friends that she should not worry or be concerned about the children, just to keep them clean and to feed them and leave them free." She felt that the nursery would support her efforts to train her children along modern lines: "Aside from the fact that she needs to work and help support them, she is very interested in having them come to groups with other children and learn to get along."[140] And a grandmother applying for care for her grandson recognized a generation gap in standards of child-rearing: "She knows that she, herself, cannot do all that is required for young children today. It is different from what it was in her day. When her children were young, it was enough to feed them well, clothe them well, and give them good attention. However, nowadays, she feels a child needs much more than that."[141]

In a reversal of earlier patterns, many parents applying to Wharton during the postwar years preferred to send their children to the day care center rather than arranging informal care with neighbors and relatives. Thelma Jackson "stated that her husband was very particular about the kind of place the children stay in and that he was satisfied with this nursery. . . . He would not consider their being placed in a private home."[142] Before coming to Wharton, Julia Ganway had left her baby daughter with a neighbor who "would lock the child in the house and go off and leave her." She told the social worker that since her daughter was at the day care center, for the first time "she has been able to be free in her working experience because she knows that Mildred is being well cared for."[143]

Conflicting Visions of Day Care

The conviction that day nurseries such as Wharton and Neighborhood Centre offered high-quality care that would provide educational and social benefits for the children who attended them shows how far the image of the nurseries had come from the early twentieth century, when they were seen as little better than orphanages. Although such positive feelings show a marked change in attitudes towards day care, older attitudes—the association of day care with charity and family pathology—also persisted.

Many day nursery workers felt defensive about day care in the postwar era; in her 1947 report, Anna Frigond of Strawberry Mansion wrote, "What we try to offer the children and their families is not a dumping ground, but an atmosphere conducive to happiness and to security."[144] The executive director of the PADN was not ready to advocate day care enthusiastically: she said at the association's 1951 annual meeting, "Day care is a mild but effective method in fighting problems our country is up against."[145] And the idea that day care should be available to everyone remained a minority opinon: despite Anna Frigond's efforts to broaden the definition of day care, her 1950 annual report still justified it as a social service for families in crisis, not a straightforward need of "normal" families.[146] A 1958 information sheet about the nursery she directed stated unequivocally, "Strawberry Mansion Day Care House is a Welfare Agency."[147]

Attempts to revise the old notion of day care as a charity conflicted with the persistent idea that families who needed day care were by definition families in crisis. When a PADN committee decided to produce a booklet that would increase public support for day care, they chose the title, "She Couldn't Cope."[148] A 1958 study of day care needs in Philadelphia's Jewish community defined day care's primary objective as "to help maintain the family unit during periods of strain or crisis, thereby preventing placement of the children [in an institution] and family breakdown."[149] Similarly, a publicity brochure printed by the Federation of Jewish Charities defined the purpose of day care as "Helping Families Stay Together . . . When Home Life Is Threatened." Next to the phrase, "When Home Life Is Threatened" was an illustration of a woman working at a machine, a person lying in a hospital bed, and a mother walking out a door with a child.[150] The idea that a mother's wage work threatened, rather than strengthened, the family was still strong. One Community Chest worker showed how little things had changed when she referred to day nursery children in 1952 as "day-time orphans whose mothers must work to pay the rent and buy the groceries."[151]

Many people continued to believe that day care should only serve desperately poor families, not mothers who might have some choice about working for wages. In 1953, as the Daughters of Charity who staffed the Cathedral Day Nursery were preparing to celebrate the nursery's fiftieth anniversary, church officials decided that the nursery should be closed instead. Although enrollments had been declining for some time, the main reason behind the decision seemed to be a change in the types of families who were relying on the nursery. Monsignor Cartwright, the rector of the cathedral, worried that the nursery offered a "temptation" to mothers to work when they did not really need to, "and both the mother and the family would be better off if she were to remain at home." Father Francis Dodd, who directed the Daughters of Charity, agreed, writing that "the number of children [at the nursery] who could really be considered 'poor,' was very small. The 'Day Nursery' had really developed into a 'Pre-school Nursery' where mothers who wanted to work could send their children with a minimum of expense." He advised against setting up a day nursery in a different location, since the order did not have any Sisters with the necessary social work training to screen out applications from mothers "who were not really obliged to work for the support of the family."[152] The Sisters who had devoted their lives to the nursery for many years were clearly disappointed (they were instructed by letter to "offer no objections whatsoever" and not to express any "signs of regret or disappointment"), and the parents were shocked, but "perfectly resigned," when they were told about the nursery's closing. Archbishop O'Hara wrote to Father Dodd that although it was difficult to close down the nursery, "We should thank God . . . that improved economic conditions have helped keep mothers in the home. Our present duty is to stress the sanctity of the home, the sacramental character of marriage, and the duties of parents to their children."[153]

These views about day care were shared by many social workers. After attending a 1956 conference of the Child Welfare League of America, St. Nicholas director Helen Lockwood wrote, "The acceptance of Day Care, . . . is not as general as we would like to think: and some really believe it is a threat to the family. Some think that if we had really good casework service, we would not need Day Care."[154] Assuming that families using day care were by definition troubled and strained, these critics insisted that day care agencies provide casework and counseling. The public day care centers in Philadelphia were criticized for failing to offer such services.[155] In 1955, the director of the city's day care program asked the First Family Day Care Association, which prided itself on the counseling it provided to mothers, to do a pilot study of the need for counseling within the public day care centers. One of the main rationales behind the study was to determine whether the addition of skilled counseling would help the centers "prevent and alleviate instability and insecurity which could lead to delinquency in families where the mothers must work outside the home."

The FFDCA's Frida Kuhlmann, who conducted the study, felt that counseling might encourage more women to stay at home with their children. She was concerned about the high number of two-parent families using the day care centers so that mothers could work to improve the family's status. She asked, "What is the implication for day care of two-parent families struggling to get ahead financially? Is the drive to improve economic status realistic and helpful to the children?" Elsewhere she wrote, "Though adults have the right to determine what they want in economic status, their drive toward economic security does not necessarily enhance family life. Could skilled counseling services be of help to evaluate this in terms of the needs of the children and whether the day care services meet these?" While Kuhlmann admitted that there were many "mature, independent, and resourceful" families using the centers who did not need counseling, she stressed that there were many who did need help. These were not only the obviously troubled families of whom the day care center staff was aware, but also families affected by marital separation, financial problems, illness, and other tensions which "must have an affect on children."[156] Although the public day care program's limited budget prevented Gingrich from acting on Kuhlmann's recommendations, the study shows the persistence of the idea that day care clients were by definition troubled and unstable, and that one of the main purposes of counseling should be to dissuade women from working.[157]

A study conducted in 1952 by the Federation of Jewish Charities also highlighted negative attitudes toward day care. The report cast day care as a less-than-ideal solution to family needs, defined it as a temporary service for families in crisis, and warned that mothers often found that combining wage work and mothering was more difficult than they had anticipated. The Strawberry Mansion Nursery objected to the report's "point of view regarding day care service" and offered an alternative perspective. While recognizing the difficulties inherent in a mother's decision to seek paid work, Anna Frigond and her board expressed their firm belief that "people have a right to make their own decisions for a way of life" and that people who chose to work rather than accept relief should be commended.

> We, in the day nurseries, therefore recognize and respect the strengths, initiative and yes, resourcefulness on the part of our parents who choose to solve their economic problems through work by using day care service despite all the hardships that this entails.

Frigond defended both the benefit of mothers' wage work to the family and the benefit of formal day care to children. She wrote, "We know it to be a fact that countless numbers of families are spared the agonies of being entirely in the class of the 'ill-fed, ill-clothed and ill-housed' by the supplementation, limited though it may be, of the woman's earnings." She was offended by the report's casual statement that school-age children could be cared for by "a nearby relative or friend," especially when school lunches were available. Frigond wrote, "We see our program as being much more than providing luncheon, and we certainly do not subscribe to the idea of the haphazard care of a reluctant neighbor or friend who certainly would not tend to give an active child the necessary understanding or a sense of belonging and being wanted as is the aim of the nursery."[158]

The 1952 report, and Anna Frigond's response to it, show how attitudes toward day care were in transition in the postwar years. While the report's generally negative tone toward day care, its assumption that day care was only used by families in crisis, and its contention that a mother's wage work was often not worth the trouble it created show the continued influence of old ideas about day care, the passion of Frigond's response suggest that the rhetorical ground had shifted since the early twentieth century. Rather than defend day care apologetically as a necessary evil, arguing that mothers' wage work was an unfortunate fact of life that nursery supporters hoped would eventually disappear, Frigond was able to take the high ground, presenting mothers' work as a noble way of contributing to the family and day care as a positive and beneficial experience for children.

Her ability to make these arguments was rooted in widespread changes in thinking about mothers' employment and about day care that were expressed by the "indignant mothers' marches" of the postwar period, as well as by the women who sought private day nursery care for their children. The protesting mothers who voiced a sense of entitlement to good day care in this period marked the most significant departure from Progressive-era understandings of day care. Their arguments that day care was a need of normal families and should become a permanent part of the public school system, available to all working mothers, suggest a vision radically different from that of the women who intially founded Philadelphia's day nurseries.

Needless to say, this new vision was not realized in the 1950s—nor has it been realized in the 1990s. Although the mothers' protests had won an important victory in keeping most of the public day care centers open, they had done so without voicing many women's positive feelings about wage work and day care. Organized day care continued to serve only a tiny fraction of the children needing care in Philadelphia and was often still associated with charity and dysfunctional families.[159] Anna Frigond's 1947 annual report reflected the discouragement of many day nursery workers during the postwar period. She asked her board members to picture a mother trying to raise a family in an overcrowded apartment.

> Imagine her feelings of worry and frustration because her husband's income does not provide for all the important needs of the children. Try as she will, she cannot find a solution to these real problems. . . . She thinks, "Am I really an adequate parent? Do I even want to try to do my best when I am so handicapped? And how dare I even feel this way when my children need me so much?"

Having painted this picture, Frigond explained that as a day nursery director (a "substitute mother," as she called herself), she shared many of the frustrations and doubts of this hard-pressed mother.

> One of the bitterest things about all this is that our culture pays such lip-service to mothers, and the importance of their role. . . . What we want is true recognition of the importance of mothers and substitute mothers; we want understanding and confidence and financial backing.[160]

But despite a lack of recognition and funding, day care's transition from charity to legitimate need was well underway by the time Frigond addressed her board with this eloquent speech. As mothers increasingly took up paid work in the 1960s and 1970s, they would rely on many of the arguments voiced by women in the postwar period to explain their need for, and right to, day care. No longer exclusively the domain of the poverty-stricken single mother, day care had become something of which it was possible to speak positively, something that women could claim a right to and fight for. This itself was perhaps the most significant change of these years—a change that lay the groundwork for more changes and struggles to come.

Conclusion

In 1960, four hundred people gathered in Washington for a national conference on day care—the first such gathering ever to be held in peacetime. The conference, which was organized by the Children's Bureau and the Women's Bureau at the urging of a new group, the National Committee for the Day Care of Children, sought to communicate to the public "what a tremendous force for national well-being a full program of day-care services for children could be."[1] Speakers at the conference explained that the numbers of mothers working had doubled in the last decade and were expected to continue growing, and proclaimed that the public needed to stop stigmatizing working mothers; that working mothers could be better mothers than those who stayed home feeling frustrated by being "nothing more exciting than a housewife"; that day care advocates needed to stop apologizing for day care and instead start "selling" it to the public; and that funding for day care needed to be dramatically expanded.

Such arguments reflected the new understanding of day care that had emerged during the 1950s: an educational, beneficial experience for children of various social classes whose mothers and fathers both worked outside the home, and a public service for which the government might take responsibility. This new definition stood uneasily next to, and often clashed with, the older understanding of day care as a private charitable enterprise, offering custodial care under less-than-ideal circumstances for the children of poor families disrupted by a mother's need to go out to work.

Throughout the time period covered in this book, day care was transformed from a charity for desperately poor single mothers to a widespread need of many families, and a legitimate public responsibility. From its origins as an elite women's effort to bring neglected children off the streets, day care had become a way for ordinary families to get help raising their children. By 1960, working mothers were no longer objects of pity, but simply members of society whose needs had to be addressed. Day care was no longer just a gift bestowed on the poor by benevolent philanthropists, but a service that mothers and child welfare advocates insisted the government had an obligation to provide. Day care programs themselves were no longer seen as day-time orphanages, but as a type of school, providing enriching experiences that would nurture children's emotional and intellectual growth. Parents spoke of day care not as a last resort in times of crisis, but as a positive force in the lives of their children.

What had caused this transformation? Clearly, changes in patterns of women's wage work—shaped by the growing demand for women's labor in the service sector of the economy—had altered attitudes toward mothers' employment. The nation's responses to the depression, World War II, and the Cold War had gradually undermined the idea that a mother's job was only in the home. As women's paid work came to be seen as a way of serving the family, it no longer seemed to pose the same threat to the social order that it had in the late nineteenth century. Day care could thus be defined as mothers had always seen it: as a way of helping women fulfill their maternal responsibilities, not as a way of avoiding them. The government's piecemeal efforts to provide day care—whether these efforts were intended to provide jobs during the depression or to help recruit women war workers during the 1940s—opened the door to defining day care as a public responsibility. At the same time, the idea that day care could be good for children gained strength, legitimizing day care by focusing on educating children rather than on liberating mothers. With the emergence of nursery schools in the 1920s, it became clear that the school was a much more palatable model for child care than the orphanage. From the 1930s through the 1950s, the idea that day care could be educational gained strength and served as a counterweight to fears that day care would encourage mothers to abandon their responsibility for their children. Nursery educators throughout this period, who saw day care as a way to benefit children, were much more effective advocates of day care than were day nursery leaders and social workers, who saw it as a means of enabling mothers to work for wages.

The maternalism that had motivated philanthropic women to establish day nurseries was not enough to bring day care into the mainstream. Although their concern with mothers and children had enabled day nursery founders to put day care on the public agenda and provide a vital service to many working mothers, the founders' narrow definition of how to value and support motherhood limited the scope of the day nurseries. Fears of freeing women from their family responsibilities thus prevented day nurseries from helping many women to fulfill the obligations of motherhood as they defined them. These fears prevented not only the philanthropic women who founded the nurseries, but also social workers, politicians, and child welfare advocates for decades afterward, from embracing day care as a way of meeting the needs of mothers and children. It was not until women's identities as workers gained public attention, and until day care could be seen as meeting children's needs, that it would begin to gain respectability.

Day care's new legitimacy was fragile in 1960, and older ideas about working mothers and day care continued to flourish. Participants at the 1960 day care conference knew that in trying to "sell" day care to the American public, they were fighting an uphill battle, for they had to contend with the mixed legacy of the seventy years of day care history explored in this book. This legacy included both the persistent conviction that day care is bad for children and the idea that educationally oriented care can be beneficial for children; that children always need their mothers and that children need to gain independence from their mothers; that mothers should devote themselves to caring for their children and that mothers should work to support their children. It included both the association of working mothers with poverty, family pathology, and welfare, and the idea that mothers of all class backgrounds had a right to work for personal satisfaction as well as to serve the family. It included the definition of day care as a private venture of female philanthropists, as a welfare measure of last resort for dysfunctional families, and as a universal entitlement similar to public education. This mixed legacy, along with new forces, has continued to shape understandings of day care since 1960, creating some of the day care dilemmas with which we struggle today.

Since 1960, day care has become an increasingly important social issue and an accepted part of everyday life. The forces that were starting to redefine day care in the post–World War II period—the acceptance of mothers' employment, growing interest in early childhood education, and a desire to reduce the welfare rolls—all developed more fully in the decades that followed, bringing day care more and more into the mainstream. But although day care has become increasingly accepted, it has not been embraced as social policy or given the resources it needs to fulfill its mission. The idea voiced by postwar protesters in Philadelphia—that day care should be provided to all working parents as a right of citizenship—has never been realized. Although it is now common for mothers across the socioeconomic spectrum of American society to work for wages and to have difficulty finding good care for their children, making day care a universally available public service is not even an issue on the public agenda.

The period since 1960 has seen changes that would seem to demand the expansion of day care. A mother's job is increasingly outside the home as well as in it, and more children are cared for in formal day care settings than ever before. The employment of married women with children under six jumped from less than 12% in 1950 to more than 30% in 1970; by the late 1980s it was about 56% (figures for mothers with school-age children are all higher).[2] This growth in mothers' employment has coincided with a decline in the number of children who are cared for by relatives. From 1965 to 1985, the percentage of children of working mothers receiving care in day care centers, preschools, and family day care settings rose dramatically, while the percentage receiving care from relatives dropped.[3] The growth of mothers' employment and of day care have been supported by the demand of second-wave feminists that women not be forced to choose between motherhood and other meaningful work. For instance, the National Organization for Women's 1966 statement of purpose called for equitable sharing of housework and child care, and its 1968 Bill of Rights called for the establishment of child care facilities on the same basis as parks, libraries, and public schools. Radical feminist groups also called for full-time childcare to be provided for all children in the public schools, as a recognition that the whole society should bear responsibility for child-rearing in order to empower and liberate women. Feminists have pushed for the establishment of child care centers while also encouraging women to expand their lives beyond the daily demands of motherhood.[4]

Coinciding with this redefinition of a mothers' job was renewed attention to early childhood education. Head Start, one of the most popular government programs of the 1960s, generated positive feelings about day care's potential to improve children's lives. Created in 1965 as part of the War on Poverty, the program's goal was not to liberate mothers, but to provide compensatory education to break the cycle of poverty for poor children. Its goals combined those of the charitable day nursery with those of the nursery school. Convinced that inadequate parenting was at the heart of poverty, supporters of the program argued that poor children needed early education in order to start school with the same skills their middle-class peers learned at home. In its emphasis on lifting children out of poverty by exposing them to a different environment, Head Start planners shared much with day nursery leaders who hoped to raise the household standards of whole families by influencing the children who attended the nurseries. Head Start planners, like day nursery leaders, felt that poor mothers were unable to meet their children's needs, and both placed a great deal of stress on parent education. When a member of Head Start's original planning committee expressed the hope that parents "will be motivated to modify appropriately the home environment," he echoed day nursery workers' attempts to reshape the housekeeping and child-rearing practices of day nursery mothers.[5] Of course, Head Start differed significantly from the early day nurseries, for it was not a charitable enterprise, but a government program born in response to mass grassroots pressure for social change. Parents and community leaders fought for Head Start programs and had a voice in governing them; some parents worked in the same programs that their children attended. Head Start also differed from the day nurseries in that its main focus was on improving the future prospects of poor children through education: like the nursery schools it was focused on children's development and was endorsed by child development experts, psychologists, and academics concerned with education. It was clearly intended to benefit children, not to meet parents' needs for day care.

The Head Start program has had its problems. Political pressures on program advocates to show that early intervention could raise poor children's IQs and make them more "teachable" when they entered the public schools led to a strong emphasis on learning preacademic skills, such as reciting the alphabet or recognizing colors.[6] While middle-class preschools held on to the nursery school idea of providing children with varied experiences that would encourage their intellectual curiosity, children in Head Start spent "half or full days in a relentless round of identifying shapes, matching colors, repeating the alphabet, and counting to ten." Activities such as dramatic play, block building, painting, and water play, seen by teachers at private preschools as the foundation of children's learning, were treated by many Head Start teachers as special rewards for good behavior, not as learning experiences in themselves.[7] Like the government nursery schools of the 1930s, Head Start's twin goals of educating children and providing employment for the poor have created lasting tension; since providing college educations for Head Start staff proved to be too expensive, Head Start staff today have less training and fewer academic credentials that the staff of centers serving middle-class children.[8] Nevertheless, Head Start's success in improving the lives of disadvantaged children through preschool education has been widely accepted, and the program has gained popularity with politicians and policymakers across the ideological spectrum. From a broader perspective, Head Start's popularity helped legitimate the idea of educationally oriented day care for all children. At a time when interest in children's cognitive development was increasing and experts were stressing the plasticity of intelligence and the vital importance of early experiences, Head Start's appeal led many people to wonder whether middle-class children might also benefit from early childhood education.[9] This new interest in the intellectual stimulation that quality preschool programs could provide for children of all classes was another potential source of support for expanding day care.

Trends in women's employment, feminism, and a new understanding of children's needs have all encouraged the expansion of day care and promoted the idea that day care is a universal social need. But rather than adopting universal child care on the grounds of women's right to work, or of children's needs for preschool education, policymakers since 1960 have linked day care to efforts to reduce the welfare rolls.[10] Day care has thus been embraced as social policy, but only for mothers receiving public assistance. As maternalism has faded and mothers' wage work has become more widespread, support for welfare programs based on keeping mothers at home with their children has disappeared. Instead, politicians and policymakers have insisted that poor mothers should be required to support their children.

The idea of compelling poor mothers to work is hardly new: indeed, it has been an important force behind the support for day care since the nineteenth century. But it took on special force in the 1960s and early 1970s as politicians in Washington sought to get mothers off welfare. In 1961, President John Kennedy persuaded Congress to pass a bill funding day care centers for mothers receiving benefits from the Aid to Families with Dependent Children program (AFDC). According to historian Mary Frances Berry, Kennedy "emphasized that day care would not be provided for anyone else for any reason."[11] Similarly, amendments to the Social Security Act passed in 1967 required able-bodied AFDC recipients to accept employment or job training, and authorized an increase in federal grants for day care. The framers of this legislation stated, "It is expected that the individuals participating in the program . . . will acquire a sense of dignity, self-worth, and confidence which will flow from being recognized as a wage-earning member of society."[12]

Tension between justifying day care for welfare mothers, on the one hand, and embracing it as social policy for everyone, on the other, became particularly acute in 1971, as Congress debated the Child Development Act. This legislation, which initially had broad bipartisan support, would have provided major federal funding for day care and established standards ensuring high-quality care; most important, it clearly stated that its goal was to lay the groundwork for universally available child care services. While proponents of the bill were interested in making public day care available to everyone, President Nixon initially supported it primarily because he saw day care as a tool for getting welfare mothers to work.[13] When it became clear that his larger welfare reform measure was unlikely to pass, however, he decided he had little use for a large-scale day care program and vetoed the bill. In a speech tailored to curry favor with right wing of his party, Nixon explained that supporting day care would weaken the family; he objected to committing "the vast moral authority of the National Government to the side of communal approaches to child rearing over against the family-centered approach."[14] But while many conservatives protested the idea of providing day care for everyone, they did not object to providing day care centers for welfare mothers. For instance, James Kilpatrick wrote that the legislation was a "nightmare proposition" that "grew out of Mr. Nixon's modest little dream of day-care centers where welfare mothers could dump their children while they went to work." Historian Robert Bremner comments on the difference in this debate between funding day care for welfare mothers and for everyone:

> Legislators and voters in the late 1960s and 1970s took it for granted that welfare mothers should be encouraged, sometimes very strongly, to go to work. Home-making and child rearing were indulgences for them, wage-earning a way of acquiring a sense of "dignity, self-worth, and confidence." Non-poor women, on the other hand, were expected by op-

> ponents of child-care legislation to be fully occupied in what Nixon called the "family-centered approach to child-rearing."

Indeed, in Senate debates on the child development bill, Senator Carl Curtis of Nebraska wanted to remind "those women who feel they are being 'wasted' by raising their children," that "the hand that rocks the cradle rules the world."[15]

In more recent debates about welfare reform, such an appeal to full-time mothering has become less popular, and it is assumed that nonpoor mothers must also work and use day care for their children. Indeed, the idea of compelling welfare mothers to work has gained popularity partly because many voters feel that staying home with their children has become a luxury they themselves cannot afford. Some employed mothers resent having their taxes go to support other women in full-time mothering. For instance, a reader of *Mothering*, a magazine that promotes natural childbirth, breastfeeding, and commitment to family, recently wrote a letter to the editor objecting to a letter from another mother who had written about going on welfare so she could stay home with her baby and breastfeed. "Why should I be subsidizing a mother nursing her child while I am *working* full-time and nursing? . . . Does [the other mother] realize that she would be living off my tax sacrifices for my own children? How does she expect me to support her in a lifestyle I myself cannot afford?"[16] As Linda Gordon has noted, the growing legitimacy of day care has undermined the ideological justification for AFDC, increasing hostility toward the recipients of the program.[17] Recent welfare reform legislation, intended to put welfare mothers to work, will create a much greater demand for day care services. But funding for day care that such a strategy requires is not adequate to meet the need, and it will be difficult for poor mothers to insist on high-quality care for their children.

While publicly supported day care has been restricted to mothers receiving welfare, most families have been left to find their own private solutions, which have public as well as private costs. Although motherhood has been redefined to include wage work, the lack of practical support for wage-earning motherhood has left many women shouldering the "double burden" that maternalist reformers of the 1910s warned against. Whatever their child care arrangements, employed mothers today continue to struggle with the combination of breadwinning and the work of nurturing children. Many fear that their deviation from the ideal of full-time motherhood makes them into "bad mothers." Failure to redefine fatherhood at the same time as motherhood has brought mothers of young children into the paid work force without altering the gendered division of labor within many American families.[18]

In the absence of universal public day care, day care programs have continued to be stratified by class. Sociologist Julia Wrigley observes that middle-class children above toddler age tend to be cared for in preschools with trained teachers and developmental goals, while low-income children are more commonly cared for by untrained providers in their homes. Both children and caregivers in day care programs are segregated by class and race to a degree that would be unacceptable in the public schools, where there is at least a general commitment to providing the same kind of education to all children. Writer Valerie Polakow reports that at one for-profit day care center she visited, the poorer children attending the day care carried signs on their backs to distinguish them from other children who attended the same center's "nursery school." And ethnographer Sally Lubeck found significant differences in resources, training, and philosophy between a preschool serving white middle-class children and a Head Start center serving low-income African-American children in the same community.[19] While poorer children are clustered in day care centers, affluent parents often solve their day care dilemmas by hiring immigrant women to act as "nannies" in their own homes. These parents thus remove themselves from the population of people who might need publicly funded day care for their children. The public outcry over Attorney-General nominee Zoe Baird's failure to pay taxes for the immigrant woman she hired to care for her children suggests the depth of class divisions between mothers who can afford different types of child care arrangements; these divisions make a united demand for universal public child care difficult to conceive.[20]

Perhaps the most damaging result of our failure to support day care is that many children spend their days in poor-quality care. A recent major study of day care centers concluded that although high-quality day care has a positive impact on all children's development, language ability, self-esteem, and ability to have warm and open relationships with others, most day care centers do not provide the level of care that can produce these results. Rather, most centers in the United States do not even "meet children's needs for health, safety, warm relationships, and learning"; 86% of the centers surveyed were classified as providing poor to mediocre care, and almost half of the infants and toddlers were receiving care rated as less than minimal quality.[21] Family day care homes, which are typically less regulated than centers, are even more uneven in quality. Several studies have concluded that since parents are unable to distinguish good from mediocre or poor care—or are unable to demand higher quality care—market forces alone will not produce good day care for children.[22] Day care workers are notoriously underpaid, especially given their level of education. Yet most parents cannot afford the full cost of the high-quality care that their children need.

Over the past hundred years, day care has become increasingly legitimate, and today it is recognized as a widespread social need. But support for day care lags far behind. We can continue to piece together individual solutions, and some of us will be more fortunate in doing so than others. But in order to "win permanent day care for our children," as one Philadelphia mother proposed in 1945, we must make a case for transforming day care once again: it must gain recognition, not just as a universal need of normal families, but as a public responsibility that reflects our society's commitment to its children.

Appendix

Table 1: Marital Status of Day Nursery Applicants

	1900–1929					1930–1939			
	N. Centre	St.Nich.	First	Baldwin	Total	N. Centre	St.Nich.	Women U.	Total
Single Mothers	27 (51%)	42 (42%)	13 (76%)	170 (58%)	252 (54%)	8 (19%)	19 (61%)	27 (53%)	54 (43%)
widow	11 (21%)	16 (16%)	4 (17%)	32 (11%)	63 (13%)	2 (5%)	9 (30%)	6 (12%)	17 (14%)
man deserted	7 (13%)	12 (12%)	7 (30%)	68 (23%)	94 (20%)	2 (5%)	4 (13%)	8 (16%)	14 (11%)
separated/divorced	6 (11%)	5 (5%)	2 (8%)	64 (22%)	77 (16%)	4 (10%)	3 (10%)	6 (12%)	13 (10%)
never married	3 (6%)	9 (9%)	—	6 (2%)	18 (4%)	—	3 (10%)	7 (14%)	10 (8%)
man in military	—	—	—	—	—	—	—	—	—
Single Fathers	—	2 (2%)	1 (4%)	6 (2%)	9 (2%)	1 (1%)	2 (6%)	5 (10%)	7 (6%)
widower	—	1 (1%)	1 (4%)	3 (1%)	5 (1%)	1 (2%)	1 (3%)	1 (2%)	3 (2%)
woman deserted	—	1 (1%)	—	3 (1%)	4 (1%)	—	1 (3%)	4 (8%)	5 (4%)
Married	26 (49%)	55 (55%)	7 (30%	112 (38%)	200 (42%)	34 (80%)	10 (32%)	19 (37%)	63 (50%)

	1940–1945					1946–1952			
	N. Centre	St.Nich.	First	Wharton	Total	N. Centre	St.Nich.	Wharton	Total
Single Mothers	3 (12%)	4 (58%)	6 (50%)	98 (47%)	111 (44%)	4 (22%)	22 (39%)	55 (40%)	81 (38%)
widow	—	—	1 (8%)	8 (4%)	9 (4%)	—	2 (4%)	6 (4%)	8 (4%)
man deserted	2 (8%)	—	—	1 (1%)	3 (1%)	—	2 (4%)	3 (2%)	5 (2%)
separated/divorced	1 (4%)	2 (29%)	3 (25%)	44 (21%)	50 (20%)	4 (22%)	16 (28%)	40 (29%)	60 (28%)
never married	—	2 (29%)	—	18 (9%)	20 (8%)	—	2 (4%)	6 (4%)	8 (4%)
man in military	—	—	2 (17%)	26 (12%)	28 (11%)	—	4 (7%)	—	4 (2%)
Single Fathers	—	—	—	2 (1%)	2 (1%)	—	—	3 (2%)	3 (1%)
widower	—	—	—	1 (<1%)	1 (<1%)	—	—	1 (<1%)	1 (<1%)
woman deserted	—	—	—	1 (<1%)	1 (<1%)	—	—	2 (1%)	2 (<1%)
Married	23 (88%)	3 (43%)	6 (50%)	109 (52%)	141 (56%)	14 (78%)	31 (54%)	82 (58%)	126 (59%)

Table 2: Day Nursery Applicants' Reasons for Applying

	1900–1929							1930–1939			
	N.Centre	St. Nich.	First	Baldwin	Lincoln	Sunnysd.	Total	N.Centre	St.Nich.	Wom. U	Total
Single mother	27 (53%)	41 (82%)	16 (57%)	163 (55%)	19 (43%)	70 (79%)	336 (60%)	7 (16%)	18 (58%)	26 (50%)	51 (40%)
Insufficient income	4 (8%)	1 (2%)	2 (7%)	41 (14%)	8 (18%)	18 (20%)	74 (13%)	16 (36%)	7 (23%)	15 (29%)	38 (30%)
Both working	—	—	—	—	—	—	—	—	—	—	—
Educational value	—	—	—	—	—	—	—	12 (27%)	—	1 (2%)	13 (10%)
Illness/maternity	15 (30%)	6 (12%)	6 (21%)	44 (15%)	6 (14%)	—	77 (14%)	4 (9%)	—	3 (6%)	7 (5%)
Unemployment	5 (10%)	—	—	20 (7%)	10 (23%)	—	35 (6%)	2 (5%)	4 (13%)	3 (6%)	9 (7%)
Needed in business	—	—	—	—	—	—	—	—	—	—	—
Debts/house	—	—	—	17 (6%)	—	—	—	—	—	—	—
Father in military	—	—	—	—	—	—	—	—	—	—	—
Other	—	2 (4%)	4 (14%)	9 (3%)	1 (2%)	1 (1%)	17 (3%)	3 (7%)	2 (6%)	4 (8%)	9 (7%)

	1940–1945					1946–1952			
	N. Centre	St. Nich.	First	Wharton	Total	N. Centre	St. Nich.	Wharton	Total
Single mother	3 (10%)	2 (25%)	4 (25%)	74 (32%)	83 (29%)	4 (22%)	49 (56%)	52 (37%)	105 (37%)
Insufficient income	5 (17%)	2 (25%)	1 (6%)	18 (8%)	26 (9%)	4 (22%)	20 (23%)	15 (11%)	39 (16%)
Both working	—	—	1 (6%)	78 (34%)	29 (27%)	—	5 (6%)	40 (28%)	45 (18%)
Educational value	12 (40%)	—	—	14 (6%)	26 (9%)	1 (5%)	—	27 (19%)	28 (12%)
Illness/maternity	3 (9%)	2 (25%)	3 (19%)	7 (3%)	15 (5%)	2 (11%)	1 (1%)	9 (6%)	12 (5%)
Unemployment	1 (3%)	—	—	—	1 (<1%)	—	2 (2%)	3 (2%)	5 (2%)
Needed in business	4 (13%)	—	—	1 (<1%)	5 (2%)	8 (44%)	1 (1%)	1 (1%)	10 (4%)
Debts/house	—	—	—	3 (1%)	3 (1%)	—	1 (1%)	9 (6%)	10 (4%)
Father in military	2 (7%)	—	6 (40%)	34 (15%)	42 (15%)	—	6 (7%)	1 (1%)	7 (3%)
Other	—	2 (25%)	1 (6%)	3 (1%)	6 (2%)	—	2 (2%)	3 (2%)	5 (2%)

Table 3: Day Nursery Applicants—Mothers' Employment

	1900–1929				
	N. Centre	St.Nich.	First	Baldwin	Total
Domestic/custodial	3 (8%)	60 (71%)	3 (25%)	13 (6%)	72 (22%)
Unskilled labor	—	—	—	—	—
Factory	27 (67%)	9 (11%)	7 (58%)	170 (76%)	213 (59%)
Defense work	—	—	—	—	—
Misc. skilled labor	—	—	—	—	—
Peddling	5 (13%)	—	—	—	5 (1%)
Family business	—	—	—	—	—
Sales/clerical	4 (10%)	1 (1%)	—	11 (5%)	16 (4%)
Professional	1 (1%)	—	—	—	1 (<1%)
Other	5 (13%)	14 (17%)	2 (16%)	27 (12%)	48 (13%)

	1930–1939			
	N. Centre	St.Nich.	Women U.	Total
Domestic/custodial	1 (4%)	26 (93%)	69 (80%)	96 (69%)
Unskilled labor	—	—	—	—
Factory	9 (36%)	1 (4%)	5 (6%)	15 (11%)
Defense work	—	—	—	—
Misc. skilled labor	3 (12%)	—	—	3 (2%)
Peddling	2 (8%)	—	—	2 (1%)
Family business	3 (12%)	—	—	3 (2%)
Sales/clerical	6 (24%)	—	3 (4%)	9 (6%)
Professional	1 (4%)	—	1 (1%)	2 (1%)
Other	—	1 (4%)	8 (9%)	9 (6%)

	1940–1945		
	N. Centre	Wharton	Total
Domestic/custodial	—	52 (30%)	52 (28%)
Unskilled labor	—	2 (1%)	2 (1%)
Factory	3 (18%)	50 (29%)	53 (28%)
Defense work	1 (6%)	33 (19%)	34 (18%)
Misc. skilled labor	—	—	—
Peddling	—	—	—
Family business	4 (24%)	3 (2%)	7 (4%)
Sales/clerical	6 (36%)	7 (4%)	13 (7%)
Professional	2 (12%)	5 (3%)	7 (4%)
Other	—	19 (11%)	19 (10%)

	1946–1952			
	N. Centre	St.Nich.	Wharton	Total
Domestic/custodial	—	7 (22%)	38 (30%)	45 (26%)
Unskilled labor	—	—	—	—
Factory	3 (19%)	5 (16%)	42 (34%)	50 (29%)
Defense work	—	—	—	—
Misc. skilled labor	1 (6%)	1 (3%)	—	2 (1%)
Peddling	—	—	—	—
Family business	8 (50%)	1 (3%)	4 (3%)	13 (8%)
Sales/clerical	4 (25%)	7 (22%)	14 (11%)	25 (14%)
Professional	—	3 (9%)	14 (11%)	17 (10%)
Other	—	8 (25%)	11 (9%)	19 (11%)

Table 4: Day Nursery Applicants—Fathers' Employment

	1900–1929				1930–1939			
	N. Centre	St.Nich.	Baldwin	Total	N. Centre	St.Nich.	Women U.	Total
Domestic/custodial	—	1 (1%)	—	1 (<1%)	1 (3%)	3 (30%)	4 (9%)	8 (9%)
Unskilled labor	4 (10%)	48 (64%)	34 (17%)	86 (27%)	1 (3%)	4 (40%)	24 (55%)	29 (32%)
Factory	14 (35%)	8 (10%)	44 (22%)	66 (21%)	2 (5%)	—	3 (7%)	5 (5%)
Defense work	—	—	—	—	—	—	—	—
Misc. skilled labor	12 (30%)	7 (9%)	73 (37%)	92 (29%)	14 (39%)	1 (10%)	5 (11%)	20 (22%)
Peddling	5 (13%)	1 (1%)	—	6 (2%)	6 (17%)	1 (10%)	—	7 (8%)
Family business	—	—	—	—	5 (14%)	—	2 (4%)	7 (8%)
Sales/clerical	4 (10%)	—	22 (11%)	26 (8%)	4 (11%)	—	1 (1%)	5 (5%)
Professional	3 (5%)	1 (1%)	—	4 (1%)	3 (8%)	—	1 (1%)	4 (4%)
Other	4 (10%)	10 (13%)	24 (12%)	38 (12%)	—	1 (10%)	4 (9%)	5 (5%)

	1940–1945			1946–1952			
	N. Centre	Wharton	Total	N. Centre	St.Nich.	Wharton	Total
Domestic/custodial	—	4 (4%)	4 (3%)	—	—	1 (1%)	1 (1%)
Unskilled labor	1 (4%)	18 (17%)	19 (14%)	1 (7%)	5 (38%)	18 (22%)	24 (22%)
Factory	4 (17%)	23 (21%)	27 (20%)	2 (14%)	2 (15%)	23 (28%)	27 (25%)
Defense work	2 (9%)	44 (40%)	46 (34%)	—	—	9 (11%)	9 (8%)
Misc. skilled labor	—	—	—	—	—	4 (5%)	4 (4%)
Peddling	—	—	—	—	—	—	—
Family business	8 (30%)	5 (5%)	13 (10%)	7 (50%)	1 (8%)	11 (13%)	19 (17%)
Sales/clerical	7 (26%)	—	7 (5%)	1 (7%)	2 (15%)	4 (5%)	7 (6%)
Professional	2 (9%)	9 (8%)	11 (8%)	2 (14%)	1 (8%)	6 (7%)	9 (8%)
Other	2 (9%)	6 (6%)	8 (6)	1 (7%)	3 (15%)	7 (8%)	11 (10%)

Notes

Figures for Baldwin, Neighborhood Centre, St. Nicholas, Wharton, and Women's Union Day Nurseries come from my analysis of case records from these nurseries; figures for First Day Nursery come from my analysis of the visitors' reports, and figures for Lincoln and Sunnyside come from those nurseries' annual reports (Lincoln 1916 and Sunnyside 1920). All the tables reflect the statements made about marital status, reasons for needing day care, and employment at the time the application was made.

In Table 1, "woman deserted""refers to women who left their husbands and children, while "separated/divorced" includes women who left their husbands, but took their children with them. There were very few official divorces in these records.

In Table 2, "insufficient income" includes married women whose husbands' wages were insufficient for the family's needs, women living with their husbands but not receiving any support, and women temporarily separated from their husbands or considering leaving their husbands because of lack of support. "Illness/maternity" includes physical or mental illness of father or mother, as well as childbirth; "debts/house" refers to women who went to work in order to pay off debts or save money for a house; and "other" includes fathers in prison and single fathers.

In Tables 3 and 4, "misc. skilled labor""is used for nonfactory work (paperhanger, tailor, carpenter) and for drivers. "Unskilled labor""includes porters and stevedores as well as laborers. "Other""includes people working in restaurants, laundries, and in unspecified government work.

Archival Sources

Archives of the Archdiocese of Philadelphia

Catholic Charities Yearbook
Catholic Register
Official Catholic Directory of the Philadelphia Archdiocese

Archives of the School District of Philadelphia

Annual Reports of the Board of Education
Handbook, School District of Philadelphia
Journal of the Board of Education

City Archives of Philadelphia

Annual Mayor's Addresses and Reports of Departments
Journal of the City Council

Daughters of Charity Archives, Northeastern Province (Albany, NY)

Cathedral Day Nursery

Historical Society of Pennsylvania, Philadelphia

Baldwin Day Nursery (Lighthouse collection)
Philadelphia Juvenile Court/Philadelphia Child Welfare Association
Society for Organizing Charity

Library of Congress, Washington, D.C.

Papers of Mary Church Terrell
Armstrong Association (Urban League collection)

National Archives, Washington, D.C.

Children's Bureau
Office of Community War Services
Office of Education
Women's Bureau
Works Projects Administration

Pennsylvania State Archives, Harrisburg

Mothers' Pension Accounts, 1913–14

Philadelphia Jewish Archives Center

Bureau for Jewish Children
Juvenile Aid Society
Neighborhood Centre
Northern Hebrew Day Nursery
Orphans' Guardians Society
Strawberry Mansion Day Nursery
United Hebrew Charities

Rockefeller Archives, Tarrytown, New York

Laura Spelman Rockefeller Memorial

Templeana Collection, Temple University Library, Philadelphia

Temple University College of Education

Urban Archives, Temple University Library, Philadelphia

Annual Report collection
Council of Social Agencies, Children's Department reports
First Family Day Care Association
  First Day Nursery
  Happy Day Nursery
  Sunnyside Day Nursery
House of Industry
Jane D. Kent Day Nursery
Newsphotograph collection
Philadelphia Association of Day Nurseries
Philadelphia Bulletin clipping file
St. Nicholas Day Nursery
  Women's Union Day Nursery case records
  National Federation of Day Nurseries newsletter *Day Nursery Bulletin*
  State Department of Welfare newsletter *Child Care Chat*
University House/Dixon House

Notes

Introduction

1. "Judge Threw Out Advice on Custody," *Detroit Free Press*, July 29, 1994, p. 1A.

2. "A Michigan Judge's Ruling Punishes Single Mothers," *Ms. Magazine*, November/December 1994, p. 93.

3. "Who Should Raise Maranda?" *People Weekly*, August 22, 1994, p. 72.

4. "Taking Jennifer Ireland's Daughter," *New York Times* editorial, August 1, 1994, p. A14.

5. "Day Care May Be Key Element in Custody Fight," *Detroit Free Press*, July 8, 1994, p. 1A.

6. "Done In By Day Care," *New York Times*, July 30, 1994, p. A19.

7. "Custody Case 'Couldn't Happen Here,'" Madison (Wisconsin) *Capital Times*, July 28, 1994.

8. Henry Reske, "Who's Minding Maranda?" *American Bar Association Journal* 82 (August 1996), p. 21.

9. "The Maranda Decision," *Washington Post*, July 30, 1994, p. D1.

10. A study released by the Families and Work Institute in New York in 1994 concluded that care by relatives was often inferior to that offered by licensed day care providers. See "Done In By Day Care," *New York Times*, July 30, 1994, p. A19, and "A Judge Who Disrespects Day Care," *Los Angeles Times*, August 8, 1994, p. B6.

11. Stephanie Cranfill to editor, *Detroit Free Press*, July 14, 1994, p. 14A; "Court Puts Custody Battle on Right Track," *Detroit Free Press*, November 11, 1995, p. 10A.

12. "Subject to Debate," *The Nation*, March 27, 1995, p. 408.

13. "Who Should Raise Maranda?" *People Weekly*, August 22, 1994, p. 72.

14. For instance, see "The Day Care Dilemma," part of a special report on child development, *Time*, February 3, 1997, pp. 58–59.

15. On new definitions of motherhood in the early nineteenth century, see Nancy Schrom Dye and Daniel Blake Smith, "Mother Love and Infant Death, 1750–1920," *Journal of American History* 73 (1986), pp. 329–353; Sylvia Hoffert, *Private Matters: American Attitudes Toward Childbearing and Infant Nurture in the Urban North, 1800–1860* (Urbana: University of Illinois Press, 1989); and Mary Ryan, *Cradle of the Middle Class: The Family in Oneida County, New York, 1790–1865* (Cambridge: Cambridge University Press, 1981). On antebellum working-class women, see Christine Stansell, *City of Women: Sex and Class in New York, 1780–1860* (Urbana: University of Illinois Press, 1987); on slave women, Deborah Gray White, *Ar'n't I a Woman? Female Slaves in the Plantation South* (New York: W. W. Norton, 1985), chapter 3.

16. Works that use day care history as a background to policy discussions include Margaret Steinfels, *Who's Minding the Children? The History and Politics of Day Care in America* (New York: Simon & Schuster, 1973), pp. 11-27; Sheila Rothman, "Other People's Children: The Day Care Experience in

America," *Public Interest* 30 (Winter 1973), pp. 11–27; Virginia Kerr, "One Step Forward—Two Steps Back: Child Care's Long American History," in *Child Care—Who Cares? Foreign and Domestic Infant and Early Child Development Policies*, ed. Pamela Roby (New York: Basic Books, 1973), p 157–171; Greta Fein and Alison Clarke-Stewart, *Day Care in Context* (New York: John Wiley & Sons, 1973). More recently, Emily Cahan, *Past Caring: A History of U.S. Preschool Care and Education for the Poor, 1920–1965* (National Center for Children in Poverty, Columbia University, 1989), and Mary Frances Berry, *The Politics of Parenthood: Child Care, Women's Rights, and the Myth of the Good Mother* (New York: Viking, 1993), have written more in-depth historical studies, also aimed at policymakers.

Historians writing about women's experiences during World War II have paid closer attention to day care, but only in a limited context. See Susan Hartmann, *The Home Front and Beyond: American Women in the 1940s*, (Boston: Twayne Publishers, 1982); Alice Kessler-Harris, *Out to Work: A History of Wage-Earning Women in the United States* (New York: Oxford University Press, 1982); and Karen Anderson, *Wartime Women: Sex Roles, Family Relations, and the Status of Women During World War II* (Westport, Connecticut: Greenwood Press, 1981). Amy Kesselman's recent book, *Fleeting Opportunities: Women Shipyard Workers in Portland and Vancouver During World War II and Reconversion* (Albany: State University of New York Press, 1990) offers the most in-depth account of day care. The best description of the legislative debates about day care policy during the war is still Howard Dratch, "The Politics of Child Care in the 1940s," *Science and Society* 38 (Summer 1974), pp. 167–204.

17. Anne Durst, "Day Nurseries and Wage-Earning Mothers in the United States, 1890–1930," (Ph.D. dissertation, University of Wisconsin-Madison, 1989); Barbara Beatty, *Preschool Education in America: The Culture of Young Children from the Colonial Era to the Present* (New Haven, Connecticut: Yale University Press, 1995); Sonya Michel, *Children's Interests/Mothers' Rights: A History of Child Care in the United States* (forthcoming from Yale University Press). See also Michel, "The Limits of Maternalism: Policies Toward American Wage-Earning Mothers During the Progressive Era," in *Mothers of a New World: Maternalist Politics and the Origins of Welfare States*, ed. Seth Koven and Sonya Michel (New York: Routledge, 1993); and "American Women and the Discourse of the Democratic Family in World War II," in *Behind the Lines: Gender and the Two World Wars*, ed. Margaret Higonnet et al. (New Haven, Connecticut: Yale University Press, 1987), pp 154-167.

Historical sociologists have also paid attention to day care history recently, advancing provocative arguments about the role of class and of changing conceptions of children's needs in shaping day care provision in different periods of U.S. history, and analyzing the political struggles over day care during and after World War II. See Julia Wrigley, "Different Care for Different Kids: Social Class and Child Care Policy," *Educational Policy* 3 (1989), pp. 421–439; Julia Wrigley, "Do Young Children Need Intellectual Stimulation? Experts' Advice to Parents, 1900–1985," *History of Education Quarterly* 29 (Spring 1989), pp. 41–75; Ellen Reese, "Maternalism and Political Mobilization: How California's Postwar Child Care Campaign Was Won," *Gender and Society* 10, no. 5 (October 1996), pp. 566–589; and Susan Prentice, "Militant Mothers in Domestic Times: Toronto's Postwar Childcare Struggle," (Ph.D. dissertation, York University, 1993).

Forthcoming works will join this book, and Susan Prentice's study of Toronto, in focusing on local experiences of day care. Kyle Ciani at Michigan State University is writing a dissertation about day care in Detroit and San Diego, and Natalie Fousekis at the University of North Carolina-Chapel Hill is at work on a dissertation about struggles over postwar day care in California.

18. The term *moral vernacular* comes from Michael Ignatieff, "Total Institutions and Working Classes: A Review Essay," *History Workshop* 15 (Spring 1983), pp. 167–173; Dana Barron, "'Illegitimately Pregnant': Unmarried Mothers and Poverty in Philadelphia, 1920–1960" (Ph.D. dissertation, University of Pennsylvania, 1995) focuses especially on the overlap between the moral codes of working-class families and those of maternity home staffers and social workers.

Linda Gordon, *Heroes of Their Own Lives: The Politics and History of Family Violence* (New York: Penguin Books, 1988) is most responsible for revising older notions of "social control"; see also Sherri Broder, "Politics of the Family: Political Culture, Moral Reform, and Family Relations in Gilded

Age Philadelphia" (Ph.D. dissertation, Brown University, 1988), and Stansell, *City of Women*, pp. 53–54. Other historians of social welfare focusing on the experience of clients include Beverly Stadum, *Poor Women and Their Families: Hard Working Charity Cases, 1900–1930* (Albany: State University of New York Press, 1992); Kathleen Jones, "'As the Twig Is Bent': American Psychiatry and the Troublesome Child, 1890–1940" (Ph.D. dissertation, Rutgers University, 1988); Anna Igra, "Other Men's Wives and Children: Anti-Desertion Reform in New York, 1900–1935," (Ph.D. dissertation, Rutgers University, 1996); Regina Kunzel, *Fallen Women, Problem Girls: Unmarried Mothers and the Professionalization of Social Work, 1890–1945* (New Haven, Connecticut: Yale University Press, 1993); and Kenneth Cmiel, *A Home of Another Kind: One Chicago Orphanage and the Tangle of Child Welfare* (Chicago: University of Chicago Press, 1995).

19. Kunzel, *Fallen Women, Problem Girls*, p. 7.

20. Robyn Muncy, *Creating a Female Dominion in American Reform, 1890–1935* (New York: Oxford University Press, 1991), Kriste Lindenmeyer, *"A Right to Childhood": The U.S. Children's Bureau and Child Welfare* (Urbana: University of Illinois Press, 1997).

21. For an overview of this literature, see Felicia Kornbluh, "Review Essay: The New Literature on Gender and the Welfare State: The U.S. Case," *Feminist Studies* 22, no. 1 (Spring 1996), pp. 171–197. The term *maternalism* was first coined in a 1990 article by Seth Koven and Sonya Michel, who used it broadly to refer to any ideology that "exalted women's capacity to mother and extended to society as a whole the values of care, nurturance, and morality." Koven and Michel, "Womanly Duties: Maternalist Politics and the Origins of Welfare States in France, Germany, Great Britain, and the United States," *American Historical Review* 95 (October 1990) pp 1076–1108. See also Koven and Michel's edited volume *Mothers of a New World: Maternalist Politics and the Origins of Welfare States* (New York: Routledge, 1993). A more specific definition that distinguishes between different types of maternalists is offered by Molly Ladd-Taylor, *Mother-Work: Women, Child Welfare, and the State, 1890–1930* (Urbana: University of Illinois Press, 1994), p. 3.

22. Scholars have differed in their assessment of maternalism's impact. For positive appraisals of the political efficacy of women's reform efforts, see Paula Baker, "The Domestication of Politics: Women and American Political Society, 1780–1920," *American Historical Review* 89 (June 1984), 620–647; Kathryn Kish Sklar, "The Historical Foundations of Women's Power in the Creation of the American Welfare State, 1830–1930," in Koven and Michel, *Mothers of a New World* pp 43–93; and Theda Skocpol, *Protecting Soldiers and Mothers: The Politics of Social Provision in the United States, 1870s to 1920s* (Cambridge: Harvard University Press, 1992), 43–93. Other historians have been critical of the limitations of maternalism. See Linda Gordon, *Pitied But Not Entitled: Single Mothers and the History of Welfare* (New York: Free Press, 1994); Eileen Boris, "What About the Working of the Working Mother?" *Journal of Women's History* 5, no. 2 (Fall 1993), pp. 104–107; Gwendolyn Mink, *The Wages of Motherhood: Inequality in the Welfare State, 1917–1942* (Ithaca, New York: Cornell University Press, 1995), and Ladd-Taylor, *Mother-Work*, p. 5.

Chapter 1

1. David Nasaw, *Children of the City At Work and At Play* (Garden City, New York: Anchor Press, 1985).

2. Christine Stansell, "Women, Children, and the Uses of the Streets: Class and Gender Conflict in New York City, 1850–1860," *Feminist Studies* 8 (Summer 1982), pp. 310–311.

3. Kathryn Kish Sklar, *Florence Kelley and the Nation's Work: The Rise of Women's Political Culture, 1830–1900* (New Haven, Connecticut: Yale University Press, 1995), p. 73.

4. Gwendolyn Hughes, *Mothers in Industry: Wage-Earning By Mothers in Philadelphia* (New York: New Republic, 1925), p. 9, 33.

5. Elizabeth Pleck, "A Mother's Wages: Income Earning Among Married Italian and Black Women, 1896–1911," in *A Heritage of Her Own: Toward a New Social History of American Women*, ed. Nancy Cott and Elizabeth Pleck (New York: Simon and Schuster, 1979), p. 372. These figures are from a government survey done in 1911.

6. Hughes, *Mothers in Industry*, pp. 46–62.

7. Barbara Klaczynska, "Why Women Work: A Comparison of Various Groups—Philadelphia, 1910–1930," *Labor History* 17 (Winter 1976), reprinted in *Ethnicity and Gender: The Immigrant Woman*, ed. George Pozzetta (New York: Garland Publishing, 1991), p. 142.

8. Forty-eight percent of the mostly Jewish immigrant women using the Neighborhood Centre nursery were in the garment industry, 19% were in other factories (garment, cigar, or paper boxes), while 13% peddled or operated a stand.

9. Introduction to Hughes, *Mothers in Industry*, p. xiii–xv.

10. Women's Industrial Conference, 1922, p. 5. *Records of the U.S. Women's Bureau, 1918–1965* [microfilm], ed. Judith Sealander (Fredrick, Maryland: University Publications of America, 1986), reel 1.

11. John Martin, "The Mother in Industry," *The Survey* 35 (March 18, 1916), p. 721.

12. Quoted in Nancy Cott, *The Grounding of Modern Feminism* (New Haven, Connecticut: Yale University Press, 1987), p. 138.

13. "The Conservation of the Home," *Outlook* 108 (1914), quoted in Mark Leff, "Consensus for Reform: The Mothers' Pension Movement in the Progressive Era," *Social Service Review* 47 (September 1973), p. 398.

14. Social worker Mary Richmond, quoted in Martha May, "'Home Life': Progressive Social Reformers' Prescriptions for Social Stability," (Ph.D. dissertation, SUNY-Binghamton, 1984), p. 149.

15. *Annual Report of the Franklin Day Nursery*, 1915.

16. *Annual Report of the Jane D. Kent Day Nursery*, 1886.

17. *Annual Report of the Baldwin Day Nursery*, 1917.

18. Helen Glenn Tyson, *The Day Nursery in Its Community Relations* (Philadelphia: 1919), pp. 25–28. Gwendolyn Hughes found similar concerns among the Philadelphia women she interviewed. Hughes, *Mothers in Industry*, p. 190.

19. Helen Glenn Tyson, *Day Nurseries In Pennsylvania: A Study Made for the Bureau of Children* (Harrisburg: Pennsylvania Department of Welfare Bulletin 17, 1925) pp. 9–10.

20. E. Digby Baltzell, *Philadelphia Gentlemen: The Making of a National Upper Class* (Glencoe, Illinois: Free Press, 1958), p. 252.

21. Sian Reynolds, "Who Wanted the Crèches? Working Mothers and the Birth-Rate in France, 1900–1950," *Continuity and Change* 5, no. 2 (1990), pp. 177–178; Sonya Michel, "The Limits of Maternalism: Policies Toward American Wage-Earning Mothers During the Progressive Era," in *Mothers of a New World: Maternalist Politics and the Origins of Welfare States*, ed. Seth Koven and Sonya Michel (New York: Routledge, 1993), p. 278.

22. By the time of the Civil War, the nursery at the House of Industry had faded from view; it would be revived in the 1890s. House of Industry/Philadelphia Society for the Employment and Instruction of the Poor, United Neighbors Association Papers, Urban Archives. Michel, "Limits of Maternalism," p. 281.

23. First Day Nursery report, April 11, 1902.

24. *Annual Report of The [First] Day Nursery*, 1902.

25. Philadelphia Association of Day Nurseries (PADN) minutes, March 18, 1898. Of seventy-six Philadelphia nurseries for which I have been able to locate founding dates, fifty-nine were founded before 1930: three were founded before 1880, nine in the 1880s, eight in the 1890s, thirteen in the 1900s, seventeen in the 1910s, twelve in the 1920s, three in the 1930s, four in the 1940s, and seven in the 1950s.

26. Anne Durst, "Day Nurseries and Wage-Earning Mothers in the United States, 1890–1930," (Ph.D. dissertation, University of Wisconsin, 1989), p. 134.

27. 1918 questionnaire, Neighborhood Centre folder 16. The Young Women's Union was renamed Neighborhood Centre in 1918; citations will refer to it by that name.

28. For First Day Nursery, see "Peggy Shippen's Diary," *Philadelphia Bulletin*, February 23, 1920; for Frankford Day Nursery, *Philadelphia Bulletin* April 2, 1964; St. Nicholas Day Nursery report, May 1950; January 22, 1957, description of history of nursery.

29. "Nursery Appeals for Aid," *Philadelphia Bulletin*, October 30, 1957; *Annual Report of Baldwin Day Nursery*, 1905. The Jane D. Kent Nursery was established by relatives as well as friends of Jane Kent, who worked "all her life among the children of her sister's and brothers' families." *Annual Report of the Jane D. Kent Day Nursery*, 1886.

30. PADN minutes, November 5, 1903.

31. PADN report read at New York conference of day nurseries, April 27, 1905.

32. The new nurseries included Sunnyside, St. Nicholas, San Cristoforo, and Southwark. PADN minutes, November 24, 1905, April 20, 1906, November 11, 1908, and April 21, 1910. At the April 21, 1910, meeting, "Mrs. Bradford moved that a vote of thanks be extended to the President, Mrs. W. W. Frazier, for her untiring labor in establishing new nurseries and the valuable work she had accomplished for DNs in general."

33. PADN minutes, November 17, 1910.

34. In the early twentieth century, Philadelphia produced more textiles than any other American city and was the world's largest textile center. Textiles continued to rank first among the city's enterprises both in amount of capital invested and in terms of number of establishments and employees. In 1904, 19% of the city's manufacturers were textile plants, and they employed 35% of the city's 229,000 workers. Nathaniel Burt and Wallace Davies, "The Iron Age, 1876–1905," in *Philadelphia: A 300-Year History*, ed. Russell Weigley (New York: W. W. Norton, 1982), p. 481.

35. Hughes, *Mothers In Industry*, p. 34. Since Hughes excluded African-American women from her study, however, this conclusion may be misleading; but certainly Kensington had the highest proportion of women employed in factories in the city.

36. Clara Beyer, *Children of Working Mothers in Philadelphia* (U.S. Children's Bureau, 1931), p. 30.

37. Pleck, "A Mother's Wages," p. 372; 57% of African-American mothers were employed, compared to 23% of white mothers. Beyer, *Children of Working Mothers in Philadelphia*, p. 6.

38. W. E. B. DuBois, *The Philadelphia Negro: A Social Study* (Publications of the University of Pennsylvania Series in Political Economy and Public Law; Philadelphia, 1899), p. 109. For occupations of women applying to St. Nicholas Day Nursery, see Table 3 in Appendix.

39. Klaczynska, "Why Women Work," pp. 146–147.

40. Roger Lane, *William Dorsey's Philadelphia and Ours: On the Past and Future of the Black City in America* (New York: Oxford University Press, 1991), p. 252, 294. The nursery is listed in the Civic Club's 1903 directory as having "A Board of Managers, under the auspices of the Woman's Union Missionary Society (colored)." *Directory of the Charitable, Social Improvement, Education and Religious Association and Churches of Philadelphia* (Philadelphia: Civic Club, 1903), p. 76. The nursery joined the PADN in 1899.

41. W. E. B. DuBois, *Efforts for Social Betterment Among Negro Americans* (Atlanta: Atlanta University Publications, No. 14, 1909).

42. Matches between the Women's Union Day Nursery Board in *Joint PADN Annual Report*, 1926, and Boyd's *Philadelphia City Directory, 1927*.

43. "Center Observes 50 Years of Devotion to Children," *Philadelphia Bulletin*, April 4, 1961.

44. A letter dated November 8, 1929, from the Bureau of Jewish Children to Dr. Ann Gibson about addressing a meeting of the Strawberry Mansion Day Nursery's mothers gave this description of the board members. On the neighborhood of Strawberry Mansion, see Robert Phillip Tabak, "The Transformation of Jewish Identity: The Philadelphia Experience, 1919–1945," (Ph.D. dissertation, Temple University, 1990). The names listed on the letterhead of the nursery suggest the East European background of its board members.

45. "Our History," reprinted in brochure celebrating dedication of a new building for the nursery, March 4, 1956.

46. The church was founded in 1851 as the first Italian Catholic church in the United States.

47. The only non-Protestant nursery that joined the PADN in its early years was a Jewish nursery, the Young Women's Union, which was founded and controlled by German Jews as part of an effort to acculturate the East European Jewish immigrants who were flocking to the city.

48. *Day Nursery Bulletin*, November 1927. Out of 328 Baldwin cases from the early 1920s that listed a parent's religion, 58% were Protestant, and 37% Catholic.

49. *Annual Report of the Baldwin Day Nursery*, 1901, 1903, and 1904.

50. John O'Grady also gives the impression that Catholic nurseries were largely inspired by fears of proselytizing Protestant nurseries; he describes a "typical" nursery in New York City that was established to counteract children's contact with Protestant nurseries. He also mentions that the Catholic Woman's League of Chicago was active in organizing day nurseries since "Protestant organizations were exceedingly active in the development of day nurseries." John O'Grady, *Catholic Charities in the United States: History and Problems* (Washington, D.C.: National Conference of Catholic Charities, 1931), pp. 312, 327.

51. Sister Frances Finley to Sister Vistation, n.d., p. 4. Cathedral Day Nursery collection, Archives of the Daughters of Charity of St. Vincent de Paul, Northeastern Province.

52. Author's correspondence with Sister Francis Marie, Franciscan Sisters Records Office, October 28, 1992. *Catholic Charities Yearbook*, p. 121.

53. *Catholic Charities Yearbook*, p. 117.

54. J. McCabe, *A History of Saint Monica's Parish, 1895–1969*, pp. 44–45, Archives of the Archdiocese of Philadelphia; *Catholic Charities Yearbook*, p. 119. St. Monica's is one of the few day nurseries founded during this period that is still in operation today. On St. Casimir's, see *Catholic Charities Yearbook*, p. 121.

55. *Catholic Charities Yearbook*, p. 111.

56. Sister Frances Finley to Sister Visitation, p. 8.

57. Sister Lizzie Patterson to Sister Carmelita, 1913, pp. 4, 6.

58. *Catholic Charities Yearbook*, p. 105. John O'Grady wrote of similar activities taken up by day nurseries in other cities as well. O'Grady, *Catholic Charities in the United States*, p. 311.

59. Sister Finley to Sister Visitation.

60. PADN minutes, April 20, 1900.

61. Child Federation, *A Study of the Day Nurseries of Philadelphia* (Philadelphia: Child Federation, 1916), p. 21; Tyson, *The Day Nursery in Its Community Relations*, p. 4. Both the Salvation Army and the Bedford Street nurseries eventually joined the PADN.

62. Child Federation, *A Study of the Day Nurseries of Philadelphia*, p. 106.

63. Tyson, *Day Nurseries in Pennsylvania*, p. 11.

64. "Commerce Chamber to Probe Day Nursery," *Philadelphia Bulletin*, February 21, 1916.

65. "Sunshine Nursery Subject of Probe," *Philadelphia Bulletin*, February 21, 1916.

66. Reporters found that the man listed as the president of the nursery had not had any contact with it for seven years, that owner Lillian Clark had raised six thousand dollars by selling a booklet in support of the nursery, but only spent six hundred on the nursery itself, and that she could not come up with names of any managers "who could be located and who did not repudiate her." "Sunshine Nursery President Considers His Office Good Joke," *Philadelphia Bulletin*, February 22, 1916; "Gorman to Close Sunshine Nursery," *Philadelphia Bulletin*, September 24, 1924.

67. In the two cases where men appear on the boards of day nurseries (at the Jane D. Kent and the Neighborhood Centre boards), they were in the role of advisory or finance committees, called on for advice in matters of money but not for regular meetings or questions of daily operation and nursery policy. At Neighborhood Centre, men formed a separate Finance Committee, while at the Jane D. Kent they were incorporated into the board but met as a separate Advisory Committee. In both cases they were dropped from the board when fund-raising was centralized in the Federation of Jewish Charities and the Welfare Federation, respectively.

68. Of Baltzell's list of "pre-Civil War First Family Founders," approximately one-third of the family names can be linked to day nursery board members. Baltzell, *Philadelphia Gentlemen*, pp. 71–77.

69. The names of board members of eighteen PADN-affiliated nurseries (taken from annual reports from 1883–1924) were matched with names in Boyd's *Philadelphia Blue Book, Elite Directory, Fash-*

ionable Private Address Directory, the Ladies' Visiting and Shopping Guide, and Philadelphia Club List (Philadelphia: C. E. Howe), for 1883–1903; and *Social Register, Philadelphia* (New York: Social Register Association), a much more exclusive listing, for 1892, 1896, 1901, 1904, 1905, 1909, 1913, 1919, and 1924.

70. Boyd's *Philadelphia City Directory*, 1913, 1927.

71. Edwin Wolf 2nd, "The German-Jewish Influence in Philadelphia's Jewish Charities," *Jewish Life in Philadelphia, 1830–1940*, ed. Murray Friedman (Philadelphia: ISHI Press, 1983), pp. 125–142.

72. *Annual Report of the Franklin Day Nursery*, 1917.

73. Wolf, "The German-Jewish Influence in Philadelphia's Jewish Charities," p. 127.

74. First Day Nursery (FDN) minutes, April 8, 1940.

75. "Model Charity's Golden Jubilee," *Philadelphia Record*, March 15, 1913.

76. On upper-class women and charity, see *Lady Boundtiful Revisited: Women, Philanthropy, and Power*, ed. Kathleen McCarthy (New Brunswick: Rutgers University Press, 1990); Lori Ginzburg, *Women and the Work of Benevolence: Morality, Politics, and Class in the 19th-Century United States* (New Haven, Connecticut: Yale University Press, 1990); and Kenneth Cmiel, *A Home of Another Kind: One Chicago Orphanage and the Tangle of Child Welfare* (Chicago: University of Chicago Press, 1995), p. 31.

77. *Day Nursery Bulletin*, December 1926.

78. Introduction to Ethel Beer, *The Day Nursery* (New York: E. P. Dutton, 1938).

79. Beer, *The Day Nursery*, p. 125.

80. *Philadelphia Bulletin*, December 2, 1960.

81. "Model Charity's Golden Jubilee," *Philadelphia Record*, March 15, 1913.

82. FDN minutes, June 5, 1916.

83. Ibid., March 4, 1918.

84. "Nursery Appeals for Aid," *Philadelphia Bulletin*, October 30, 1957.

85. *Annual Report of the Young Women's Union*, 1896.

86. BDN minutes, June 1915.

87. For instance, parents' fees made up 14% of the total receipts of the Jane D. Kent Nursery in 1886, and 7% of those at the Lincoln in 1915.

88. BDN minutes, June 12, 1922.

89. Sometimes donations were made as a memorial, drawing on the devotion of elite women to their female kin and friends; for instance, the baby room at the Baldwin Nursery "was furnished by Miss Elizabeth Pugh as a memorial to her friend Emma Jaynes Wrightman, who dearly loved little children." BDN minutes, February 1911. The entire Jane D. Kent Nursery, as we saw earlier, was founded as a memorial to Jane D. Kent "through the exertions and benevolence of" her relatives and friends. *Philadelphia Ledger*, December 3, 1883. Since the founders of the nursery raised enough money to buy a building, the nursery only had to pay interest on the mortgage. *Annual Report of the Jane D. Kent Day Nursery*, 1886.

90. BDN minutes, January 1911, January 1913, September 1915, and May 1917.

91. Typescript history of FDN, April 11, 1902.

92. "Model Charity's Golden Jubilee," *Philadelphia Record*, March 15, 1913.

93. *Annual Report of the Young Women's Union*, 1896.

94. BDN minutes, May 1921.

95. Ibid., October 1903.

96. Ibid., March 1909, March 1917.

97. *Annual Report of the Baldwin Day Nursery*, 1902.

98. Ibid., 1904.

99. BDN minutes of special meeting, December 10, 1906.

100. "Frankford Served 52 Years by Independent Day Nursery," *Philadelphia Bulletin*, April 2, 1964.

101. *Catholic Charities Yearbook*, p. 121.

102. Sister Frances Finley to Sister Visitation, pp. 4–10.

103. *Catholic Charities Yearbook*, p. 113.

104. Ibid., p. 121.

105. Sister Lizzie Patterson to Sister Carmelita, 1913, p. 7.

106. *Annual Report of the San Cristoforo Day Nursery*, 1907.

107. *Annual Report of the Franklin Day Nursery*, 1912.

108. *Catholic Charities Yearbook*, p. 121.

109. Tyson, *Day Nurseries in Pennsylvania*, p. 11.

110. PADN minutes, March 21, 1923.

111. *Annual Report of the Baldwin Day Nursery*, 1916.

112. "Our History," reprinted in brochure for dedication of new building, March 4, 1956, Strawberry Mansion Day Nursery.

113. *Catholic Charities Yearbook*, p. 101.

114. Neighborhood Centre, Annual Report of Day Nursery, 1913.

115. Ibid., 1914.

116. *Annual Report of the Baldwin Day Nursery*, 1900. Among the applicants to the nursery during the years for which we have case records (1922–25), 21% of women were working because their husbands earned insufficient wages or were unemployed, while only 2% of applications came from single fathers.

117. Tyson, *Day Nursery in Its Community Relations*, p. 26.

118. *Annual Report of the Baldwin Day Nursery*, 1914.

119. Neighborhood Center Day Nursery (NCDN), Annual Report of Nursery and Shelter, 1914, p. 3; this phrase is also found in a 1919 report on child care.

120. NCDN, Annual Report of Nursery and Shelter, 1915, p. 6.

121. *Annual Report of the Baldwin Day Nursery*, 1918, p. 5.

122. FDN visitor's report, February 23, 1917. Emphasis in original. This success story, however, was only temporary: when the visitor called next, she found Mr. Fowles drunk and not working, Mrs. Fowles supporting the whole family. He ended up in prison again, and things got better for the mother only when her children started to work.

123. Report of Franklin Day Nursery, *Joint Annual Report of PADN*, 1926, p. 19.

124. NCDN, Annual Report of Day Nursery, 1914.

125. Linda Gordon, "Putting Children First: Women, Maternalism, and Welfare in the Early Twentieth Century," in *U.S. History as Women's History: New Feminist Essays*, ed. Linda Kerber et al. (Chapel Hill: University of North Carolina Press, 1995), p. 76.

126. Eileen Boris makes this critique of maternalism in her contribution to the "Maternalism as Paradigm" roundtable, "What About the Working of the Working Mother," *Journal of Women's History* 5, no. 2 (Fall 1993), pp. 104–107.

127. *Annual Report of the Baldwin Day Nursery*, 1917.

128. Ibid., 1914.

129. Ibid., 1904.

130. Ibid., 1910.

131. *Annual Report of the Lincoln Day Nursery*, 1916.

132. *Annual Report of the First Day Nursery*, 1890.

133. NCDN, Annual Report of Nursery and Shelter, 1915, p 2.

134. *Annual Report of the Baldwin Day Nursery*, 1902.

135. On the different meanings of the threshold of the home in nineteenth-century British culture, see John Gillis, "The Ritualization of Family Life in Nineteenth Century Britain," *International Journal of Politics, Culture, and Society* 3 (Winter 1989), pp. 224–225.

136. *Annual Report of the Franklin Day Nursery*, 1917.

137. *Annual Report of the First Day Nursery*, 1888, p. 4.

138. Philadelphia Society for the Employment and Instruction of the Poor, *Annual Report of the House of Industry*, 1916.

139. Child Federation, *A Study of the Day Nurseries of Philadelphia*, pp. 18–19.

140. *Annual Report of the Franklin Day Nursery*, 1917.

141. *Catholic Charities Yearbook*, p. 109.

142. *Annual Report of the Baldwin Day Nursery*, 1913.

143. Gwendolyn Mink, "The Lady and the Tramp: Gender, Race, and the Origins of the American Welfare State," in *Women, the State, and Welfare*, ed. Linda Gordon (Madison: University of Wisconsin Press, 1990), pp. 103–105. Mink's argument is more fully developed in *The Wages of Motherhood: Inequality in the Welfare State, 1917–1942* (Ithaca, New York: Cornell University Press, 1995). For African-American women reformers, the term *uplift* carried a somewhat broader meaning, although it similarly included a desire to reshape motherhood and home life.

144. John Emlen, "The Movement for the Betterment of the Negro in Philadelphia," *Annals of the American Academy of Political and Social Science* 49 (1913), p. 85.

145. Tyson, *Day Nursery in its Community Relations*, p. 14. With its heritage of Quaker abolitionism and its substantial African-American middle class, Philadelphia probably provided more day nurseries for black children than most areas of the country. In 1930, sociologist Ira De Reid reported that in the entire country there were fewer than forty day nurseries for African-American children, while Ethel Beer reported that there were eight hundred nurseries in the country in 1931. Mary Frances Berry, *The Politics of Parenthood: Child Care, Women's Rights, and the Myth of the Good Mother* (New York: Viking, 1993), p. 105; Beer, *The Day Nursery*, p. 5.

146. *Philadelphia Bulletin*, October 18, 1928. On African-American migration to Philadelphia, see Sadie Mossell, "The Standard of Living Among One Hundred Negro Migrant Families in Philadelphia," *Annals of the American Academy of Political and Social Science* 98 (November 1921), pp. 173–222; Emlen, "The Movement for the Betterment of the Negro in Philadelphia"; and Fredric Miller, "The Black Migration to Philadelphia: A 1924 Profile," *Pennsylvania Magazine of History and Biography* 108 (July 1984), pp. 315–350. See also Lloyd Abernethy, "Progressivism, 1905–1919," in Weigley, *Philadelphia: A 300-Year History*, p. 531.

147. Eileen Boris, "The Power of Motherhood: Black and White Activist Women Redefine the 'Political,'" *Yale Journal of Law and Feminism* 2 (1989), p. 27.

148. Mink, *The Wages of Motherhood*, p. 120. The phrase "excluded from assimilation" is credited to Gunnar Myrdal.

149. Elisabeth Lasch-Quinn, *Black Neighbors: Race and the Limits of Reform in the American Settlement House Movement, 1890–1945*, (Chapel Hill: University of North Carolina Press, 1993), pp. 14–19.

150. Boris, "Power of Motherhood," p. 30.

151. Quoted in Boris, "Power of Motherhood," p. 36.

152. Mary Church Terrell, "The Duty of the National Association of Colored Women to the Race," address at Second Convention of the NACW, 1899. Mary Church Terrell Papers, Library of Congress.

153. Emily Cahan, *Past Caring: A History of U.S. Preschool Care and Education for the Poor, 1920–1965* (National Center for Children in Poverty, Columbia University, 1989), p. 18; Durst, "Day Nurseries and Wage-Earning Mothers," p. 159.

154. *Joint Annual Report of PADN*, 1926, p. 55.

155. PADN minutes, April 20, 1906. A similar statement was made about the Jenkintown Nursery, PADN minutes, April 17, 1903.

156. Ibid., April 28, 1902.

157. PADN minutes, November 20, 1903. Since no organizational records of the Women's Union Nursery have survived, it is impossible know for sure where control of this nursery rested. Given the description of the nursery in the 1903 Civic Club's guide as being "under the auspices of the Woman's Union Missionary Society (colored)," the description of the nursery's board as governed by African-Americans in the 1926 report, and the occupations of the board members found in the 1927 city directory, it seems fairly clear that the board itself was made up of African-American women.

158. *Annual Report of the Lincoln Day Nursery*, 1915 and 1916.

159. This event was so successful that a "Second Pickaninny Dance" was held the same year, and together these dances raised more money than any other source of income for the nursery. *Annual Report of the St. Nicholas Day Nursery*, 1915.

160. *Report of the Members of the PADN*, 1926, p. 26. These groups are not listed in any particular order.

161. St. Anthony's Day Nursery accepted "white children of any nationality," but since it was located in the middle of an Italian immigrant neighborhood, most of its children were Italians; the same was true at St. Mary Magdalen de Pazzi, which was the first church in the country "for the special and exclusive use of an Italian congregation." St. Casimir's Nursery, on the other hand, was founded specifically for Lithuanian children. *Catholic Charities Yearbook*, 1923, p. 117, 121; *Historical Sketches of the Catholic Churches and Institutions of Philadelphia* (Philadelphia: Daniel Mahony, 1895), p. 99.

162. *Catholic Charities Yearbook*, p. 107. Because the word *race* was commonly used to mean "nationality" or "ethnicity," it is impossible to know whether the Catholic nurseries also accepted African-American children. St. Anthony's Kindergarten and Day Nursery at the Church of Our Lady of Good Counsel, as well as St. Anthony's Day Nursery, specified "Only white children are received," but this may have been a general rule. Decades later, St. Simon's Church, dedicated to African-American Catholics, opened a day nursery.

163. Ibid., p. 115–123.

164. *Annual Report of the Franklin Day Nursery*, 1915.

165. Joy Day Nursery, *PADN Joint Annual Report*, 1929.

166. *Annual Report of the House of Industry*, 1917.

167. Ibid., 1916.

168. Ibid., 1917.

169. Quoted in Durst, "Day Nurseries and Wage-Earning Mothers," p. 147.

170. *Annual Report of the San Cristoforo Day Nursery*, 1913.

171. Mary Church Terrell, "The Duty of the National Association of Colored Women to the Race," address at Second Convention of the NACW, 1899.

172. *History of the Young Women's Union of Philadelphia, 1885–1910* (Philadelphia: Young Women's Union, 1910), p. 3.

173. Ibid., p. 15.

174. Elizabeth Rose, "From Sponge Cake to *Hamentashen*: Jewish Identity in a Jewish Settlement House, 1885–1952," *Journal of American Ethnic History* 13 (Spring 1994), pp. 3–23.

175. NCDN report, June 1912; NC case 114.

Chapter 2

1. Katharine Anthony, *Mothers Who Must Earn* (West Side Studies of the Russell Sage Foundation, New York: Survey Associates, 1914), p. 153.

2. *The Share of Wage-Earning Women in Family Support* (U.S. Women's Bureau Bulletin 30, 1923), p. 86. This study of Manchester, New Hampshire, was one of twenty-two such investigations conducted by the bureau from 1888 to 1923. See Nancy Cott, *The Grounding of Modern Feminism* (New Haven, Connecticut: Yale University Press, 1987), pp. 128–130.

3. Linda Gordon, *Pitied But Not Entitled: Single Mothers and the History of Welfare* (New York: Free Press, 1994), p. 32.

4. Gwendolyn Hughes, *Mothers In Industry: Wage-Earning By Mothers in Philadelphia* (New York: New Republic, 1925), p. 13.

5. Ibid., p. 101.

6. Caroline Manning, *The Immigrant Woman and Her Job* (U.S. Women's Bureau Bulletin 74, 1930), pp. 50–53, 57.

7. Clara Beyer, *Children of Working Mothers in Philadelphia* (U.S. Children's Bureau, 1931), p. 13.

8. Helen Glenn Tyson, *Day Nurseries In Pennsylvania: A Study Made for the Bureau of Children* (Harrisburg: Pennsylvania Department of Welfare Bulletin 17, 1925), p. 12.

9. Part of the reason for the discrepancy may be that Hughes excluded African-American women, as well as Italian and Jewish women, from her study. See Table 2 in Appendix.

10. Helen Glenn Tyson, *The Day Nursery in Its Community Relations: A Study of the Day Nurseries of Philadelphia* (Philadelphia: Philadelphia Association of Day Nurseries, 1919), pp. 17–19.

11. Quoted in Kenneth Cmiel, *A Home of Another Kind: One Chicago Orphanage and the Tangle of Child Welfare* (Chicago: University of Chicago Press, 1995), p. 18.

12. Neighborhood Centre (NC) case 857.

13. NC case 135.

14. First Day Nursery (FDN) Visitor's Report, September 1919.

15. NC case 20.

16. Ellen Ross, "Good and Bad Mothers: Lady Philanthropists and London Housewives Before the First World War," in *Lady Bountiful Revisited: Women, Philanthropy, and Power*, ed. Kathleen McCarthy (New Brunswick, New Jersey: Rutgers University Press, 1990), p. 180.

17. Hughes, *Mothers In Industry*, p. 177.

18. Tyson, *Day Nursery in Its Community Relations*, pp. 24–25.

19. NC case 920.

20. Sharon Harley, "When Your Work Is Not Who You Are: The Development of a Working-Class Consciousness Among Afro-American Women," in *Gender, Class, Race and Reform in the Progressive Era*, ed. Noralee Frankel and Nancy Dye (Lexington: University Press of Kentucky), p. 45.

21. Anne Durst, "Day Nurseries and Wage-Earning Mothers in the United States, 1890–1930," (Ph.D. dissertation, University of Wisconsin-Madison, 1989), p. 69.

22. Quoted in Gordon, *Pitied But Not Entitled*, p. 135.

23. W. E. B. DuBois, *The Philadelphia Negro: A Social Study* (Philadelphia: Publications of the University of Pennsylvania Series in Political Economy and Public Law, No. 14, 1899), p. 194.

24. Hughes, *Mothers in Industry*, p. 190.

25. NC case 253.

26. Manning, *Immigrant Woman and Her Job*, p. 52.

27. Report of the Committee on Day Nurseries of the Bureau for Jewish Children. Bureau for Jewish Children, Box 1, Folder 10, Series 5. Philadelphia Jewish Archives.

28. Manning, *Immigrant Woman and Her Job*, pp. 56–59.

29. Elizabeth Pleck, "A Mother's Wages: Income Earning Among Married Italian and Black Women, 1896–1911," in *A Heritage of Her Own: Toward a New Social History of American Women*, ed. Nancy Cott and Elizabeth Pleck (New York: Simon and Schuster, 1979), pp. 387–388.

30. Pleck, "A Mother's Wages," p. 372.

31. DuBois, *Philadelphia Negro*, p. 111.

32. Hughes, *Mothers In Industry*, p. 196.

33. "New Nursery Plan May Help 50,000," *Philadelphia Bulletin*, March 24, 1927.

34. Manning, *Immigrant Woman and Her Job*.

35. Durst, "Day Nurseries and Wage-Earning Mothers," p. 71; Barbara Klaczynska, "Why Women Work: A Comparison of Various Groups—Philadelphia, 1910–1930," *Labor History* 17 (Winter 1976), reprinted in *Ethnicity and Gender: The Immigrant Woman*, ed. George Pozzetta (New York: Garland Publishing, 1991), p. 144; Mary White Ovington, *Half a Man: The Status of the Negro in New York* (New York: Hill and Wang, 1911), p. 143.

36. Elizabeth Clark-Lewis, *Living In, Living Out: African-American Domestics in Washington, D.C. 1910–1940* (Washington, D.C.: Smithsonian Institution Press, 1994), pp. 79–80 and 64–65.

37. NC case 957.

38. NC case 756.

39. Of the forty-one siblings whose admission to the nursery was not requested, twenty were cared for by relatives; of the nineteen cases that described other child care arrangements, eight mentioned relatives. At Neighborhood Centre, fourteen out of twenty-eight cases that described other child care arrangements mentioned relatives.

40. NC case 1147.

41. Tyson, *Day Nursery in Its Community Relations*, pp. 25–28.

42. FDN Visitor's report, January 1919.

43. NC case 785.

44. NC case 872.

45. NC case 867.

46. Ardis Cameron, "Landscapes of Subterfuge: Working-Class Neighborhoods and Immigrant Women," in *Gender, Class, Race and Reform in the Progressive Era*, ed. Noralee Frankel and Nancy Dye (Lexington: University Press of Kentucky, 1991), p. 60.

47. Sherri Broder, "Child Care or Child Neglect? Baby Farming in Late-Nineteenth-Century Philadelphia," *Gender and Society* 2, no. 2 (June 1988), pp. 137–138.

48. Helen Russell Wright, *Children of Wage-Earning Mothers: A Study of a Selected Group in Chicago* (Children's Bureau publication no. 102, 1922), p. 22.

49. Manning, *Immigrant Woman and Her Job*, p. 42.

50. NC case 140.

51. Baldwin Day Nursery (BDN) case 192.

52. Child Federation, *A Study of the Day Nurseries of Philadelphia* (Philadelphia: Child Federation, 1916), pp. 109, 104.

53. Tyson, *Day Nurseries in Pennsylvania*, p. 6.

54. NC case 837.

55. Manning, *Immigrant Woman and Her Job*, p. 43.

56. Jacqueline Jones, *Labor of Love, Labor of Sorrow: Black Women, Work and the Family from Slavery to the Present* (New York: Vintage, 1985), p. 371 (footnote 28).

57. Pleck, "A Mother's Wages," pp. 386–387; Beard quoted in Durst, "Day Nurseries and Wage-Earning Mothers," p. 107.

58. Clark-Lewis, *Living In, Living Out*, p. 41.

59. Wright, *Children of Working Mothers*, p. 24.

60. Manning, *Immigrant Woman and Her Job*, pp. 43–44.

61. NC Shelter case 198.

62. For instance, only 13% of the applications to Philadelphia's Jewish Foster Home from 1882–1912 were for "full orphans." Reena Sigman Friedman, *These Are Our Children: Jewish Orphanages in the United States, 1880–1925* (Boston: Brandeis University Press, 1994), p. 156. Most orphanages were largely populated by half-orphans; at the Chicago Half-Orphan Asylum, more than half the children had both parents still living. Cmiel, *A Home of Another Kind*, p. 18. Sociologist Julia Wrigley estimates that in New York City in the 1890s, at least one in every thirty-five children lived in a public orphan asylum. Julia Wrigley, "Different Care for Different Kids: Social Class and Child Care Policy," *Educational Policy* 3 (December 1989), p. 423.

63. Friedman, *These Are Our Children*, p. 161.

64. NC cases 705, 263, 180.

65. *A Bintel Brief: Sixty Years of Letters from the Lower East Side to the Jewish Daily Forward*, ed. Isaac Metzger (Garden City, New York: Doubleday, 1971), p. 83.

66. NC case 211.

67. Anthony, *Mothers Who Must Earn*, pp. 151–153. Similarly, Helen Tyson noted, "most mothers are afraid of any type of institutional care for their children, even the part-time care of the nursery." Tyson, *Day Nursery in Its Community Relations*, p. 28. Helen Wright's study of working mothers in

Chicago found a higher proportion of families using day nurseries (23%), but she noted that her findings were skewed in favor of the nurseries, since some of the records of mothers for her study came from the day nurseries themselves, while a larger group came from the United Charities, which "put constant pressure on the families under its care to take the children to a day nursery when the mother was obliged to work outside the home." Wright, *Children of Wage-Earning Mothers*, p. 20.

68. Hughes, *Mothers in Industry*, p. 194.

69. "New Nursery Plan May Help 50,000,"*Philadelphia Bulletin*, March 24, 1927. If Hughes's sample of working mothers' child care arrangements was typical, most of the children who were left without supervision were over ten years old.

70. Tyson, *Day Nursery in Its Community Relations*, p. 27.

71. The ages of the youngest child in a family attending these nurseries clustered around less than one to four years, while even the ages of the oldest child in a family attending these nurseries clustered around two to seven years at the Baldwin and St. Nicholas; at Neighborhood Centre there were more older children.

72. "New Nursery Plan May Help 50,000," *Philadelphia Bulletin*, March 24, 1927.

73. Tyson, *Day Nursery in Its Community Relations*, pp. 22, 28.

74. An average of 55% of families at Baldwin, Neighborhood Centre, First, and St. Nicholas had only one child; 24% had two children.

75. Tyson, *Day Nursery in Its Community Relations*, p. 8.

76. Tyson, *Day Nurseries in Pennsylvania*, p. 13.

77. Sonya Michel, "The Limits of Maternalism: Policies Toward American Wage-Earning Mothers During the Progressive Era," in *Mothers of a New World: Maternalist Politics and the Origins of Welfare States*, ed. Seth Koven and Sonya Michel (New York: Routledge, 1993), p. 284.

78. Sister Frances Finley to Sister Visitation, p. 5. Cathedral Day Nursery collection, Archives of the Daughters of Charity of St. Vincent de Paul, Northeastern Province.

79. *Annual Report of the Baldwin Day Nursery*, 1901.

80. Ibid., 1905.

81. Child Federation, *A Study of the Day Nurseries of Philadelphia*, p. 22

82. Annual Report of the Strawberry Mansion Day Nursery (SMDN), 1949.

83. Cmiel, *A Home of Another Kind*, p. 26.

84. Wrigley, "Different Care for Different Kids," p. 424.

85. Bureau of Jewish Social Research, "Report on Jewish Day Nurseries of Philadelphia," (December 1920), Neighborhood Centre collection.

86. Out of twenty-seven recommendations for improving the city's day nurseries, only one concerned providing better play space; the others aimed to improve hygiene, food, and management of the nurseries. Child Federation, *A Study of the Day Nurseries of Philadelphia*, pp. 7–16.

87. Quoted in Sonya Michel, "Children's Interests/Mothers' Rights: Women, Professionals, and the American Family, 1920–1945." (Ph.D. dissertation, Brown University, 1986), p. 171.

88. Annual Report of the SMDN, 1949.

89. Child Federation, *Study of the Day Nurseries of Philadelphia*, p. 57.

90. Tyson, *Day Nursery in Its Community Relations*, p. 28.

91. Cmiel, *A Home of Another Kind*, p. 27. Similarly, Reena Friedman argues that children in Jewish orphanages during this period lived in surroundings designed to maximize efficiency and promote order: they ate silently on long benches in great dining halls; slept in barracks-style dormitories, and were marched to activities in silent rows to the clanging of a bell. Friedman, *These Are Our Children*, pp. 36–43,

92. Child Federation, *Study of the Day Nurseries of Philadelphia*, p. 38; typescript report on First Day Nursery, n.d.

93. NC case 925.

94. Matron Anna Frigond was described this way in "Our History," poem read at twenty-fifth anniversary celebration of the Strawberry Mansion Nursery and reprinted in a brochure celebrating the dedication of a new building, March 4, 1956.

95. *Annual Report of the Baldwin Day Nursery*, 1900.

96. Forty-ninth Street Station Day Nursery Application for Reinstatement in the PADN, Report of the Visiting Committee, February 20, 1928, PADN.

97. BDN minutes, June 1908.

98. *Annual Reports of the Baldwin Day Nursery*, 1913 and 1916.

99. *Annual Report of the Jane D. Kent Day Nursery*, 1886.

100. Child Federation, *A Study of the Day Nurseries of Philadelphia*, p. 71. See also Elizabeth Perrine, "The Public Health Nurse and the Day Nursery," *Day Nursery Bulletin*, August 1927, who reported that while some matrons had training in nursing, social work, or kindergarten work, many had no special training and "ranged from 'good housekeeper,' 'no training' down to 'bedraggled little widow with three children of her own,' 'kind old woman,' 'matron immoral, possibly insane.'"

101. Annual Report of the SMDN, 1945.

102. Child Federation, *Study of the Day Nurseries of Philadelphia*, p. 106.

103. Annual Report of the SMDN, 1949.

104. Child Federation, *Study of the Day Nurseries of Philadelphia*, p. 71.

105. PADN minutes, October 21, 1920.

106. NC case 315. After sending for their furniture from Williamsport, Pennsylvania, the couple found that the Hebrew Day Nursery was not willing to take their five children as part of their employment contract. This is the only instance I have found of a man being employed for child-care duties at a day nursery; since this was an immigrant institution, advertised in the Yiddish press, its practices may have differed.

107. Child Federation, *A Study of the Day Nurseries Of Philadelphia*, pp. 71–72.

108. For instance, the Baldwin report for 1906 mentioned that the new matron and her daughter would "make their home at the nursery." Flora Lockwood, matron of the St. Nicholas Day Nursery, brought her daughter Helen up at the nursery; Helen later became the nursery's visitor and ultimately director.

109. BDN minutes, September 1915.

110. St. Nicholas minutes, Feruary 8, 1924.

111. Sunnyside minutes, December 5, 1910.

112. BDN minutes, February 1917.

113. Minutes of PADN executive committee, November 8, 1899.

114. PADN minutes, February 20, 1920.

115. NC, Annual Report of Day Nursery, 1916.

116. Sister Frances Finley, p. 5.

117. See Ellen Ross, *Love & Toil: Motherhood in Outcast London 1870–1918* (New York: Oxford University Press, 1993), pp. 209–215, for a discussion of mothers' feelings about school medical inspections and for the argument that working-class mothers did not take seriously medical conditions that they did not consider to be possibly life-threatening.

118. PADN minutes, April 22, 1909.

119. FDN Visitor's report, July 1919.

120. Child Federation, *Study of the Day Nurseries of Philadelphia*, p. 29.

121. Ross, "Good and Bad Mothers," p. 186.

122. Cmiel, *A Home of Another Kind*, p. 26.

123. *Annual Report of Jane D. Kent Day Nursery*, 1888.

124. Ibid., 1913.

125. Julian Greifer, "Philadelphia Jewish Philanthropy, Its Evolution and Maturation," in

Philadelphia Jewish Life, 1940–1985., ed. Murray Friedman (Ardmore, Pennsylvania: Seth Press, 1986), p. 281.

126. *Catholic Charities Yearbook*, p. 123.

127. Ellen Ross, "Hungry Children: Housewives and London Charity, 1870–1918" in *The Uses of Charity: The Poor on Relief in the Nineteenth-Century Metropolis*, ed. Peter Mandler (Philadelphia: University of Pennsylvania Press, 1990), p. 187.

128. *Annual Report of the Baldwin Day Nursery*, 1922.

129. Hyman Bogen, *The Luckiest Orphans: A History of the Hebrew Orphan Asylum of New York* (Urbana: University of Illinois Press, 1992), p. 80.

130. FDN Visitor's report, January 1917 and January 1919.

131. NC, Day Nursery Committee minutes, September 1913.

132. *Annual Report of the Baldwin Day Nursery*, 1913.

133. NC case 761.

134. NC case 735.

135. Tyson, *Day Nursery in Its Community Relations*, p. 27.

136. NC case 857.

137. NC case 908.

138. NC case 10.

139. NC case 735.

140. NC case 20.

141. NC case 369.

142. NC case 12.

143. NC cases 6, 2, and 10.

144. NC Day Nursery Committee minutes, May 5, 1924 and October 6, 1924.

145. NC Shelter case 198.

146. Hilda Satt Polacheck, *I Came a Stranger: The Story of a Hull House Girl* (Urbana: University of Illinois Press, 1989).

147. NC case 6.

148. NC case 9.

149. NC case 14.

150. FDN Visitor's report, July 1919.

151. Ibid., August 1919.

152. NC case 425.

153. NC case 640.

154. Among the important recent works critiquing, complicating, and/or revising an argument about social welfare institutions as agents of class control are Linda Gordon, *Heroes of Their Own Lives: The Politics and History of Family Violence, Boston 1880–1960* (New York: Penguin Books, 1988); Sherri Broder, "Politics of the Family: Political Culture, Moral Reform, and Family Relations in Gilded Age Philadelphia" (Ph.D. dissertation, Brown University, 1988); Mary Odem, *Delinquent Daughters: Protecting and Policing Adolescent Female Sexuality in the United States, 1885–1920* (Chapel Hill: University of North Carolina Press, 1995); and Christine Stansell, *City of Women: Sex and Class in New York, 1789–1860* (Urbana: University of Illinois Press, 1982), especially chapter 3.

Chapter 3

1. Neighborhood Centre (NC) case 751.

2. Sonya Michel makes a similar argument in "The Limits of Maternalism: Policies Toward American Wage-Earning Mothers During the Progressive Era," in Seth Koven and Sonya Michel, eds., *Mothers of a New World: Maternalist Politics and the Origins of Welfare States* (New York: Routledge, 1993), p. 307.

3. Gwendolyn Mink, *The Wages of Motherhood: Inequality in the Welfare State, 1917–1942* (Ithaca, New York: Cornell University Press, 1995), p. 151.

4. Linda Gordon, *Pitied But Not Entitled: Single Mothers and the History of Welfare* (New York: The Free Press, 1994), pp. 24–28.

5. Helen Glenn Tyson, *The Day Nursery in its Community Relations: A Study of the Day Nurseries of Philadelphia* (Philadelphia: Philadelphia Association of Day Nurseries, 1919), p. 39.

6. PADN minutes, April 9, 1908.

7. "Widows' Allowance Act in Kansas City" (1914), in *Selected Articles on Mothers' Pensions*, ed. Edna Bullock (New York: H. W. Wilson, 1915). Similarly, according to the investigations of Barbara Bartlett in 1918, one faction of the Boston Association of Day Nurseries thought that nurseries could be eliminated by strengthening the mothers' aid society and placing children in private homes, whereas "the other side" believed that nurseries were needed and should be established. Barbara Bartlett to Grace Meigs, November 30, 1917, File 4-15-4-6, Children's Bureau (CB) records, Record Group 102, National Archives.

8. Nancy Fraser and Linda Gordon, "'Dependency' Demystified: Inscriptions of Power in a Keyword of the Welfare State," *Social Politics* 1, no. 1 (Spring 1994), pp. 10, 22.

9. Alice Kessler-Harris, *A Woman's Wage: Historical Meanings and Social Consequences* (Lexington: University Press of Kentucky, 1990), especially chapter 1.

10. Commonwealth of Pennsylvania, *A Ten Year Program for the Department of Welfare* (Harrisburg: 1936), p. 23.

11. Nationally, the Jewish charities were at the forefront of this trend. Public officials in California (1906) and New Jersey (1910) decided to allow state aid to be used to "commit" children to their mothers. Mark Leff, "Consensus for Reform: The Mothers' Pension Movement in the Progressive Era," *Social Service Review* 47 (September 1973), p. 399. The New York bill, however, did not become law, as the mayor, pressured by private charities, persuaded the governor not to sign it. In Philadelphia, a test case was brought in January 1913 to see if the courts would support such an interpretation of the law, but it was not successful. *The Survey* (March 22, 1913), p. 850.

12. Quoted in Leff, "Consensus for Reform," p. 400.

13. *Report of the United Hebrew Charities*, 1912, p. 7. The New York Association for Improving the Condition of the Poor also pensioned a group of widows and used this experience to argue in favor of public mothers' pensions. NYAICP, *Shall Widows Be Pensioned?* (New York: 1914).

14. The first mothers' pension legislation was passed in Jackson County, Missouri, (which included Kansas City) in 1911; the first statewide measure was passed in Illinois a few months later. Joanne Goodwin, "The Differential Treatment of Motherhood: Mothers' Pensions, Chicago 1900–1930," paper presented at the Conference on Gender and Social Policy, Minneapolis, 1990, p. 13; Theda Skocpol, *Protecting Soldiers and Mothers: The Politics of Social Provision in the United States* (Cambridge: Harvard University Press, 1992), p. 31. See also Joanne Goodwin, *Gender and the Politics of Welfare Reform: Mothers' Pensions in Chicago, 1911–1929* (University of Chicago Press, 1997), and her article, "An American Experiment in Paid Motherhood: The Implementation of Mothers' Pensions in Early Twentieth Century Chicago," *Gender and History* 4 (Autumn 1992), pp. 323–342.

15. Quoted in Skocpol, *Protecting Soldiers and Mothers*, p. 23.

16. *Selected Articles on Mothers' Pensions*, ed. Edna Bullock (New York: H. W. Wilson, 1915), pp. 28, 108.

17. Barnard is quoted in Molly Ladd-Taylor, *Mother-Work: Women, Child Welfare, and the State, 1890–1930* (Urbana: University of Illinois Press, 1994), p. 146; Cavin's comment is found in the Orphans Guardians Society (OGS) minutes, February 26, 1925. Philadelphia Jewish Archives. For reformers' hopes for the pension programs, see Wendy Sarvasy, "Beyond the Difference versus Equality Policy Debate: Postsuffrage Feminism, Citizenship, and the Quest for a Feminist Welfare State," *Signs* 17 (Winter 1992), pp. 340–345 and 347–351; Katharine Anthony, *The Endowment of Motherhood* (New York: B. W. Huebsch, 1920).

18. Both quoted in Michel, "Limits of Maternalism," p. 294.

19. Ladd-Taylor, *Mother-Work*, pp. 141–142. Linda Gordon refers to mothers' aid as "a kind of child custody reform for the poor" in *Pitied But Not Entitled*, p. 39.

20. Gordon, *Pitied But Not Entitled*, p. 59.

21. Sonya Michel writes that some estimated it cost half as much to support children with their mothers than in institutions or foster homes. Michel, "Limits of Maternalism," p. 295.

22. This is Joanne Goodwin's argument in "An American Experiment in Paid Motherhood."

23. Gordon, *Pitied But Not Entitled*, p. 49.

24. A 1922 study showed that eleven out of thirty agencies made these kinds of calculations; another account reveals that social workers in Washington, D.C., had two different standard budgets for mothers' aid recipients, a higher one for whites and a lower one for African-Americans. Gordon, *Pitied But Not Entitled*, pp. 47–48.

25. Hall, *Mothers' Assistance in Philadelphia* , pp. 1–2.

26. Helen Russell Wright, *Children of Wage-Earning Mothers: A Study of a Selected Group in Chicago* (Children's Bureau publication no. 102, 1922), p. 52.

27. Gordon, *Pitied But Not Entitled*, p. 49. In New York City, the Board of Child Welfare rejected applications for mothers' pensions from women who used tobacco, didn't attend church, drank, were dishonest, housed a male lodger, had extramarital relations, exercised poor discipline, engaged in criminal behavior, or had delinquent children. Anne Durst, "Day Nurseries and Wage-Earning Mothers in the United States, 1890–1930" (Ph.D. dissertation, University of Wisconsin-Madison, 1989), pp. 33–34.

28. Hall, *Mothers' Assistance in Philadelphia* , p. 89.

29. "How Philadelphia Helps Her Poor: An Abstract of the Report of the Philadelphia Relief Study," (1926), p. 9. Urban Archives Vertical File.

30. Orphans Guardians Society (OGS) minutes, December 19, 1918 and May 9, 1922.

31. OGS minutes, September 30, 1920.

32. Ibid., September 26, 1929.

33. The SOC was often torn between meeting the needs of particular clients and realizing that "in the interest of ultimately obtaining adequate appropriations" for the MAF, the SOC must not supplement pensions from its funds. They tried to encourage private individuals to help specific families by contributing to the MAF. Society for Organizing Charity (SOC) Case Work and Special Relief Committee minutes, January 19, 1920, April 19, 1920, and May 3, 1920. Historical Society of Pennsylvania.

34. For instance, Edith Glenn, registrar of the Mothers' Assistance Fund, to Carrie Yonkers at Neighborhood Centre, July 24, 1931.

35. Quoted in Janet Wedel, "The Origins of State Patriarchy During the Progressive Era: A Sociological Study of the Mothers' Aid Movement" (Ph.D. dissertation, Washington University, 1975), p. 375.

36. OGS minutes, February 26, 1925.

37. Goodwin, "Differential Treatment of Motherhood," pp. 14–15.

38. Gordon, *Pitied But Not Entitled*, p. 50.

39. Wright, *Children of Wage-Earning Mothers*, p. 30.

40. Mrs. Walter MacDonald to Julia Lathrop, January 9, 1918, CB.

41. Margaret Murphy to Children's Bureau, January 21, 1920, CB.

42. *Monthly Register of the Philadelphia Society for Organizing Charitable Relief and Repressing Mendiancy* 1 (November 1879).

43. *Annual Report of the Jane D. Kent Day Nursery*, 1888.

44. PADN minutes, January 30, 1899.

45. For example, in 1920, two weeks after the board of the First Day Nursery had resolved not to accept families where two parents were working, it considered an individual case and decided "that if the wage of father didn't cover the expenses of family it was duty of nursery to care for children." First Day Nursery (FDN) minutes, January 15, 1920 and February 2, 1920.

46. See Table 2 in appendix.

47. Tyson, *Day Nursery in Its Community Relations*, p. 41.

48. Margaret McMillan, "The Nursery of Tomorrow," in *Women and the Labour Party*, ed. Marion Phillips (London: Headley Bros., 1918).

49. Helen Brenton to Julia Lathrop, September 16, 1917, CB.

50. *Day Nursery Bulletin*, June 1928; Judith Raftery, "The Invention of Modern Urban Schooling: Los Angeles, 1885–1941" (Ph.D. dissertation, UCLA, 1984), p. 49.

51. Quoted in Martha May, "'Home Life': Progressive Social Reformers' Prescriptions for Social Stability" (Ph.D. dissertation, SUNY-Binghamton, 1984), p. 228.

52. On Kelley's arrangements for her children, see Kathryn Kish Sklar, *Florence Kelley & the Nation's Work: The Rise of Women's Political Culture, 1830–1900* (New Haven, Connecticut: Yale University Press, 1995), pp. 178–180, 223–225, and 290.

53. Quoted in Michel, "The Limits of Maternalism," p. 291. In Pennsylvania, Helen Glenn Tyson, who had served both as the executive secretary of the Philadelphia Association of Day Nurseries and as head of the state's Mothers' Assistance Fund, shared Addams's strong preference for mothers' aid. She concluded that day nurseries, suffering from the stigma of charity, could not meet the need for child care; family allowances or mothers' pensions were the "chief hope of relief for the working mother." Helen Tyson, "Foreword," to Gwendolyn Hughes, *Mothers in Industry: Wage Earning by Mothers in Philadelphia* (New York: New Republic, 1925), pp. xv–xvii.

54. See, for example, the recommendations at the end of Helen Wright's 1922 study of wage-earning mothers in Chicago. Wright, *Children of Wage-Earning Mothers*, pp. 76–88.

55. Robyn Muncy, *Creating a Female Dominion in American Reform, 1890–1935* (New York: Oxford University Press, 1991); Ladd-Taylor, *Mother-Work*, chapter 3; Lindenmeyer, "*A Right to Childhood.*"

56. For information on the unconventional personal lives of many of these reformers, see Gordon, *Pitied But Not Entitled*, pp. 67, 71-84

57. "Memorandum on Day Nurseries," July 15, 1918, CB.

58. Clara Savage, "The Children's Bureau and You," *Good Housekeeping* (January 1918), p. 54.

59. Julia Lathrop to Helen Sabin Anderson, July 2, 1918, CB.

60. Julia Lathrop to Helen Brenton, September 25, 1917, CB.

61. Julia Lathrop to Miss Peck, June 22, 1920, CB.

62. Barbara Bartlett to Grace Meigs, May 16, 1918, CB.

63. Helen Glenn Tyson, *Day Nurseries in Pennsylvania: A Study Made for the Bureau of Children* (Harrisburg: Pennsylvania Department of Welfare Bulletin 17, 1925), p. 9.

64. Michel, "Limits of Maternalism," p. 304.

65. *Annual Report of the Baldwin Day Nursery*, 1912, p. 5.

66. PADN minutes, February 18, 1921. In Chicago, Barbara Bartlett reported that a conservative group of nursery directors who resisted incorporating social investigation and casework into their nurseries were also opposed to mothers' pensions, but no such opposition was ever voiced in Philadelphia. Barbara Bartlett to Grace Meigs, February 7, 1918, CB.

67. *Annual Report of the Baldwin Day Nursery*, 1914, p. 5.

68. NC Annual Report of Day Nursery and Shelter, 1916, p. 4.

69. NC Day Nursery questionnaire, 1918.

70. NC Day Nursery and Shelter Report, February 1915, p. 3. Given her feelings about the relative merits of day nurseries and pensions, it is not surprising that when Kohn left Neighborhood Centre in 1925, she went to work for the Orphans Guardians Society, a private agency that supported mothers in their homes with private funds as well as with funds from the MAF.

71. Tyson, *Day Nursery in Its Community Relations*, p. 40.

72. *Day Nursery Bulletin*, August 1926.

73. NC Annual Report of Day Nursery and Shelter, 1916.

74. PADN minutes, February 16, 1922.

75. Barbara Bartlett to Grace Meigs, May 16, 1918, CB.

76. Emily Cahan, *Past Caring: A History of U.S. Preschool Care and Education for the Poor, 1920–1965* (New York: National Center for Children in Poverty, Columbia University, 1989), p. 22.

77. Durst, "Day Nurseries and Wage-Earning Mothers," p. 282.

78. Tyson, *Day Nurseries in Pennsylvania*, p. 25.

79. Dodge was a founder of the National Association Opposed to Woman Suffrage and was married to a founder of the New York Charity Organization Society, which opposed government involvement in charity work. Michel, "Limits of Maternalism," p. 285.

80. Michel, "Limits of Maternalism," p. 307.

81. "New Nursery Plan May Help 50,000," *Philadelphia Bulletin*, March 24, 1927.

82. She thus had a certain advantage over mothers receiving pensions, for, despite the language that referred to these mothers as employees of the state, they differed from employees in that they could not be fired—their claim to mother their children existed independent of their relationship to the state.

83. "Experimental Work of the First Day Nursery of Philadelphia," *Biennial Conference of the National Federation of Day Nurseries*, 1929, pp. 43–44.

84. FDN minutes, June 7, 1932.

85. In 1935, the First Day Nursery was the only nursery in the state doing foster day care work; the Morton Street Day Nursery had adopted the plan, but then gave it up when the nursery turned into a settlement house. FDN minutes, May 13, 1935.

86. FDN minutes, December 3, 1928.

87. Ibid., November 4, 1929.

88. Daniel Walkowitz, "The Making of a Feminine Professional Identity: Social Workers in the 1920s," *American Historical Review* 95, no. 4 (October 1990), pp. 1051–1075.

89. Linda Gordon, *Heroes of Their Own Lives: The Politics and History of Family Violence* (New York: Penguin Books, 1988), pp. 62–63.

90. Tyson, *Day Nurseries in Pennsylvania*, p. 5.

91. PADN minutes, December 28, 1925.

92. Tyson, *Day Nurseries in Pennsylvania*, p. 5.

93. PADN minutes, April 25, 1939.

94. Tyson, *Day Nursery in Its Community Relations*, p. 33.

95. Durst, "Day Nurseries and Wage-Earning Mothers," p. 258.

96. *Annual Report of the Baldwin Day Nursery*, 1903.

97. Quoted in Julia Wrigley, "Different Care for Different Kids: Social Class and Child Care Policy," *Educational Policy* 3 (December 1989), p. 424.

98. *Annual Report of the Franklin Day Nursery*, 1912.

99. Child Federation, *A Study of the Day Nurseries of Philadelphia*, pp. 65–67.

100. Tyson, *Day Nursery in Its Community Relations*, p. 9.

101. Ibid., p. 35.

102. Ibid., p. 31.

103. *Annual Report of the Jane D. Kent Day Nursery*, 1913.

104. Annual Report of the Strawberry Mansion Day Nursery, 1949.

105. NC Day Nursery report, March 1914.

106. Kenneth Cmiel makes this point about the Chicago Half-Orphan Asylum in the 1920s. Cmiel, *A Home of Another Kind: One Chicago Orphanage and the Tangle of Child Welfare* (Chicago: University of Chicago Press, 1995), p. 79.

107. NC and Franklin Day Nurseries, *PADN Joint Annual Report*, 1928 and 1926.

108. NC Day Nursery report, January 1928.

109. NC Day Nursery, *PADN Joint Annual Report*, 1925.

110. Mary Julia Grant, "Modernizing Motherhood: Child Study Clubs and the Parent Education Movement, 1915–1940," (Ph.D. dissertation, Boston University, 1992), p. 165.

111. NC Day Nursery, Report of Family Worker, December 1927.

112. Sunnyside Day Nursery, *PADN Joint Annual Report*, 1926.

113. *Annual Report of the Baldwin Day Nursery*, 1901, 1903, and 1904. The success of these abstinence meetings is an example of Julia Grant's finding that successful mothers' groups among poorer women were run by the women themselves and often reflected the design of other community groups, such as the church or mutual aid associations. Grant, "Modernizing Motherhood," p. 173.

114. Judith Trolander, *Professionalism and Social Change: From the Settlement House Movement to Neighborhood Centers, 1886 to the Present* (New York: Columbia University Press, 1987), argues that membership in charity federations or Community Chests was responsible for the decrease in social activism among settlement house workers in the 1920s. Susan Traverso, "The Politics of Welfare: Boston, 1910–1940," (Ph.D. dissertation, University of Wisconsin-Madison, 1995), sees Boston's Council of Social Agencies as an attempt by the more conservative Protestant welfare agencies to consolidate their power when Catholic and Jewish agencies began to challenge them. Kenneth Cmiel, in *A Home of Another Kind*, argues that in Chicago, the Council of Social Agencies represented the voice of professional social workers and reformers who sought greater control over the city's private welfare institutions.

115. Eighteen of the PADN nurseries joined either the Welfare Federation or the Federation of Jewish Charities; only three PADN nurseries clearly did not: the Frankford, the Jenkintown, and the Salvation Army day nurseries. Information was not available for eight other nurseries that were PADN members at some point during this period. Although the Federation of Jewish Charities initially excluded East European Jewish charitable groups, including two day nurseries, it eventually expanded to include charities founded by immigrants, including the Downtown Hebrew and Strawberry Mansion Day Nurseries. Philip Rosen, "German Jews vs. Russian Jews in Philadelphia Philanthropy," *Jewish Life in Philadelphia, 1830–1940*, ed. Murray Friedman (Philadelphia: ISHI Press, 1983).

116. Annual Report of Strawberry Mansion Day Nursery, 1945.

117. FDN minutes, April 8, 1940.

118. "Experimental Work of the First Day Nursery of Philadelphia," *Biennial Conference of the National Federation of Day Nurseries*, 1929, pp. 44–45.

119. PADN memo, November 21, 1916; PADN minutes, November 22, 1920.

120. Tyson, *Day Nursery in Its Community Relations*, p. 32.

121. NC case 140.

122. PADN medical regulations committee, April 13, 1920. Colbourne offered her services "to any matron or visitor needing information or advice as to the particular agency to whom the mother should be referred in order to be enabled to keep her child at home for the prescribed time."

123. Tyson, *Day Nursery in Its Community Relations*, p. 16.

124. Ibid., p. 35.

125. Durst, "Day Nurseries and Wage-Earning Mothers," p. 258.

126. Annual Report of the Strawberry Mansion Day Nursery, 1949.

127. NC case 963.

128. FDN minutes, December 3, 1928.

129. Ibid., February 4, 1929.

130. NC Nursery School report, September 1928.

131. NC case 837.

132. NC case 20.

133. FDN Visitor's report, July 1919.

134. NC case 740.

135. Bureau of Jewish Social Research, "Report on Jewish Day Nurseries of Philadelphia," (December 1920), Neighborhood Centre.

136. *Catholic Charities Yearbook*, p. 105.

137. Tyson, *Day Nursery in Its Community Relations*, p. 6.

138. Forty-ninth Street Station Day Nursery Application for Reinstatement in the PADN, Report of the Visiting Committee, February 20, 1928; PADN minutes February 23, 1928.

139. Ruth Ferguson Weaver, *Children's Progress: A Study of Some Accomplishments of Day Nurseries in Philadelphia* (Philadelphia: PADN, 1931), pp. 47–50.

140. Weaver, *Children's Progress*, pp. 10–11.

141. Ibid., p. 53.

Chapter 4

1. Before the common school system was fully standardized, young children did sometimes attend the new public primary schools alongside their older siblings. For instance, in 1839–40, an estimated 40% of three-year-olds were enrolled in public schools in Massachusetts. Barbara Beatty, *Preschool Education in America: The Culture of Young Children from the Colonial Era to the Present* (New Haven, Connecticut: Yale University Press, 1995), p. 23. Although "infant schools" for poor children had been part of the charity school movement in Philadelphia and other cities, in the process of consolidation and systematization over the course of the nineteenth century, the public schools defined their responsibility as beginning only at the age of five. Both infant schools and common schools had an academic mission, teaching even very young children how to read and write. Caroline Winterer, "Avoiding a 'Hothouse System of Education': Nineteenth-Century Early Childhood Education from the Infant Schools to the Kindergartens," *History of Education Quarterly* 32, no. 3 (Fall 1992), pp. 289–314. Carl Kaestle, *Pillars of the Republic: Common Schools and American Society, 1780–1860* (New York: Hill and Wang, 1983), traces the rise of the public elementary school and discusses infant schools in Philadelphia and elsewhere, pp. 47–51; see also John Trevor Custis, *The Public Schools of Philadelphia: Historical, Biographical, Statistical* (Philadelphia: Burk & McFetridge, 1897), pp. 15–16.

2. Sociologist Sorca O'Connor describes the evolution of a "child-rearing partnership between mothers and schools," in which mothers have been assigned responsibility for the total care of very young children as well as for the primary physical and emotional care of children of all ages, while schools have taken on the task of teaching older children specific skills and socializing them to become good workers and citizens. Sorca O'Connor, "Rationales for the Institutionalization of Programs for Young Children," *American Journal of Education* (February 1990), p. 115.

3. Ann Taylor Allen, "Gardens of Children, Gardens of God: Kindergartens and Day-Care Centers in Nineteenth-Century Germany," *Journal of Social History* 19 (Spring 1986), p. 438; Beatty, *Preschool Education in America*, pp. 42–47.

4. In Nina Vandewalker, *The Kindergarten in American Education* (New York: Macmillan, 1908; rpt Arno Press, 1971), pp. 61–63.

5. Beatty, *Preschool Education in America*, p. 63.

6. Michael Shapiro, *Child's Garden: The Kindergarten Movement from Froebel to Dewey* (University Park: Pennsylvania State University Press, 1983), p. 86. In Philadelphia, for instance, kindergartens could be found in twenty-seven different churches, at the headquarters of the Children's Aid Society and of the Women's Christian Temperance Union, and in many other locations. Vandewalker, *The Kindergarten in American Education*, p. 78; Shapiro, *Child's Garden*, p. 96

7. *History of the Kindergarten Movement in the Southeastern States* (Atlanta: Association for Childhood Education, 1939), p. 38.

8. Custis, *The Public Schools of Philadelphia*, p. 61. By the same date, the city had thirty charitable day nurseries.

9. Francis Wayland Parker, quoted in Beatty, *Preschool Education in America*, p. 74.

10. Philadelphia day nurseries that had kindergarten instruction as part of their program included Baldwin, House of Industry, Jane D. Kent, and San Cristoforo.

11. A survey in 1903 indicated that the two types were about evenly represented. Vandewalker, *Kindergarten in American Education*, p. 78.

12. Shapiro, *Child Garden*, p. 150.

13. Abbie Gordon Klein, *The Debate Over Child Care 1969–1990: A Sociohistorical Analysis* (Albany: State University of New York Press, 1992), p. 270.

14. Shapiro, *Child Garden*, p. 134.

15. In surveying more than a thousand articles about children, sociologist Julia Wrigley found a rapid increase from the 1910s to the 1920s in the number of articles focusing on social and emotional development. Julia Wrigley, "Do Young Children Need Intellectual Stimulation? Experts' Advice to Parents, 1900–1985," *History of Education Quarterly* 29, no. 1 (Spring 1989), p. 47.

16. Quoted in Barbara Ehrenreich and Deirdre English, *For Her Own Good: 150 Years of the Experts' Advice to Women* (New York: Anchor Books, 1978), p. 209.

17. Quoted in Mary Julia Grant, "Modernizing Motherhood: Child Study Clubs and the Parent Education Movement, 1915–1940," (Ph.D. dissertation, Boston University, 1992), pp. 1, 91, 118–119.

18. Ehrenreich and English, *For Her Own Good*, pp. 207–208.

19. Steven Schlossman, "Before Home Start: Notes Toward a History of Parent Education in America, 1897–1929," *Harvard Educational Review* 46 (August 1976), p. 455.

20. Nancy Cott, *The Grounding of Modern Feminism* (New Haven, Connecticut: Yale University Press, 1987), p. 170.

21. Cott, *Grounding of Modern Feminism*, p. 169. Emphasis in original.

22. Christina Hardyment, *Dream Babies: Child Care from Locke to Spock* (London: Jonathan Cape, 1983), p. 164.

23. He wrote, "Mother love is a dangerous instrument . . . which may inflict a never healing wound, a wound which may make infancy unhappy, adolescence a nightmare, an instrument which may wreck your adult son or daughter's vocational future and their chances for marital happiness." John Watson, *Psychological Care of Infant and Child* (New York: W. W. Norton & Company, 1928), p. 87.

24. Watson, *Psychological Care*, p. 85.

25. Julia Wrigley, "Different Care for Different Kids: Social Class and Child Care Policy," *Educational Policy* 3 (December 1989), p. 427. The phrase "laboratory for parents" comes from a 1944 article in *Parents' Magazine*.

26. Dr. Smiley Blanton, "Functions of the Nursery School," *Biennial Conference of the National Federation of Day Nurseries* (NFDN), April 1929, p. 17.

27. Remarks of Dr. Patty Hill, *Biennial Conference of the NFDN*, p. 28.

28. These institutions included Columbia University's Teachers' College, Iowa State, Cornell University, Ohio State, Mills College, Vassar, Smith, and Antioch. Lawrence Cremin, *American Education: The Metropolitan Experience, 1876–1980* (New York: Harper & Row, 1988), p. 302; Women's Bureau, *Employed Mothers and Child Care* (Bulletin no. 246, 1953), p. 13.

29. Emily Cahan, *Past Caring: A History of U.S. Preschool Care and Education for the Poor, 1920–1965* (New York: National Center for Children in Poverty, Columbia University, 1989), p. 32. For instance, in Philadelphia, laboratory nursery schools were established at Temple University, the University of Pennsylvania, Babies Hospital, and at Drexel Institute of Technology; by 1928 there were fifteen parent-cooperative nursery schools in the city and suburbs. The figure on cooperative nursery schools is found in a proposal from Temple University to the Laura Spelman Rockefeller Memorial, July 6, 1928. Rockefeller Archive Center, Tarrytown, New York.

30. Josephine Foster and Marion Mattson, *Nursery School Procedure* (New York: D. Appleton and Company, 1929), pp. 5–12.

31. Immigrant and other working-class parents came into contact with Merrill-Palmer stu-

dents through public health programs and nutrition classes, but were not invited to use the nursery school. Kyle Ciani, "'Great, Wonderful Years': Professional Training at the Merrill-Palmer School, 1920–1940," paper presented at the Berkshire Conference on the History of Women, Chapel Hill, North Carolina, 1996. The first quote is from Florence Willson Duhn, a student at Merrill-Palmer in the late 1920s; the second is from the school's annual report in 1940.

32. Grant, "Modernizing Motherhood," p. 222.

33. Blanton, "Functions of the Nursery School," p. 23.

34. Foster and Mattson, *Nursery School Procedure*, pp. viii, 2.

35. Harriet Johnson, *Children in the Nursery School* (New York: John Day Company, 1928) pp. 45–49. Beatty, *Preschool Education in America*, pp. 138–142. See also Claudia Lewis, *Children of the Cumberland* (New York: Columbia University Press, 1946), which compares the Harriet Johnson Nursery School with Lewis's experience conducting a WPA nursery school in the mountains of East Tennessee.

36. Sally Lubeck, *Sandbox Society: Early Education in Black and White America, A Comparative Ethnography* (Philadelphia: The Falmer Press, 1985).

37. The size of groups and the ratio of staff to children varied enormously, but a model nursery school, such as the one conducted by Harriet Johnson in New York, had two teachers on duty for a group of eight children (with a third teacher whose time was devoted to record-keeping), while the typical day nursery belonging to the Philadelphia Association of Day Nurseries had about three adults to minister to a group of fifty children. Johnson, *Children in the Nursery School*, p. xviii..

38. Blanton, "Functions of the Nursery School," pp. 16–20.

39. *Biennial Conference of the NFDN*, 1929, pp. 16–17.

40. Quoted in Wrigley, "Different Care for Different Kids," p. 427.

41. Miss May Workinger, Oregon State Agricultural College, to Carrie Younker, Neighborhood Centre, May 9, 1930.

42. Beatty, *Preschool Education in America*, pp. 138–139.

43. This privileging of middle-class parents as more promising targets of professional attention is clear at the Merrill-Palmer School, where students did some outreach work with working-class families, but faculty reserved their real attention for the "cream of the crop" parents in the nursery school and in local child study groups. Ciani, "'Great, Wonderful Years.'"

44. Beatty, *Preschool Education in America*, p. 139.

45. *Day Nursery Bulletin*, November 1927.

46. Blanton, "Functions of the Nursery School," p. 22.

47. Preface to Foster and Mattson, *Nursery School Procedure*, p. ix.

48. Johnson, *Children in the Nursery School*, pp. 97–98.

49. Cott, *Grounding of Modern Feminism*, p. 197; Lois Scharf, *To Work and To Wed: Female Employment, Feminism, and the Great Depression* (Westport, Connecticut: Greenwood Press, 1980), p. 32.

50. This phrase was used by Paul Klapper in the preface to Foster and Mattson, *Nursery School Procedure*, p. ix; Harriet Johnson wrote, somewhat defensively, "We are not proposing to substitute the nursery school for the home." Johnson, *Children in the Nursery School*, p. 98. Abigail Eliot, founder of the Ruggles Street Nursery School, told an interviewer that many social workers were hostile to the nursery school idea, fearing that it would "undercut family life." James Hymes, Jr., *Early Childhood Education Living History Interviews, Book 1: Beginnings* (Carmel, California: Hacienda Press, 1978), p. 20.

51. Kathleen Jones, "'As the Twig Is Bent': American Psychiatry and the Troublesome Child, 1890–1940," (Ph.D. dissertation, Rutgers University, 1988).

52. A 1931 report estimated that there were about five hundred nursery schools throughout the country, compared to about eight hundred day nurseries. White House Conference on Child Health and Protection, *Nursery Education: A Survey of Day Nurseries, Nursery Schools, and Private Kindergartens in the United States* (New York: The Century Company, 1931), pp. 7–10. Barbara Beatty, noting that

these schools enrolled a tiny fraction of the total preschool population, suggests that resistance to making nursery schools public came from awareness of their expense, concerns about forcing children to develop early, and fears of taking children away from their mothers and placing them in the control of the state. Beatty, *Preschool Education in America*, p. 167.

There were a few public nursery schools in the 1920s, mostly demonstration schools relying on outside funding or tuition payments. The first one was established in Chicago under the auspices of the Chicago Women's Club; Rose Alschuler also directed another in Winnetka, Illinois. Most others were run by high-school home economics departments, although in Grand Rapids, Michigan, three nursery schools were funded by the school board to demonstrate the value of nursery education. But these public nursery schools remained exceptions to the rule. Hymes, *Early Childhood Education Living History Interviews*, p. 21; Beatty, *Preschool Education in America*, pp. 174–176.

53. *Day Nursery Bulletin*, November 1927.

54. Ibid., January 1928.

55. Ibid:, February 1928.

56. Mrs. Hermann Biggs, *Biennial Conference of the NFDN*, 1929, p. 14.

57. *Biennial Conference of the NFDN*, 1929, pp. 7, 14.

58. Ibid., pp. 76–81. This careful record-keeping was typical of many research-oriented nursery schools who sought a better understanding of each child and a way to provide "scientific" information to researchers through the painstaking accumulation of information on each child's behavior. Record-keeping was a major activity at the Harriet Johnson Nursery School, where three teachers alternated between working with the children and recording their observations. Johnson, *Children in the Nursery School*, p. xviii.

59. *Biennial Conference of the NFDN*, 1929, pp. 27–29, 72.

60. Hymes, *Early Childhood Education Living History Interviews*, pp. 11–16.

61. Beatty, *Preschool Education in America*, pp. 142–144.

62. These included San Cristoforo, Willing, Joy, and Sunnyside day nurseries; the nursery school at Sunnyside was used for observation by students at Temple University until Temple established its own nursery school in 1929. Temple University College of Education, *Annual Reports*, 1927 and 1929, Templeana Collection, Paley Library.

63. Neighborhood Centre (NC) Report of Head Worker on Day Nursery, February 1925.

64. "Neighborhood Centre to Have Nursery School," October 1925.

65. NC Report of Executive Director, September 29, 1925.

66. NC Head Worker's Report of Day Nursery, March 1925.

67. NC Annual Report of Day Nursery, 1927, p. 2.

68. NC Nursery Report, October 1928.

69. Ibid., December 1928.

70. Indeed, in one case, a Neighborhood Centre board member applied to place her grandson in the nursery school during the summer while the university-affiliated nursery school he usually attended was closed. Before the creation of the nursery school, it would have been unthinkable for a board member to consider enrolling a member of her family in the day nursery. NC case 1118.

71. NC case 1033.

72. NC case 1137.

73. NC case 1152.

74. NC case 1064. For more on the treatment of mothers in child guidance clinics, see Jones, "'Mother Made Me Do It': Mother-Blaming and the Women of Child Guidance," in *"Bad" Mothers: The Politics of Blame in Twentieth-Century America*, ed. Molly Ladd-Taylor and Lauri Umansky (New York: New York University Press, 1998) pp. 99–124; and Margo Horn, "The Moral Message of Child Guidance, 1925–1945," *Journal of Social History* 18 (1984), pp. 25–36.

75. NC case 1187.

76. NC case 1239.

77. NC case 1152.

78. NC case 1325.

79. NC case 1132.

80. Jacquelyn Litt, "Mothering, Medicalization, and Jewish Identity, 1928–1940," *Gender and Society* 10, no. 2 (April 1996), pp. 188–190.

81. Litt, "Mothering, Medicalization, and Jewish Identity," p. 194.

82. NC case 1193.

83. NC case 1347.

84. NC Day Nursery Report, November 1938.

85. NC Nursery School Annual Reports, 1939, 1940, and 1941.

86. NC Nursery School Annual Report 1942; also monthly report, February 5, 1942.

87. Neighborhood Centre Day Nursery Policies, November 13, 1942.

Chapter 5

1. Linda Gordon makes this argument in *Pitied But Not Entitled: Single Mothers and the History of Welfare, 1890–1935* (New York: Free Press, 1994), p. 291.

2. Margaret Tinkcom, "Depression and War, 1929–1946," in *Philadelphia: A 300-Year History*, ed. Russell Weigley (New York: W. W. Norton, 1982), p. 612.

3. Alice Kessler-Harris, *Out To Work: A History of Wage-Earning Women in the United States* (New York: Oxford University Press, 1982), pp. 259–261.

4. *Maytime in Midwinter* (Report of the Children's Department of the Council of Social Agencies, 1931), p. 13.

5. Ibid., p. 27.

6. Ibid., p. 43; St. Nicholas minutes, October 24, 1935.

7. Lizabeth Cohen, *Making a New Deal: Industrial Workers in Chicago, 1919–1939* (Cambridge: Cambridge University Press, 1990), p. 247.

8. Kessler-Harris, *Out To Work*, pp. 254–261.

9. Quoted in Ibid., p. 255.

10. Quoted in Cohen, *Making a New Deal*, p. 247.

11. Laura Hapke notes that although thousands of women in families like the Joads worked in the fields, there is only one occasion in Steinbeck's book, described as a dire emergency, when Ma Joad takes up this work. Hapke, *Daughters of the Great Depression: Women, Work, and Fiction in the American 1930s* (Athens: University of Georgia Press, 1995), pp. 19–20, 30, 36.

12. Historian Elaine Tyler May observes that during the depression, "public praise was reserved for self-supporting single women, or for frugal and resourceful homemakers whose domestic endeavors helped their families through the crisis." Elaine Tyler May, *Homeward Bound: American Families in the Cold War Era* (New York: Basic Books, 1988), p. 50.

13. Hapke, *Daughters of the Great Depression*, pp. 18–19, 29–31, and 24–25.

14. Ruth Ferguson Weaver, *Children's Progress: A Study of Some Accomplishments of Day Nurseries in Philadelphia* (Philadelphia: Philadelphia Association of Day Nurseries, 1931), p. 34.

15. Hapke, *Daughters of the Great Depression*, p. 11.

16. Quoted in Susan Ware, *Holding Their Own: American Women in the 1930s* (Boston: Twayne Publishers, 1982), p. 27.

17. Kessler-Harris, *Out To Work*, p. 257; Lois Scharf, *To Work and To Wed: Female Employment, Feminism, and the Great Depression* (Westport, Connecticut: Greenwood Press, 1980), p. 60.

18. NC case 1113.

19. NC case 1079.

20. Hapke, *Daughters of the Great Depression*, p. 7, 30.

21. Weaver, *Children's Progress*, p. 17.

22. NC case 1079.

23. NC case 1106.

24. NC case 1132.

25. NC case 1177.

26. NC case 1069.

27. Jacqueline Jones, *Labor of Love, Labor of Sorrow: Black Women, Work and the Family from Slavery to the Present* (New York: Basic Books, 1985), p. 200.

28. Patricia Hill Collins, "The Meaning of Motherhood in Black Culture and Black Mother-Daughter Relationships," in *Double-Stitch: Black Women Write About Mothers and Daughters*, ed. Patricia Bell-Scott et al. (Boston: Beacon Press, 1991), p. 48; Lucille Abney, "Black Mothers' Perceptions of Their Childrearing Practices from 1945 to 1955: A Cohort of Southern Black Mothers Born in the 1930s" (Ph.D. dissertation, Texas Women's University, 1991).

29. Brenda Clegg Gray, *Black Female Domestics During the Depression in New York City, 1930–1940* (New York: Garland Publishing, 1993), p. 141.

30. Women's Union (WU) case 710/368.

31. WU case 712/370

32. Quoted in Ware, *Holding Their Own*, p. 28

33. *Maytime in Midwinter*, p. 27.

34. Neighborhood Centre minutes of Day Nursery Committee, March 5, 1935.

35. WUDN case 703/361.

36. WUDN case 714/372.

37. Jacqueline Jones reports that by 1935, Philadephia domestics had to work as much as ninety hours a week to earn the same small wages (five to twelve dollars) they had earned for forty-eight to sixty-seven hours of work just three years before. Jones, *Labor of Love, Labor of Sorrow*, p. 207.

38. *Skipping Over 1933* (Report of the Children's Department, Council of Social Agencies, 1933), p. 10.

39. See report of federal Women's Bureau investigator, quoted in Lois Helmbold, "Making Choices, Making Do: Black and White Working-Class Women's Lives and Work During the Great Depression," (Ph.D. dissertation, Stanford University, 1983), p. 247.

40. Bonnie Thornton Dill, *Across the Boundaries of Race and Class: An Exploration of Work and Family Among Black Female Domestic Servants* (New York: Garland Publishing, 1994 [originally published as Ph.D. thesis, 1979]), p. 101.

41. Gray, *Black Female Domestics During the Depression*, p. 61. The practice of turning back the clock was so common that domestic workers were urged to bring their own clocks with them.

42. Helmbold, "Making Choices, Making Do," p. 29.

43. Darlene Clark Hine argues for the emotionally devastating effects of the depression in "The Housewives' League of Detroit: Black Women and Economic Nationalism," in *Visible Women: New Essays on American Activism*, ed. Nancy Hewitt and Suzanne Lebsock (Urbana: University of Illinois Press, 1993), p. 223, although she does not specifically address the issue of mothers' wage-earning.

44. NC case 1357.

45. NC case 1069.

46. NC case 1157.

47. NC case 998.

48. WU case 720/378.

49. NC case 1074.

50. NC case 1069.

51. NC case 1113.

52. WU case 703/361.

53. WU case 703/361.

54. NC case 1111.

55. WU case 714/372.

56. NC case 1069.

57. For instance, the Baldwin Day Nursery reported in 1931 that since there was more work for women than for men in Kensington, fathers instead of mothers were picking children up from the nursery. *Maytime in Midwinter*, p. 13. There were probably more fathers who took on child care duties at least temporarily than show up in these records, since the people who applied to day nurseries were by definition people who had been unable to make satisfactory arrangements for their children. Nevertheless, the assumptions made by these families, and by nursery social workers, about who would naturally take on responsibility for child care shed light on broader patterns.

58. NC case 1091.

59. Quoted in Elizabeth Clark-Lewis, *Living In, Living Out: African American Domestics in Washington, D.C., 1910–1940* (Washington, DC: Smithsonian Institution Press, 1994), pp. 79–80.

60. WU case 163/346. William Wilson may have been another "unusual" father: when his family first came into contact with the nursery, he was described as taking "quite an interest in his home"; he "shares in the housework and cooking when his wife is employed." When he was laid off from his WPA job in December 1936, he planned to care for the children at home. But two months later, his wife applied to readmit the children to the nursery since William was leaving the house regularly to look for work, returning at night drunk. WU case 703/361.

61. "Father is Mother for Day Nursery," *Philadelphia Bulletin*, May 13, 1935.

62. This finding is also supported by Lois Helmbold's study, which found no evidence of "role reversals" between unemployed husbands and employed wives. Helmbold, "Making Choices, Making Do," p. 142. Of course, since the families applying to day nurseries were by definition those who were unable to make other satisfactory arrangements for their children's care, it is possible that unemployed fathers were more involved than this data suggests.

63. NC case 1085.

64. *Maytime in Midwinter*, p. 13.

65. Ibid., p. 21.

66. *Skipping Over 1933*, p. 9.

67. *Maytime in Midwinter*, p. 27. Nurseries that bent this rule included the Baldwin, Frankford, Joy, Jane D. Kent, Lincoln, Salvation Army, and Willing.

68. *In a Nutshell* (Report of the Children's Department of the Council of Social Agencies, 1932), p. 2.

69. *Children, Preferred* (Report of the Children's Department of the Council of Social Agencies, 1930), pp. 45, 33.

70. St. Nicholas minutes, January 23, 1935.

71. "Made Work at Neighborhood Centre," (press release February 27, 1933).

72. *In a Nutshell*, p. 2; *Maytime In Midwinter*, p. 49.

73. *Children, Preferred*, p. 13; *Maytime In Midwinter*, p. 27.

74. NC case 998.

75. NC case 1069.

76. NC case 1091.

77. WU case 106/325.

78. Tinkcom, "Depression and War, 1929–1946," pp. 609–610.

79. Joanne Goodwin, "Work and Welfare: Reinterpreting the Origins of Social Provision for Indigent Mothers," paper presented at the Organization of American Historians meeting, April 1993, p. 6.

80. Mimi Abramowitz, *Regulating the Lives of Women: Social Welfare Policy from Colonial Times to the Present* (Boston: South End Press, 1988); Linda Gordon, "What Does Welfare Regulate?" *Social Research* 55

(Winter 1988), pp. 609–630; Virginia Sapiro, "The Gender Basis of American Social Policy," in *Women, The State, and Welfare*, ed. Linda Gordon (Madison: University of Wisconsin Press, 1990).

81. On women's experiences with WPA projects, see Susan Ware, *Beyond Suffrage: Women in the New Deal* (Boston: Harvard University Press, 1981), pp. 104–110, and Ware, *Holding Their Own*, pp. 39–41.

82. Cohen, *Making a New Deal*, p. 269. Kenneth Cmiel also finds that the Community Chest and the Council of Social Agencies began to exert more control over child welfare agencies in Chicago during the 1930s, solidifying the influence of professional social workers that had been growing since the 1910s. Kenneth Cmiel, *A Home of Another Kind: One Chicago Orphanage and the Tangle of Child Welfare* (Chicago: University of Chicago Press, 1995), p. 112. The Federation of Jewish Charities was the umbrella agency for Jewish welfare agencies (especially those founded by German Jews), while the Welfare Federation was composed mostly of agencies with Protestant background; the Catholic Charities represented a similar effort at centralization, but exercised less control. The Council of Social Agencies, which was closely linked with the Welfare Federation, provided social work expertise and guidelines to the city's child welfare agencies, issued annual reports on child welfare institutions, and played a role in whatever publicity was deemed necessary.

83. The board of the First Day Nursery had particular problems with this ruling, and the Executive Committee of the PADN registered the feeling that each family should be considered separately. First Day Nursery minutes, February 12, 1934, February 11, 1935, March 23, 1935, and April 9, 1935; PADN minutes, April 20, 1934.

84. *Between Ourselves* (Report of the Children's Department of the Council of Social Agencies, 1934), pp. 5–6.

85. *Stepping Stones to Better Citizenship* (Report of the Children's Department of the Council of Social Agencies, 1935), p. 5.

86. Annual Report of the Strawberry Mansion Day Nursery, 1936, p. 1.

87. *Maytime In Midwinter*, pp. 47, 51, 23, 41.

88. Ibid., p. 43.

89. NC case 5001.

90. NC case 1177.

91. NC cases 1132, 1106.

92. NC case 1069.

93. NC case 1091.

94. NC case 5001.

95. NC case 1106.

96. In a 1938 study, social worker Emily Bartlett found that 94% of the families she interviewed preferred WPA work relief to direct relief from the County Relief Board. Emily Bartlett, "WPA Employment As Viewed By the Clients of a Family Agency," *Smith College Studies in Social Work* (March 1938), p. 276.

97. NC case 1111.

98. NC case 1058.

99. NC case 1069.

100. WU case 713/371.

101. WU cases 144/352, 132/348.

102. WU case 163/346.

103. Annette Moser Hodess, "A Study of the History of the WPA Nursery Schools of Boston," (Ed.D. dissertation, Boston University, 1983), p. 26. Funds for other aspects of the nursery schools' operation came from states and local communities.

104. The schools were housed at Wharton Settlement, Southwark Settlement, the House of Industry, and the Germantown Settlement. "4 Schools Cater To Tiny Children," *Philadelphia Inquirer*, August 10, 1934.

105. Yvonne Perry, "Historical Development of Day Care Service at the Wharton Centre," Wharton Centre collection.

106. House of Industry Annual Report, 1935.

107. Press release on the housing project from Public Works Administration, December 8, 1935, in "Organizations—Juniata Park Housing," Newsphotograph Collection, Urban Archives.

108. Memo from Audrey Hardy, January 3, 1936, Box 3; Memo from Grace Langdon, December 9, 1935, Box 5, Records of the Emergency Education Program (EEP), Subject Series 1935–1939, Records of the Works Projects Administration, National Archives.

109. L. R. Alderman to W. H. Smith, December 20, 1933, Box 10, Records of the Federal Emergency Relief Administration (FERA), National Archives.

110. "Summary of Meeting at Washington," May 13, 1939, Folder 291, University House collection, Urban Archives.

111. Beatty, *Preschool Education in America*, pp. 177–184.

112. Ibid., p. 181. A survey by Mary Dabney Davis in 1930 estimated two hundred nursery schools, while the report of the White House Conference on Child Health and Protection in 1931 estimated there were five hundred, including nursery schools combined with kindergartens and "relief" nursery schools. White House Conference on Child Health and Protection, *Nursery Education: A Survey of Day Nurseries, Nursery Schools, and Private Kindergartens in the United States* (New York: Century Company, 1931), p. 10.

113. Indeed, all the WPA educational programs sought to make themselves "indigenous in the states and communities in which it flourishes," rather than establishing a separate federal educational structure. Report of Emergency Education Division of FERA At the End of the First Year of Operation; Report on Educational Program of the WPA As of October 1936, memo from L. R. Alderman to Aubrey Williams, Box 2, Records of the EEP.

114. Julia Wrigley, "Do Young Children Need Intellectual Stimulation? Experts' Advice to Parents, 1900–1985," *History of Education Quarterly* 29, no. 1 (Spring 1989), p. 61.

115. Langdon and Stoddard quotes are found in Beatty, *Preschool Education*, p. 184.

116. Records of the EEP, State Series, 1933–35—Pennsylvania, Box 19. The goal of locating the nursery schools in public school buildings was achieved in about two-thirds of the nursery schools across the country, although in Philadelphia, as in New York and Chicago, almost all the schools were housed in settlement houses. Grace Langdon, "Coordination of Agencies in Carrying on WPA Nursery Schools," *Progressive Education* 15, no. 6 (October 1938), pp. 479–480.

117. Grace Langdon to J. Banks Hudson, June 14, 1938, WPA Box 74.

118. Hodess, "History of the WPA Nursery Schools of Boston," p. 15.

119. Beatty, *Preschool Education*, p. 181.

120. Catherine Landreth, Gladys Gardner, Bettie Eckhardt, and Anne Prugh, "Teacher Child Contacts in Nursery Schools," *Journal of Experimental Education* 12, no. 2 (December 1943), pp. 85–90. The authors were affiliated with the Institute of Child Welfare at the University of California-Berkeley.

121. "Defense Babies," *Philadelphia Bulletin*, October 20, 1941. The story explained that the nursery had initially kept children until the end of their mothers' work day, but the director decided to change to shorter hours so that the children could have more "home life." She explained that working mothers relied on neighbors or made other arrangements to care for their children in the late afternoon hours.

122. Wharton case 19702. The form written up by the social worker categorized her reasons for admitting Howard as "anorexia—child contact."

123. Wharton cases 19701, 19602.

124. House of Industry Annual Report, 1935.

125. Correspondence with Annette Murphy, January 7, 1935; January 10, 1935; and January 24, 1935; Dixon House Nursery School, Folder 289, University House collection.

126. Minutes of Mothers' Club, September 1937–September 1941, Wharton Centre.

127. Langdon, "Coordination of Agencies," p. 474.

128. Folder A-E 1935, Records of the EEP.

129. Hodess, "History of the WPA Nursery Schools of Boston," p. 62; Barbara Harned, "Relationships Among the Federally Sponsored Nursery Schools of the 1930s, the Federally Sponsored Day Care Program of the 1940s, and Project Head Start," (Ph.D. dissertation, Rutgers University, 1968), p. 30.

130. Standards Committee for Employees in WPA Nursery Schools, University House Folder 293.

131. In Boston, for instance, local administrators were satisfied with a two-day training session that taught specific activities rather than nursery school philosophy and pedagogy. Hodess, "History of the WPA Nursery Schools of Boston," p. 66.

132. Claudia Grant to Margaret Stone, February 23, 1943, Wharton Centre.

133. Minutes of the Early Childhood Committee, December 18, 1939, discussing efforts to remove the eighteen-month ruling; letters between Gertrude Kaufman and Annette Murphy, April 29, 1939, Folder 291; September 27, 1940 WPA to Murphy, Folder 293; Nursery School parents to Dr. Lewis Rohrbaugh, January 11, 1940 about deletion of Ruth Dick and Sadie Bynum; all in University House Box 31.

134. Perry, "Historical Development of Day Care Service at the Wharton Centre."

135. William Henry Welsh to headworker of Wharton Centre, May 12, 1934.

136. Welsh to headworker, July 9, 1934.

137. Wharton Centre Folder 8, Box 1.

138. House of Industry Annual Report, 1935.

139. Ibid., 1937.

140. Mothers' Club minutes, September 20, 1939; December 6, 1939, December 13, 1939, and December 15, 1939, Wharton Centre. Early Childhood Education Committee, June 19, 1940, Dixon House, Folder 293.

141. Conference Summary—Dixon House Pre-School Group, June 26, 1939; Minutes of Preschool Sponsoring Committee February 13, 1940; Report to Early Childhood Education Committee on Dixon House Sponsoring Committee; Sponsoring Committee to Medaglia D'Oro Coffee Company October 15, 1940; Julia Abbott to Annette Murphy April 17, 1941; Florence Kerr to Robert Hetler May 24, 1941; Annette Murphy to Colonel Philip Mathews June 26, 1941; Charles Mechiorre to Annette Murphy July 1, 1941; and Murphy to Robert Nedtler July 3, 1941, Dixon House.

142. The Germantown, Southwark, and Kensington High School nursery schools all had active sponsoring committees. Minutes of Early Childhood Committee, June 19, 1940, Dixon House.

143. "Kensington Nursery School," *Philadelphia Inquirer*, March 11, 1940.

144. The committee also discussed ways to revoke the rule limiting employment of nursery school teachers to 18 months; they finally decided to ask the National Association of Early Childhood Education to draft an amendment and present it to Congress at the proper time. Meeting of Early Childhood Committee WPA, January 22, 1940, and February 19, 1940, Dixon House.

145. Agenda for Early Childhood Education meeting March 17, 1941, Dixon House.

146. Wharton Centre, for instance, transformed its nursery school into a day nursery supported by private funds from the settlement and the city's Community Chest when the WPA finally cut off all funding in 1942.

147. "Kensington Nursery School Teaches Mothers, Too," *Philadelphia Bulletin*, July 16, 1943.

Chapter 6

1. Gwendolyn Mink, *The Wages of Motherhood: Inequality in the Welfare State, 1917–1942* (Ithaca, New York: Cornell University Press, 1995), p. 156.

2. Lenroot to public relations firm for Jacksonville cigar plant, September 13, 1939; Lenroot to

president of Florida Congress of Parents and Teachers, September 29, 1939; Elizabeth Woodruff Clark to Lenroot, July 11, 1940; Lenroot to Clark, August 5, 1940. File 4-9-10, Box 114, Records of the Children's Bureau (hereafter CB).

3. Grace Abbott, acceptance speech at awarding of medal by the National Institute of Social Sciences, 1931. Quoted in Kriste Lindenmeyer, *"A Right to Childhood": The U.S. Children's Bureau and Child Welfare, 1912–1946* (Urbana: University of Illinois Press, 1997), pp. 175-176.

4. Unpublished summary of conference on day care for children of working mothers, November 14, 1941, CB Box 114.

5. March 5, 1942, statement from Mary Anderson, Office Files of the Director, 1918–1948, Government, Box 21, "Children's Bureau" file. Records of the Women's Bureau, Department of Labor, National Archives. Anderson may have been paraphrasing Secretary of Labor Frances Perkins, whose words on the subject are quoted in a Children's Bureau policy statement, "Policies Regarding the Employment of Mothers of Young Children in Occupations Essential to the National Defense," January 26, 1942, in the same folder.

6. Memo from Bessie Trout to Katharine Lenroot, August 10, 1944, CB Box 116. Emphasis in original.

7. Angelo Patri, "Children Look for Mother's Affection," *Philadelphia Evening Bulletin*, October 18, 1943. This advice column was placed strategically next to a story about how mothers were making ends meet through part-time work and other strategies when their husbands were serving in the military. For more on Patri, a nationally syndicated columnist whose parenting advice was popular, see Robert Griswold, *Fatherhood in America: A History* (New York: Basic Books, 1993).

8. Quoted in Elaine Tyler May, *Homeward Bound: American Families in the Cold War Era* (New York: Basic Books, 1988), p. 74. Emphasis in original.

9. Emma Lundberg to Elizabeth Clark, April 6, 1942, CB Box 114.

10. Susan B. Anthony II, *Out of the Kitchen—And Into the War: Women's Winning Role in the Nation's Drama* (New York: Stephen Daye, 1943), pp. 135–136.

11. Sonya Michel, "American Women and the Discourse of the Democratic Family," in *Behind the Lines: Gender and the Two World Wars*, ed. Margaret Higgonet (New Haven, Connecticut: Yale University Press, 1989), pp. 155–157.

12. Children's Bureau, *A Children's Charter in Wartime* (Bureau Publication No. 283), p. 1.

13. Linda Kerber coined this term in "The Republican Mother: Women and the Enlightenment—An American Perspective," *American Quarterly* 28 (1976), pp. 187–205, and *Women of the Republic: Intellect and Ideology in Revolutionary America* (Chapel Hill: University of North Carolina Press, 1980). For critique of Kerber's emphasis on motherhood in the immediate post-Revolutionary period, see Jan Lewis, "The Republican Wife: Virtue and Seduction in the Early Republic," *William and Mary Quarterly* 44 (October 1987), p. 690.

14. Linda Kerber, "A Constitutional Right to be Treated Like American Ladies: Women and the Obligations of Citizenship," in *U.S. History As Women's History: New Feminist Essays*, ed. Linda Kerber, Alice Kessler-Harris, and Kathryn Kish Sklar (Chapel Hill: University of North Carolina Press, 1995), pp. 23, 31.

15. Katharine Lenroot to Secretary of Labor, November 5, 1943, CB Box 116. The child care centers at the Kaiser shipyards were generally of very high quality, following or exceeding standards established by child welfare experts, and conducted by specialists in child development and nursery education who had been recommended by the Children's Bureau. But their primary commitment to facilitating mothers' employment put them at odds with the bureau on this issue. See Amy Kesselman, *Fleeting Opportunities: Women Shipyard Workers in Portland and Vancouver During World War II and Reconversion* (Albany: State University of New York Press, 1990), pp. 75–86, and interview with Lois Meek Stolz in James Hymes, Jr., *Early Childhood Education Living History Interviews—Book 2: Care of the Children of Working Mothers* (Carmel, California: Hacienda Press, 1978), pp. 27–56. Stolz explained that she had initially wanted to restrict the centers to serving children older

than two, but the need for care was so great that she decided to lower the admission age to eighteen months.

16. The conference, held in 1944, adopted a policy statement: "Policy of the Children's Bureau on the Care of Infants Whose Mothers Are Employed," December 1, 1944, CB Box 114.

17. Emma Lundberg, "A Community Program of Day Care for Children of Mothers Employed in Defense Areas," December 1941, Box 3, Records of U.S. Office of Education, National Archives.

18. Barbara Gray, "Child Care Problems of Forty-Six Working Mothers," (M.A. thesis, Smith College School of Social Work, 1943), quoted in Michel, "American Women and the Discourse of the Democratic Family," p. 165.

19. Children's Bureau, *Proceedings of Conference on Day Care of Children of Working Mothers, With Special Reference to Defense Areas, Held in Washington, D.C. July 31 and August 1, 1941* (Bureau publication no. 281, Washington, D.C. 1942), pp. 30–31.

20. Ibid., p. 32.

21. Report on meeting held in Harrisburg, January 9, 1942, Neighborhood Centre.

22. Report on the conference of the National Association for Nursery Education, held October 1941. December 1941 report to the Nursery School Committee, Neighborhood Centre.

23. Memo from Evelyn Wood to Bessie Trout, July 4, 1945, CB Box 115.

24. Anthony, *Out of the Kitchen*, p. 130.

25. Karen Anderson, *Wartime Women: Sex Roles, Family Relations, and the Status of Women During World War II* (Westport, Connecticut: Greenwood Press, 1981), p. 124. The Women's Bureau Advisory Committee policy statement, January 22, 1942, is in "Policies Regarding the Employment of Mothers of Young Children," Children's Bureau folder, Box 21, Office Files of the Director, 1918–1948, Women's Bureau records.

26. Susan Hartmann, *The Home Front and Beyond: American Women in the 1940s* (Boston: Twayne Publishers, 1982), p. 58.

27. Report of meeting held January 9, 1942, in Harrisburg, Neighborhood Centre.

28. Lundberg, "Community Program of Day Care," p. 17. At the Harrisburg meeting, Maud Morlock also suggested that day care was needed by skilled and professional workers as well as by "the economically undeprivileged."

29. Lundberg, "Community Program of Day Care." Others also expressed the hope that the war would be an opportunity to get public schools to take responsibility for preschool children. At the Children's Bureau's 1941 conference on day care, social work educator Edith Abbott argued forcefully for the need to make day care a free service provided by the schools, although her position that parents should not be required to pay a fee was disputed by others in attendance. Katharine Lenroot explained, "We don't want in any way to break down the idea that education, free public education, has responsibility for the preschool child," but also felt that parents should bear part of the expense. CB, *Proceedings of Conference on Day Care*, pp. 51–58.

30. "Memorandum on Responsibilities of Schools and Social Agencies," October 24, 1944, CB Box 114.

31. Although the First and Sunnyside Day Nursery remained an active member of the PADN, it was no longer really a day nursery: the difference in its program distanced the agency from the concerns of the institutional day nurseries and brought it into closer alliance with other child welfare organizations who were quite critical of conventional day nurseries. The nursery was the first in the country to be admitted to membership in the Child Welfare League of America and remained the only one out of the Philadelphia nurseries to be represented in that organization during the war years. First and Sunnyside Day Nursery (FSDN) minutes, June 7, 1932.

32. For instance, in December 1928 the agency's social worker reported to the board that "the work now really consists more of a Bureau for Working Mothers than a day nursery, as nearly as much work is done on cases not taken as those that are." She described a mother with two children whom she persuaded not to go out to work, instead taking in boarders and keeping the chil-

dren with her at home. "In some cases," she reported, "it would be easier to take the children than to make these adjustments, but that does not mean lasting help." In 1929 she explained that in about half the cases of women applying for child care, a "more suitable plan" was found. Minutes of FSDN, December 3, 1928, and February 4, 1929.

33. FSDN Annual Report, 1942.

34. Ibid., 1943.

35. Ibid., 1945.

36. Ibid., 1944.

37. Mary Rogers to John Dawson, December 10, 1945, FSDN.

38. Minutes of PADN Executive Committee, June 15, 1942, Box 1, Folder 15.

39. Lynn Weiner, *From Working Girl to Working Mother: The Female Labor Force in the United States, 1820–1980* (Chapel Hill: University of North Carolina Press, 1985), p. 111.

40. Employer-sponsored day care does not seem to have existed in Philadelphia; no mention of any industry-sponsored day care center was made in any records of the PADN, reports of the public day care program, or newspaper articles about day care during the war. Frieda Miller of the Women's Bureau explained in a 1951 letter that there were only a handful of employer-run child care facilities in the country during the war, although employers sometimes contributed financially to the operating costs of community-run day care centers. Frieda Miller to Margaret Ackroyd (Rhode Island Department of Labor), February 16, 1951. Folder 3-1-2-4-2, Box 28, General Correspondence, Office of the Director, Women's Bureau.

41. Day care teachers were often invited to celebrations when new ships were launched from the yards and displayed their role in the production process by christening the ship with champagne. Hymes, *Early Childhood Education Living History Interviews*, pp. 46–47.

42. Ethel Beer, "Help Mothers Win the War," *The Trained Nurse and Hospital Review* 108, no. 3 (March 1942).

43. Maureen Honey, *Creating Rosie the Riveter: Class, Gender and Propaganda During World War II* (Amherst: University of Massachusetts Press, 1984), pp. 89–91.

44. Robert Westbrook, "Fighting for the American Family: Private Interests and Political Obligation in World War II," in *The Power of Culture: Critical Essays in American History*, ed. Richard Wightman Fox and T. J. Jackson Lears (Chicago: University of Chicago Press, 1993), p. 203 and passim. Robert Griswold makes a similar argument in *Fatherhood in America*, p. 164. For examples of how women's war work was cast as an obligation to their men, see Honey, *Creating Rosie the Riveter*, pp. 126–128.

45. Westbrook, "Fighting for the American Family," p. 213.

46. Honey, *Creating Rosie the Riveter*, pp. 49–50, 78–79.

47. Ibid., pp. 130–137. Government directives specifically instructed magazine writers to focus on recruiting women with children over the age of fourteen for war work.

48. Ibid., pp. 54–55.

49. For the argument that most women workers would have entered the work force even without the war, and that most went to work to seize opportunities rather than out of patriotism, see Alice Kessler-Harris, *Out to Work: A History of Wage-Earning Women in the United States* (New York: Oxford University Press, 1982), pp. 276–279.

50. Fanny Christina Hill, quoted in Sherna Gluck, *Rosie the Riveter Revisited: Women, The War, and Social Change* (Boston: Twayne Publishers, 1987), p. 23.

51. "Mothers, Ready for Jobs, Welcome First 'War Nursery,'" *Philadelphia Evening Bulletin*, February 7, 1942.

52. Howard Dratch, "The Politics of Child Care in the 1940s," *Science and Society* 38 (Summer 1974), p. 197.

53. Honey, *Creating Rosie the Riveter*, p. 81.

54. Ibid., p. 191.

55. Press release from the United War Chest, n.d. *Philadelphia Bulletin* clipping collection, Urban Archives.

56. Emma Lundberg to Florence Thorne, AFL, November 6, 1942, asking her to send letter from her office to presidents of affiliated unions; similar letter to CIO; internal CB memo May 7, 1943, enclosing list of unions to be included in a conference of organized labor to consider day care problems (this conference did not materialize). CB Box 114.

57. UAW to affiliated unions of UAW-CIO, 6/10/43, CB Box 116. Later that year, the union wrote to the Children's Bureau for information that would help some of their locals start child care centers. UAW to CB, 12/1/43, CB Box 114.

58. Anthony, *Out of the Kitchen*, pp. 135–136.

59. Dratch, "Politics of Child Care," p. 185.

60. Congress of Women's Auxiliaries of the CIO, Third Annual Conference, November 4, 1943, in CB Box 114. Unions represented at this conference included the United Auto Workers, The United Federal Workers of America, the United Electrical Workers, and National Miners' Union, and the Textile Workers' Union; the auxiliary women were not themselves workers.

61. Dratch, "Politics of Child Care," p. 185.

62. Susan Hartmann, "Women's Organizations During World War II: The Interaction of Class, Race and Feminism," in *Women's Being, Woman's Place: Female Identity and Vocation in American History*, ed. Mary Kelly (Boston: G. K. Hall, 1980), p. 321.

63. Michel, "American Women and the Discourse of the Democratic Family," p. 166.

64. Anthony, *Out of the Kitchen*, p. 3.

65. Ibid., p. 130.

66. Dratch, "Politics of Child Care," p. 177.

67. Hartmann, *Home Front and Beyond*, p. 84.

68. Report of National Commission for Young Children, October 1943, Records of the Office of Community War Services (OCWS), National Archives, Box 3.

69. This was in May 1942. Donald Davis to H. F. Alves, U.S. Department of Education, April 14, 1942; Sara Walsh, Teachers Union of Philadelphia to Martha Wood, Children's Bureau, July 25, 1942, Office of Education Box 3.

70. "Child Care Center Plan Expanded," *Philadelphia Bulletin*, December 28, 1943.

71. *Journal of the Board of Education*, December 27, 1943, pp. 369–371.

72. School District of Philadelphia, "Child Care Centers: Report of Twenty Years of Operation, 1944 to 1964," Urban Archives. The *Annual Report of the Board of Public Education, School District of Philadelphia* shows that in 1944 and 1945, the city appropriation covered 15% of the total budget for the day care centers, while the federal appropriation accounted for 64% in 1944 and only 44% in 1945.

73. "Mothers, Ready for War Jobs, Welcome First 'War Nursery,' *Philadelphia Evening Bulletin*, December 7, 1942.

74. Tinkcom, "Depression and War," p. 642.

75. "Child Care Fund Boosted $83,652," *Philadelphia Bulletin*, August 16, 1944.

76. "City To Get $152,862 U.S. Child Care Aid," *Philadelphia Bulletin*, January 19, 1945.

77. School District, "Child Care Centers," p. 19.

78. The board closed one center, moved six into more adequate quarters, and opened ten new centers.

79. School District, "Child Care Centers," p. 1.

80. Anderson, *Wartime Women*, p. 133.

81. Emily Cahan, *Past Caring: A History of U.S. Preschool Care and Education for the Poor, 1920–1965* (National Center for Children in Poverty, Columbia University, 1989), p. 42–46. By contrast, the Kaiser centers served about 22% of employee families needing child care, thus suggesting that parental hesitation to use day care centers could be overcome. Kesselman, *Fleeting Opportunities*, p. 87.

82. Hymes, *Early Childhood Education Living History Interviews*, p. 10.

83. Kesselman, *Fleeting Opportunities*, p. 84.

84. Fact sheet on "Good Child Care," OCWS Box 3.

85. *Journal of the Board of Education*, December 27, 1943, p. 370. Federal guidelines specified that parents' fees, along with local contributions, had to defray at least 50% of the day care centers' operating costs; these fees were calculated according to parents' employment and marital status. FWA Administrator, War Public Services Letter No. 8 ("Policies Governing Review of Lanham Applications for Services for Children"), Office of Education Box 3. In the Philadelphia centers, the same amount was charged to families where both parents were employed and to families where the mother was employed and the father was in the service; mothers who were the sole supporters of children were charged less. School District, "Child Care Centers," pp. 6-7.

86. Anthony, *Out of the Kitchen*, pp. 142–143.

87. Response to questionnaire sent out by the National Commission for Young Children, August 8, 1942, OCWS Box 3.

88. The bill thus built on the Children's Bureau's longstanding preference for state rather than federal programs, and their ties to state departments of welfare. On this preference, see Linda Gordon, *Pitied But Not Entitled: Single Mothers and the History of Welfare* (New York: The Free Press, 1995), p. 101.

89. Dratch, "Politics of Child Care," pp. 181–182.

90. "Mothers and Children Come First in Good Community Day Care Programs," May 11, 1944, CB Box 114.

91. Wharton Settlement Annual Report, 1942 and 1944, Box 1, Folder 1A.

92. A 1942 guide to prioritizing needs for admittance to the Day Nursery put family needs before the emotional needs of the child and put a family's economic needs before other types of needs. Box 2, folder 7, "Neighborhood Centre Day Nursery Policies," November 13, 1942.

93. Speech of outgoing president, Strawberry Mansion Day Nursery (SMDN) annual meeting, June 12, 1945.

94. FSDN Board meeting minutes, annual meeting minutes, 1943.

95. Karen Anderson argues that African-American women were generally more responsive to the call for war workers than were white women. Anderson, *Wartime Women*, p. 39

96. SMDN Annual Report, 1941.

97. FSDN Annual Report, 1942, p. 2.

98. Ibid., 1943, p. 3.

99. "Presenting Neighborhood Centre," January 1943, February 1944, and October 1944, Series 1, Box 2, Folder 7, Neighborhood Centre.

100. Wharton case 19210/639.

101. Wharton case 19308/650.

102. Wharton case 19421/677. Ultimately the mother decided to go on Mothers' Assistance and stay home from work. For similar concerns, see also Wharton cases 20303/737 and 22205/864.

103. Wharton case 22003/829.

104. Wharton case 19406/663.

105. NC case 1381.

106. Wharton case 22302/868.

107. This article appeared in the *Philadelphia Evening Bulletin*, October 18, 1943.

108. NC case 1366.

109. Twenty-eight percent were born in Philadelphia; 15% in Virginia; 15% in North Carolina; 12% in South Carolina; 8% in Georgia, 3% in Florida, Maryland, Texas, and New Jersey; and less than 3% in Pennsylvania, Alabama, New York, Illinois, Kentucky, Louisiana, Delaware, Missouri, West Virginia, Canada, Ohio, Liberia, and the West Indies. By contrast, of the thirty-nine people applying to Neighborhood Centre who listed a birthplace, 54% were natives of Philadelphia and another 19% were born in New York, New Jersey, Illinois, or Michigan; 15% were born in Russia, 5% in Germany, and 3% each in England, Hungary, and Turkey.

110. Wharton case 21202/798.

111. Wharton case 22007/833.

112. Wharton case 19415/671.

113. NC case 1397.

114. Wharton case 20503/752.

115. Wharton case 22410/886.

116. FSDN Annual Report, 1943, p. 3.

117. These figures are based on the social worker's contact with the Social Service Exchange for 268 cases during the war years and 128 cases during the 1930s.

118. Memo from Bessie Trout to Katharine Lenroot, August 10, 1944, CB Box 116.

119. FSDN visitors' reports, October 1943–November 1944.

120. One family (NC case 1407) had hired a practical nurse to help with the children, but found her unsatisfactory; when they withdrew the children from Neighborhood Centre, they sent them instead to a private nursery school and kindergarten. Another family (NC case 1284) considered sending their child to Temple University's nursery school instead of Neighborhood Centre's.

121. Wharton case 19409/666.

122. NC case 1347.

123. Wharton case 19804/688.

124. Wharton case 19901/690.

125. Wharton case 22302/868.

126. Wharton case 21908/820.

127. NC case 1315.

128. NC case 1284.

129. Wharton case 22002/828.

130. Wharton case 23002/934. See also Wharton case 22008/834.

131. Wharton case 22207/866.

132. Wharton case 19416/672.

133. Wharton case 20807/778.

134. William Chafe, in *The American Woman: Her Changing Social, Economic, and Political Roles, 1920–1970* (New York: Oxford University Press, 1972), argued that the war represented a turning-point in ideas about women's paid work. Works such as Anderson, *Wartime Women*, Kessler-Harris, *Out To Work*, and Leila Rupp, *Mobilizing Women for War: German and American Propaganda, 1939–1945* (Princeton: Princeton University Press, 1978) tend to emphasize the more conservative impact of the war on women's roles.

Chapter 7

1. See the essays collected in *Not June Cleaver: Women and Gender in Postwar America, 1945–1960*, ed. Joanne Meyerowitz (Philadephia: Temple University Press, 1994).

2. "What About Day Nurseries?" *Philadelphia Bulletin*, June 2, 1948.

3. Summary of Meeting of Social Workers and Supervisors of Day Nurseries, August 28, 1945, Neighborhood Centre.

4. PADN minutes, October 16, 1945.

5. In contrast to the child care campaign in California, which was spearheaded and coordinated by early childhood educators, directors of day care centers, and welfare agency staff, such professionals do not seem to have played a leading role in the Philadelphia protests. On the California campaign, see Ellen Reese, "Maternalism and Political Mobilization: How California's Postwar Child Care Campaign Was Won," *Gender and Society* 10, no. 5 (October 1996), p. 573.

6. "Mothers Appeal for Child Care," *Philadelphia Bulletin*, August 30, 1945.

7. "Women Threaten March on Council," *Philadelphia Bulletin*, September 6, 1945.

8. "Mothers Heckle City Council," *Philadelphia Bulletin*, September 13, 1945.

9. "$65,000 To Be Asked for Child Care: Council Member Will Seek Grant as Result of Mothers' Demands," *Philadelphia Bulletin*, September 14, 1945. In making this demand for public school adoption, Bloomfield echoed the demands of women in the United Electrical Workers of America (UE) who resolved at a convention in 1944, "A real child care program for peacetime must become an integral part of our nation's school system." Howard Dratch, "The Politics of Child Care in the 1940s," *Science and Society* 38 (Summer 1974), p. 187.

10. "City Lacks Funds for Child Centers," *Philadelphia Bulletin*, September 15, 1945.

11. "Child Care Centers" editorial, *Philadelphia Bulletin*, September 15, 1945.

12. National-level protests included resolutions passed by groups like the Chicago War Service Corps, which called for the continuation of day care funding in September 1945 since servicemen's wives still needed to support their families, and other women were needed for reconversion and were "the support of their families" just as in the war period. September 24, 1945, resolution, CB Box 115. The executive director of the Child Welfare League of America wrote and met with President Truman, referring to forty-four communities where children would suddenly be without day care and calling for the extension of federal funding. Howard Hopkirk to President Truman, September 28, 1945, CB Box 115. Parents' protests in New York City and in Toronto were also successful in keeping day care centers open in those cities. See Lynn Weiner, *From Working Girl to Working Mother: The Female Labor Force in the United States, 1820–1980* (Chapel Hill: University of North Carolina Press, 1985), p. 136; Dratch, "The Politics of Child Care"; and Susan Prentice, "Militant Mothers in Domestic Times: Toronto's Postwar Childcare Struggle" (Ph.D. dissertation, York University, 1993).

13. "Demonstrating for Child Care Centers Here," *Philadelphia Bulletin*, October 11, 1945; "Child Centers Reprived Till March 1 by U.S. Aid," *Philadelphia Bulletin*, October 12, 1945

14. Mrs. Albert Nalle to Frederic Garman, City Council, November 30, 1945, Wharton Collection. Emphasis in original.

15. "Care Center Funds Voted for Vets' Children Only," *Philadelphia Bulletin*, November 16, 1945.

16. "Council Will Drop Nursery Limit," *Philadelphia Bulletin*, December 10, 1945.

17. The rates, which used to range from $1.80 to $3 a week for one child, would now range from $2 to $7 a week, depending on family income. "Education Board Set To Carry On Child Care Plans," *Philadelphia Bulletin*, January 29, 1946. Centers at the Wharton Settlement and at the Tasker and Johnson housing projects were closed, leaving a total of thirteen operating in the city. Add Anderson of the Board of Education explained that it was felt that private community agencies could carry on the work of these centers. This only actually happened in two cases: Wharton's day care program continued with funding from the settlement and the Community Chest, and the Westside Day Care Center was taken over by Salvation Army, later dropped, and then continued temporarily by a community group that in 1950 was successful in persuading the public day care program to take over the center once again. PADN minutes, September 12, 1946, June 23, 1949; *Child Care Chat* [newsletter of the Pennsylvania Department of Welfare's child care consultant], June 1950, St. Nicholas, Box 2.

18. "$75,000 Child Care Fund Is Sought," *Philadelphia Bulletin*, May 23, 1946; *Journal of the Board of Education*, June 27, 1946, p. 167.

19. "School Aid Centers Fought," *Philadelphia Bulletin*, April 2, 1947. Obermayer wrote to the Children's Bureau in February 1947 asking how many Boards of Education had terminated child care centers and what agency took them over. Obermayer to Children's Bureau, February 6, 1947.

20. In addition to the mothers' protest, the Teachers Union of Philadelphia also voiced opposition to closing the centers, as did parents and social workers of the South Philadelphia Coordinating Council, who pointed out that all the centers had waiting lists. "20 Reassured on Child Centers," *Philadelphia Bulletin*, June 18, 1947; "Mothers Press Plea to Council," *Philadelphia Bulletin*, June 19, 1947; "Closing of Child Centers Assailed by Civic Group," *Philadelphia Bulletin*, June 21, 1947.

21. "150 Mothers Besiege City Hall To Win Child Care Fund Pledge," *Philadelphia Bulletin*, April 22, 1948.

22. "What About Day Nurseries?" *Philadelphia Bulletin*, June 2, 1948.

23. *Journal of the Board of Education*, June 10, 1947; July 1, 1947; June 8, 1948; September 14, 1948; and December 14, 1948.

24. FFDCA President's report, June 13, 1949; PADN minutes, June 23, 1949.

25. Leah Gingrich to Evelyn Smith, September 13, 1949, CB Box 409.

26. *Journal of the City Council*, November 14, 1949 and November 13, 1950; earlier appropriations from the Mayor's special fund can be seen in budgets approved on December 13, 1945 and November 12, 1946.

27. During a PADN meeting in 1949, someone referred specifically to a day care center parents' association, saying, "The parents' association of the Public Day Care Centers has been very active and will do all that it can." PADN minutes, June 23, 1949. The mothers, however, never identified themselves as part of an organization in any of the press coverage about the protests. In California, child care workers helped mobilize parents, holding meetings about day care legislation, organizing parents' associations, and organizing potluck dinners during which mothers could write letters and send telegrams to public officials (while teachers watched the children). A similar process may have been at work in Philadelphia, although no evidence of it remains. Reese, "Maternalism and Political Mobilization," p. 574. Photographs of the demonstrations show a racially mixed group, with white women in the majority.

28. On the food demonstrations and rent strikes, see articles in *Philadelphia Bulletin* clipping file, May 11, 1946–July 27, 1946. They mention the Consumers and Tenants League, which was formed to combat soaring prices, and show members of different labor unions in the city protesting high prices, as well as a female member of the Communist Party carrying a petition to save the Office of Price Adjustment . There was also at least one meat boycott during the war, in August 1942. Fredric Miller, Morris Vogel, and Allen Davis, *Philadelphia Stories: A Photographic History, 1920–1960* (Philadelphia: Temple University Press, 1988), p. 132.

29. Annelise Orleck, *Common Sense and a Little Fire: Women and Working-Class Politics in the United States, 1900–1965* (Chapel Hill: University of North Carolina Press, 1995), pp. 267–269.

30. Amy Swerdlow, "The Congress of American Women: Left-Feminist Peace Politics in the Cold War," in Meyerowitz, ed., *Not June Cleaver*, pp. 296–312.

31. "What About Day Nurseries?" *Philadelphia Bulletin*, June 2, 1948.

32. "Readers Favor Continuing City's Child Day Care Centers," *Philadelphia Bulletin*, June 13, 1948.

33. California was the only state that continued a sizable program, with 288 centers operated as of February 1949; Massachusetts only had four state-funded centers in 1948; New York City had 91 centers as of August 1949, and Washington, D.C., and Detroit were each operating six centers. Evelyn Smith to Mrs. Felix Gentile, CB Box 407.

34. *Handbook, School District of Philadelphia, The Board of Public Education*, 1944–49; *Annual Report of the Board of Public Education, School District of Philadelphia*, 1944–59. Archives of the School District of Philadelphia.

35. "For Working Mothers," *Philadelphia Daily News*, April 14, 1958, Strawberry Mansion Day Nursery collection. Tellingly, while coverage of struggles over day care funding in the 1940s had been reported in the front section of the newspaper, this series of stories was published in the Women Today section. The only other local press coverage of day care I have located was in 1951, when there was national concern about mobilizing for defense production for the Korean War, although the story itself does not refer to any special wartime needs, nor to the public protests over funding the day care centers. "Care Center Keeps Boys and Girls Busy, Happy and Healthy While Mothers Work," *Philadelphia Bulletin*, January 21, 1951.

36. Wharton Centre Day Nursery Auxiliary Committee, November 2, 1949. A thirteenth center was added in 1950, when the Westside Center, which had originally been one of the public centers, was again adopted by the public day care program.

37. Enrollment was 1,085 in 1945 and reached 1,111 in 1952, growing to 1,188 by 1963. School District

of Philadelphia, "Child Care Centers: Report of Twenty Years of Operation, 1944 to 1964," p. 19. Urban Archives.

38. In 1949 program director Leah Gingrich told a group at the Wharton Center that the existing centers were not adequate to meet the demand for child care. Wharton Centre Day Nursery Auxiliary Committee, November 2, 1949.

39. "Finding Good Day Care Centers Is Working Mothers' Problem," *Philadelphia Bulletin*, September 3, 1957.

40. School District, "Child Care Centers," pp. 32–33.

41. *Annual Report of the Board of Public Education, School District of Philadelphia*, 1944–1959. Parents' fees made up 15% of the budget of thirteen day nurseries listed in the annual report of the Council on Social Agencies in 1940 and 16% in 1941. Report of the Children's Department of the Council on Social Agencies, 1940, 1941. A 1957 study of the Strawberry Mansion Day Nursery showed that parents' fees made up 30% of its budget in 1953, but only 18% in 1956, as lower-income families started making use of the nursery.

42. St. Nicholas minutes, April 1955.

43. Nancy Fraser, "Struggle Over Needs: Outline of a Socialist-Feminist Critical Theory of Late-Capitalist Political Culture," in *Women, the State, and Welfare*, ed. Linda Gordon (Madison: University of Wisconsin Press, 1990), p. 199.

44. NC case 1501. Parents did organize and protest when the Nursery School was being shut down in 1942 in order to reestablish a Day Nursery at the settlement. Perhaps parents were more likely to protest the replacement of an educational program with a custodial one than to demand the continuation of a custodial program.

45. Rose Bloomfield to Katharine Lenroot, August 31, 1945, and Michael Weintraub to CB, September 6, 1945, CB Box 117.

46. Mrs. Max Weintraub to CB, September 7, 1945, CB Box 117. Mrs. Weintraub was probably related to Michael Weintraub: in addition to sharing the same last name, these two letters appear to have been written on the same typewriter and were sent within a few days of each other.

47. Daisy Glass to Katharine Lenroot, September 5, 1945, CB Box 117.

48. Rose Bloomfield to Katharine Lenroot, August 31, 1945, CB Box 117.

49. One of the placards at the 1945 demonstration read, "American Legion—Why have you neglected our pleas and letters to Congress to support child care centers?" Photographs of demonstrations on October 11, 1945, and April 22, 1948, Newsphotograph Collection, Urban Archives.

50. "Readers Favor Continuing City's Child Day Care Centers," *Philadelphia Bulletin*, June 13, 1948.

51. For instance, Leah Gingrich's comments to a community group in 1946, and Mrs. Albert Nalle's (of the Council of Social Agencies) plea to City Council to extend funding for the day care centers through 1946 both used this language. "Group Fights Closing Child Care Centers," *Philadelphia Bulletin*, November 19, 1946; Mrs. Albert Nalle to Frederic Garman, City Council, November 30, 1945, Wharton Centre. Emphasis in original.

52. Minutes of the PADN, June 23, 1949.

53. Minutes of the PADN, January 30, 1951.

54. Benjamin Spock, *Baby and Child Care* (New York: Duell, Sloan & Pearce, 1945), pp. 569–570.

55. For instance, in response to a 1945 letter, Katharine Lenroot explained that government aid was not generous enough to replace mothers' wages, nor did everyone accept the idea of subsititing aid for wages. Nevertheless, she wrote of working with labor unions to "develop educational materials which will reemphasize the importance of the contribution made by the mother in the home, as well as developing measures that are needed to provide the best possible means of caring for children when mothers must be employed." Response to letter from Dr. James Wilson, July 18, 1945, CB Box 115.

56. "Readers Favor Continuing City's Child Day Care Centers," *Philadelphia Bulletin*, June 13, 1948.

57. Ibid.

58. Wharton case 23003/935.

59. Wharton case 21901/814.

60. "Readers Favor Continuing City's Child Day Care Centers," *Philadelphia Bulletin*, June 13, 1948.

61. Negatives from April 22, 1948, demonstration, Newsphotograph collection, Urban Archives.

62. "150 Mothers Besiege City Hall To Win Child Care Fund Pledge," *Philadelphia Bulletin*, April 22, 1948.

63. School District, "Child Care Centers," p. 31. Gingrich also saw widespread fears of juvenile delinquency as an explanation for the gradual rise in the age of children attending the public centers. In the early years of the program, preschoolers had made up two-thirds of the children attending the centers, but the proportions gradually shifted, so that by 1964 school-age children were in the majority. School District, "Child Care Centers," p. 19.

64. Rose Bloomfield to Katharine Lenroot, August 31, 1945, CB Box 117.

65. Tregua Mack to Katharine Lenroot, September 6, 1945, CB Box 117.

66. Elaine Tyler May, *Homeward Bound: American Families in the Cold War Era* (New York: Basic Books, 1988), p. 149, 142.

67. Quoted in Alice Kessler-Harris, *Out to Work: A History of Wage-Earning Women in the United States* (New York: Oxford University Press, 1982), p. 302.

68. Agnes Meyer, "Women Aren't Men," *Atlantic* 186 (1950), pp. 32–36; Adlai Stevenson, commencement address at Smith College, 1955, Smith College Archives; both reprinted in Ruth Barnes Moynihan, Cynthia Russett, and Laurie Crumpacker, *Second To None: A Documentary History of American Women*, Volume 2 (Lincoln: University of Nebraska Press, 1993), pp. 240–245.

69. Nancy Pottishman Weiss, "Mother, the Invention of Necessity: Dr. Benjamin Spock's *Baby and Child Care*," *American Quarterly* 29 (Winter 1977), p. 533.

70. Maureen Honey, *Creating Rosie the Riveter: Class, Gender and Propaganda During World War II* (Amherst: University of Massachusetts Press, 1984), pp. 56, 124.

71. Weiner, *From Working Girl to Working Mother*, pp. 114–115.

72. Spock, *Baby and Child Care*, p. 569.

73. May, *Homeward Bound*, p. 140.

74. Throughout 1951, child welfare professionals and day care planners met to discuss how to address the new wartime need for child care. The Children's Bureau held a conference on "planning for day care and extended services in areas affected by defense mobilization" in January 1951. Philadelphia day nursery directors met later that month to discuss "the responsibility of the Day Nursery in the present national crisis." St. Nicholas Social Service Report, January 1951. After surveying nine critical defense cities, Child Welfare League consultant Dorothy Beers announced that day care facilities for children of mothers being asked to take defense jobs were "grossly inadequate," explained that no community had adequate facilities or adequate financing for the centers they did have, and called for federal and state funds to help solve the problem. *Child Care Chat*, December 1951, St. Nicholas Box 2.

75. CB memo, January 18, 1951, CB Box 407.

76. Susan Hartmann, "Women's Employment and the Domestic Ideal in the Early Cold War Years," in Meyerowitz, *Not June Cleaver*, pp. 91–93.

77. Kessler-Harris, *Out To Work*, pp. 300, 308.

78. Susan Rimby Leighow, "An 'Obligation To Participate': Married Nurses' Labor Force Participation in the 1950s," in Meyerowitz, *Not June Cleaver*, pp. 48–49.

79. Mrs. John Weich to Frieda Miller, Women's Bureau, February 26, 1952. Folder 3-1-2-4-1, Box 28, General Correspondence 1948–1963, Office of the Director, Women's Bureau records.

80. Eisenhower's initial proposal, which was part of a larger tax-reform bill, would have covered only widows, widowers, divorced or legally separated individuals, and mothers who provided most of the family's support. Congress expanded the measure, extending coverage to any employed mother whose annual family income did not exceed $4,500 (roughly half of all families had

incomes below that level in 1954.) Hartmann, "Women's Employment and the Domestic Ideal," pp. 94–97; Mary Frances Berry, *The Politics of Parenthood: Child Care, Women's Rights, and the Myth of the Good Mother* (New York: Viking, 1993), p. 122.

81. Joanne Meyerowitz, "Beyond the Feminine Mystique: A Reassessment of Postwar Mass Culture, 1946–1958," in Meyerowitz, *Not June Cleaver*, pp. 231, 238–240. For another critique of women's magazines as promoters of the "feminine mystique" during this period, see Eva Moskowitz, "'It's Good to Blow Your Top': Women's Magazines and a Discourse of Discontent, 1945–1965," *Journal of Women's History* 8, no. 3 (Fall 1996), pp. 66–98.

82. Susan Hartmann, *The Home Front and Beyond: American Women in the 1940s* (Boston: Twayne Publishers, 1982), p. 24.

83. Weiner, *From Working Girl to Working Mother*, p . 91.

84. Kessler-Harris, *Out to Work*, pp. 302–303.

85. "Finding Good Day Care Centers Is Working Mothers' Problem," *Philadelphia Bulletim*, September 3, 1957.

86. May, *Homeward Bound*, pp. 18–20, 167.

87. History of Neighborhood Centre Day Nursery, November 1946.

88. First Family Day Care Association (FFDCA) Annual Report 1946, 1947.

89. Ibid.

90. Leah Gingrich, speaking at Wharton Centre Day Nursery Auxiliary Committee, November 2, 1949.

91. Hartmann, *The Home Front and Beyond*, p. 93.

92. At a 1956 Child Welfare League of America meeting on day care, a day care worker commented on this shift : her clients were no longer families receiving assistance, but "pretty independent families—parents who want to buy a home, who want a higher standard of living." St. Nicholas Executive's Report, March 1956.

93. The three nurseries are Neighborhood Centre, St. Nicholas, and Wharton. The information for the FFDCA comes from "Children Under Care of First Family Day Care Association," December 1952, p. 12.

94. See Table 2 in appendix. The shift in the mission of the day care program at Neighborhood Centre meant that there were more single mothers and women working to supplement an insufficient income than there had been during the war, when the center accepted children for educational reasons.

95. The public day care centers had similar proportions of two-parent families in 1946, but within two years the percentage of single parents using the public centers rose to 49.2%, and by 1963, it had grown to 55%. Leah Gingrich to Evelyn Smith, October 1, 1948, CB Box 117; School District, "Child Care Centers," p. 22. "Pilot Study of Child Care Centers of Philadelphia, PA," May 1956, p. 5. FFDCA.

96. Wharton case 20107/726.

97. Wharton case 20506/755.

98. Wharton case 22807/925.

99. Wharton case 22801/919.

100. Wharton case 22415/891.

101. Wharton case 20701/764.

102. NC case 1461.

103. NC case 1481(B).

104. May, *Homeward Bound*, p. 25.

105. NC case 1437.

106. Ethel Beer, "Should Mothers Stop Working?" *Unity* (November–December 1952), p. 2. Women's Bureau Office of the Director, General Correspondence, Box 28, Folder 3-1-2-4-2.

107. Wharton case 21910/822.

108. Wharton case 22001/827.

109. Wharton case 22507/898.

110. Although the day care program had officially changed from nursery school back to day nursery, parents and staff seemed to have used the terms interchangeably. The Planned Parenthood broadcast combined a dramatic public interest story related to family planning with an interview about more general family life issues in Philadelphia.

111. WHAT, June 23, 1950, typescript. Neighborhood Centre.

112. FFDCA Annual Report, 1950, p. 3.

113. See appendix for parents' occupations at the different nurseries.

114. Doris Campbell Phillips, "Why Day Care?" *Child Welfare* (December 1949), p. 11.

115. Anna Frigond to Dorothy Beers, 1949, Strawberry Mansion Day Nursery (SMDN).

116. Frigond, paper presented at the Day Nursery Council, March 29, 1951.

117. Report of Day Care Committee, Children's Division, Health and Welfare Council, June 1954. FFDCA.

118. St. Nicholas Social Service Committee minutes, March 1952.

119. Quoted in Weiner, *From Working Girl to Working Mother*, p. 137.

120. Ruth Pearson Koshuk, "Developmental Records of 500 Nursery School Children," *Journal of Experimental Education* 16 (December 1947), pp. 134–148.

121. Neighborhood Centre Day Nursery Report, January 21, 1946, Series 1, Box 2.

122. CWLA to CB, October 26, 1954, CB Box 616.

123. Quoted in Weiner, *From Working Girl to Working Mother*, p. 136.

124. St. Nicholas Exeuctive's Report, May 1957. Similarly, at a meeting of the PADN in 1951, "the question of public versus private agencies arose," and one of those present noted, "The money-giving organization [i.e., the Community Chest] tells us that it is the government's responsibility. This is a nation-wide topic, a general trend." PADN minutes, September 26, 1951.

125. Rhoda Kellogg, Golden Gate Kindergarten Association, to Elsie Wolfe, Women's Bureau, January 17, 1951. Folder 3-1-2-4-2, Box 28, General Correspondence, Office of the Director, WB. Emphasis in original.

126. PADN minutes, March 26, 1952.

127. PADN minutes, September 26, 1951.

128. Neighborhood Centre, Box 17.

129. Although the families using the Bustleton Avenue Nursery School were probably more affluent than those in the settlement's old location, their middle-class status was tenuous, and several applied for scholarships in order to pay the nursery school fee.

130. Wharton case 21206/802.

131. School District, "Child Care Centers," p. 25.

132. WHAT, June 23, 1950, typescript. Neighborhood Centre Box 2, Folder 9.

133. *Child Care Chat*, June 1950, St. Nicholas Box 7.

134. Wharton case 20706/769.

135. Wharton case 20513/762.

136. Wharton case 21005/788.

137. Wharton case 20708/771.

138. NC case 1437.

139. Wharton case 22408/884.

140. Wharton case 21910/822.

141. Wharton case 23104/945.

142. Wharton case 22801/919.

143. Wharton case 21005/788.

144. SMDN Annual Report, 1947.

145. PADN minutes, May 24, 1951.

146. SMDN Annual Report, 1950.

147. "Questions and Answers Pertaining to the Use of the Service at the Strawberry Mansion Day Care House," July 1958.

148. Minutes of the PADN, November 22, 1949.

149. "A Study of Jewish Community Day Care Needs in Philadelphia," (1958), p. 5. SMDN.

150. "Keeping Families Together," n.d., SMDN.

151. Quoted in Weiner, *From Working Girl to Working Mother*, p. 136.

152. John F. O'Hara, archbishop of Philadelphia, to the Very Reverend Francis Dodd, director of the Daughters of Charity, Emmitsburg Province, May 25, 1953; Dodd to O'Hara, May 28, 1953. Records of the Cathedral Day Nursery, Daughters of Charity Archives, Northeastern Province, Albany, New York.

153. Letter to Sister Genevieve (author unclear), May 28, 1953; Sister Genevieve to Father Dodd, May 29, 1953; Sister Genevieve to Sister Visitatrix, June 12, 1953; O'Hara to Dodd, June 2, 1953.

154. St. Nicholas Executive's Report, March 1956.

155. Minutes of Meeting of Day Nursery Council, April 25, 1946, Neighborhood Centre.

156. "Pilot Study of Child Care Centers of Philadelphia, PA," May 1956, pp. 6, 10, 17. FFDCA.

157. In her 1964 report, Leah Gingrich referred to the need for casework in the public day care centers as the major gap in a day care program that was otherwise of high quality; she noted that both the Child Welfare League of America and the Children's Bureau had declared case work service to be an essential part of good day care. Although she did point out that not all families who used the centers required case work, she wrote that "the need for case work is apparent from the very nature of day care," and called for hiring four or five case workers to staff the thirteen centers. School District, "Child Care Centers," pp. 30–31.

158. Typescript, n.d. (response to report dated November 1952), SMDN.

159. Private as well as public day care programs reported a rise in applications and their inability to serve all the families who needed care. The 1949 FFDCA Annual Report shows increase in applications, higher than any point except during the war; applications remained at that high level throughout the 1950s. PADN January 26, 1949, minutes reported that a survey of twenty day nurseries in Philadelphia found that there was a preschool capacity of 637 and waiting list of 308.

160. SMDN Annual Report, 1947.

Conclusion

1. *Day Care Services: Form and Substance, A Report of a Conference November 17–18, 1960* (Children's Bureau, 1960), p. 1. The National Committee for the Day Care of Children was made up of professional social workers and early childhood educators, including Philadelphia public day care program director Leah Gingrich. James Hymes, Jr., *Early Childhood Education Living History Interviews—Book 2: Care of the Children of Working Mothers* (Carmel, California: Hacienda Press, 1978), p. 20.

2. Lynn Weiner, *From Working Girl to Working Mother: The Female Labor Force in the United States, 1820–1980* (Chapel Hill: University of North Carolina Press, 1985), p. 93. The figure for 1988 is from the Children's Defense Fund, "Child Care: Key Facts," (1988), cited in Anne Durst, "Day Nurseries and Wage-Earning Mothers in the United States, 1890–1930," (Ph.D. dissertation, University of Wisconsin-Madison, 1989), p. 305.

3. Children's Defense Fund, "Child Care: Key Facts," (1988), cited in Durst, "Day Nurseries and Wage-Earning Mothers," p. 305; Mary Tuominen, "Caring for Profit: The Social, Economic, and Political Significance of For-Profit Child Care," *Social Service Review* (September 1991), p. 452.

4. Lauri Umansky, *Motherhood Reconceived: Feminism and the Legacies of the Sixties* (New York: New York University Press, 1996), pp. 46–50.

5. Quoted in Julia Wrigley, "Different Care for Different Kids: Social Class and Child Care Policy," *Educational Policy* 3 (1989), p. 429.

6. For an account of how measuring IQ came to be a focus in evaluating the program's effectiveness, see Edward Zigler and Susan Muenchow, *Head Start: The Inside Story of America's Most Successful Educational Experiment* (New York: Basic Books, 1992), pp. 51–75

7. Eveline Omwake, quoted in Wrigley, "Different Care for Different Kids," p. 431. Sally Lubeck argues that in the Head Start program she observed, teachers do not fully subscribe to their supervisors' stress on the creative value of play. Their own priority (one often shared by the parents they serve) is to teach children preacademic skills they will use in school. Lubeck, *Sandbox Society: Early Education in Black and White America, A Comparative Ethnography* (Philadelphia: Falmer Press, 1985).

8. Wrigley, "Different Care for Different Kids," pp. 433–434.

9. Julia Wrigley, "Do Young Children Need Intellectual Stimulation? Experts' Advice to Parents, 1900–1985" *History of Education Quarterly* 29, no. 2 (Spring 1989), p. 67.

10. Sonya Michel makes a similar point in "Should Mothers Work? Finding a Rationale for Public Child Care in the 1950s," paper presented at the Berkshire Conference on the History of Women, University of North Carolina, June 1996, p. 18.

11. Mary Frances Berry, *The Politics of Parenthood: Child Care, Women's Rights, and the Myth of the Good Mother* (New York: Viking, 1993), p. 131.

12. Robert Bremner, "Other People's Children," *Journal of Social History* 16 (Spring 1983), p. 90.

13. Zigler and Muenchow, *Head Start*, pp. 123–128.

14. Berry, *Politics of Parenthood*, p. 138. Patrick Buchanan, who wrote the veto message, was instructed to "put in what the right wing wants to hear." Zigler and Muenchow, *Head Start*, p. 146.

15. Bremner, "Other People's Children," p. 92.

16. Yasmin Cooper to editor, *Mothering* 72 (Fall 1994).

17. Linda Gordon, "How 'Welfare' Became a Dirty Word," *Chronicle of Higher Education*, July 20, 1994.

18. Arlie Hochschild, *The Second Shift: Working Parents and the Revolution at Home* (New York: Viking, 1989); for a similar point about Italy, see Chiara Saraceno, "Shifts in Public and Private Boundaries: Women as Mothers and Service Workers in Italian Daycare," *Feminist Studies* 10, no. 1 (Spring 1984), p. 26.

19. Wrigley, "Different Care for Different Kids," p. 422; Valerie Polakow, *The Erosion of Childhood* (Chicago: University of Chicago Press, 1992 [2nd edition]); Lubeck, *Sandbox Society*.

20. See Diane Sampson, "Rejecting Zoe Baird: Class Resentment and the Working Mother," in *"Bad" Mothers: The Politics of Blame in 20th-Century America*, ed. Molly Ladd-Taylor and Lauri Umansky (New York: New York University Press, 1997), pp. 310-318. For a recent sociological study of families employing nannies, see Julia Wrigley, *Other People's Children* (New York: Basic Books, 1995). Wrigley argues that such arrangements represent a "private solution to a public problem," one which ignores the need to redistribute the work of child-rearing within the family and also takes pressure off employers to create more "family-friendly" work situations.

21. Suzanne Helburn et al, *Cost, Quality, and Child Outcomes in Child Care Centers: Executive Summary* (January 1995).

22. Helburn et al., *Cost, Quality, and Child Outcomes*, and Angela Browne Miller, *The Day Care Dilemma: Critical Concerns for American Families* (New York: Plenum Press, 1990) both found that parents rate their day care services very highly even though trained observers find the same day care settings to be poor or inadequate.

Index

Printed in the United States
1017000002B